'It offers something fresh and pure and notably fair. Early on, the authors call the tale they have to tell 'this story of magic and manipulation.' It is greatly to their credit that they have managed to resist being blinded by that magic or succumbing to that manipulation . . . DIANA: STORY OF A PRINCESS has a remarkably clear-sighted vision.'
Mail on Sunday

'Ground-breaking. The most penetrating portrait yet . . . the real story behind the lies and propaganda.'
Daily Mail

'The best account yet of the tragedy . . . A world away from the synthetic soap-opera of most royal accounts. Anyone who advises royalty – not just those on the official payroll – would benefit from reading it.'
Patrick Jephson, former Private Secretary to Princess Diana

'DIANA: STORY OF A PRINCESS is a good, plain, lucid, responsible (book)'
Observer

'A convincing and at times moving portrait.'
Sunday Telegraph

'Intelligent and well-researched . . . the best account so far of the unlucky lady and her mystifying cult.'
Ben Pimlott, New Statesman Books of the Year

'A real achievement. They find something new and interesting to say about a subject we thought we all knew backwards.'
Ian Hislop

Also by Tim Clayton and Phil Craig

Finest Hour

DIANA

STORY OF A PRINCESS

Tim Clayton & Phil Craig

CORONET BOOKS
Hodder & Stoughton

For Frances, Juliette, Alex,
Helen, Jenny and William.

First published in Great Britain in 2001 by Hodder and Stoughton
A division of Hodder Headline

A Coronet paperback

1 3 5 7 9 10 8 6 4 2

A CIP catalogue record for this title is available from the British Library

ISBN 0 340 82179 5

Typeset in Monotype Sabon by
Rowland Phototypesetting Ltd,
Bury St Edmunds, Suffolk
Printed and bound in Great Britain by
Clays Ltd, St Ives plc

Hodder and Stoughton
A division of Hodder Headline Ltd
338 Euston Road
London NW1 3BH

Contents

Picture Credits

SECTION I

Look at me! (*Penny Walker*); What Diana wrote in a cupboard at West Heath school (*Brook Lapping*); Outside the Young England kindergarten, Pimlico, September 1980, Arthur Edwards (*The Sun*); Jayne Fincher's first photograph of Diana, November 1980; Diana enters St Paul's Cathedral with Earl Spencer, July 1981; On honeymoon at the Braemar Highland Games, September 1981 (*Photographers International*); Diana in Brecon, November 1981 (*April Games*); Ken Lennox's long-lens shots of Charles and Diana in the Bahamas, February 1982 (*Ken Lennox*); Australia's new princess at Sydney Opera House, spring 1983 (*Photographers International*); With John Travolta at the White House, November 1985 (*Ronald Reagan Library*); The puppet from the television series *Spitting Image*, November 1985 (*Ken Lennox*); A family day out at the Guards Polo Club, Windsor, May 1987 (*Photographers International*); Diana presents the Captains and Subalterns Cup, summer 1988 (*News International*); Her favourite photograph: autumn 1991, Diana greets the children on *Britannia* in Canada, and Charles hugging them too; The Six Acres Day Centre, Taunton, Somerset, April 1991; RAF Cranwell, June 1991; The winner's kiss, Valentine's Eve, February 1992 (*Photographers International*)

SECTION 2

Lech, Austria, March 1994 (*PA Photos*); Diana shows her anger towards photographers, March 1994 (*Big Pictures*); Avoiding photographers, July 1994 (*London Features*); Diana passes Glenn Harvey, Mark Saunders makes way as Glenn Harvey 'whacks' her; then Diana breaks down as Mark Saunders waits for her to turn (*Mark Saunders; Mark Saunders; Big Pictures*); The *People* newspaper, 1993, and *His Highness in Fitz* (*The People, Andrew Edmunds, London*); Lord Palumbo meets Diana outside the Serpentine Gallery, 29 June 1994, (*Photographers International*); Following Diana's *Panorama* interview, *Private Eye* devoted an entire issue to the royal marriage (*Private Eye*); Diana leaves the English National Ballet 28 August 1996 (*Photographers International*); Diana at Huambo, Angola, January 1997 (*Christina Lamb*); Floral tributes outside Kensington Palace, September 1997 (*Photographers International*); The cover of *Private Eye* that led to the magazine attracting a record number of complaints (*Private Eye*)

Acknowledgments

The narrative in this book is based principally on research and filming undertaken for the television series *Diana: Story of a Princess*. We would first of all like to express our deep gratitude to the gifted producers responsible for these programmes: Sally Brindle, Janice Sutherland and Nick Ward. We also want to thank the ever-resourceful and hard-working production team of Sarah Gowers, Valerie Hetherington, Susan Horth, Delphine Jaudeau, Melody Lander, Beth Serota and Steve Thomas. Our executive producer, Brian Lapping, was at his judicious best throughout.

We are especially grateful to all those who gave interviews: Victor Adebowale; Mike Adler; Ronald Allison; Harry Arnold; Jane Atkinson; Jacques Azagury; Elsa Bowker; Carolan Brown; J. Carter Brown; Graydon Carter; David Chipp; Mary Clarke; Annick Cojean; Derek Draper; Frances Drayton; Arthur Edwards; Gwanwyn Evans; Janet Filderman; Jayne Fincher; Valerie Harris; James Hewitt; Shirley Hewitt; Stuart Higgins; Christopher Hitchens; Anthony Holden; Margaret Jay; Penny Junor; Andrew Knight; Christina Lamb; Ken Lennox; Felix Lyle; Jean-Louis Macault; Frederic Mailliez; Lana Marks; Neville Marks; Ed Mathews; Thierry Meresse; Verona Middleton-Jeter; Sami Naïr; Nick Owen; Peter Palumbo; Vivienne Parry; Anne Rachlin; Shirley Reese; Jenny Rivett; Joseph Sanders; Mark Saunders; Muriel Stevens; Kay Seth-Smith; Jon Snow; Robert Spencer; Richard Stott; Stephen Twigg; Judy Wade; Penny Walker; Mike Whitlam; Dean and Jane Woodward.

A number of others asked that their contributions should remain non-attributable, in particular those who have worked, or still work, for the Royal Family. We hope they know how much we appreciate their help.

We were kindly granted access by Blakeway Productions to material filmed for their excellent television series *Royals and Reptiles*. Our thanks go to Leonie Jameson and Kate Macky there. Brook Lapping opened up its own archives to give us access to material filmed for its previous royal series *The Windsors*.

A number of writers and photographers have been especially helpful. We thank Jayne Fincher, Martyn Gregory, Christopher Hitchens, Anthony Holden, Penny Junor, Sally Bedell Smith, Kate Snell and Judy Wade, all of whom have been generous with time and advice, even if their interpretations do not always dovetail with our own.

Ian Paten copy-edited the book in record time; Diana LeCore did the index likewise; Sarah Byrt, Catherine Bristow and Jane Phillips gave us legal advice; Frances Craig helped us collate and edit the material; hoteliers supreme, James and Sue Murray at the Lewtrenchard Manor, provided an ideal Devonian hideaway for some of our more sensitive meetings; Valerie Hetherington took time away from her TV work to help us find the right photographs, and Susan Horth did likewise with newspaper cuttings; Christine Craig provided a Mediterranean backdrop for writing our first drafts and Peter and Avice Clayton a Norfolk one for the second; the *Private Eye* office dug enthusiastically through its dustier filing cabinets; and the Diana, Princess of Wales Memorial Fund was sympathetic and accommodating – we thank Victoria Rae and Andrew Purkis there. The Fund exists as a memorial to Diana. For more information about the Fund, visit their website www.theworkcontinues or write to them at The County Hall, Westminster Bridge Road, London SE1 7PB.

Every reasonable effort has been made to acknowledge the ownership of copyright material included in this book. Any errors that may have occurred are inadvertent and will be corrected in subsequent editions provided notification is sent to the authors.

Lastly our thanks to Rupert, Roland, Briar, Elizabeth and all at Hodder & Stoughton for another fine job under pressure.

Preface

This book has an ambitious objective: to evaluate the story of Diana, Princess of Wales, fairly.

Divorce provokes twisted stories. It is clear that, in the destructive phase of *their* marriage, Princess Diana and Prince Charles allowed, and in some cases caused, prejudicial accounts to be published. Because Diana became a figure of almost universal impact – with more power to win supporters and donors to a cause worldwide than all the rest of the royals put together – an attempt to weigh and get behind the rival versions of her story is long overdue.

It is hard to judge the right moment for a biography. If this book and the television series it accompanies are too early, the fault is mine.

Brook Lapping is not the obvious television production company to make programmes – and generate an associated book – about Princess Diana. Britain's independent television network asked Brook Lapping to do it, curiously, because our reputation lies in a quite different area. We have specialised in recent history: Gorbachev's Soviet Union in eight hours, Nixon's Watergate in five, the death of Yugoslavia in six, the Beirut hostage crisis in four, Israel and the Arabs in six. The techniques we have developed in such productions led ITV in Britain, the Learning Channel in the US, Canal Plus in France and a number of other broadcasters around the world to decide that we could bring to the biography of Princess Diana something previous coverage of her life has lacked. Perhaps judiciousness was what they were after. It is certainly what we have attempted.

Some people argue that royalty is not a fit subject for serious writers or programme-makers. In general we reject that view as pompous – in Princess Diana's case, vehemently so. With simple acts she effected significant changes. When many believed AIDS could be passed on by the slightest casual contact, she touched a patient in front of cameras and made people around the world realise that they had no need to shun AIDS sufferers. When the British government hesitated about the sale of anti-personnel mines, she strode across the world to campaign for a ban. Her walk through a minefield in Angola caused apoplexy among ministers in London. It also won the cause, for the first time, the attention of the world.

Whatever she did, Diana made an impact; but in no area more powerfully than in destabilising her husband's family. Effortlessly she outshone Guy Fawkes.

When Queen Elizabeth II called 1992 an *annus horribilis*, she was referring partly to the fire at Windsor Castle. But above all she was upset by a Princess who had declared open war on her in-laws. When, in her *Panorama* interview in 1995, Diana said, 'It's a very demanding role being King and would be a little suffocating, and I would think that the top job would bring enormous limitations to him and I don't know whether he could adapt to that', she was seeking to deny Prince Charles the office for which his whole life had been a preparation. When, after Diana's death, the police warned the Queen that if members of the Royal Family returned to London they risked being booed or worse, they were demonstrating how far Diana had undermined the monarchy's popularity. Then, at Diana's funeral, her brother Earl Spencer promised to ensure 'that their [William's and Harry's] souls are not immersed by duty and tradition'. The sound of applause from the crowd outside startled the invited mourners in Westminster Abbey, suggesting that Spencer and the popular mood were united against the Palace.

To the Royal family, Diana, alive or dead, was *dangerous*. The threat she represented arose largely from one of her great virtues: she seemed able to be genuinely sympathetic to ordinary people who were suffering. From lepers to drug addicts to the homeless, from crippled children to pensioners incapacitated by dementia, her capacity for kindly interest seemed endless. Clever people scoffed. But Diana had something they lacked. It resembled the 'king's touch', the power monarchs were once held to possess to cure the sick. She just made people feel cared about – and feel better. Such a remarkable power could surely have been an asset to the Royal Family, winning them enhanced public enthusiasm. But her magic with those in need, like her magic in front of the camera, repeatedly upstaged her husband and in-laws.

The process by which Diana's story reached the public is also a legitimate subject for further exploration. Diana secretly briefed journalists and lied to the Queen's private secretary (her own sister's husband) about the extensive help she gave Andrew Morton with his biography of her. Prince Charles's friends also briefed the press unattributably. And his closest friend, Camilla Parker Bowles, surprised some senior people in Fleet Street with regular off-the-record chats. All these whisperings, the War of the Waleses, lay behind the two incompatible versions of the Diana story that became current, his and hers.

Generally Diana was the more successful at winning public sympathy, establishing herself as the victim. But some of Prince Charles's friends and advisers put about reports that the Princess was mentally unstable. As a result several writers have diagnosed Diana as suffering from a mental illness called Borderline Personality Disorder. This piece of amateur psychiatry is now widely believed, leading to the conclusion that Diana's husband was the stoical victim of her erratic behaviour.

The mechanism by which such dynamite was stacked by both sides beneath their royal rivals, possibly threatening the succession and even the Constitution, seemed worth uncovering while memories are fresh, since, by their nature, off-the-record chats leave no reliable written record.

An argument against undertaking the series and book was

that researching fresh data about Princess Diana and her problems risked becoming prurient. I hope viewers and readers will judge that we have shown restraint.

Brian Lapping
Executive Producer, *Diana: Story of a Princess*

I
Look at Me

With a light knock on the door, Lady Diana Spencer came into the office. She looked first at her feet, then towards the royal official who was now standing before her. It was obvious she had been crying. Would he mind if she asked him a delicate question? Of course not.

She hesitated for a moment and then asked whether he knew someone called Camilla Parker Bowles. He said yes immediately. He knew her as a friend of Prince Charles who was married to an officer in the Household Cavalry. He had met her several times; all the senior staff had.

Then Diana said in a quiet but serious voice that she had just asked the Prince of Wales whether he was in love with Camilla Parker Bowles. He had not said no. As the tears returned, but still looking him full in the face, she asked another question: 'What am I going to do?' The courtier had no idea what to say. In his years of royal service, no one had ever spoken to him like this. He wasn't alone. Within hours one of his closest colleagues, another senior member of the royal household, was asked exactly the same question.

The wedding was only ten days away. What were they *all* going to do? After urgent consultations in a corridor, the courtiers suggested to Diana that she should talk it over with Camilla face to face. One of them arranged a lunch at her favourite restaurant. It was called *Ménage-à-trois*.

> So we had lunch. Very tricky indeed. She said: 'You are not going to hunt are you?' I said: 'On what?' She said: 'Horse. You are not going to hunt when you go and live at

> Highgrove are you?' I said: 'No.' She said: 'I just wanted to know.'

Inside Buckingham Palace they awaited the outcome apprehensively. When Diana came back she said, 'It was brilliant. We all understand each other.' One of the courtiers told us:

> We all heaved a sigh of relief. I do think Camilla and Charles backed off in the early years. But an atmosphere soon developed. Some of us put it down to Diana being spoilt. I put it down to different backgrounds.

Diana Spencer's background *was* different to Prince Charles's, but not that different. She was born into one of the grandest families in England, a family that for two hundred years had been intimate with the court and its slowly ossifying traditions.

'The Lord Chamberlain ventures most respectfully to hope that the heart-stirring though silent sympathy of the vast crowds of Your Majesty's subjects may have somehow helped Your Majesty in his crushing sorrow,' wrote Diana's great-grandfather to George V. Edward VII had just died and Earl Spencer was looking forward to arranging the new King's coronation. He made urgent notes regarding the forthcoming ceremonials: 'Queen's robes – Are they safeguarded from moth in the Tower?'

Diana's grandfather was the first of his family for several generations not to take a place at court. But this was chiefly owing to his devotion to a more urgent duty: to preserve his own decaying heritage. In 1922, as a young officer in the Life Guards, Albert Edward John, 7th Earl Spencer, inherited the palace and estates of Althorp in Northamptonshire and the urban palazzo called Spencer House in St James's Place, overlooking Green Park. Both were packed with priceless fittings, furniture and paintings, all of which needed care and restoration.

There were debts, mortgages, death duties and the buildings were in disrepair. He raised £300,000 by selling six masterpieces by Reynolds, Gainsborough, van Dyck and Frans Hals to the United States. This solved the immediate problem. During the war, 'Jack', as the seventh earl was known, emptied Spencer House, to save its fabulous contents from Hitler's bombers, and he crowded more evidence of the affluence of his ancestors between the fading silk wall hangings of his country home. As time went by Althorp became increasingly museum-like. In 1957 he opened it to the public, the condition for receiving government grants to save the fabric of the house from dry rot and death-watch beetle. But even though Jack Spencer was preoccupied with the conservation of one of the largest fortunes made in the days when Britannia truly ruled the trade routes, his wife, Lady Cynthia, kept up tradition. In 1936 she was made a Woman of the Bedchamber and she later became a lady-in-waiting to Queen Elizabeth II. She was still a courtier when her granddaughter Diana was born.

Diana's first home, Park House, is in the grounds of Sandringham House, the Royal Family's country seat in Norfolk. To Prince Charles, Diana was the girl next door – the youngest of three Spencer sisters, along with Sarah and Jane, who were all spoken of from the nursery as possible brides for Britain's three young princes.

This privileged proximity to the royal home was owed to Diana's maternal grandparents. In the 1930s Diana's grandfather, the Irish-American Maurice Roche, Lord Fermoy, had settled in King's Lynn and had befriended the shy, stammering Duke of York, later King George VI. Fermoy's wife, Ruth, was even closer to the Duchess, later Queen Elizabeth (now the Queen Mother). When the Fermoys had children, the King and Queen invited them to take the lease of Park House. Later it passed to their daughter, Frances Roche, Diana's mother.

Diana's father, Johnny Spencer, Viscount Althorp, was educated at Eton and Sandhurst. As an officer in the Royal Scots Greys, he fought in Normandy after D-day. After the war he became equerry to King George VI, and after the King's death in February 1952 he was appointed equerry to his daughter, Queen Elizabeth II. He met the bright and lively Frances Roche on a visit to Sandringham. After her coming-out ball in April 1953 the twenty-nine-year-old Johnny and the seventeen-year-old Frances began an intense love affair.

After their engagement Johnny accompanied the Queen on her coronation tour of Australia while the bride's family arranged the wedding. With both bride and groom so closely connected to the Windsors, it was natural that there should be a royal presence at the ceremony on 1 June 1954. It took place at Westminster Abbey, a rare privilege. Seventeen hundred people were invited to the service, including Queen Elizabeth and Prince Philip, the Queen Mother and six other members of the Royal Family. The *Daily Mail* called it the wedding of the year. Through a tunnel formed by the raised swords of the Scots Greys, the bride and groom left the abbey for a reception at St James's Palace.

Johnny and Frances's first daughter Sarah was born within a year. But, like generations of the great county families before them, what the Spencers really wanted was a son and heir. Jane, their second daughter, was born in 1957. The third child *was* a son, John, but he died within ten hours of his birth on 12 January 1960. The event was shattering for both parents, and rather than bringing them together it did the opposite. Johnny Spencer could not conceal his disappointment. Frances has confirmed that she was sent by her family (in which she included mother-in-law Cynthia Spencer and her mother Ruth) to be seen by specialist obstetricians in the belief that there must be something wrong with her.

When Frances became pregnant again (after a miscarriage that she kept secret) there can be little doubt that both parents were hoping for a boy. At each successive confinement Jack Spencer had built bonfires at Althorp to celebrate the birth of an heir. But the result was Diana. She later told her biographer Andrew Morton that she had felt unwanted from a very early age because her parents so clearly wanted *her* to be *him*. Frances says that this was an idea implanted in the adult Diana by therapists. And since an heir, Charles Spencer, was finally born on 20 May 1964, when Diana was still only three, she had little time to develop such an understanding of her parents' secret feelings of disappointment when she was young.

Charles Spencer's birth did not cure the tension at Park House. Johnny and his wife had drifted apart. Perhaps, having finally produced a son, Frances felt that she had discharged her responsibilities and could look to her own happiness. Still young and financially independent, she began to spend more time in London.

In 1966 Frances met Peter Shand Kydd over dinner. The heir to a thriving wallpaper business, he was adventurous, Bohemian and bright. The Althorps and the Shand Kydds met frequently, culminating in a joint skiing holiday. But the attraction between Frances and Peter was at the heart of the friendship between the families. Eventually Peter left his wife and met Frances secretly during her visits to London. She told Johnny about the affair in September 1967, and he agreed to a trial separation. She found a flat in Cadogan Place. In October, Diana, Charles and their nanny went to join their mother in London. Sarah and Jane were by now away at boarding school. Frances had found places for Diana at a local school and Charles at a kindergarten. Their father visited at weekends. It's likely that the children did not know of their parents' separation. The family was united at Park House in Norfolk for Christmas 1967, but then Johnny refused to allow the children to return to London with their mother and she left alone.

On 10 April 1968 Janet Shand Kydd sued her husband for divorce on the grounds of his adultery with Frances Spencer. In

September 1968 Frances went to court with her plea for custody of her children. Lady Fermoy gave evidence against her daughter and she lost. A generous view of Lady Fermoy's behaviour is that she felt the children would be better off in Norfolk. A less generous view is that she set a high value on the Spencer connection and was appalled that her daughter had run off with a tradesman. On 12 December Frances sued for divorce. Johnny cross-petitioned, citing her already proven adultery. He won his case and received custody of the children.

Lady Fermoy is one of the minor villains of the Diana story: tough, ambitious, inflexible and steeped in the culture of another era. But since she followed her friend the Queen Mother's policy of remaining 'utterly oyster' and never defended herself on the record, she has made an easy target. The majority of royal writers assume that she exerted a malign influence, and she is damned in most accounts.

It's easy to create caricatures – Diana modern, classless, open and emotional, the world of her grandmother snobbish, secretive, repressed and sinister; Diana's childhood ruined by the same deadening forces that she would later confront from inside the heart of the establishment.

Except that it wasn't. Certainly there was a nasty divorce, which strained relationships between Frances and her mother for many years, but Diana knew nothing about what had been said in court. And she was to see plenty of both parents, who went out of their way to be civilised about access and not to drag her into their private recriminations.

The divorce was made absolute on 2 May 1969. A month later Frances and Peter Shand Kydd were married. At first they divided their time between Buckinghamshire and Cadogan Place, but soon they bought a house in Itchenor on the West Sussex coast.

In practical terms the custody arrangements did not deprive Frances of visits from her children, and she phoned them every day. The elder girls were free to spend their time where they wished. Sarah chose mostly to go to Park House in Norfolk and Jane to be in London with her mother. Some weekends Diana and Charles Spencer shuffled between London and Norfolk, and holidays were divided equally between the two parents.

Robert Spencer – Johnny's cousin and close friend – maintains that the atmosphere was not particularly unhappy:

> Well, of course, any divorce is bound to affect children. But I don't think it affected Johnny and Frances Althorp's children any more or any less than any others. After all, they were not particularly short of cash and they had two loving parents . . . They were fortunate in that they had two happy homes, and despite the parents being divorced as far as I can remember they were as happy as could be expected.

Against this it might be argued that the children were materially spoiled and, though not starved of parental affection, were perhaps given it in unpredictable doses. Diana always tended to have a dramatic side which may have been nurtured by many tearful partings and the sympathy she felt for each parent as she left to be with the other.

July 1971. Mary Clarke turned right off the Diss road and into the tree-lined avenue that led to Riddlesworth Hall. The twenty-one-year-old nanny had started at Park House in February, looking after Charles Spencer. Her other charge, nine-year-old Diana, was in her second term boarding at Riddlesworth, a prep school about an hour's drive from Sandringham, and Mary had still not met her. Now the Easter holidays had started, and Viscount Althorp had sent Mary off alone to collect Diana and bring her home. She was distinctly nervous because other staff had already told her some alarming stories about the way the children could behave:

> Childish escapades such as going into the nanny or au pair's room and throwing all her clothes out of the window on to the roof, because the house is built in such a way that there's different levels of roof. And then poor old Smith would have to get up and get them down. Or else locking one of them in the toilets.

Mary didn't think she would enjoy this sort of treatment. But perhaps the older staff were just trying to tease her. She had had a wonderful time so far looking after Charles, so she had set off for Riddlesworth Hall with an open mind, hoping for the best.

> I arrived at Riddlesworth and it was a typical end-of-term scenario really – little girls standing round in their uniforms, surrounded by trunks and all their bits and pieces and in Diana's case her guinea-pig in its cage as well. And I walked towards her, because obviously I'd seen pictures of her so I knew who to look out for. And I saw this little girl walking towards me, a real English rose with her eyes downcast, and blushing furiously. And she was very polite and shook my hand and then we were able to lose ourselves in all the fuss of loading up the car.

On the way home Mary asked Diana about her school. She said what she liked best was swimming. By the time Mary got back to Park House she was reassured, and felt she had struck up some kind of understanding. She had already spent six weeks alone with Charles and was worried that Diana might feel like an outsider, something she did everything possible to avoid. Diana's room was all ready for her. As they got nearer to Park House, Diana was getting more and more excited to be home again. She asked Mary, 'How are the Smiths? And how is Mrs Petrie?' They arrived in a jumble of trunks, cages, hockey sticks and tennis rackets, and Diana went dashing off to reacquaint herself with her brother and father and all the staff at the house, as well as all the animals.

Park House is a ten-bedroom yellow-brick Victorian pile, surrounded by wide lawns and trees and close to the church that divides it from Sandringham House. It's a holiday home for old people now. To reach it you drive through the royal estate up an avenue lined with trees, then branch off on to a gravel drive with lawns on one side and the house facing you.

There, Viscount Althorp led the life of a country gentleman, with gun dogs curled up by the fire and piles of *Country Life* and the *Field* on the coffee table. Diana grew up surrounded by cats and dogs, and the precious guinea-pigs that she used to show in late July in the local flower show's 'fur and feathers' tent. She had a fierce ginger cat called Marmalade, and her bed was covered with a variety of furry toy animals. She grew nervous of horses after a fall from a pony, but she went riding with Mary Clarke in order to be with Sarah. She admired her vivacious elder sister very much. She was a healthy child who loved her food and hated wearing dresses. She liked to be outside in muddy jeans climbing trees and making dens and going for long walks with the dogs. Even as a child she had a practical side and helped Mary Clarke with housework in the nursery, which it was the nanny's responsibility to keep tidy. Housework was not Mary Clarke's strong point so when, as he did now and again, Johnny Spencer came to run a finger along a picture frame, Diana always ensured she was there before him, dusting down the pictures and tidying things up.

When the weather looked good, Mary Clarke would plan an excursion to nearby Brancaster beach, where the Spencers had an old wooden beach hut. They would get the cook to pack up a big picnic basket and they would fill the Land Rover with dogs and children – Diana, Charles and their friends. Other local families had huts there, and sometimes the excursions would involve several nannies and all their children. It was a thrill for everyone. The first excursion to Brancaster in the spring was always a big event. Since the previous autumn the winter winds would have reshaped the sand dunes and blown them all over the huts. All the way there, the children would be guessing how many steps to the hut would have been covered and how much digging would have to be done to excavate them.

> At the beginning of the track to the beach huts Diana would shout, 'Let the dogs out! Let the dogs out!' And they would all rush along, having a race to see who had arrived at the beach hut first. As soon as we got there Diana would rush out to get water for the dogs to drink. We'd be trying to scrape away at the steps of the beach hut, seeing which of us had won the competition to see how many steps would be covered by the winter winds. And when we got to the hut and unloaded the Jeep, Diana would be rushing around setting everything up, getting the water on so that we could all have a drink, and rushing off to the sea. Diana was always trying to do about a hundred things all together, just to get everyone settled in and organised. She did like everything to be totally organised. And then they would rush down – the beach huts were built in the dunes – so you ran down from the dunes on to the beach and they would have competitions to see who could take off from the top, and jump the farthest down on to the beach. Some of them used to roll the whole way down on to the beach.
>
> They were really happy, carefree times down at the beach because you were free to roam anywhere. The sea was safe when the tide was in. And if the tide was out it would leave pools of water to swim in and huge expanses of sand. They would wander round collecting shells too.
>
> I would tell them stories. We'd find the conch-type shells and hold them to our ears and see who could hear the sea the loudest. Diana, of course, always heard the sea the loudest.

> And I would tell them stories of different places, of different seas. Diana loved to live in an imaginary world where everything was happy. She always wanted everything to be happy. And we were very happy down at Brancaster.

But the children did not need to go to the seaside to play. The house was big and full of toys and the wrought-iron banisters were perfect for sliding down. There was a grand piano in the music room at the back of the house from which the windows looked out over the climbing frame to the lawn, and beyond that the fenced hard tennis court. Behind the tennis court, up against the park fence, was a swimming pool with two diving boards and a slide. On baking summer days, Park House was very popular with the children who lived near by on the Sandringham estate, girls like Alexandra Lloyd, daughter of the Queen's land agent, and Penelope Ashton, the vicar's daughter, and even with the Royal Family. Although Diana and Charles only visited Sandringham House by invitation, Princes Andrew and Edward frequently dropped by unannounced at Park House. Mary Clarke used to watch Diana play with them.

> Diana knew she was a very good swimmer and she used to take every opportunity to show off. She used to love nothing more than when we had crowds of people round the pool. Much against her father's wishes – and she knew she wasn't really allowed to do this – she'd run to the top of the slide and stand there poised – and she was beautiful and slim – and shout to everyone, 'Look at me! Look at me!' knowing that her father wouldn't reprimand her in front of everyone else, and execute this beautiful dive into the pool.

They took it out of context! This is the most common complaint about journalists. An incident, a memory, one portion of a half-remembered conversation lifted out of the jumble and contradiction of real experience and used to make a telling point in a television programme or a book. 'Look at me! Look at me!' – who hasn't shouted that at the top of a diving board? But childhood stories like this have been used to build up a picture of the young Diana as an attention-seeker, a prima donna in the making.

Diana was thirty when she told Andrew Morton that she had a very unhappy childhood. By then she was fluent in the language of psychotherapy, and the rooting of later troubles in childhood trauma. She herself is the sole source of the received impression that her early life was lonely and sad. But Diana didn't tell the story straight. She took *herself* out of context, exaggerating for effect when constructing a story of her early life that made her out to be more unusual and disturbed than she actually was.

There were, no doubt, unhappy moments as the children were shuffled between parents, but most remember Diana as a cheerful, tree-climbing tomboy: a bit overindulged, a bit lackadaisical at schoolwork, but otherwise unremarkable. A nice upper-class little English girl with good manners, neat handwriting and a deep affection for guinea-pigs; a girl who got excited about picnics on the beach and standing on a diving board. Like thousands of others, destined to move smoothly from boarding school to finishing school, a secretarial course, maybe some cooking and a stint in a ski chalet, and then marriage to a well-bred young man from a good county family.

Diana loved to read romantic novels and Barbara Cartland was her favourite author. Nanny Mary Clarke thought she had a very simple vision of the future:

> What Diana really wanted to do when she grew up was very simple, it was a dream shared by many little girls, to marry someone who really loved her and who she really loved and to have lots of children. Diana had in mind anything from four

to six children and just to have a normal happy life. It was immaterial to her who the person that she married was, the important factor was that he should really love her and she love him because otherwise the marriage would end in divorce.

She wanted to be a ballet dancer, but at twelve years old Diana was already five foot nine and far too tall. Lady Fermoy had been a concert pianist and her sister Sarah was also a talented musician, but though she played a lot at home, Diana was not as good.

In 1973 Diana changed schools, following her sisters to West Heath, a small private boarding school for about 120 girls in Sevenoaks in Kent, surrounded by charming countryside and set in its own beautiful grounds. Its fees were very high, its facilities were magnificent, and its goals were not primarily academic.

During her first term at West Heath, Diana was, by her own admission, something of a bully. At least one of her smaller contemporaries claims to have suffered at her hands. In her second term she was treated to some of her own medicine, being picked on by some older girls, and then she settled down into boisterous popularity as the leader of a small gang in her class of about fifteen.

Diana was daring – she mounted nocturnal raids on the school kitchens and enjoyed midnight swims. The headmistress almost expelled her for wandering about the school after lights-out. Her teachers soon discovered that she had difficulty concentrating for any length of time. Penny Walker, Diana's music teacher, felt that this was due to a number of factors, one being troubles at home:

> Her mind, you often felt, was elsewhere. Her sisters were fairly good academically. Sarah was a brilliant pianist. Jane wasn't far behind. So she had a lot to live up to. She also came late to the school, which is always a disadvantage. Friendships are already formed, everybody knows the staff already. They've

already started on their course of work. So she had that to cope with as well.

Occasionally in repose her face would look sad, but I wouldn't have said that she was a sad person. She was always full of fun and very, very lively and always doing things. She wasn't moping around or anything like that. I think she was quite happy at West Heath.

The Shand Kydds bought a romantic hill farm on the Isle of Seil near Oban on the west coast of Scotland. Diana had a poster of Seil over her bed at West Heath and took friends there in the holidays, spending her time playing with lobster pots on the beach. She still saw Princes Andrew and Edward regularly in Norfolk. Diana's sisters had it in mind that she might make a suitable bride for Prince Andrew and she did, for a while, correspond with him at school. Their teasing ambition for her in this direction is one of many explanations that have been produced for her nickname 'Duch', short for Duchess. Her brother Charles denies this version, saying that they named her Duchess after the elegant leading feline in Walt Disney's cartoon *The Aristocats*.

Aristocat was certainly appropriate for the Spencers. About three hundred and fifty years before her birth, the family bought their peerage for £3,000 in hard cash from the impoverished James I. The first Lord Spencer's introduction to the House of Lords infuriated another member so much that he interrupted Spencer's speech on the conduct of affairs in previous reigns, saying with heavy sarcasm: 'When these things were doing the noble Lord's ancestors were keeping sheep!'

But measured in ready cash, that newly ennobled Spencer soon became the richest man in the land. Having founded their wealth on wool, his family captured the London meat contracts and grew richer. With enough gold to fund dynastic ambitions, they acquired a genealogy from the College of Heralds that traced their line through the Despensers to the retinue of William the Conqueror. It was not until 1901 that their right to the Despenser coat of arms was declared a fraud and their pedigree exposed as near-total fabrication. But by then they had been playing a leading role in the affairs of Great Britain for a good century more than the present Royal Family.

Indeed, the Spencers had helped place the Royal Family on the throne. It was another Spencer who, in 1693, brokered the deal by which William III received the support of the noble families that had fought on the Parliamentarian side in the Civil War. Spencer, described as 'the most subtil working villain on the face of the earth', hosted a conference at Althorp, a conference of 'Great Men'. There, King William accepted the principles of limited monarchy. When his successor Queen Anne died in 1714 without producing the requisite Protestant heir, the Spencers were among the same great families who imported the Elector of Hanover from Germany to be King George I.

The new German royals found themselves in a country famed for removing inconvenient monarchs, with a parliament that regarded itself as sovereign and a haughty aristocracy that could match them for wealth. For three generations they spent as much time as possible in Hanover. Admittedly, through the long reign of Victoria, the people became less boisterously critical of their imported royals. But a Spencer, in particular, was always liable to remember that meeting at Althorp in 1693 where aristocracy and royalty had met eye to eye.

2
I'm a Lady

In April 1975 Jack Spencer died at the age of eighty-three. Althorp was in the hands of Diana's father at last. Overnight he became an earl, and his children lords and ladies. Penny Walker remembers Diana hearing the news: 'She rushed along the corridor with her dressing gown billowing out behind her, saying "I'm a Lady, I'm *Lady* Diana now". She was so excited.'

The family moved into their new home, 121 rooms and 13,000 acres set in gently rolling English farmland north-west of Northampton. To deal with four-million-pound death duties, the new Earl Spencer sold two van Dycks. He also introduced a new member to the family: his girlfriend, Raine, Countess of Dartmouth, daughter of Barbara Cartland. Johnny had met Raine when she had been working on *What Is Our Heritage?*, a book produced by the London County Council. They soon began an affair. In 1975 Lord Dartmouth divorced her and in July 1976 she married Johnny, becoming Countess Spencer. She was a fixture at Althorp from the moment Johnny took over, and was the driving force behind the reforms that were soon under way there. Raine imposed her own exacting standards on the household servants and the tenants.

The children hated Raine at first sight. She was larger than life, a cartoon aristocrat, all frills and furs but with an iron will. And their father was putty in her hands. Diana had been introduced to Raine in Norfolk when she was eleven. At that time she, her sisters and the nanny had all been summoned to lunch to meet their father's new girlfriend. She did not make a very good impression. After a few edgy exchanges, Sarah burped loudly. Her father sent her out of the room, and Diana followed in sisterly solidarity. They made no effort to conceal their detestation for the extraordinary woman who now claimed their father's time and affections.

After the family moved to Althorp, Diana and Charles Spencer were mostly away at school. They went to Northamptonshire only for part of the school holidays and on those weekends when they did not visit their mother. For Jane and Sarah visits were even rarer.

At West Heath, Diana's teachers had discovered a sphere in which she excelled. The Sevenoaks Voluntary Service sought to persuade local schools to make visits to Darenth Park, a large hospital for the mentally and physically handicapped. West Heath willingly joined in and appealed for volunteers. Diana was one of the first in her class to raise her hand.

Muriel Stevens organised the visits. Every Tuesday and Thursday evening about seven o'clock their minibuses would pull up outside the main doors and slightly apprehensive teenagers dressed in jeans would tumble out. It was not an experience for the faint-hearted. The hospital was isolated – a huge, looming Victorian Gothic edifice surrounded by high walls. Muriel remembers that when the children came through the great doors into the bright light the patients would be waiting for them, noisy, their voices echoing in the high-ceilinged hall:

> It was intimidating to walk into that huge place with the level of noise and to see some of the very severely handicapped people that we did have. Some of them would be in wheelchairs. Some of them would be sitting on chairs and needed encouragement to move to get off them. Others would rush up and that in itself can be quite frightening, because they were just so delighted to see these young people they would rush up and of course they would touch their hair, grab their hands. And if you're actually not used to it, that can be very

> frightening. Diana was never frightened. She was extremely relaxed in that setting which, for a young person of her age, was incredible.

She would immediately make friends and she would laugh. Diana's echoing laughter is a sound that Muriel has never forgotten.

> That tremendous laugh! That joyous sound! And it was wonderful because you wouldn't actually know what she was laughing at, or have any idea at all what had amused her, but at the sound alone you would find yourself smiling, and as you got closer and you heard it more, you'd find yourself laughing. It was a terrific sound . . .

Then the dancing would begin. All the volunteers were told that it was important to bend down to the level of the people in the wheelchairs and hold their hands. Dancing with people in wheelchairs was not easy and most could do no more than push their partners from behind. Diana was different. She was tall and lithe and enthusiastic and she had been trained to dance:

> Diana actually danced backwards and drew the wheelchair towards her, by holding the arms of the wheelchair. Now that is incredibly agile and clever and there are not many people who could maintain their balance. And she kept an extremely good rhythm.

At Darenth Park, Diana was taught the principles of how to communicate with such vulnerable people in a way that would put them at their ease:

> Touch was the main means of communication and Diana actually took that very much to heart, and we never had to remind Diana of that. We did have to remind some of the other young people – you know, 'Look it would be better if you hold hands, stroke' – Diana we never had to remind.

One of Diana's relatives told us she had seen something special in her too.

> It was an indefinable quality, something very rare and rather beautiful. I was not surprised years later when she emerged as a great communicator. Even as a young child she had a strange way of getting through to people.

Later in her life Diana would make similar visits in secret, satisfying a desire for contact with people in distress. Few feel this need to give and receive instant emotional contact, to go straight to the heart of a stranger's deepest feelings. Normally we hold back, embarrassed, scared of saying the wrong thing. But not Diana.

In 1995, two years before she died, Diana told *Panorama* interviewer Martin Bashir and a billion others: 'I know I can give love for a minute, for half an hour, for a day, for a month, and I want to do that.' In our interviews we repeatedly invited people from the medical and charity worlds to criticise such an overblown idea. How could this girl from the inner circle of privilege give love to the world, this girl who had never known poverty or hunger? Time and again we were asked in turn, 'Who are *you* – who haven't seen her in action, who haven't felt it – to contradict her?'

On the dormitory walls horses were giving way to pop stars. But Diana Spencer's pin-up wasn't a singer: he was Charles, Prince of Wales.

In the mid- to late 1970s there was nothing peculiar about this. The Prince of Wales was very much in the news and widely regarded as the most eligible bachelor in the world. The newspapers called him 'Action Man'. His image was daring and athletic, that of a man prepared to compete at anything. He had served with the RAF, the Navy and the Fleet Air Arm and done his best to undergo the most dangerous trials in their respective training programmes. And like the adaptable military toy from which he took his nickname, Charles was regularly seen in the appropriate uniforms in which to dive, parachute, pilot planes and helicopters, ride polo ponies, captain boats or ski. He was photographed and filmed with a variety of glamorous women – actresses, models and pop singers. Dark-haired, tanned and muscular, he would be striding confidently across a polo field wearing expensive sunglasses and the most sharply cut of navy blazers. He was known to be looking for a bride, and speculation in the press had already focused on several suitable aristocrats, including Lady Jane Wellesley and Davina Sheffield.

In the late 1970s one writer was allowed to sample Charles's lifestyle. A *Sunday Times* journalist named Anthony Holden was researching a biography to mark the Prince's thirtieth birthday. He flew in Charles's helicopter, dined at Buckingham Palace, met many of Charles's friends:

> I spent eighteen months, while doing the book, travelling all over the place with him . . . there was a trip through the Amazon where I was the only journalist, and we had dinner together in the hotel – it's unthinkable all these years later.

Holden wrote of the glittering junior court that was gathering around the Prince of Wales and predicted that 'a place at his table will be the most sought after in the land'. He wrote about Charles's 'magic', the way he was the instant focus of attention at any party or meeting, the flurry of charged excitement that accompanied him everywhere he went.

Property developer Peter Palumbo had known Prince Charles since he was sixteen. They played polo together at Windsor.

> He had all the aces – he had everything. He was the future King of England, he was wealthy, he was good looking, he was

> intelligent, he was sporting, he was a man of action, and he was a very considerable person. He was immensely eligible. I thought the Prince of Wales was quite wonderful. I mean, he was funny, he was obviously full of his responsibility in terms of public duty, but he was amusing and he was kind. He was a compassionate person and we had some good times at Windsor Park playing polo. There was enormous speculation all the time in the press and in social circles about who he might marry – after all, it was a very topical interest – and as the years went by and he had not married, speculation became even more fevered.

Penny Walker remembers that Diana idolised the Prince from the age of about thirteen or fourteen, and had a picture of him near her bed. Other West Heath girls remember that Charles was much discussed in their school. Most of the girls in Diana's peer group were expected to marry well and he was, without doubt, the most eligible man they could imagine. Diana could already boast of him as a family friend. And then, during 1977, in the summer after Diana sat for her O-levels, he was a particularly close friend of her elder sister Sarah. The press called it a romance, so that was how everyone thought of it, but Diana's uncle Robert Spencer told us that Charles knew perfectly well that Sarah was in love with Gerald Grosvenor, who had just broken up with her, and that he was helping her through a difficult time.

For Diana the most exciting thing was that her sister spent the summer 'dating' the heir to the throne. And in the autumn Charles accepted an invitation to go shooting on the estate at Althorp. It was November 1977 and Diana was sixteen. Having failed all of her five O-levels the previous summer, she was revising for a second attempt, but she made sure she was at home that weekend. In a ploughed field near the village of Nobottle, Charles met Sarah's little sister. She made an immediate impression. He found her 'jolly' and 'bouncy', the same slightly plump, noisy teenager that West Heath friends recall. And she was unfazed by his celebrity, chatting away happily without a trace of embarrassment.

Once she got back to school she couldn't wait to show off about it, as Penny Walker recalls:

> She rushed into school on the Monday after her weekend away, saying, 'I've met him. I've met him at last.' And she had. She'd met him in the ploughed field, and her dream had come true. She'd come face to face. It was just something that you knew was part of her life. She had this idealistic crush if you like on Prince Charles and it was always there, but I never dreamt that it would actually happen.

Diana failed her O-levels again so, instead of moving on to the sixth form she was hurriedly booked into the Institut Alpin Vidamanette near Gstaad in Switzerland, an old-fashioned finishing school, where skiing and cookery were high on the curriculum. She had never been confident about schoolwork. When she was small her clever brother Charles had taunted her, 'Brian! Brian!' after the slow snail in the children's programme *The Magic Roundabout*. Throughout her life she would make self-deprecating asides about her dimness ('brain the size of a pea, I've got', 'in the academic department you might as well forget about it').

The finishing school conducted its business entirely in French. Diana was one of only nine English-speaking girls out of seventy-two. Her French was far from fluent and she was shy about making mistakes. Consequently she had difficulty fitting in. The only thing she did enjoy was the skiing. Mary Clarke says that Diana wrote to her soon after arriving in Switzerland about what a miserable time she was having. Diana also wrote long, pleading letters to her parents saying how unhappy she was and asking them to let her come back immediately.

As she continued to blush in silent embarrassment rather than mumble bad French, Sarah came to nearby Klosters on a much-publicised skiing holiday with Prince Charles. There was speculation back home about whether Charles was going to propose but, on her return, Sarah appeared to sabotage any possibility. She had what seemed a harmless conversation with the press. Asked whether she would marry the Prince, she replied that when she did marry it would be for love and that it didn't matter whether the man concerned was a prince or a dustman. If there had been any possibility of romance, these unexceptional words were enough to end it. Just talking about him was, it seemed, enough to disqualify an entrant in the royal marriage stakes. Diana watched and took careful note.

Her second sister Jane *was* getting married. Her match was less ambitious, but it still brought her within the ambit of the Royal Family. She was to wed Robert Fellowes, son of the land agent who ran Sandringham, and now the Queen's assistant private secretary.

In April, after a term and many begging letters, Diana was allowed to leave her finishing school and return to her mother's home in Cadogan Place. The family considered what to do. She needed a social life and she needed some interests. First came a ten-week cookery course in September 1978. And then, just as she began it, she learned that her father was dangerously ill.

That September, Johnny Spencer nearly died. He collapsed after complaining of a headache and was rushed to Northampton General Hospital. It was a brain haemorrhage. Raine and the four children were summoned to his bedside and told that his chances of survival were slim.

But Raine was not prepared to allow Johnny to die without a fight. She took charge and gambled, insisting that he be moved to London and insisting that the doctors operate straight away. He survived, but only just. Raine then kept him alive, according to family legend, by the pure force of her willpower, literally ordering him to get better. Her constant presence by the bedside made the children feel excluded. Then she took two steps that may have saved him. One was to obtain an untested drug from Germany; the other was to get the vicar of All Saints Church, Northampton to exorcise the ghost of his father.

Whether through intercession pharmaceutical or spiritual, Johnny Spencer *did* recover, though he remained physically weak and heavily dependent on his wife. As he recuperated at home, Raine decided that now was the moment to leave her mark on Althorp for ever. She began a process of modernisation, installing *en suite* bathrooms with central heating. She carpeted the long corridors, she replaced faded, water-stained silk wall coverings with new ones in lurid pinks. All that she put in was frilly, garish and expensive. To achieve this transformation of the interior decor, she sold what Charles Spencer later estimated to be one fifth of the contents of the house. Most was disposed of privately to Bond Street dealers, and some large profits were made from subsequent resale. As all this happened, Earl Spencer beamed his weak approval while his heir and his daughters looked on, steaming with sullen fury. The final affront to family pride came when the famous portrait of Robert, 1st Lord Spencer, which had dominated the grand staircase for centuries, was replaced by a full-length picture of Raine in her beauteous youth.

If 1978 was not a happy year for Diana, 1979 began promisingly. Having married Robert Fellowes, Diana's sister Jane travelled with the court. In January she invited Diana for a weekend at Sandringham. Prince Charles was occupied with Amanda Knatchbull, to whom he proposed that summer. But Diana, remembering her earlier encounter in the ploughed field, felt herself smitten once again. That month she started to train as a dancing teacher. She wrote to Madame Betty Vacani, who ran a school where children of the Royal Family had learned to dance, and was accepted. She supervised the youngest toddlers and accompanied them on the piano. But in March she went on holiday and never returned to the school.

Diana joined a chalet party at Val Claret in the French Alps, where she was able to polish the outdoor skills she had picked up at the Institut Alpin. She enjoyed herself so much that she decided to stay for an extra week with another group she had run into, which included Simon Berry from the family of wine merchants. There were twenty in Berry's party, all strangers to Diana, but she soon became the life and soul of their chalet. One of the skiers told us, 'She knew nobody, she was the youngest by a good year or more, but that didn't throw her at all. She had this ability to get on with everybody. She was interested in everybody, it was not a studied craft.' One of the young men was medical student James Colthurst, who had a brief romance with Diana amid the snowball fights and sledge races. Colthurst's party piece was a full-volume impersonation of Martin Luther King's 'I have a dream . . .' speech at 7 a.m.

Diana tore the ligaments in her left leg. Unable to ski, she could have the tea and cake ready for when the rest came back hungry from the slopes. This only added to her popularity. The same leg injury gave her the excuse to stay in the Alps since, with her leg in plaster, she was unable to dance. One member of the group described her to us as 'fresh and unsuperficial, totally disarming . . . and fascinated in other people . . . she could just sit down and make you laugh'. He also remembers Diana hating having her picture taken, because, she said, her nose was too big.

Diana at eighteen, happy in the snow. It's an arresting image of the kind of life that could have been her fate. Colthurst, Berry, one of the other old Etonians in the chalet – young men of promise, the perfect partners for a life of country houses and happy family holidays, the Range Rover bursting with children and nannies, the ski rack on the roof. But although she fitted so easily into the group, she told one of them that she already had a very different sense of her future.

> She was quite clear about her destiny. She said she was going to get married to the Prince of Wales – not 'I want to' or 'I'd like to', but 'I'm going to' – and she'd only met him properly once by then! She was extremely sure of herself. It was fate: she had a strong sense of her own destiny. Then I said, 'Why would you want to do that? What's the attraction?' And she said, 'He's the one man on the planet who is not allowed to divorce me.'

On 27 August 1979 Lord Louis Mountbatten was killed in an IRA bomb attack. The younger brother of Amanda Knatchbull, Charles's guest at Sandringham the previous January, had also been killed by the bomb that blew up Mountbatten's boat on a fishing holiday near his Irish home. Amanda's mother and father were injured, her grandmother died of her wounds. Diana watched the state funeral on television. Prince Charles was visibly distraught.

By then Diana had settled in London and kept in touch with the boisterous group of slightly older friends that she had met while skiing. Life had taken a marked turn for the better. To keep occupied during the day she worked for Sarah and her friend Lucinda Craig-Harvey as a cleaner for one pound an hour. The money was irrelevant. On her eighteenth birthday, on 1 July, Diana had received a bequest from her great-grandmother, the American Frances Work. And, as a coming-of-age present, her parents wanted to buy her a flat. Sarah, then working for Savills estate agents, found Diana a £50,000 mansion flat, no. 60 Coleherne Court, at the junction of the Old Brompton Road and Redcliffe Gardens – the very heartland of the young rich set that congregated around Sloane Square. Diana officially joined the ranks of these 'Sloane Rangers' when she moved in, playing landlady to a varying group of girlfriends. Her other sister Jane found her a proper job, three afternoons a week with Kay Seth-Smith at the Young England kindergarten in Pimlico, a private pre-school with a wealthy clientèle.

Diana succeeded there from the start. Soon parents were remarking how often their children spoke about the pretty new teacher. She was invited to work mornings as well. Diana's colleagues were impressed with her flair for bringing out the best in the children. Although she had never received so much as an hour of teacher training, Diana's 'natural patience, good humour and intuition' shone through. Kay Seth-Smith was delighted:

> She was very good at getting down to the children's level both physically and mentally. She was quite happy to sit on the floor, have children climbing all over her, sit on the low chairs beside them, and actually talk to them. That's very important, to be able to talk to them, at their level. And they responded incredibly well to her. She would then go and help clear up in the kitchen. She was happy to put on the Marigolds as she called them [rubber gloves]. She would prepare lunch and just generally mucked in.

To occupy the other two days in her week, Diana had signed on with several nannying agencies. In February 1980 one of them, Occasional Nannies, found her a job with an American businesswoman called Mary Robertson, looking after her baby son, Patrick.

> The agency read her references and they described her as 'sweet tempered, wonderful with children and willing to do whatever she's asked'. When she came to the apartment I was expecting a nanny but I wasn't expecting this vision of perfect English beauty standing on my doorstep.

> During the interview, what I liked most was that she focused totally on Patrick, she looked up at me and answered my questions about hours and duties and pay, just the ordinary things. But she was ruffling his hair or handing him toys or giving him a little squeeze or a pat, just absolutely an instant connection between the two of them. I never even checked her references: I hired her on the spot.

The only thing about Diana that seemed less than perfect was her lack of academic qualifications. Robertson, a graduate of the Harvard Business School, was amazed to hear that this well-mannered English girl had, by American standards, not even graduated from high school. It was something Diana often complained about, blaming herself for a lack of talent at exams. It was nerves, she said.

Diana and Patrick soon established a routine. Building blocks on the floor, long walks in the London parks, she spooning jars of baby food, he splashing in his bath with the shiny yellow duck she bought him, she reading 'Where's the bunny?' over and over again. When Robertson returned from work, she would find her washing up done, her flat tidied, her child clean and contented and snuggling up to his nanny.

> It was a huge step to hand over Patrick to a stranger in a strange city where we had no neighbours, we really didn't know anybody. But Diana just struck me as so sensible and grounded and committed to Patrick. I really had no concerns about her being flighty or irresponsible.

Mary Robertson's words directly contradict those who insinuate that Diana was an emotional mess long before she met her future husband.

In fact, during these few months before she started dating Prince Charles, Diana was happier, more successful and more confident than at any time since she had first failed her O-levels three years before. She'd put Switzerland behind her and she was getting on with a pleasant life as a young Sloane about town, holding down two jobs that might not have needed great academic skill, but certainly required concentration, tact and a good feel for personal relations.

Mary, a businesswoman with a sharp mind, says that her baby son was the most precious thing in her life and she would not have trusted him with anyone she even suspected of being 'not quite right in the head'. None of this means that Diana at eighteen was cool and stable all the time. But in the months before her sudden fame, Mary Robertson had a powerful reason to examine her very closely, and so had an unusually good view of Diana then and, because they kept in touch, of the way she quickly changed.

When not tending to babies and toddlers, Diana mixed with other people who lived in this most exclusive part of west-central London. So recognisable was its resident class of affluent young people that a book called the *Sloane Ranger's Handbook* was published, describing how they dressed, where they shopped and ate, their upper-class English accent and the peculiar way that they signified agreement with 'OK, yah'. Sloanes tended to dress in country clothes in town – Barbour jackets, headscarves and green wellies – and sometimes tore around SW3 in country four-wheel drives. The Volkswagen Golf GTi was the preferred smaller car. They shopped at Harvey Nics and the General Trading Company. Around Sloane Square and the King's Road in Chelsea, they were as conspicuous as the punks who posed on street corners for the American tourists.

Their routine was dinner dates, charity balls and weekends in the country. It was a lifestyle little changed from that of the young rich of the 1950s, or even the 1930s. Parties often involved high spirits and heavy drinking, caught on the pages of society magazines like the *Tatler*. Diana's boyfriends came from this same set – young bankers, stockbrokers and soldiers from the smarter regiments. Adam Russell, reading languages at Oxford, dated Diana briefly, as did Rory Scott, a Scots Guardsman. Scott later said that his relationship with Diana was 'not platonic in my eyes but unfortunately it remained so'. Whatever it was in *hers*, she thought enough of him to iron his shirts every weekend. She also had a relationship with James Gilbey, of the London gin dynasty, that several of her friends believed was the most serious of her life so far.

Just what these relationships amounted to did not really matter when Diana was being vetted as a possible royal bride. What mattered was not having any untrustworthy ex-boyfriends who would run to the papers with embarrassing stories at the wrong moment. On these grounds Diana was safe. In fact, when the press began to dig the most damaging stories that emerged about her teenage love life concerned not sex but bad temper. She may have been an angel with Mary Robertson and her baby, but when James Gilbey stood her up one evening Diana made her displeasure very visible. She mixed a paste of flour and egg and poured it over his shiny Alfa Romeo.

There was a lot of talk of men and marriage inside Colherne Court. Diana told her friends that she was waiting for Mr Right and believed there was a good chance he would also be Mr Royal. Andrew seemed most likely, but it was Charles she really wanted.

The musicians are tuning up in the Regent's Gallery. As the evening light thins, elegant young men admire the dreamy view down the sloping lawns, past the fountain and out over the misty Vale of Belvoir. Down the grand staircase come the young ladies in their ballgowns; they glide through the Elizabeth Salon, between the silks, tapestries and porcelain. A buffet dinner is laid out under the chandeliers, to be eaten on laps between the Italian sculptures, underneath the Gainsboroughs, Reynoldses and Holbeins. Drinks are carefully placed on fine eighteenth-century French furniture, and then the dancing begins.

Behind Belvoir Castle's battlements and turrets, the Duke of Rutland is holding his annual summer ball. As the tempo of the music increases, and some of the older guests prepare to leave, Robert Spencer looks across the ballroom and catches sight of his favourite young cousin.

> The time I remember her best was the big ball at Belvoir Castle. Quite lovely. She looked magnificent whenever I saw her that summer in fact, and she seemed to have a great number of admirers. I lived rather farther to the south near Market Harborough and I had a large house party for this dance. I remember even some of the young men who were staying with me who knew Diana remarking on how absolutely lovely she looked. She certainly was great to me that night because she wanted to talk to me and we had delightful little chats. Prince Andrew was at that dance and he danced with Diana a lot.

Prince Charles was on the same circuit. Since November 1979 he had been romantically attached to Anna Wallace, the very pretty twenty-five-year-old daughter of a wealthy Scottish landowner. She was nicknamed 'whiplash Wallace' for her fearsome enthusiasm on horseback and her ready wit. It was rumoured that he had proposed and she had turned him down. Then in early summer 1980 the couple had a furious argument at a party at Stowell Park. The story ran that she borrowed her hostess's car to leave in a rage after he had paid rather too much attention to a married woman named Camilla Parker Bowles.

A few weeks later, in July, Diana met Charles again during a weekend party at the country home of Commander Robert de Pass near Petworth. His son Philip invited Diana to come along at the last minute. They went to Cowdray Park to watch the Prince playing polo for Les Diables Bleus, one of his teams.

Polo matches were good places at which to get a shot of Prince Charles with a girl, and for this reason polo grounds were haunted by teams of journalists on Charles-watching duty. Thirty-eight-year-old Harry Arnold had been on the royal beat with the *Sun* for five years. With tinted glasses shading his eyes against the sun, he was scouring the crowd at Cowdray Park for potential love interest that day with his cameraman, Arthur Edwards:

> Every weekend in the summer we would go along to the polo matches where he would always take his current girlfriend. But of course you didn't always know which one it was. Sometimes the girl would be very close to him, on his arm, talking to him between 'chukkas' and that kind of thing. But this particular weekend came where there didn't appear to be a current girlfriend and we went to this particular match and Arthur spotted this girl sitting in the crowd with a 'D' round her neck and had a vague recollection he'd seen her somewhere before. We talked about it and thought: Well, perhaps she's the latest one. So Arthur took just one frame of her, just one snap. And that was the very beginning of it.

After the match, and safely away from Edwards's camera, Diana sat next to Charles on a bale of hay during a barbecue back at Petworth. Both later recalled that she led the conversation. Dispensing with small talk, she raised one of the most sensitive subjects imaginable, telling Charles that she had really felt for him during the televised funeral of Lord Mountbatten, and asking him how he had coped with his evident unhappiness. It was an arresting moment for Charles, who was not used to being dealt with so directly. Always suspicious of flatterers, and uneasy with the insincerities of royal life, he found this woman surprisingly down to earth and very easy to confide in.

As the evening wore on, their conversation became very intense very quickly, as conversations with Diana often did. She told Charles how she sensed his loneliness and his need for someone to care for him. Charles found it hard to break away from this beguiling and rather beautiful young woman who seemed to understand so much about him. And, as he later recalled, he was moved by her patient and tender sympathy, her ability to go straight to the heart of things without fuss or embarrassment. Here was somebody he wanted to see again.

3
Eminently Suitable

> I'm sure that one of the things that appealed to Prince Charles about Lady Diana was just how unsophisticated she was. There was a naivety about her . . . she was just so young and beautiful, and great fun to be with – in that sense, I imagine, very different from most of the other young women that he's developed some sort of friendship with.
>
> Ronald Allison, former Buckingham Palace press secretary

Diana's sympathy over the murder of his great-uncle hit a soft spot in Charles. The World War II commander and former Viceroy of India had been like a father to the Prince. Although some regarded Mountbatten as vain and domineering, he was the most charismatic figure in the Windsor family, and Charles came to respect his advice. As Charles grew older this advice included tips about how to treat women and how to arrange his routine to accommodate a little discreet sexual experience. When Charles first began dating, Mountbatten offered his own country estate at Broadlands, safely away from the eyes of the press and the Palace.

In a series of letters, the older man gave the younger the benefit of his wisdom: enjoy your bachelor years, play the field, sow your wild oats and then, at about thirty, settle down with a nice aristocratic girl about ten years your junior, a girl who knows the royal scene and for whom you will be her first love. The advice may have been well meant, but it came as no surprise to Mountbatten's more cynical friends that his own granddaughter, Amanda Knatchbull, was a precise fit for the kind of bride

Mountbatten recommended. He had spent years trying to get the Royal Family named Mountbatten-Windsor, and he was not one to give up easily.

For years he made sure that Amanda and Charles were thrown together whenever it could be engineered, and was delighted when Charles first reported how attractive she had become, at age fifteen, on holiday in the Caribbean. Charles continued to find her attractive, and in the summer of 1979 he proposed to her, but Amanda said no. Neither this gentle rejection nor Mountbatten's murder a few weeks later diminished the old hero's influence. As Diana mentioned Mountbatten's name, Charles would have seen before him another perfect example of his great-uncle's ideal bride.

Soon after their conversation on the hay bale, Charles invited Diana to a performance of Verdi's *Requiem* at the Royal Albert Hall, followed by supper at Buckingham Palace. Lady Fermoy accompanied them as chaperone. The same week Mary Robertson discovered her nanny's true identity:

> I was cleaning up after my day at work and I found a bank deposit slip tucked under the skirt of the sofa in the living room where Patrick's toys were sprawled all over the floor. It was a deposit slip from Coutts & Company, which I knew from my job was the bank to the privileged, and her name was stamped on it, *Lady* Diana Spencer. And I did a double-take – by then we had been in London long enough so I knew this was not just a title, but a fabulous title. I took the slip along to my job the following day, I said nothing to Diana, and my office had a copy of either Burke's or Debrett's, I don't remember which, and I looked her up and discovered that she was as blue-blooded and aristocratic as you could possibly be.

Before finding the bank slip Mary Robertson had supposed that when Diana talked of weekends in the country she meant sleeping on the couch in a friend's cottage. After Robertson had extracted a promise that one day she might visit Althorp, Diana asked her employer whether she would be able to take her next two days off. She was planning a trip to Scotland. What she didn't tell Robertson was that she was going up to the royal estate at Balmoral to stay with her sister Jane Fellowes, ostensibly to see her new baby.

Prince Charles was at Birkhall, the Queen Mother's house near Balmoral, and made a point of inviting Diana to join him on several of his favourite Scottish walks. They got to know each other better. By the time that Diana accepted a personal invitation to the royal yacht *Britannia* for the week of the Cowes regatta in August, Charles was already telling friends that he thought he might have met the woman he would marry. Those who had not already met her were keen to. They were 'all over me like a bad rash', as Diana later put it, using one of her favourite phrases. Charles's assistant private secretary, Oliver Everett, received an early impression that this romance might go the distance. Robert Spencer remembers his cousin Johnny telling him at the same time that 'he was thrilled that Prince Charles seemed to be so keen on Diana'.

Charles asked Diana to return to Balmoral for the weekend of the Braemar Games in early September as part of his house party. Charles had several friends staying in or around Balmoral Castle.

> Mr and Mrs Parker Bowles were there. I was the youngest there by a long way. Charles used to ring me up and say: 'Would you like to come for a walk, come for a barbecue?' so I said 'Yes, please.' I thought this was all wonderful.

As well as Camilla Parker Bowles and her husband Andrew, the guests included Charles Palmer-Tomkinson and his beautiful wife Patti. At the centre of their party was Prince Charles, with his valet, Stephen Barry, fussing over his personal comfort. By now Barry and the servants were also speculating, but could pick up no sign that Diana was being accorded special treatment. Nevertheless, Charles's friendly but intimidating friends, all much older than Diana, were certainly vetting her closely.

Charles taught Diana to fish. They marched off with picnics to distant cottages. In the evening, after drinks with the Queen at six, they would dress for dinner at eight. Charles's brothers vied with him to sit next to Diana. She did her best to behave perfectly in the presence of the Queen, to whom even Charles deferred.

Charles told his friends that he found Diana warm, approachable and enthusiastic. He very much appreciated how easily she went along with his plans and mixed in with the group. Most of the friends, like Patti Palmer-Tomkinson, quickly came to share Charles's view of the pretty teenage girl who had suddenly come among them. She was great fun to have around and she appeared to be devoted to Charles. It was delightful to see, and it certainly seemed to make Charles happy, which wasn't always easy. The Prince confessed to one of these friends that he was not *yet* in love with Diana, but felt that he might come to fall in love with her in time.

Diana was excited by this new insight into the private life of the Prince of Wales, of whom she was still very much in awe. Once he was away from his mother, life revolved around him. His valet sorted his clothes, picnics appeared from the kitchen, everyone fell in with his wishes. In September at Balmoral he liked to walk in the hills and fish in the Dee. So this was what his friends did too.

It was fun being a friend of the Prince of Wales, moving around the beautiful estates that housed the van Cutsems and the Romseys, the Parker Bowleses, Soameses and Palmer-Tomkinsons. Life was relaxed and stylish: riding horses through woods or along riverbanks, early evening drinks in the garden, an excellent dinner to follow. It was pleasant for Charles too.

For inside the walls of his friends' country homes he could escape from the aspects of royal life that he found tedious or stressful: the crowds, the flowers, the 'and what do you dos?', the pestering journalists and the pompous local dignitaries. Broadlands and Bolehyde, Eaton Hall and Bowood: these were oases of relaxed pleasure where he could read and think, paint and fish; where he could be himself.

'From his childhood this boy will be surrounded by sycophants and flatterers by the score, and will be taught to believe himself as of a superior creation.' Thus the veteran socialist Keir Hardie had prophesied on the birth of another Prince of Wales, the future Edward VIII. Twenty years earlier the constitutional historian Walter Bagehot had explained that

> All the world and all the glory of it, whatever is most attractive, whatever is most seductive, has always been offered to the Prince of Wales of the day, and always will be. It is not rational to expect the best virtue where temptation is applied in the most trying form at the frailest time of human life.

Nothing much had changed. Charming as he was at the centre of his own charmed circle, Charles enjoyed having things his own way. 'He had a lot of charisma but he was a very selfish and old-fashioned man. Everything rotated around him,' we were told by a courtier of the late 1970s. Diana would soon begin to realise that the Prince of Wales, his friends and his servants all had an interest in preserving the lifestyle they had grown to know and love.

Royal photographer Arthur Edwards of the *Sun* was driving the last few miles on his way to the Highland Games at Braemar. With him were his friends and rivals from the *Daily Star*, flamboyant James Whitaker, and his photographer, Ken Lennox. Fixed in Edwards's mind was the usual target – a snap of Prince

Charles with a girl – when they suddenly saw Charles's car parked by the side of the road:

> We were driving along the River Dee and I spotted the green Range Rover. And there he was fishing. And there was this girl. She was dressed like a man but you could tell. She had green wellies on, one of these Barbour coats and a cap. We got closer and this lady ran up into the trees and hid behind a tree. And a colleague of mine – Ken Lennox – said, 'Look, if you go that way, I'll go that way. We'll get her in a pincer movement and she'll have to come out of the trees.' Which we did. And we saw her with her vanity mirror looking round at us. And at the point where we would have photographed her, she made a dash up through the trees. And all I had was these pictures of this girl's rear end rushing to the car.
>
> Prince Charles was absolutely livid. He put his fishing gear away and stomped off to drive back on to the estate somewhere.

Ken Lennox thought, 'My God! Who is this he's got? This is interesting.' He was so impressed by the woman's cunning evasion tactics that he wondered whether Charles might have something to hide. She had put a tree between him and her and all he had was a very fuzzy picture of her face that would not do for the paper. Edwards was more dogged. That afternoon at the Highland Games he made his usual enquiries of his usual sources. He was told that the mysterious she-male was Lady Diana Spencer and that she was following Prince Charles around like a lamb. The moment he heard the word 'Diana', he put two and two together: it was the girl at the polo with the necklace with the 'D'. He had a photo already! 'I rang the office immediately, and said, "That picture I sent back from the polo – can you get it out, it's her!"' Then he rang Harry Arnold, who was at a party in Kent. Arnold filed the story with sounds of disco music in the background. And so, on 8 September, beside 'Yippee! It's Wild West Week . . . see page 3', the *Sun* had the scoop: 'He's in Love Again! Lady Di is the new girl for Charles'. Edwards's polo photo was on the front page.

Diana came back from Scotland for the start of the new term at the Young England kindergarten to find that she had become a celebrity. The press quickly found out where she lived and followed her to Mary Robertson's mews house.

> She burst into my bedroom and said, 'I have something important to tell you, Mrs Robertson.' And I was blowing my hair dry and I said, 'OK, go ahead, tell me, Diana,' and she said, 'No, I'd like your full attention please.' So I put the hairdryer down and I can still see her – she was standing in the bedroom doorway and she was blushing and looking down. And she told me that when I left for work I would see photographers and reporters at the end of the mews. I couldn't imagine what they were doing there and she admitted that they were following her.
>
> I did a double-take and said, 'Good heavens, Diana, what have you done?' And she said, 'Well, I spent last week up at Balmoral Castle.' I asked if it was with Andrew because I knew they were the same age. And she said, 'No,' and she was blushing and looking down at the floor and very modest, very demure, you know, very Diana, very understated. She said, 'No, actually I've been with Prince Charles.' And I just couldn't believe it, I said, 'Oh, that's terribly exciting, do you think anything's gonna develop?' And she blushed again and said, 'No, I really don't think so. After all, he's thirty-one, I'm only nineteen. I don't think he'd ever seriously look at me.' And I said, 'Well, I wouldn't be too sure.'

Kay Seth-Smith was just back from holiday and hadn't seen the picture of Diana in the paper. She was shocked when she arrived at her Pimlico school to find photographers mingling with the new parents outside. Pushing her way through, she asked the staff what on earth was going on, and Diana blushed and giggled and said, 'I'm afraid it's my fault. I was photographed with Prince Charles at Balmoral.' Harry Arnold and Arthur Edwards were soon at the door, determined to develop their scoop by constructing a portrait of this latest fetching candidate for the Prince's hand.

> We went down to about half a dozen nurseries – we knew she was a nursery school teacher – and we found this nursery school, the Young England kindergarten. I knocked on the door: 'Does Lady Diana Spencer work here?' 'Yes.' 'Would she come out and have a photograph taken?'

Kay Seth-Smith told Edwards that she would go inside and ask Diana:

> And I said to her, 'How do we get rid of them? What about if you go and have your photograph taken?' And we were both very naïve in those days, and didn't realise this was not the way to get rid of photographers.
>
> So she said yes she would do that, but could she please take some children with her. And I said – well, yes, I suppose that's fine, but I'd better ring their parents up and say, you know, did they mind if their children were photographed. So I selected I think it was four children who I thought wouldn't be totally fazed by strange people thrusting cameras in their faces. I rang their parents up and said, 'We've got a rather unusual situation here – one of the teachers has been photographed with Prince Charles – you probably didn't know this and, um, they're now very anxious to get another photograph of her. Would you mind if your son or daughter was photographed outside with her?' And then I laughed and said, 'You never know, she may be the Queen of England.' And anyway, Diana went out, very embarrassed, clutching these children with her.

The photographers were delighted she was using the children as props and even more delighted, Edwards says, at their next stroke of luck: 'That was the picture where the sun came out halfway through the photographs and we saw her wonderful legs. And of course she blushed when she heard about that . . . She was very good at blushing.'

Kay Seth-Smith recalls that it did not take long for the pictures to appear:

> Later that afternoon, I suppose just after lunch, the doorbell rang, and somebody thrust a copy of the *Evening Standard* at me. And there on the front was this picture of her, in the see-through skirt. And I remember thinking, Oh dear, I think I've really blown this for her. And she took one look at it, went bright red, and put her hands up to her face in absolute horror.

But the picture of the shy girl with children in the see-through skirt didn't ruin it for Diana. Charles is said to have commented, 'I knew your legs were good but I didn't realise they were that spectacular.' The sunlight effect may have been luck rather than guile on the part of the photographers – Edwards says the weather changed. But the image with its triple message – naïve, sexy, homely – had a lasting impact. The siege of the kindergarten intensified:

> More and more press descended on us. And every day it got worse, we had television crews front and back, we had photographers hanging out of trees peering in windows. It was actually a fair nightmare to live with and of course Diana had no help, we had no help, none of us knew what we were doing.

On Diana's third visit to Balmoral in early October she stayed with the Queen Mother at her house at Birkhall. The rhythms of life there had altered little during the twentieth century. While the men went out stalking deer, Diana remained at Birkhall doing her needlepoint with the ladies. The Queen Mother and her close friend Lady Fermoy, Diana's grandmother, were soon entirely in agreement with Mary Robertson. Something might well develop. From now on the Queen Mother's London home, Clarence House, would become a powerful source of pro-Diana sentiment inside the Royal Family.

Like the young Elizabeth Bowes-Lyon, Diana offered youth, vitality and British blood to the still largely Germanic Royal Family In the twentieth century the Battenbergs had become Mountbattens and the Saxe-Coburgs had become Windsors. If accepted into the Royal Family, Diana would be the first English-born bride for an heir to the British throne for nearly three hundred years, since Lady Anne Hyde married the future James II. Diana was all English on one side and on the other a mix of Scottish, Irish and American.

Diana was an old friend of the family with links to the court on both her mother's and father's sides. Her parents, grandmother and sister all had experience of life inside Buckingham Palace. And she showed every sign of being eager to adapt to whatever challenge royal life might bring. Above all she appeared to love Charles. He would be lucky to find anything better than this.

A senior courtier working directly for Prince Charles told us that just two weeks after Diana had been spotted on the Dee, the Queen's private secretary, Sir Philip Moore, told him, 'I do hope he gets a move on and proposes to her for God's sake, the Queen is very keen.'

With newspaper photographs of Diana now appearing daily, the pace began to quicken. Camilla Parker Bowles invited Diana to her home, Bolehyde Manor, the weekend after she returned from Balmoral. Stephen Barry, Charles's valet, had his suspicion that Diana was a serious love interest confirmed when Charles rang him one morning to ask him to drive her to the country. On 24 October Diana appeared at Ludlow and stood, side by side with Camilla, watching the Prince race his horse, Allibar, in the

Clun Handicap. On Sunday Charles and Andrew Parker Bowles joined the Beaufort Hunt while Diana spent the morning talking with Camilla. Charles had just bought nearby Highgrove House. That afternoon he showed Diana round it and invited her to suggest ideas for its redecoration. Camilla was giving Diana advice on how to please Charles. As Diana later said, it was advice that revealed just how well the older woman knew him.

> I couldn't understand why she kept saying to me, 'Don't push him into doing this, don't do that.' She knew so much about what he was doing privately . . . I couldn't understand it.

Diana and Charles spent the following weekend at Bolehyde too.

It is not clear just when Diana began to worry about the nature of Charles's relationship with Camilla Parker Bowles, or indeed when she learned about its history.

Charles first met Camilla Shand in the summer of 1972 when he was twenty-three, and fell for her with the intensity of a true first love. Andrew Parker Bowles, her on-off boyfriend since 1966, had been posted to Germany in 1971. Charles had embarked on a career in the navy, and he had to join HMS *Minerva* three weeks before Christmas. They did not have much time together, and at that time neither he, nor even the press, was thinking seriously about marriage. He entertained Camilla on board twice and then, still very much infatuated, left for the Caribbean on an eight-month tour of duty. In April he learned that she had accepted an offer of marriage from Parker Bowles. Charles suffered a terrible 'feeling of emptiness', as he later confided to his biographer Jonathan Dimbleby.

Marrying Andrew did not remove Camilla from Charles's circle. As a Household Cavalry officer, Parker Bowles was frequently included in parties at Balmoral and Windsor. As his wife, Camilla was invited to the same events. Charles came to regard her as one of his best friends. Charles and Camilla frequently exchanged long telephone calls. Some people began to think they were having a clandestine affair, and in 1979, by Charles's own account, they were. When Andrew Parker Bowles went to Rhodesia, Charles spent a lot of time with his wife and, when Parker Bowles returned, Charles attended the ceremony for Rhodesian independence, taking Camilla with him as his official escort. Gossip about this web of relationships was only very occasionally aired in public, but it was not kept entirely secret.

At that time the satirical magazine *Private Eye* had a reputation for printing what even the tabloids dared not. The *Eye*'s staff endeavoured not to reveal whether its columns were a conduit for journalistic speculation, leaks from friends, or sheer fantasy – the mystery of what was truth or fiction was part of the joke. But *Private Eye*'s contributors, and especially its editor, Richard Ingrams, were intelligent and well connected. It reported early in 1980:

> No sooner had Lord Soames been appointed Governor of Rhodesia than the subject of jobs for the boys arose. Among the lucky ones: Major Andrew Parker Bowles, now a colonel and in charge of British liaison with the guerrilla forces. Andrew, 39, is married to a former (?) Prince Charles fancy, Camilla Shand, and if I should find the royal Aston Martin Volante outside the Parker Bowles mansion while the gallant colonel is on duty overseas, my duty will be clear.

In the early summer of 1980 Charles attended the Cirencester Polo Club ball. Andrew and Camilla were there too. Charles and Camilla danced together and were seen to be kissing enthusiastically. Camilla's husband, when told of this, is reported to have said: 'HRH is very fond of my wife, and she appears to be very fond of him.'

Camilla was not the only friend of Prince Charles upon

whose name society gossip lingered. Dale Tryon, known as 'Kanga', the Australian wife of Anthony, Lord Tryon, was also rumoured to be a current mistress, and appeared frequently in that guise in *Private Eye*. Innuendo about Dale Tryon had started in 1978:

> What a sport Lord Tryon is!!
>
> A loyal subject whose late father was Treasurer to the Queen, Anthony Tryon, 38, seems only too happy to let his Australian-born wife Dale act as hostess to Prince Charles when he is on holiday . . . Now the threesome are in Iceland where Brian [the *Eye*'s name for Charles] has taken a salmon river to indulge in his favourite sport, and Dale looks after the house.

These two women were very much part of Charles's circle during his courtship of Diana. Camilla and 'Kanga' were said to be mistresses in the classic court tradition, open and friendly with each other about their position in the Prince's life, even to the extent of discussing whom he might eventually marry. Charles evidently liked to remain friends with ex-girlfriends and was determined not to exclude them from his warm, supportive circle. As Louis Mountbatten might have put it, 'a man of the world' should not feel uncomfortable in situations like this.

PENNY JUNOR: He used these friends and he and Diana went and spent weekends with . . . with these people. I don't find anything particularly strange . . . particularly strange about that. Charles at that time was not having a relationship with Camilla – he had been certainly, but when he . . . when he began his . . . his pursuit of Diana that finished. I am abs . . . I am in no doubt about that.

AUTHOR: Seems a little bit convenient and, er, clean, clean and simple and . . . um, relationships often aren't any of those things.

PENNY JUNOR: What seems clean? That he stopped his relationship with . . . with Camilla? I think that would have been very, very two-faced and I don't think that the Prince of Wales is that kind of man. I think he . . . I think he's honourable and I think he would have regarded that as pretty dishonourable – to have an affair, to carry on an affair with an old mistress while courting a new . . . a new woman. On top of which don't forget . . . I mean, I believe that Charles at that time was head over heels in love with Diana. I think he was. When I say head over heels in love, I don't know whether love was the right word . . . *He* doesn't know whether love was the right word . . .

She [Diana] looked back years later on that early period with the Prince of Wales . . . and said that she had been a sacrificial lamb and how ghastly life had been and all his horrible friends and all his horrible family. I don't believe that at the time . . . I think she rewrote history.

During the week in London, away from Charles's safe houses, Diana was at the mercy of the press. Not that her pursuers were hostile. On the contrary, the royal journalists took an instant liking to Diana. They did their best to court her and she courted them right back. There were smiles and winks, but nothing too intimate or indiscreet and no repeat of Sarah's *faux pas*. Lennox, like other press photographers, took to sleeping in his car outside her flat.

> She was good fun. I mean, she invited me up for a cup of cocoa one night, as they were going to bed and she knew I was bedding down in the car outside. And I got up to the landing of the flat, the girls were standing in their jim-jams. And I just laughed, and she said, 'Are you laughing 'cos it's funny seeing us all in our pyjamas?' And I said, 'No, I thought you were gonna invite me in.' She said, 'What, and have a detailed description of the flat in the paper tomorrow? Do you think I'm stupid, Mr Lennox?'

Although most of the attention was friendly, royal staff were anxious to protect Diana.

> She was young, insecure, shy, not like the others. His previous playmates were all hard, capable of looking after themselves. But she was very different, she was kept out of the way until it leaked out, then all hell let loose.

Privately, they gave her advice on how to handle the media, what to say to them, how to hide her face when she did not wish to be photographed. Her combination of shyness and flirtatiousness won yet more hardened Fleet Street hearts, though they were frustrated by her habit of walking around with her head down.

Jayne Fincher was a young freelance photographer and, in 1980, one of the few women on the royal beat. She had been in America when the *Sun* exposed Diana and had missed the excitement about the new girl in Charles's life. Her first impression came in November:

> I went to the Ritz Hotel to photograph Princess Margaret's fiftieth birthday party, and I was standing outside and this girl came up behind us, a very quiet sort of young girl, and said, 'Excuse me, excuse me, can I get through?' And one of the other photographers said, 'I'm sure that's that girl, you know, what's her name? Diana Spencer.'
>
> So we all camped outside the Ritz and there were about three of us left, I suppose, and it was about two o'clock in the morning on a very cold freezing night. And suddenly she came out and she was all huddled up in this really unattractive green woolly coat that really looked very sort of dull and dowdy – not the sort of thing an eighteen-year-old girl would wear at all. And I looked at her and I thought, No, I'm sure these stories can't be true, because all the other girls that I'd photographed with Prince Charles at the polo matches had all been quite sophisticated women of the world.
>
> And Diana looked so young and she was so embarrassed and shy and looked like a little scared mouse coming out. And she

> scurried down the road and we followed her down and she, you know, she just wanted to die really.

Ken Lennox remembers that one of the things that was fun about staking out Diana was their informal exchanges about the progress of the courtship:

> If we put the cameras down, she would laugh and giggle with us – ask us what *we* thought was going on. She'd even sit in the front seat of my car and read *Private Eye* because they had twigged to it and the 'Sylvie Krin' column was full of all sorts of nonsense. And Diana would hoot with laughter when she read some of that, about Prince Philip kicking corgis up and down the corridor and stuff.

If it is true that Diana read *Private Eye*, this is possibly more significant than it might first appear. From early December, *Private Eye* ran a spoof romance about the royal courtship called 'Born to be Queen' by 'Sylvie Krin'. It was full of jokes at the expense of Prince Philip, Raine Spencer and Barbara Cartland, but, to Diana, it could also have been rather disturbing. Prince Charles was portrayed as having a great deal of red-blooded fun, and distinctly ambivalent about the idea of marriage. While his parents were determined that he should marry the sweet-natured but naïve Lady Diana, the heir to the throne was constantly on the phone to a character called Venetia Barkworth-Smythe, a married woman of the world.

Some of the dailies were producing innuendo of a similar nature. Nigel Dempster, the *Daily Mail*'s gossip columnist, reported that Diana's romance with Charles had been approved by the Prince's two married 'friends', Camilla Parker Bowles and Lady Dale 'Kanga' Tryon. If Diana did not already know what was being said about the nature of Charles's past friendship with these two women, she learned about it now, for she admitted that she read this column.

At the beginning of November a much more dangerous story broke, a story far worse than that which had sunk Sarah's chances with the Prince. The *Sunday Mirror* published a piece headlined 'Love in the Sidings', written by reporter Wensley Clarkson. It claimed that Diana had spent the nights of 5 and 6 November with the Prince on the royal train while it was parked in a siding at Holt in Wiltshire. When the *Sunday Mirror* rang her the night before they printed the story, Diana swore that she had not been on the train, but the paper was so confident that they failed even to mention her denial. In a most unusual intervention, Buckingham Palace, rather than maintaining its habitual dignified silence, demanded an apology. Michael Shea, the Queen's press secretary, announced that the only true fact in the story was that the Prince of Wales had used the train on the nights in question. The *Sunday Mirror*'s editor, Bob Edwards, believed his secret source – almost certainly a royal policeman – to be utterly dependable and refused to retract the story. In the end the Palace backed away from confrontation, but their intervention on behalf of Diana sent out a signal that she really was a potential bride.

Meanwhile every royal journalist wondered who the mystery blonde might have been if it was *not* Diana.

In the early 1980s the British tabloid press was changing character. Its new face had sharper fangs and a more derisive smirk. Rupert Murdoch had bought the *Sun*, previously a title owned by the Mirror group, and turned it into a garish rival to the *Daily Mirror*. The *Mirror* itself was acquired by Robert Maxwell and competed with the *Sun* in the search for sensation. A fierce circulation war ensued. Hyperbole was one weapon, and a newly intemperate tone crept into the newspapers' comments on those they liked and those they didn't. The 'build 'em up one week, knock 'em down the next' treatment became a salient feature. England football managers, soap opera stars, television quizmasters, all came in for the treatment. *Private Eye* invented a caricature tabloid columnist called Glenda Slagg. Within the same column Slagg would sing someone's praises and tear them apart.

Murdoch, at that time an outspoken republican, had no intention of bowing and scraping to British royalty. Royal stories sold newspapers and an imaginatively embellished story was better than no story at all. The new breed of editors had much less respect for the Royal Family too. Kelvin Mackenzie, who would take over the *Sun* in June 1981, positively enjoyed annoying the royals. Wearing a contrite expression at the morning conference, he would announce, 'I'm afraid we've upset the Palace yesterday.' Then his expression would change, as he demanded, 'How can we do it today?' Spurred on by their editors, reporters began to take what the Palace old guard considered to be an impertinent tone.

After the train story, the papers rallied round Diana again, the *Sun* to the fore. They implored Charles not to let a catch like this slip through his fingers. At the kindergarten, Diana continued to play cat-and-mouse with the press, and, according to Kay Seth-Smith, seemed to relish it:

> Diana was on a high, I would say, through all of this, there was an element of excitement, it was rather like the chase. At lunch-time, she would often be the one to say, 'Well, I'll go out and get it' – I mean, never a question of 'would *you* mind?' Because we all knew what she was going to come up against. But I think she quite enjoyed belting out of the school – and in fact one of my favourite photographs is of her running flat out with something for lunch under her arm.

One of Diana's friends also remembers her excitement.

> She rang up one day and said, 'I've always wanted to go around Westminster Abbey. You can teach me about architecture.' We

> went around and I was banging on about architecture, the Gothic arches, features, et cetera, and she wasn't listening to a word I was saying. She was walking up the aisle very slowly. I said, 'What are you doing?' And she said, 'Just practising.'

In late November and December Charles visited India and Nepal with more than the regular complement of royal reporters in tow. As usual the tour began with a cocktail party for the press, on this occasion at the British High Commission in New Delhi. Prince Charles seized the opportunity to sound out journalists on their view of Diana Spencer. One was Harry Arnold:

> There we were sipping drinks on the lawns of the British High Commission and Charles came over and terribly embarrassed me by saying, 'I hear you've been ringing up my friend Nicky asking when I'm going to get married,' meaning Nicky Soames. And I was very flustered and said something like, 'Well, you've given away my best contact now.' And he then said, 'Why do you think Lady Diana Spencer is the one?'
>
> And I think we all misunderstood the question because we didn't know what was going on in his mind. I thought he meant 'How did you detect that she was the one I have chosen?' And he then said, 'You mustn't rush me.' He said, 'It's all right for you chaps, you can live with a girl before you marry her, but if I get it wrong you'll be the first to criticise me in a few years' time.'
>
> And now, of course, with the benefit of hindsight, one looks back and thinks, well, what he really meant was, why do *you* think she's the one I should marry? It was as though he was seeking our approval. And now I think that we all rushed him into it, we urged it along and no one could stop the runaway train.

As a child Prince Charles had been diffident and sensitive. He admired his bold and confident sister Anne in much the same way that Diana admired her clever brother Charles. His childhood had often been lonely and his experience of school had, for the most part, been unhappy.

The Queen was distanced from her son by a busy schedule, a requirement to travel and the ritual formality of her job. Relations with Prince Philip were strained and, according to his authorised biographer, Charles had the impression that he had never been able to live up to his father's expectations. From an early age a sense of the importance of duty and self-control had been drilled into him. In a famous photograph that later moved his wife to tears, Charles stood looking lost in a little boy's suit, waiting in a queue to greet the mother he had not seen for several months. He got a handshake.

Charles redoubled his efforts to please, trying to adapt to a childhood rhythm that seemed calculated to create confusion. In the palaces and the castles, he was the centre of attention, fawned upon by courtiers and nannies, taught to command with confidence and grace, cooed over by thousands of strangers whenever he accompanied his parents on royal duty. For the rest of the time he was a desperately miserable boarding schoolboy, picked on and isolated by the boys at Gordonstoun, the tough Scottish school that his father insisted he attend and from which he wrote a series of upsetting letters home about his loneliness and mistreatment.

> The people in my dormitory are foul. Goodness they are horrid, I don't know how anyone could be so foul. They throw slippers all night long or hit me with pillows or rush across the room and hit me as hard as they can . . . I still wish I could come home. It's such a HOLE this place!

Beyond being a prince with big ears, his crime had been to snore.

The bewildered sadness and introspection of the Gordonstoun letters stayed with Charles, emerging later at moments of stress.

The biographer Penny Junor, who has spent a lot of time with Charles's circle, says that 'he is one of the saddest people I have ever encountered. He has a pitifully low opinion of himself and a debilitating lack of confidence in his own worth.' She puts the blame squarely on his father: 'Prince Philip is bluff, outspoken, hearty, tough and something of a bully, and he has no patience with his eldest son's soul-searching. Sensitivity is not one of the qualities he expects in a man, and although he undoubtedly has great affection for Prince Charles, he has spent a lifetime criticising him and quietly undermining his self-esteem.'

Charles returned from India in time for Christmas at Windsor. He had spent some time trekking in the mountains where the solitude had helped clear his mind. It needed to be clear because, by the time he got back home, not only Diana but the entire Royal Family were showing signs of strain. The Duke of Edinburgh wrote to his son, advising him that Diana's honour was at stake and that he could not leave her in doubt for much longer. Charles interpreted this as an ultimatum with an implied instruction to marry. At a dinner party soon after, Charles's friend Nicholas Soames upbraided the Duke's private secretary, Rupert Neville, for allowing the Duke to impose a match on his son. The Prince, who described himself as being in a 'confused and anxious state of mind', confided to a friend, 'I do very much want to do the right thing for this country and for my family – but I'm terrified sometimes of making a promise and then perhaps living to regret it.'

For Diana the excitement of having the press permanently camped outside her door and following her down the street whenever she left her house was beginning to wear off. At times she cracked under the strain, as a royal official recalls:

> The truth is she got swamped. Yes, she listened, but it was so overwhelming. I remember being in a car with her coming over

> Vauxhall Bridge and there was this huge hoarding with 'Di – the real story' and she broke down in tears and said, 'I can't take this any more.'

There had been days when she had phoned Mrs Robertson to excuse herself from work, saying she just couldn't face the attention. But now that job was over. The Robertsons had returned to America and she had waved Patrick off from Heathrow. Christmas was coming, bringing a different excitement and the prospect of escape to the privacy of Althorp. Ken Lennox was still on duty outside Diana's flat.

> She knew my family were still in Scotland at that stage, and she said, 'Mr Lennox, are you going home for Christmas to be with your family?' She knew enough about it, our families, and she would quiz us when she was sitting around with us. And I said, 'I don't think so.' And she said, 'Whyever not?' I said, 'Because we all reckon you're going to marry Prince Charles, and my task is to find some very good close-ups of you to use for a whole front page when the announcement's made.' And she said, 'But there's nothing like that happening yet.' I said, 'Well, we think there is.' And she said, 'Are you serious? You're staying down here to get that photograph?' I said, 'I am.' She said, 'But you must have lots?' I said, 'Yes, but they're all head down – they're not very good. I want a full-face, big, smiling picture for us, that we can drop over the whole front page of the paper.' And she said, 'I'll look out of the window tomorrow morning at six-thirty, and if you're the only one here, I will come down and get into my car. I'll put the window down, and let you have some close-ups, with a big smile. And that'll allow you to get home for Christmas.' I said, 'Right, I'll be here.' And she did it.

Robert Spencer joined the family for Christmas. He says that the relationship was not much discussed, but Raine Spencer told a friend that Diana was walking alone around the grounds of Althorp in tears.

The Royal Family went to Sandringham for New Year, where Diana joined them, spirited by back roads through a horde of reporters and photographers. They pressed so close that even the Queen lost her temper, snapping, 'Why don't you go away?' Prince Charles wished reporters 'a happy New Year and your editors a particularly nasty one'. At the beginning of January press secretary Michael Shea let it be known that the Queen was 'very distressed' at the way her family had been harassed during their winter holiday. The Queen urged Charles to take action soon but did not recommend one course or another.

Diana planned a trip to Australia with her mother to escape from the pressure and persuade the Prince with her absence.

Charles put a great deal of faith in the Queen Mother. She and her lady-in-waiting, Lady Fermoy, seemed firmly behind the match. Many years later Lady Fermoy admitted to Charles's biographer Jonathan Dimbleby that she had privately worried that Diana might not be up to the job. At the time she had tried to hint to Diana that she might be making a mistake: 'Darling you must understand that their sense of humour and their life-style are different, and I don't think it will suit you,' but, to her lasting regret, she had warned no one else. Robert Spencer told us that any reservations were overwhelmingly outweighed by delight at the apparent suitability of the match.

> Well, I don't remember any reservations at that time at all. I remember just celebrating, because it did appear then how eminently suitable Diana was. She'd never had any serious affairs, she was nineteen and a half, extremely beautiful and most popular, and she seemed to share interests with the Prince of Wales. She gave the impression of loving the country life, in particular staying at Balmoral. She seemed to be madly in love

with him and, after all, she did come from stock of a family who had worked with and supported the Royal Family for many generations.

And it seemed even more suitable because the Prince seemed like somebody who would want a younger girl to be his wife. She was young enough to be trained, and young enough to be helped, and young enough to be moulded.

Of Charles's friends, only two spoke out against Diana. Nicholas Soames, Churchill's grandson and a heavyweight in every sense, thought the couple too unlike each other to get on and felt that, above all, she did not share his serious social and political interests. Penny Romsey, wife of Mountbatten's grandson, also realised how little Charles and Diana had in common. She worried that Diana was courting press photographers and posing for them to put herself in the best possible light. She thought that the nineteen-year-old had fallen in love not with the Prince but with the idea of being Queen. After she had tried to hint as much to Charles, to no effect, her husband, Norton, stated her views more bluntly during a horse ride at Broadlands. Charles lost his temper.

His mother and father were urging him to act and seemed to be in favour of the match. Charles made clear in a letter that he wanted to make the right decision for himself and for the country, but he was being given no time to think and no opportunity to get to know the girl. An aide told us:

> Charles was an insecure person. He bounced around from one thing to another. He was captivated by this nice young thing, but he was never one for reaching a decision. The Queen told him, 'You can't keep on delaying coming to a decision. It's not fair on the girl, when the world's press is looking on the whole time. Come to a decision.'

Other royal officials remain convinced that Charles felt under pressure:

> He was a bachelor, loved the single life, travelling around the world. He didn't want to get married. But then his father issued an ultimatum, and told him to marry her, and so he did what he was told. He was forced into it.

And another courtier told us:

> He got bounced into this, make no bones about it. The combination of press and public pressure, he conned himself into thinking he was in love with her. Alarm bells should have been ringing all over the place. We are as guilty as everybody else.

While she awaited developments, Diana revisited West Heath. Penny Walker says that:

> She burst into our sitting room, and just beamed, and of course we said, 'What are these rumours? Are they true about you and Prince Charles?' And the beam got bigger and bigger, and she just said, 'I can't possibly say.' And she continued to beam for the rest of the afternoon. So we actually weren't quite sure what was happening, but she was obviously very, very happy.

Some of the press followed Charles to Switzerland. Harry Arnold was at Klosters, and he too was feeling the strain:

> I was under tremendous pressure to find out if there was going to be an engagement. I remember telephoning her from a hotel in Switzerland. All the calls in those days went through the switchboard. So I got through to the flat and one of the other girls answered, so I simply said, 'I have a call from Klosters.' Lots of girlish squealing in the background and on came Diana. I said, 'Oh, hello, Diana, it's Harry Arnold here.' There was this gasp and I said, 'Who did you think it would be?'

In the clear mountain air Charles was making his final deliberations. He had been close to Diana for only six months but his parents had told him that he could not keep her waiting much longer. It was his duty to let her go if he was not sure. And in many ways she seemed so perfect.

While skiing in Klosters he talked his problem through again with his hosts, Patti and Charles Palmer-Tomkinson. Both had been early supporters of Diana, and it's likely that they encouraged the match at this critical moment. Had Charles gone skiing with Nicholas Soames or the Romseys, it is conceivable that the story may have ended differently.

On his return to London, on 6 February, Charles invited Diana to Windsor Castle and asked her to marry him. He told her to take some time to think it over. She accepted immediately. Charles explained how horrendous some of the pressures would be and said that it would not be an easy life. She barely listened and rushed back to Colherne Court to tell the girls. Unable to celebrate in public, and yet needing an outlet for their excitement, the four of them went for a late-night drive around Buckingham Palace in Diana's Mini Metro.

As they sped up and down Birdcage Walk and round and round the Victoria Memorial, they talked about the great occasions that were to come. Diana standing on the balcony and waving at the crowds pouring down the Mall, Diana showing her young princes to their people, Diana, *their* Diana, riding in an open carriage. She was going to be the Queen of England.

As Diana and her friends sped dreamily past the gates of her future home, Charles was inside Windsor Castle making a series of telephone calls. According to Penny Junor, one was to Camilla Parker Bowles, who was aware that he was planning to propose to Diana that evening and was keen to know the result.

In New York, Mary Robertson had been scanning the English newspapers anxiously. Then she got a call from a friend in London:

> 'Mary, your girl made it.' I just shrieked for joy. I couldn't have been prouder of her than if she'd been my own daughter. And I *was* happy for her, because this was truly what she wanted.

Arthur Edwards was on holiday in Ireland that February, but he had left a number with Harry Arnold. He'd only just arrived at his cottage when the phone rang.

> It was Harry and he said, 'Listen to the one o'clock news. I think they're going to get engaged.' I said, 'Why?' He said, 'Well, I'm at the Foreign Office and he's cancelled the engagement here and there was a piece in *The Times* this morning suggesting it was going to be today.' And I said to my wife, 'I'm sorry. I've got to go back to London.' I went straight to the flat, Colherne Court, and got a really nice picture of her leaving for the last time. She gave a smile, I promise you it just lit up the whole street. She was such a happy girl.

4
New Billing

> I thought that it was a match made in heaven and I think most of us did. I thought that the Prince of Wales would take Princess Diana under his wing and teach her the ways of the Royal Family and the direction that she should follow, and I couldn't think of a better tutor.
>
> Lord Palumbo

Within a week of Prince Charles's proposal on 6 February, Lady Diana was in session with *Vogue* fashion editor Anna Harvey choosing clothes. Harvey had rung round various leading designers asking for samples for an anonymous celebrity. Elizabeth Emanuel, five years out of the Royal College of Art but already a favourite at Harrods and Harvey Nichols, sent in a pink blouse and skirt. Diana loved them. A few days later she went to Elizabeth and David Emanuel's Brook Street studio and asked for an evening dress for her first public appearance. At the time all they had was a strapless, backless, black taffeta silk gown with a plunging front. She loved this too and said that she thought black was the smartest colour a girl could wear.

She consulted Kevin Shanley about her hair. Twenty-five-year-old Shanley ran a stylish Kensington studio called Head Line. He had been doing Diana's hair since 1978, and her current short look was his creation. Now she was worried that it wouldn't go with the Spencer tiara for her wedding. She could only grow her hair two inches before July: he assured her it would be fine.

With the announcement of the engagement on 24 February 1981, large crowds converged on Buckingham Palace. The band of the Coldstream Guards played 'Congratulations' and Diana's father and stepmother beamed their delight to reporters at the Palace gates. At Westminster, Margaret Thatcher interrupted Prime Minister's Question Time to congratulate the couple.

They were interviewed for television that day. The Prince declared himself 'positively delighted and frankly amazed that Diana is prepared to take me on'. The BBC interviewer pressed them, 'And in love?' Diana's 'Of course', delivered with rolled eyes and a self-conscious giggle, was immediately qualified by Charles's 'Whatever "in love" means'. Much has been made of Charles's odd remark. Ronald Allison, who was Buckingham Palace press secretary through the seventies, told us the Prince was merely being clumsily flippant. But Diana noticed the comment. She later claimed that it echoed what her new fiancé had said to her seconds after she had accepted his proposal of marriage: 'I said, "I love you so much, I love you so much." He said: "Whatever love means." He said it then.'

PENNY JUNOR: But I think that he ... he could have handled the situation better, he could have explained more to Diana, he failed to realise that she was a ... a jealous ... I mean the jealousy is perfectly understandable and perfectly normal in a nineteen-year-old girl and I think that he failed to see that and when asked whether he was in love he said ... he answered – absolutely typically – 'Yes, in love, whatever love means.' This man is not like the rest of us, he can't tell a little white lie, he can't just say, 'Yes, of course we're madly in love,' he thinks too hard about everything and feels compelled to articulate what he's thinking. He's ... And if something is difficult or deep or complicated he will spell it out, whereas the rest of us will just be two-dimensional about things.

AUTHOR: Would you have bought it if you'd been Diana? And how would you have felt if you'd been standing next to him –

international television, you adore him, he's been the object of your teenage crush, you're about to marry him and he says that, what would you have said?

JUNOR: I would have been devastated. I mean, I think it was a terrifically insensitive thing to have done, but in some areas he's a . . . I think he was . . . He was insensitive.

Whatever Diana thought in retrospect, Charles's lack of emotional enthusiasm was probably not her most unsettling experience that spring. Or rather, perhaps, his reserve mirrored the coldly orchestrated formality of court life as it was suddenly revealed to her. She found herself under constant pressure to perform in circumstances dictated by protocol and the rigidly old-fashioned officials responsible for determining it.

The night before her engagement was announced, Diana had been moved to the Queen Mother's home, Clarence House, and three days later to her own apartment in Buckingham Palace, where she stayed until the wedding on 29 July. A courtier told us that the move was made:

> partly because of the press but partly as a result of her determination to come to terms with the huge challenge. She was trying terribly hard to get it right. She cut herself off from her Sloaney friends, which was part of her attempt to try and get it right. That was the streetwise Diana. She would have realised all her old chums and kindergarten friends would have stuck out like sore thumbs in the Palace. Once she was in there, what does she do? Who does she talk to?

But the pace was so fast that the problems did not emerge immediately. There was very little time for preparation before Diana's first public engagement on 3 March 1981, a musical recital at Goldsmiths Hall in aid of the Royal Opera House Development Appeal. The one highlight of this evening was meeting Princess Grace of Monaco, who sympathised with

Diana's predicament. Next week came Diana's first state occasion, a banquet given by the Queen for the President of Nigeria. The weekend was spent at Balmoral and was followed by a photo call with the Queen after ratification of the marriage by the Privy Council.

Diana wanted to please Charles, have him take pleasure in her progress, give her an encouraging pat or a kiss, as courtiers who first worked with her recall vividly. But in mid-March, he went off on a long-planned official visit that took him to Australia for three weeks, New Zealand for two weeks, and then on to Venezuela, Washington and Williamsburg. The tour had been arranged months before and could not now be cancelled. Nor, apparently, could Diana be worked into the tight schedule, although she longed to travel with him. Perhaps everyone felt that she needed to be in London to arrange the wedding. But it was an unfortunate time for her to be deprived of Charles's support.

Diana accompanied Charles to Heathrow and telephoto pictures of her as she left revealed a head bowed in tears.

'Never underestimate the Palace establishment,' we were told. 'When I first arrived there the footmen had their rooms tidied by the maids. They are deeply conservative.'

With over six hundred rooms and two hundred staff, Buckingham Palace is more like a large office building with an attached hotel than anything resembling a family home. Members of the Royal Family each have their own apartment, and Diana too was assigned a suite with a sitting room, bedroom, bathroom and small kitchen. The rooms had the impersonal feel of an Oxbridge college with ugly furniture, pictures drawn from the less celebrated corners of the royal collection, and old-fashioned electric-bar heaters fixed to the walls. The sense of temporary incumbency was emphasised by the typed names inside brass holders attached to the door frames. With the flat came a maid and a footman.

The Palace is a very gossipy place and Diana was soon made aware that staff provided information to the newspapers. It was difficult to know who to trust, and it did not come naturally to Diana to remain distant and buttoned up. They had rescued her from the press, but she soon found herself bewildered and lonely inside an alien institution with its own arcane rules.

To demonstrate that she was taking her new life seriously and was determined to rise to the challenge, Diana saw little of her friends from Colherne Court. Instead she strengthened friendships within the royal circle, notably with Sarah Ferguson (whose father managed Charles's polo team), with whom she had lunch once a week, Sarah Armstrong-Jones, Viscount Linley, and Princes Andrew and Edward. But none of them provided Diana with a soul mate to make the atmosphere less oppressive.

When Sarah Ferguson eventually married Prince Andrew in 1986, she also found life in Buckingham Palace intimidating:

> Over the four months that led up to our wedding, I was swept along with the tide. Every person I met seemed powerful to me: the ladies in waiting, the protection men, even the housemaids. I assumed they must know what to do, as they had all been at it much longer than I.

Royal press officer Ronald Allison recalls that:

> Once the engagement was announced, the focus of the press was even sharper on Lady Diana Spencer than it had been before. They were no longer speculating about who the Prince of Wales was going to marry, they were absolutely concentrating whole-heartedly, one hundred per cent, on the person he *was* going to marry.

The black dress she had bought from the Emanuels received a mixed reception. As Diana stooped low to climb out of the royal car, the photographers snapped the shot they had most wanted

– soon-to-be-royal cleavage to match September's legs. Diana was blushing again. A few days later she was photographed in Cheltenham having her hand kissed by gallant sixth-former Nicholas Hardy. Innocent enough, but laden with the sexual innuendo that was now creeping into coverage of the royal couple. Edmund, Lord Fermoy, Diana's uncle, asserted to journalist James Whitaker that she was a virgin, tempting *Private Eye* to dig for dirt. They unearthed the name James Boughey and the insinuation that he was not known in his regiment for pursuing platonic relationships, but nothing more damaging. Other friends were targeted by the press, and to Diana's annoyance Simon Berry's pictures of their skiing holiday appeared in the *Sunday Mirror*.

Journalist Christopher Hitchens remembers the fevered atmosphere in the build-up to the royal wedding:

> A story of this kind will always find the G-spot in our great profession. She was quite pretty, she was young and blushing and innocent. There was an undertone of the salacious which doesn't hurt the circulation . . . It's actually brilliantly caught in Martin Amis's novel *Money*, which is set at the time when the royal wedding's about to occur. And there's a big discussion down the pub about whether he's 'given her one' or not. And I certainly remember those kinds of discussions, they were inevitable, they were all part of it.

From Charles's tour, meanwhile, came the unsurprising news that everybody wanted to see Diana. Charles was constantly apologising for her absence and was embarrassed by various incidents with women, including a posse of fake Dianas and a bikini-wearing girl rising for a kiss from the waves of Bondi Beach.

For photographers Diana was a gold mine and for the most part they, like Jayne Fincher, were

> Just very excited about it. I mean, all the men were madly in love with her instantly and we all adored her straight away because she was great fun to photograph. We had this very pretty girl and it was a fairy story and we all loved the story and obviously it was very good for us because, you know, it kept us really busy. Everyone in the world wanted pictures of her.

Unfortunately, Diana was not always prepared to co-operate:

> She was so painfully shy. And every magazine in the world wanted a picture of Diana on the cover – you know, a nice head on the cover – and her head was down the whole time. We'd all say, 'Did you get her head up? Did you see her eyes?' I think I had one picture of her with her head up before she got married.
>
> She did make a comment about it to me later. She said that if she heard the ladders – because we all have these aluminium ladders that we stand on to get over the heads of the crowd – she knew that we were all in front of her so she'd keep her head down. And then if she heard the sound move away she could put her head back up again.

However well meaning the photographers were, the persistence of their pursuit and the constant worry that she might provide the wrong sort of photograph were stressful. Press officers recall Diana coming into their offices in tears, begging them to get the press to leave her alone. They had meetings with police chiefs at Scotland Yard about the problem, but they judged that it was simply impractical to shut the door.

During March and April, Diana got to know the staff of the various offices and began to get a sense of the royal establishment within which she now had to live and work.

At the top of the pyramid of royal service were the private

secretaries, one for each member of the family. They governed with the assistance of deputies and equerries. Many of the jobs were semi-hereditary, although most courtiers had a background in the armed forces and some were on secondment from the Foreign Office. The latter, though often gifted individuals, were in the job too short a time to be able to bring much experience to bear, and this may explain what look like some rather poor decisions on royal tours.

In *My Story*, Sarah Ferguson provides a hostile account of the palace 'grey men', as she called them. Where some speak tactfully of a desire not to rock the boat, or of inflexibility, she condemns self-serving inertia, downright laziness, pompous mediocrity. She refers to levels of pay that attracted snobbery more than talent, to suits, polished shoes, old-school or regimental ties (Guards for preference). She speaks of umbrellas handed to footmen at the Privy Purse entrance, of days devoted to the control of information, the careful channelling of messages through at least four secretaries. Gin and tonic in the Equerries' Room at 12.30 sharp would precede lunch in the Household Dining Room, the most senior of the three staff dining rooms at the Palace. In their own common rooms the ruling secretaries could joke about their masters and mistresses in private. Sarah's account is unlikely to be fair, but many of the details are corroborated by what Patrick Jephson, Diana's private secretary in the nineties, said about the Palace establishment in his book *Shadows of a Princess*.

Prince Charles's immediate staff were hardly ideal company for her. The Hon. Edward Adeane, born in 1939, bald and bespectacled, had been private secretary to Prince Charles since 1979. He was a precise and intellectual bachelor, whose father and grandfather had also been royal private secretaries. He was very conservative and was already engaged in a rearguard action against the Prince, for whose enthusiasms he felt little instinctive sympathy. It was about the Prince, not the Princess, that he once remarked, 'If I hear the word "caring" again, I'm going to be sick.' Diana flirted with him and teased him and at first they got on quite well. His assistant, Francis Cornish, on secondment from the Foreign Office, had been with the Prince only since May 1980. He was thirty-nine and a much more approachable figure than Adeane, but his first loyalty was to the Diplomatic Service, and he was not anxious to get too involved in the personal lives of the Royal Family. Cornish's precursor in this job, Oliver Everett, was less reserved. He abandoned his Foreign Office career and accepted the Prince's offer to become Diana's unofficial private secretary. He liked both Charles and Diana, and made every effort to be friendly to his young charge. He was tall, dark and square-shouldered with a strong jaw – quite Diana's sort. But his endeavours to get her to read up on the Constitution and the role of the monarchy met with scant success. Dull, difficult books were not Diana's thing.

Charles had his own differences with Palace bureaucracy, and his private affairs were handled by his own man – the Secretary of the Prince's office, Michael Colborne. In place since 1975, Colborne had served with Charles in the navy and was – most unusually in this environment – a grammar school boy. He also spoke his mind in a manner that was uncommon in the circles around Prince Charles. He was twenty-seven years older than Diana but soon became one of her closest friends in the Palace.

Lady-in-waiting Lady Susan Hussey was brought in to teach Diana how to be royal. She was devoted to the Queen, whom she had served since 1960, was deeply versed in protocol and possessed a powerful, no-nonsense personality. At the time Diana wrote of Lady Susan as of an elder sister, but later recalled feeling that she had seemed hostile to her. What she most certainly was *not* was a girlish confidante.

Diana's immediate concern was the wedding. She fixed on the Emanuels for her wedding gown. They were ecstatic, if slightly surprised that the job had not gone to a traditional outfit like

Belville Sassoon or Hardy Amies. Diana told them she wanted something romantic. It had to be stunning but classic so that she didn't disappoint anyone. They laid out their entire range for her and finally found a design she loved. Her mother came to the second session, and they all sat on the floor and pored over sketches. They went through books and pictures of previous royal weddings, determined to outdo them all. They found the royal dress with the longest train and created one that was longer.

Preparations for the wedding brought Diana into frequent collision with other, even more intimidating parts of the royal establishment. A courtier told us that:

> It wasn't long before the apparatus of the Palace got to work over the wedding plans. That part of the Palace is deeply embedded in the Guards, staffed by older people, pretty reactionary. If I found them frustrating, what could it have been like for her?

The wedding was the province of the Lord Chamberlain, Lord Maclean, the head of the royal household. For him and his staff, this would be the biggest event of their career, a moment of defining glory. All agreed that it was to be a splendid occasion, but their ideas of what was splendid did not always coincide.

Charles wanted the wedding to take place in St Paul's Cathedral, rather than the traditional venue, Westminster Abbey. He preferred the architecture and acoustics of St Paul's, a church big enough for the orchestras that he wanted to provide music and with space for more guests. The Lord Chamberlain's staff worried that there were no precedents for the use of St Paul's. They worried too about the cost – particularly the cost of the extra policemen and soldiers who would be required to guard the much longer processional route that would now stretch all the way from the Palace to the City. Only two years after Mountbatten's death, the threat from the IRA could not be taken lightly, and the longer route meant that the soldiers would be more widely spaced than the security advisers wished. The Lord Chamberlain's anxieties were heightened when on the Queen's official birthday, 13 June, she was shot at by a lone gunman. The assassin turned out to be a seventeen-year-old firing blanks, but for Diana, watching the Trooping of the Colour for the first time, it was a forcible reminder of another of the strains of royal life.

The cogs may have squealed but the royal machine moved efficiently. By the end of June the order of service and the complete programme of processions were ready. Eleven carriages had been selected and prepared, with three closed ones in case of rain. Three thousand policemen and three thousand soldiers had been designated to line the route. Meanwhile the media went into a frenzy of excitement. ITV and the BBC were planning the biggest outside broadcasting event ever on television, and each of them spent £500,000 on coverage. Teams from the American networks descended on London to secure strategic positions on the route to the cathedral. Fees of £2,000 were negotiated for the use of a desirable window on the day. CBS paid £8,000 for a balcony. Both ABC and NBC transmitted their breakfast programmes from Britain throughout the week of the wedding. The BBC arranged to broadcast live to seventy-four countries to a worldwide audience of 750 million people. What the Coronation had done for television sets, the royal wedding did for home video recorders. In 1980 the British video market doubled to around 700,000. For this new market taped souvenirs were made such as *The Story of Prince Charles and Lady Diana* and *Prince Charles: A Royal Portrait*. In the full flush of enthusiasm for the royal couple, the BBC screened the first royal quiz show, *So You Think You Know about Royalty?*, on 19 July, with Cliff Michelmore and Magnus Magnusson as quizmasters.

The commemorative industry was working overtime. At the official level there were stamps and coins; at the commercial, plates and mugs and playing cards, bookmarks and beach balls, place mats and tea towels. The most popular image was that of Charles placing his arms protectively around his fiancée's shoulders. Since she was slightly taller than him, he had to stand on a box to achieve this effect.

Diana's dress needed constant alteration because all the time she was getting slimmer. She lost two stone between her engagement and the wedding. She had been disappointed when she saw the engagement photographs because she looked chubby, an effect only attributable in part to the frumpy blue dress that she was wearing. She showed off her newly glamorous attire and attenuated figure at Ascot and at Wimbledon. The *Sun* approved of 'Lady Di-et'.

Few things in Diana's life story are as contentious as the date of the onset of her bulimia. Old friends support Diana's own account that it began now, under the sudden pressure of life inside the Royal Family, her mounting anxiety about Charles's true feelings and her worries about her weight.

Bulimia experts point to the family history of eating disorders – Diana's sister Sarah had been anorexic for a while – and say that generally this condition begins in the mid-teens. Those who portray Diana as unbalanced before she met her husband naturally seek to root the bulimia in the past, but there is scant evidence of it. Mary Robertson is emphatic that Diana showed no sign of an eating disorder while she shared a fridge and a bathroom with her family. And the first photographs that could possibly be said to show Diana looking unhealthily thin were taken in Wales in October 1981, some months after the wedding.

She was certainly anxious to look slim in order to be a credit to her husband and to live up to her new billing as a beautiful princess. She was a teenage girl thrown into this world of palace and sexual intrigue alongside older and more worldly people, all of whom were confident in their familiar environment. She was insecure and unknowing. The excitement of having been chosen to be the Princess of Wales was quickly buried in a misery of worry about what marriage to Charles might be like and whether he really loved her – an agony of jealous, anxious teenage first love exacerbated a million times over by its national significance. Enough to make anybody sick.

Charles returned to London at the beginning of May, but if Diana thought she would now have him entirely to herself she was soon disappointed. According to a senior member of the royal household:

> Lovely chap though he was, her fiancé gave no indication of thinking through what getting married to this person would be like for her. He carried on with his merry ways, his extracurricular bachelor life, one night in Scotland, one night somewhere else. In her case, it was a massively bigger thing.

They did spend some time together. A round of joint engagements began with a visit to Broadlands where he opened an exhibition of Mountbatten memorabilia on 9 May. Diana spoke to children and cuddled babies. Five days later she was at Windsor for lunch with the President of Ghana. Later in the month came a state visit from King Khalid of Saudi Arabia.

On 22 May the couple went walkabout in Tetbury. Jayne Fincher was there with her camera:

> He took her down to Tetbury, their future home town. He introduced her to the locals. They did a walkabout and visited the local hospital. And, you know, she was very nervous and he was sort of gently cajoling her round and showing her what to do. She was obviously very new to it, and very shy about it, and he was like the proud peacock showing her off. But he was very gentle and he always had an arm round her showing

her what to do, watching her all the time. And obviously was sort of gently nurturing her into it.

But by now Diana was fretting about Camilla. *Private Eye* had become more brazen in its accusations against Prince Charles, although its sources and its seriousness remained as ambiguous as ever. At Christmas it reported that White's Club (venue for Charles's stag night) had voted him 'Shit of the Year':

> It was Brian's behaviour to his girlfriends that clinched matters . . . Now Brian is trying to lead the innocent Lady Diana Spencer up the garden path. In giving him their vote, White's members have taken into consideration that he will probably be equally beastly to her.

On 3 July, 'Grovel' produced another disquieting and apparently authoritative report:

> Bets are being taken among Prince Charles's male friends as to how long Aussie harpie Lady Tryon will last as the Heir to the Throne's 'confidante' when he returns from honeymoon in September. Melbourne publisher's daughter Dale Tryon (nee Harper) arrived in England a decade ago with the sole ambition of marrying into the aristocracy, and quickly ensnared Anthony Tryon, whose late father the 2nd Baron, was Keeper of the Privy Purse and Treasurer to the Queen for 25 years. Through him she met Prince Charles and their friendship became close.
>
> But not for much longer, I can reveal.
>
> Lady Diana has yet to meet Dale – Charles calls her 'Kanga' – but she has become friends with her fiance's other 'confidante', Camilla Parker-Bowles, whose husband Andrew has recently been made Commanding Officer of Knightsbridge Barracks, where the Household Cavalry is stabled.

It then repeated the story of how Charles and Camilla were supposed to have met, drawing back the curtain to reveal a tantalising glimpse of an *ancien régime* world of '*liaisons dangereuses*' in which the naïve Lady Diana was a potential laughing-stock. Camilla had indeed done her best to befriend Diana, but it is not surprising that such stories undermined the younger woman's trust in the older woman's motives.

Diana was well aware of *Private Eye*'s vivid coverage of the Royal Family. With little other evidence to go by, its insinuations may have given darker significance to a series of incidents that she cited ten years later to Andrew Morton as signs that her fiancé's relationship with his 'confidante' was not as innocent as she had been told. When she first moved in to Clarence House, she said that she found a note waiting on her bed. It was from Camilla: 'Such exciting news about the engagement. Do let's have lunch soon . . . I'd love to see the ring.' Then, within days of entering Buckingham Palace, she discovered that Charles had recently sent some flowers to Camilla when she was ill with a message using what she claimed were the couple's pet names for each other: 'To Gladys from Fred'.

In mid-July Diana discovered a bracelet in Michael Colborne's office with the initials 'G' and 'F' cut into it. It was intended for Camilla. Diana stormed out of the room. According to Charles, it was a thank-you present for years of friendship and G F meant 'Girl Friday', his nickname for the supportive Camilla. But Diana believed the letters stood for 'Gladys' and 'Fred', and that the characters were intertwined on the bracelet when she saw it, suggesting a relationship more intimate than the one Charles was implying with his Robinson Crusoe analogy. This incident was witnessed by courtiers, and only the interpretation of it is in doubt: Charles's apologists go with the G F explanation, Diana's with G and F intertwined.

Diana and Charles had a heated row that afternoon. Diana pleaded with him not to give Camilla the present out of respect for her feelings. He insisted on doing so, in person, on 27 July, two days before their wedding.

Charles had already admitted to a relationship with Camilla

but maintained it was now in the past. A number of royal officials have told us that Diana questioned them repeatedly about Camilla. Embarrassed, they would change the subject. Diana struck the Parker Bowleses and the Tryons off the invitation list to the wedding breakfast. She and Charles argued again. She asked him outright whether he still loved Camilla. He said yes he did, just as he loved many old friends, but insisted upon his word of honour that from now on he would remain faithful to Diana. It was then that Diana panicked the office into arranging the *Ménage-à-trois* lunch in a bid to clear the air.

At the time it seemed to have worked, but Diana evidently went over her conversations with Camilla again and again in her mind. Her analysis suggested that Camilla saw hunting and country life as her opportunity to maintain her affair with Charles. She appears to have interpreted Camilla's 'Will you hunt?' as a code for 'Do you accept he will be mine some weekends?' Penny Junor, who has heard Camilla Parker Bowles's side of the story, believes that anything that might have touched on hunting was simply small talk: a friendly part of a friendly occasion that both women – at the time – felt had gone very well. Camilla says that she thought Diana was a good match for Charles and accepted that her relationship with him was over for ever.

Charles was away touring the Duchy of Cornwall on 20 and 21 July. He rejoined Diana on 22 July for a wedding rehearsal followed by his stag night at White's Club. On Saturday, 25 July, four days before the wedding, Charles played polo in the annual cup match between the navy and the army. There were those who thought he should not have done it. The repercussions of a fall could have been serious, and a team of doctors with ambulances stood by, watching anxiously from the sidelines. Playing for the army that day was a young officer named James Hewitt:

> Prince Charles was playing for the navy, and the army lost by one goal. Actually I'd fouled him just before the end of the last chukka which gave away a penalty, a forty yard penalty, from which he was able to score. So, it was my fault that they lost, really. He got the goal and I said, 'Well, there's your wedding present, Sir.'

Diana was biting her nails. The press was out in force for the last pictures of the single girl. Her every gesture was accompanied by the whirring of cameras. To add to her anxiety, Charles was planning to deliver his bracelet on Monday. She watched under visible strain and then, halfway through the match, fled the field in tears, hurried away by Lady Romsey. Prince Charles came over and tried to comfort her. Then he lost his temper with members of his staff, shouting angrily for his car to be brought round. David May, a reporter for the *Sunday Times*, had been standing away from the main press pack. Diana had stormed right past him and he had seen everything else that followed. His story led the following day's paper, with Diana's tears ascribed to pre-nuptial tension.

Diana's doubts were mounting, as Robert Spencer confirms:

> I am sure that Diana did have reservations about getting married at that stage because her father told me so. But her father and I never discussed the question of Camilla Parker Bowles, her name never came up. We just felt that it was a natural thing to happen because her husband had gone off on a pre-planned trip, she had moved into Buckingham Palace, which was strange and lonely, and there was the tremendous strain of getting ready for the wedding. That was enough to make any girl think 'Gosh, I can't go through with this'.

'Uniform or Evening Dress. Tiaras optional,' read the note at the bottom of the silver-edged card. Mary Robertson knew that she was to be invited to the wedding because Diana had written to tell her so, but an invitation to a ball at Buckingham Palace as well! She packed her husband's new tuxedo alongside her lavender ballgown and long white gloves and flew back to London on 24 July.

> The joy and excitement were just palpable. By the time we got here, there were people camping out on the streets already, to have a good view of the procession to St Paul's. The weather was beautiful, flags flying everywhere; you couldn't imagine a more joyous event.

The night of the ball was 27 July, the Monday before the Wednesday wedding. It was a warm, light summer's evening. The Robertsons were driven through the crowds that clustered around the gates of Buckingham Palace. As they swept in, Mary was pinching herself and thinking about Cinderella. The receiving line stretched right up the Grand Staircase, and the nervous Americans stood under the shiny domed skylight alongside duchesses and bishops, presidents and princesses. Everywhere Mary looked were lace-trimmed gowns, dazzling jewels and tall, handsome men in ribbons and medals. Charles looked regal in his red dress uniform, Diana was ravishing in deep pink ruffled taffeta with the most enormous diamond necklace sparkling at her neck. She cried out, 'Mrs Robertson, I'm so glad you are here,' gave her a tight hug, and then introduced her and Pat (her husband) with a loud 'Oh look, Charles, it's Patrick's parents from America'.

They wandered through a succession of elegant reception rooms. There were mirrors, chandeliers, gilded frames, carved wood, velvets, silks and brocades, columns, marble and stone. Everything was rich, ornate and royal. They saw the red-and-gold Throne Room, converted into a spare butler's pantry for the night. An orchestra struck up a gentle repertoire of waltz and foxtrot. The ballroom soon filled with twinkling tiaras and swirling silk. Mary almost bumped into Prime Minister Margaret Thatcher, standing alone at the edge of the dance-floor, surveying the scene and looking as if she felt a little out of place among the cream of Europe's aristocracy.

A smaller music room had a disco playing pop. Nearby the Queen stood talking. Having failed to pluck up the courage to talk to Mrs Thatcher, a woman she admired greatly, Mary considered an even braver step.

> I was longing to walk over to Her Majesty, the Queen, and tell her, mother to mother, 'Your Majesty, we've known Lady Diana quite well for the past year and a half. We'd like you to know what a truly lovely young woman your son is about to marry.'

But protocol forbade it, and Mary was afraid of embarrassing Diana.

Midnight came and went and, despite her persistent Cinderella fantasy, Mary's gown had still not turned into rags. Now the music was hotting up and Princess Margaret was one of many bopping enthusiastically with a balloon tied to her tiara. Outside, through the happily waving arms and bobbing balloons, Mary could see moonlight playing on the Palace garden.

But she could not see Diana, although she searched every room. It seemed odd for her to disappear like that, especially after her vivacious mood on the receiving line.

Earlier that day Charles had given the bracelet to Camilla and Diana had confessed her fears to her sisters, said she was not sure whether her fiancé truly loved her and announced that she wanted to pull out of the wedding. According to Diana, Sarah remarked, 'Well, bad luck, Duch, your face is on the tea towels so you're too late to chicken out.'

The next morning, 28 July, the dress was delivered to Clarence House in a hired van. Everything had been carefully packed in pink boxes monogrammed 'D'.

In the evening the Robertsons walked over to Hyde Park,

where in perfect balmy summer weather a firework display was held. It was modelled on the Royal Fireworks of 1749, for which Handel had written the music. The fireworks were set off against a mock palace façade. There were massed bands and choirs, huge rockets and a giant Catherine-wheel. The Prince of Wales began the evening by lighting the first in a chain of 101 beacons that marked out a line of celebratory fire on hilltops between Land's End and the Shetland Islands.

Diana had decided to get to bed early, so she missed the show. Charles watched the fireworks and then, unable to sleep, talked with Lady Susan Hussey late into the night.

5
The Queen's Ship

This was Kevin Shanley's biggest day too. When he arrived at Clarence House, Diana was watching the live coverage of the crowd outside on television. She took one look at his suit and T-shirt and suggested that today was a day when her hairdresser might wear a tie. With only three hours to go, she was on top form.

Shanley washed her hair and put it in rollers so that Barbara Daly could do her make-up. David and Liz Emanuel were hovering around anxiously as the bridesmaids' dresses came off their hangers. Soon, Diana had her ivory silk dress on. She looked stunning. Shanley set the Spencer tiara in its place. The Queen Mother tiptoed in and said, 'My dear you look simply enchanting.' Then she left for Buckingham Palace. It was time. The Emanuels packed Diana and her train into the Glass Coach. The last few feet of it had to be piled on Earl Spencer's lap. Diana gave them a chorus of 'Just One Cornetto!' Doubt was banished as she took the stage. She was really enjoying herself.

Charles was woken by the buzz of the crowd outside Buckingham Palace. The sky was bright blue flecked with cloud. The Palace balcony was draped in crimson. From the windows he could see the Mall decorated with 150 union flags hanging from flagstaffs crowned and tasselled in gold. Lampposts were hung with flowers. Red, white and blue banners and bunting could be glimpsed hanging from every distant building. The people in the crowds outside were wearing silly paper pork-pie hats in red, white and blue and cheering every twitch of the Palace curtain.

Friends, staff and foreign dignitaries drifted towards St Paul's.

Just after ten, minor royalty left Buckingham Palace by car. Ten minutes later a procession of black limousines carried away members of the world's reigning royal families in strict order of seniority. The bridesmaids left Clarence House. Shortly after 10.20 the Queen's carriage set out, followed by the Queen Mother and the two princesses, Anne and Margaret. Royalty, politicians, Guardsmen on their horses, even stray balloons: all were cheered by a million enthusiastic voices.

Diana shared the famous Glass Coach with her father. They waved continuously as they passed through the crowds. In Trafalgar Square there were so many people, and the cheering grew so loud, that Earl Spencer confused St Martin's-in-the-Fields with St Paul's and prepared to get out. Diana held him back protectively with a huge smile on her face. The general feeling of optimism and pleasure was washing over her. 'Everyone hurraying, everybody happy.' She could hear voices from the crowd: 'Good luck, Diana', 'You look fabulous', 'Congratulations'. Some threw flowers at her coach as it passed them by. She was wearing a signet ring that Charles had sent over to Clarence House the night before, along with a note which read: 'I'm so proud of you and when you come up I'll be there at the altar for you tomorrow. Just look 'em in the eye and knock 'em dead.'

Jayne Fincher had got herself into the perfect position for the dress shot, the one all the papers wanted most. As Diana stepped out of the carriage, Fincher could barely hear the crowd's cheers for the staccato rattle of motor drives all around.

> I looked at her dress and I thought, Oh no, it's awful. Because it was all scrunched up, it looked terrible. I just remember thinking, It doesn't look like it's been ironed.

The Emanuels reacted the same way and dashed to the rescue. Once the train was properly spread out on the carpeted steps, it looked as dazzling as the young woman who was wearing it.

India Hicks, a ten-year-old bridesmaid, couldn't take her eyes off Diana.

> She was extremely gentle, very shy, and she was someone that as a young girl you thought was everything a princess should be. Very beautiful, very young, very calm – and yet there was a kind of nervousness about her. But the feeling inside the cathedral was just enormous. It's a very hollow place but it was filled with so much warmth and excitement . . .

Perched on a piece of precarious scaffolding opposite the cathedral, Anthony Holden, by now features editor for *The Times*, was covering the wedding for ABC television.

> For the American networks this was the biggest coast-to-coast, live, open-ended broadcast there'd ever been. There were huge briefing books about every detail, down to the history of the paving stones around St Paul's.

Holden was only one of 180 staff backing up Barbara Walters, who fronted the ABC network's coverage. ABC deployed hundreds of cameras, mobile studios, 750 miles of cable, satellites and a balloon floating a thousand feet overhead for the USA's biggest ever pre-breakfast audience. Like ABC, the BBC employed a woman to anchor their coverage of a royal occasion, rare in 1981. Angela Rippon was backed up by sixty outside broadcast cameras, twelve mobile control rooms and three hundred staff. The UK audience was the biggest ever – thirty-nine million, six and a half million more than had watched the 1970 World Cup match between England and Brazil. The CBS network chose Lady Antonia Fraser to join Dan Rather and David Frost for their five-hour commentary. NBC advertised *The Wedding of the Century* – 'When England's future King says "I do" a shy 20-year-old girl turns into a royal princess. Watch the fairy tale come true!'

Diana walked gracefully down the aisle, her snowy twenty-five-foot train billowing behind her, held in place by her heirloom diamond tiara. Forty-five feet of ivory silk taffeta had gone into her dress, made by a single seamstress working secretly in a locked room. Ten thousand pearls and mother-of-pearl sequins had been hand-sewn into her white bodice. In her hand she held a waterfall bouquet with orchids and odontoglossum, pale Earl Mountbatten roses, stephanotis, gardenia, freesia and myrtle.

Six hundred and fifty feet of carpet, with the notes of Jeremiah Clarke's trumpet voluntary from the resounding organ. She was ready to support her father, still shaky after his stroke, but Earl Spencer was walking with pride. This was his family's moment of greatest glory. As Diana walked towards her prince, she was scanning the congregation for family and old friends. 'I remember being so in love with my husband. I absolutely thought I was the luckiest girl in the world. He was going to look after me.'

To her right, Margaret Thatcher; to her left, some rows back:

> Camilla, pale grey pill-box hat. Saw it all, her son Tom standing on a chair. To this day, you know. Vivid memory. 'Well, there you are, let's hope that's all over with.'

Nearer the front now. To her left and right the massed royalty of the world. Three steps and at the top the Archbishop of Canterbury. This was it. On her right the Queen, Prince Philip, the Queen Mother. On her left her mother, Frances Shand-Kydd, and her grandmother, Ruth, Lady Fermoy. She reached Prince Charles. The Archbishop, Robert Runcie, had taken his cue from NBC: 'This is the stuff of which fairytales are made; the Prince and Princess on their wedding day.'

Runcie and his chaplain had met Charles and Diana a week before the wedding and had both felt uneasy about the couple they were due to marry. The chaplain, Richard Chartres, noted that Charles appeared to be 'seriously depressed'. Runcie thought that Diana was in awe of her husband-to-be. And the Archbishop was one of many in the cathedral who knew all about the woman wearing the pill-box hat in the third pew back. 'Oh yes,' he said years later, 'I knew about *that* already.' The union, Runcie privately concluded, was not a fairytale at all, but an 'arranged marriage'.

Christopher Hitchens agreed and, unlike the Archbishop, he had published his opinion. Hitchens suggested that Charles had just spurned an opportunity to connect the monarchy with the modern world. The Prince could have chosen a career woman, but instead had allowed himself to be fixed up with what Hitchens called an under-educated 'brood mare', a product of 'that warm bath of snobbery in which the English upper classes marinade their young'.

Untroubled by such thoughts, an even larger crowd cheered the couple all the way back to the Palace in an open carriage. Andrew Parker Bowles rode guard behind them. The barriers were lifted, and hundreds of thousands of people streamed down the Mall, spilled around the Victoria Memorial and washed down both sides of Buckingham Palace. The Royal Family came out on to the balcony to face an ocean of chanting, singing, waving delight. The loudest chants of all called for a kiss. On the balcony Prince Andrew goaded Charles, and a rather chaste clinch followed. The *Sun*'s Harry Arnold had a good contact inside the Palace who was standing just behind the balcony.

> He telephoned me from inside Buckingham Palace and said that Andrew had said, 'Go on, give her a kiss,' and Charles replied, 'I'm not getting into that caper.' And Andrew said, 'Oh yes, go on, give her a kiss.' And Charles said to his mother, 'May I?' And the Queen said, 'Yes.'

A rival tabloid had hired a professional lip-reader to check the words uttered on the balcony and they confirmed Harry Arnold's source word for word. Such scrutiny would continue.

The couple enjoyed the wedding breakfast and left in high spirits, taking the train from Waterloo to Romsey and then travelling by car to Broadlands. It had all gone fantastically well. Martin Charteris, the Queen's former private secretary, said: 'I looked at the marriage as one of the greatest things I've seen. I saw no clouds on the horizon. I saw nothing but sunshine and happiness.' At the *Sun* all the journalists celebrated with wedding cake and lots of champagne.

Walter Bagehot had declared that 'a princely marriage is the brilliant edition of a universal fact, and, as such, it rivets mankind'. The Windsors were the national emblem family, and this wedding gave many, perhaps most, of their subjects a moment of vicarious joy during a summer of unemployment and inner-city rioting. There were street parties and special newspaper editions and hundreds of different souvenirs. Six thousand people queued on the first day of an exhibition to see a selection of the couple's wedding gifts.

After two nights at Broadlands, the Prince and new Princess flew to Gibraltar to board the royal yacht for the honeymoon proper. Departure from the contested peninsula was taken by the Spanish government as a calculated insult, but the people of Gibraltar turned out in force, showering the royal couple with confetti as they drove down to the harbour.

The royal couple and a handful of courtiers were the only passengers on the 5,700-ton HMS *Britannia*, alongside 277 sailors in pristine white uniforms. The only female company for Diana was her dresser, Evelyn Dagley. Real privacy remained difficult. To dine alone was to be serenaded by a Royal Marine band two dozen strong. Precedent dictated that royal guests were expected to dine in black tie with the ship's twenty-one officers.

Versions of the voyage differ. Charles's valet, Stephen Barry, said that the couple spent a lot of time alone as the ship sailed down the coast of Italy, across to Ithaca and via Cephalonia, Kythira and Santorini towards Crete and then Cairo. Diana recalled that being a princess on honeymoon with a prince was not what she had imagined. She thought that Charles was avoiding her.

It quickly became clear that the royal party would have to fall in with the customs of the royal yacht. One afternoon Diana and Charles were having coffee and discussing the upcoming visit to Egypt. The Flight Officer approached and said to Prince Charles, 'Church as usual, around nine a.m. tomorrow, sir?' Diana's face fell. Honeymoons and early church services evidently did not go together in her mind. The Prince looked troubled for a second but said, 'Yes.' Some of the officers, who shared their memories with us, realised that the Princess did not appear to enjoy the regular formal dinners and one suggested that the couple should be allowed more evenings alone. To this suggestion the Admiral said, 'This is how it's done on the Queen's ship.'

Once more Diana was face to face with the tedium of the royal machine. Although Charles thought much of it was irksome too, he had long ago found his own way of ignoring it all. Those accompanying him thought that he did not know whether to break the rules to please his wife or try to coax Diana into coming to terms with the necessary facts of royal life. After all, as he had warned her at the moment of his proposal, she would have to learn to live a very odd kind of life.

This was the first time that Charles and Diana had been in each other's company for more than a few hours, and Diana was beginning to discover new and unexpected sides to her husband's character.

Charles's recent ancestors had been proudly philistine. His great-grandfather, King George V, when visiting an exhibition of famous Impressionist artists, called over to his queen: 'Oh, look here, May, this one will really make you laugh.' His grandmother, Queen Elizabeth, was utterly bemused when T.S. Eliot came to read *The Waste Land* at Buckingham Palace. But Charles read serious literature, tried his hand at painting, and took a keen interest in architecture and art history. Having been the first Windsor to suffer school, he insisted on going to university, taking a place to read archaeology and anthropology at Trinity College, Cambridge. Anthropology introduced Charles to the writings of Laurens van der Post, who became a mentor during the 1970s. He now hoped to share these enthusiasms with his young wife. But Charles's attempts to read Laurens van der Post aloud to Diana, and his attempts at intellectual discussion, triggered her inferiority complex and she left him to it. A witness told us:

> He did a lot of reading and painting. She got bored and wandered down to the mess decks. She was eating ice cream, surrounded by lots of sailors. Along comes the Admiral: 'No, no, this has got to stop!' 'Why?' 'Because they all walk around naked.' She was doing something innocent but there was gossip and disapproval.

Being told off by people she did not want on her honeymoon, and having to share Charles with naval officers, did not please Diana. But at other times witnesses recall that she and Charles looked as though they were besotted with each other.

Diana's spontaneity was a permanent threat to protocol. One afternoon Charles appeared disappointed with her after she embarrassed him in front of the crew:

> It was terribly difficult for Prince Charles. They'd gone on an excursion and landed on a deserted beach. Next thing I know the Princess is careering across the beach, pissed out of her mind – she'd discovered Pimms. She had seaweed all over her. The poor old Prince is standing around, talking about the navy.

> She was hustled back to base. He was very gloomy. As they climb up the steps, she tips a bucket of water over him. He gets very angry, and looks like a hurt spaniel. You can see why – he's the heir to the throne.

Towards the end of the voyage the Camilla question re-emerged. Photographs of her fell from Charles's diary as they compared engagements. A few days later Diana spotted that Charles was wearing a pair of cuff links decorated with entwined Cs. She rightly divined that these were a gift from Camilla. In the face of what he considered to be his wife's unreasonable anger, Charles refused to change them.

Diana told the stories about the photos and the cuff links many times. Writers sympathetic to Charles have never denied them. Penny Junor repeats both stories but tries to explain Charles's point of view:

> Diana screamed and shouted and burst into tears. The Prince – though perfectly capable of losing his temper and shouting at the people who work for him and even throwing ornaments – had never experienced anyone shouting at him before . . . and was completely nonplussed.

Jonathan Dimbleby – Charles's authorised biographer – mentions neither story. Instead he sums up the problems on the cruise:

> . . . the Prince was perplexed by her sudden shifts of mood, which he ascribed to the transient pressures of adapting to her new and exacting role as his consort.

One reason for Diana's moodiness was her bulimia. In 1991 she told Andrew Morton that on board *Britannia* she was bingeing on anything she could find and making herself sick immediately afterwards. 'The bulimia was appalling, absolutely appalling. It was rife, four times a day on the yacht. Very tired. So of course, that slightly got the mood swings going.'

From Egypt the newlyweds flew to Lossiemouth and drove to Balmoral for the next and longest stage of the honeymoon, a month living on Charles's favourite royal estate. Here the holiday was shared with Diana's new in-laws and a collection of Charles's old friends.

Charles had his books and his fishing rod and he relaxed immediately into his time-honoured Balmoral routine. Over drinks and dinner, Diana had another taste of the rules of royal precedence, and later said she was infuriated when Charles offered his mother and grandmother drinks before her. By the rules, the Queen and her mother were the senior ladies present. She felt that as his new wife she should come first. At a press conference by the Brig o'Dee, the Princess, dressed in tartan and looking tanned and relaxed, said she could 'thoroughly recommend married life', but in reality things were already strained. Charles's long walks up the hills did not fit into Diana's image of a honeymoon:

> His idea of enjoyment would be to sit on top of the highest hill at Balmoral. It is beautiful up there. I completely understand; he would read Laurens van der Post or Jung to me, and bear in mind I hadn't a clue about psychic powers or anything . . . So anyway we read those and I did my tapestry and he was blissfully happy . . .

After a few weeks Diana announced that she wanted to go to London, telling Charles that Balmoral was wet and boring. Charles reminded her that a year ago she had said it was her favourite place on earth. He pointed out that the court was now at Balmoral and that was where they had to be, it went with the job. She tried again, and when that didn't work she complained, 'If you loved me you'd put me first.'

> I remember crying my eyes out . . . At night I dreamt of Camilla the whole time . . . Everybody saw I was getting thinner and thinner . . . Didn't trust him, thought every five minutes he was ringing her up . . . It rained and rained and rained . . .

Diana had been obliged to conform to the rules of royal behaviour on the royal yacht. Now she was presented with family life the Windsor way, and she did not like what she saw. For their part, Diana's new relatives were concerned that she did not deliver the politely neutral performance expected of her. According to one witness, the Queen was alarmed at the evident signs that Diana was unhappy with her lot. An early dinner guest told us about the uneasy atmosphere around the Balmoral dinner table:

> At dinner one night the Queen cornered me and said, 'I don't know what we can do. Look at her, sitting at the table glowering at us! The only time she bucks up is when Charles speaks to her.' I said to her, 'Perhaps if you look around the table – they're all so much older than her.' . . . She said, 'I don't care. She'll just have to buck up.'

'It was all done with the best intentions,' we were told by a courtier. 'It was all to do with duty. It got off to a bad start. She had nobody to talk to.'

In public Diana did buck up. The couple made a second public appearance for the Highland Games at Braemar in early September, and she still looked healthy, happy and not noticeably thinner. But behind the scenes the jolly girl in green wellies who, a year before, had endeared herself to Charles and his friends with her love of the countryside now made it clear that she wanted no part of it. She took every opportunity to complain about Balmoral – the incessant rain, the muddy barbecues, the ugly furniture, the antique bathrooms. Longing to have her husband to herself, Diana was cross and bored while Charles was hurt and embarrassed by her ill-concealed resentment, and disappointed that she no longer wanted to share the pursuits he enjoyed.

Partly because she was so histrionic about it, Diana's unhappiness was soon the property of the ever-resourceful press. A courtier told us that 'brown envelopes of ten-pound notes were being waved at junior members of staff. The *Sun* had a huge number of leaks.'

In late September the first stories of Diana's rows with Charles and dislike of Balmoral were printed in the *Sun* and the *News of the World*. It was said that she went off on her own for walks to escape the 'stuffed shirt' atmosphere of royal functions, and that she was 'deeply unsettled'. She was reluctant to go on shooting parties and left royal dinners early. Ironically, her bad press was compounded when the League against Cruel Sports accused the Princess of being present at the disembowelling of a stag. This was awkwardly and ambiguously denied by the Palace, who were no doubt trying to tell the world that she was willing to go stalking with Charles and his friends but did not butcher deer. Diana must at this point have begun to wonder who in her entourage was leaking damaging stories to the press. By coincidence, if his own account can be believed, Stephen Barry resigned.

Charles asked his secretary, Michael Colborne, to travel up from London to look after Diana on a day he was due to go out stalking deer. From nine in the morning to four in the afternoon, Colborne sat with Diana as she poured out her anger about her absent husband, his family, the boredom, Balmoral. Colborne saw Diana kick furniture and then lapse into long brooding silences. Sandwiches came and were left untouched. At one point Colborne timed a gap in their conversation at almost an hour as they sat on either side of a drawing room listening to the clock ticking and the rain spilling down a broken gutter pipe. Charles was feeling the strain too. Later that day, after another shouting match with his wife, he lost his temper with Colborne over a trivial misunderstanding about the carpet in his new Range Rover, and yelled at his friend for over an hour.

In October Charles persuaded Diana that she needed professional help and they left Balmoral for London. On the train on the way back, the Prince had a five-hour conversation with Colborne. Charles was baffled and despondent, unable to grasp what had gone wrong or how to cope. To the doctors Diana said that she needed time to adapt. She did not admit to bulimia, nor did she accept that she might be seriously ill. They prescribed Valium, which she rejected, believing they only wanted to remove her as a problem by sedating her. Charles, who disapproved of drugs, was appalled. She later commented bitterly that all the officials and their doctors were interested in was being able to 'go to bed at night and sleep, knowing the Princess of Wales wasn't going to stab anyone'.

Amid the turmoil, Diana discovered she was pregnant. At court, everyone was relieved, hoping that her sickness, her changing moods and her spells of depression might be due to the pregnancy. For a while the news was not relayed to the general public.

On 27 October the Prince and Princess of Wales set out on their first joint venture, a short tour of their own principality. Anne Beckwith-Smith was appointed as a lady-in-waiting to look after Diana and provide some support and female companionship. The visit again brought home the occupational hazards of royal life. There were threats from Welsh nationalists to contend with, and the visit was preceded by a huge security operation, made more serious when an incendiary device was found at Pontypridd. There were some anti-English and anti-royal banners on display, some chanting, some stink bombs and a successful attack on the royal car with an aerosol can, but these were swamped by a wave of popular interest in the Royal Family, or rather in the new Princess.

The tour began at the Deeside Leisure Centre and moved on to Caernarfon Castle on an austere, windy day. The Princess wore the red and green of Wales. Jayne Fincher studied her through the camera lens:

> The first thing that struck us was how ill she looked. She looked dreadful. She'd gone from this lovely tanned, healthy, robust girl to looking really quite tired and thin and pale.

But Diana immediately endeared herself to the crowds with her lack of reserve. She had learned enough Welsh to say '*Diolch yn fawr*' in response to gifts. She liked to touch people: she embraced a child with spina bifida, was kissed by a seven-year-old. It came naturally to her. She liked to smile. She made people want to smile back, and ever since the Darenth Park visits she had been able to talk to strangers without conveying condescension. Jayne Fincher was impressed:

> Instead of just sort of doing a very gentle regal handshake she'd go out of her way to really reach into the crowd and touch people. She was a very touchy person and that became apparent very quickly because she was touching everybody. I think she quickly worked out that this is the best way to deal with it . . . If you see the Queen doing a walkabout it's very dignified and quite formal. She'll walk down the edge of a barrier and she'll take some flowers very gently and elegantly, and maybe occasionally she might shake a hand. But they normally don't shake hands. And normally the royal ladies would always have these long white gloves on. Diana didn't wear gloves. It was completely different.

Judy Wade, an Australian, was covering the tour for the *Sun*.

> We were used for so many years to royal ladies swanning through jobs and being rather aloof, and they certainly didn't

> swap chit-chat with people. Their conversation extended to 'Aren't the flowers lovely?' and 'Have you been waiting long?' But Diana was much more personal, and she would get down, bend down and talk to small children, and make sure they weren't getting crushed in the crowd, and – she was just so different, so much closer to the people. It was brilliant for us – it provided good stories every single day.

According to one of those who shared the royal car with her in Wales, Diana frequently broke down in tears and was sick between engagements. At one time she protested to her husband that she could not face another crowd. But she did. The second day began with a service at St David's Cathedral. Diana's head drooped when she could not join Charles in his lusty rendition of 'Land of My Fathers' in Welsh. She was evidently desperate not to let him down in any way. Then, as she walked among crowds at Carmarthen, the rain came down in torrents. The royal couple carried on, thanking those they met for waiting to see them in such hideous weather. Jayne Fincher kept snapping away.

> She had all these outfits that she turned up in and it just rained non-stop and all the feathers were all bedraggled over her face and all her new coats were all soaking and it was really tough going for her. When you're not feeling well the last thing you want to do is walk down Carmarthen High Street in a thunderstorm with your new John Boyd hat all ruined.

On the third day Diana looked more cheerful. Pressed against the railings lining Brecon High Street, Valerie Harris and her daughter Beverley had been waiting all morning. 'It was very cold but people didn't seem to notice the cold because they were so excited by Diana coming. And then we heard all the cheering from downtown.' Mayor Gwanwyn Evans was walking with the royal couple.

> Prince Charles indicated to me that they would each take a side of the road and at a certain stage he would take the initiative

> and he would decide to go over. And every time this happened you had this huge 'Oaoah' from the people that she was leaving. And all the time people keep calling, 'Di, Di . . .'

'Di, Di, over here please, Di, Di.' The sound echoed through the town. After a while she did double back and swap sides, to the biggest cheer of the day. Charles was beaming at her pleasure and her popularity as his arms filled up with the flowers that were being pressed upon him to pass to his wife. 'Yes, of course, of course, I know, she is lovely, isn't she? Thank you so much for coming, and in this foul weather too . . .'

'Di, Di, over here.' The Princess of Wales seemed about to lose herself in the crowd, seemed almost to be absorbed by it. She was moving through a blur of smiles and waves and handshakes. Someone kissed her hand and she blushed. Someone threw her a rose. She caught it and blushed again. As her car drove slowly past Ken Lennox in the pouring rain she looked at him through the window and mouthed: 'How am I doing, Ken?' Lennox burst out laughing, let both cameras dangle at his neck and gave her a double thumbs-up as he shouted 'Okay!'.

By the end of the day, Charles had started to make self-deprecatory jokes to the crowd. 'Well, at least I know my place now – I'm a carrier of flowers for my wife.' But Jayne Fincher saw his face fall from time to time.

> It would be really embarrassing sometimes because she'd be on one side of the road and they'd all be excited and screaming, and on the other side of the road they'd all be going, 'Oh no!' because they'd got him. He'd just turn round and say, 'I'm really sorry, she'll be here in a minute.'

Even at this early stage, Charles was privately hurt by the public preference for his wife. Someone who accompanied the royal couple on this tour told us that:

> I caught Charles kicking a pebble around. He said, 'They don't want to see me.' He was wobbly. He seemed schizophrenic,

> deeply caring followed by deeply selfish. Diana said, 'Isn't it great! They love us. I hope I can keep going, my feet are wet.' She said, 'It's a bit embarrassing, what can we do about it? They keep moving to my side.' We all adored working with her.

Diana was a natural, a sensation. One local paper printed a special edition commemorating the visit. Their headline was 'Diana: the Queen of Hearts'.

The Prince of Wales now returned to his habitual schedule. It took him all over the country, and only a few engagements were shared with the Princess. On 1 November there was a concert at Blenheim, on 3 November the National Film Festival's gala opening, the next day the State Opening of Parliament followed by the opening of the 'Splendours of the Gonzaga' exhibition at the Victoria and Albert Museum. On 5 November Diana's pregnancy was announced and the planned 1982 tour to New Zealand, Australia and Canada was postponed. The mayor of Tetbury drank champagne beneath the union flag. Over lunch at the Guildhall, the Prince thanked the City of London for the wedding. He paid tribute to Diana, attributing the nation's warm response 'entirely to the effect my dear wife has had on people'.

But his wife was not happy with the way he had resumed the pattern of his pre-nuptial life, dashing from engagement to engagement and spending time away from home – if you could call Buckingham Palace home. Someone who worked, but did not have to live there, told us:

> Moving into Buck House with the in-laws was a disastrous start to the marriage. Why nobody thought about it, goodness knows. They had a suite of rooms, but they didn't even have a kitchen. They should have got Kensington Palace ready for them after the wedding. Every time you wanted to order tea,

a footman was summoned. There was an element of 'Why's she ringing the bell again?'

By now Diana was experiencing morning sickness or bulimia or both, and most of her engagements were cancelled as a result. She attended the Remembrance Sunday service and on 12 November made visits to York and Chesterfield, where she was showered with gifts of soft toys for the expected child. But she failed to go to church at Sandringham that weekend and cancelled a visit to Bristol on 18 November. In late November, appearing on her own for the first time, she switched on the Christmas lights in Regent Street.

One reason why Diana was unhappy about appearing in public was that she did not want to be photographed looking ill, not out of vanity – according to one of her aides – but because she considered that looking good was part of her duty:

> She was terribly conscious of her image. She would get disproportionately pissed off by a silly headline. She thought it was her job to bring credit to her husband. She thought that was what it was all about.

Diana supervised the decoration of Kensington Palace. But most days there was little for her to do except brood, and she was still brooding about Camilla. Charles would return home to face a litany of doubts, recriminations and anxieties. Whatever he said, he could not persuade her that her fears were groundless.

Diana suspected that Charles was seeing Camilla during hunting excursions from Highgrove. There are contradictory accounts from Gloucestershire journalists, some of whom believe they saw the pair riding together at this time. Charles is reported to have rounded on a group of them, angrily asking: 'When are you going to stop making my life a misery?' Seeing Camilla, riding with Camilla, talking to Camilla on the telephone, none of this meant any kind of an affair was taking place. But Diana believed it did.

During the autumn royal officials began to consider a full-time public role for her. But they did so without much enthusiasm. Relations with the courtly and old-fashioned Adeane, the private secretary, were strained. He was very busy keeping what he saw as the Prince of Wales's wild enthusiasms and unwelcome advisers at bay. He did not approve of the Prince visiting summer camps full of teenagers on probation, for example. Frustrated with the Prince's reluctance to listen to his advice, he had little patience to spare when it came to considering a new role for the Princess. Something to do with Wales and something to do with children were vaguely suggested, but in the Household Dining Room they complained that she had no serious interests to build on. And when Adeane tried to talk to her about such matters, she delighted in teasing him with lines such as 'Oh, don't be so stuffy, Edward'. The Prince was frequently called upon to assure his private secretary that his wife meant no insult.

Diana was troubled by her intellectual shortcomings; she wanted to learn and improve. And yet she reacted badly to instruction, believing that she was being patronised. It was obvious to her that Charles felt she was stupid since he had Everett trying to educate her all the time. According to the courtiers, Charles tried to tell her that she had a natural flair for the job but with a little work she could be better. She chose to take that as criticism; chose too to point out that the press and the population clearly thought she was wonderful already. Charles – it appeared – began to avoid her because he couldn't tell whether she would be friendly or argumentative. The outbursts of temper only made him more reserved when what she wanted, what she said she wanted, was his loving attention. But the more demanding she became, the more Charles viewed her with distaste. A courtier gave us his view:

> Prince Charles is somebody who is very caring, but to have a wife around who was constantly throwing wobblies when he couldn't understand why drove him almost demented. That

> stems also from the bulimia thing, but back then nobody had even heard of bulimia. And then friends reacted to his reaction.

Her friends say that she felt rejected and worthless. Charles's friends say that however emotional, affectionate and attentive he was, it was never enough. They were both reacting in ways that made it impossible for them to be good for each other.

It was clear to everyone close to Diana that something needed to be done to relieve the pressure. In December 1981 the pregnant Princess left Highgrove to visit a Tetbury sweet shop to buy some wine gums. She was cornered by photographers and the resulting pictures were published the following day. The Queen's press secretary invited all Fleet Street and television news editors to Buckingham Palace. It was the first time that this had happened in twenty-six years, since Charles's first term at Cheam preparatory school. They all turned up except Kelvin Mackenzie of the *Sun*. He had a more pressing engagement with his boss, Rupert Murdoch. David Chipp of the Press Association was one of those who attended:

> We had a briefing and a discussion with Michael Shea, who was the Queen's press secretary, and he made the point that could we lay off a bit, give them some freedom? And we chatted about this and then he said, 'Would you like to come for a drink?' And so we all went in next door, and in came the Queen and the Duke of Edinburgh and talked to us in small groups. They came round, and the Queen made it clear that Diana was not from a family that had been used to this sort of press coverage, unlike her family which had from childhood. And she said it was very difficult for her, and said, for example, if she goes down to the local shop, near Highgrove, there'll be photographers and reporters there, covering her buying a bag of sweets or something. And one of my colleagues from the Sunday papers said, 'Well, ma'am, couldn't she send a foot-

man?' And the Queen looked up at him and said, 'Do you know, I think that's the most pompous remark I've ever heard in my life.'

The *Sun* did not take the Queen's intervention very seriously. According to Harry Arnold, 'We had no reverence for the Royal Family. We didn't believe in following rules laid down by the old guard at the Palace, we went our own way. Kelvin printed my stories whether they liked them or not.'

Christmas at Windsor was happy and relaxed. There were carols and turkey and stockings hanging over the hearth, and much talk about how next year there would be a new baby to share it all with. But Diana's mood changed suddenly as the extended family went to Sandringham for New Year. At the beginning of 1982, the *Sun*, acting on a detailed tip-off from a royal servant, reported that Diana had fallen down the stairs at Sandringham. A doctor was called but pronounced no harm done to mother or baby.

Years later this episode assumed great significance in Diana's account of her marriage's disintegration. Andrew Morton's 1992 biography told how she was at the end of her tether, overwrought at the cruel indifference of the Prince of Wales. She confronted Charles in a tearful row that was audible all over Sandringham. She told Morton that in her despair she threatened suicide. He coldly called her bluff, mocked her melodramatic style and refused to listen. He said he was going riding and left the room. Diana, three months pregnant, threw herself down the main staircase at Sandringham, landing at the feet of the Queen, who was ashen pale and shaking with fear. When Charles heard what had happened he went out riding, and when he came back he was just as dismissive as ever. To a friend called Elsa Bowker, Diana amplified her tale: she had broken into Charles's desk and found love letters between Charles and Camilla. 'She said that is why she threw herself down the stairs at Sandringham. She said she didn't think it was worth living or having a baby.'

In 1994 Jonathan Dimbleby repeated the story that Diana threw herself down a staircase, citing Morton, and lending further credence to this version of events. He tried to explain how Charles might have become frustrated with Diana's refusal to be pacified by him. Then there was a plot twist. The writer Lady Colin Campbell announced that in an interview with *her* in 1995 Diana denied that any of this had happened at all and blamed Morton for distorting what she had told him. He had invented the 'cry for help', she said. Only a man would write such a thing, since it was obvious that no woman would do anything to harm her unborn child. Morton's eventual response was to publish the transcripts of the tapes that Diana had recorded for him. This is what she had said:

> I threw myself down the stairs. Charles said I was crying wolf and I said I felt so desperate and I was crying my eyes out and he said: 'I'm not going to listen. You're always doing this to me. I'm going riding now.' So I threw myself down the stairs. The Queen comes out absolutely horrified, shaking – she was so frightened. I knew I wasn't going to lose the baby; quite bruised around the stomach. Charles went out riding and when he came back, you know, it was just dismissal, total dismissal. He just carried on out of the door.

That there was a bitter argument is not in doubt. *That* detail was part of the original story supplied to the *Sun*. The paper decided not to ignore it. Their informant, a royal servant, had seen the argument and then saw Diana trip and stumble down three steps before holding on to the banister. The *Sun*'s informant added that Charles had stayed with Diana until a doctor arrived to pronounce that no harm had been done.

The *Sun*'s photographer, Arthur Edwards, who knew the witness well, was philosophical:

> It's just the sort of thing you expect. In any marriage there are rows. Of course, they were royal and they were not supposed to row, and certainly not in public and certainly not where the servants can hear. But you see, Diana was very volatile, she just let it rip when she felt she should. Now she didn't fall down, as it has been suggested, a whole flight of stairs: she fell down three. And of course Prince Charles was very concerned and called the doctor because she was pregnant to see if the baby was fine and it was fine. But that was interpreted later as Diana trying to commit suicide. Well, of course it wasn't that, she just fell down three stairs.

Joseph Sanders, a close friend of Diana's in the 1990s, says that she told him she slipped and there was no suicide bid.

It's a familiar story. Two people not getting on, blaming each other for the problems and then exaggerating later when they want outsiders to take their side. Selectively quoting incidents from the past to justify their current behaviour; writing off all the happy moments: 'You never loved me', 'I was never happy', 'You were always unfaithful'. The great difference is that this particular failing marriage was to be played out inside an echo chamber.

Jonathan Dimbleby's book was published when the battle between the couple was at its height, the echoes of their past arguments at their loudest and least reliable. Nevertheless, his account is the closest thing we have to Charles's side of the story. Dimbleby writes of Charles devoting hours 'haplessly trying to soothe her back to cheerfulness' at the time of the staircase incident, and goes into detail about Diana's dark moods, calling them 'unfathomable', 'inexplicable' and 'aberrant'.

Dimbleby also gives us a telling account of the attitude of Charles's friends at this time. Some of them, 'those of their friends who had sympathy for them both',

> did not rush to judgement but did their limited best to help, knowing that to attribute blame in such a predicament would do nothing to solve what they regarded as an awful plight for them both.

But others were evidently less sympathetic:

> As her pregnancy advanced, a sense of despair lurked about the Princess. Her bouts of misery lasted longer and her outlook seemed bleaker than ever. The Prince confided his anxiety only to a tiny circle of his most trusted friends, one or two of whom urged him to be tougher with what they interpreted as her self-pity. They said that she needed to 'pull herself together', and that would not happen if he indulged her bouts of gloom with tender words.

Dimbleby is careful to put the 'self-pity' line into the mouths of Charles's friends, but he allows that Charles sometimes took their advice. It seems likely that in these early difficult months of her royal life, the pregnant, insecure twenty-year-old was told to 'pull herself together' rather a lot.

Diana quickly came to believe that Charles's friends, 'the Highgrove set' as she called them, were out to get her. She thought they saw her demands on his time as a threat to their own role in his life, and so to their position in society. She was also convinced that they were bad for him: 'They were all oiling up, basically, kissing his feet and I thought it was so bad for an individual to receive all that.' She was determined that family life would be different from the royal existence she had known up to now. She wanted Charles to herself in her own home. Things would change when her baby was born.

6
Mood Swings

> The marriage was not unhappy at the beginning, just tempestuous. Loving at times and confused at times. But two things screwed the relationship. The Queen and his family constantly siding with him . . . and the Camilla relationship. Diana was extremely interested, always asking about it.
>
> It *was* spelt out to Diana. She was told that a lot of the time she would be on her own, that she was expected to be his consort, but everyone was telling her 'You're the future of the Royal Family'. A young girl like that, it turned her head.
>
> Two senior members of the royal household, early 1980s

Janet Filderman didn't think that Diana made the best of her looks. She had often wondered if she would get the chance to do something with that lovely face. Now, thanks to a recommendation from Diana's sister Jane, the top beautician was about to get her opportunity.

'Oh, so this is where it all goes on, is it?'

The young woman was a bit gangling in a way. Breezy and funny but rather unsure of herself.

Filderman's beauty parlour was crammed into the basement of a hairdresser's salon in Porchester Place. She busied herself with her lotions and face flannels, looking respectfully away as the Princess discarded her blouse and lay on her treatment table. There was always something intimate in the relationship between beautician and half-naked client. But between Diana and Janet there soon developed an unusual closeness. 'On the third visit she said, "Do you think you could call me Diana?" and I said, "If it's not presumptuous, yes, I would love to."'

> She became the daughter I have never had and a very delightful friend. I liked her humour, I liked her sense of purpose, her determination, her caring. I think she was a special person in that respect because she had this magic of making you feel that you were the most important thing in her life. She made you feel that she was grateful for seeing you, which was really the other way around
>
> We talked on the telephone a great deal. She would phone me up in the evenings, probably nine o'clock or something like that when she was on her own, she would just have a little chat about her day. And we would have a little giggle. She had a tremendous sense of humour. On one occasion when she was going to a state dinner and she came to me that afternoon and I said 'Oh, marvellous, marvellous, what are you going to wear, what are you going to do?' 'Dah dah, dah dah,' she said. 'I always end up sitting next to the oldest person and they are usually deaf.'

Filderman came to love her new friend's style and spontaneity. Some mornings she would come in after swimming twenty lengths of the Buckingham Palace pool, her hair still wet and wearing cowboy boots and jeans. With a smile and a kiss on the cheek, she would throw her things off and get on to the table, sometimes sleeping as Filderman worked on her back and neck.

> Yes, she had times when she was unhappy but usually I think if you were to ask her that she would probably say, 'Oh, it is not as bad as all that.' She wasn't by any stretch of the imagination a miserable person.

After the anxiety caused by the fall at Sandringham it seemed unwise to take Diana skiing so the February holiday of 1982 was scheduled instead for Eleuthera in the Bahamas, a genuinely glamorous royal hideaway that Charles hoped Diana would like. There they would stay with Norton and Penny Romsey at their secure beachside estate for a complete break, utterly secluded from crowds and prying eyes.

As a result of the Queen's recent hospitality at Buckingham Palace, most newspaper editors fell in with the royal demand to give Diana a break. But one or two intrepid journalists had other ideas. James Whitaker spoke to Palace press officer Michael Shea, who said, 'By all means come along, James, but you'll get nothing. The Bahamian police have promised us complete seclusion.' The editor of the *Daily Star* said, 'Go for it! See what you can get.' So Fleet Street's finest took the plane to the Caribbean. Whitaker and his photographer Ken Lennox got there in plenty of time to watch the royal plane land and follow the couple's car down a causeway on to the peninsula where the Romseys had their beach house. Charles and Diana disappeared past a policeman, who politely turned the curious public back.

Lennox and Whitaker chuckled to themselves. They had got on to the peninsula the day before, photographed the house and sent back the pictures of the seven-bathroomed 'beach hut' love nest. They had also bought an Ordnance Survey map that showed that the house was only half a mile away from another, unguarded spit of land. That night Ken Lennox shouldered his camera bags and his biggest lens and set off:

> This spit of land butted on to a piece of very thick thorn jungle. So we did some compass bearings and made for the nearest part. We set off at two o'clock in the morning and we were in position by eight. We were torn to shreds by this stage, but we got there. We knew that Arthur Edwards and Harry Arnold would be doing their utmost to get there because Arthur had been telling us that he'd once photographed Prince Charles water-skiing on Eleuthera, but wouldn't tell us how.

In those times Arthur and I were deadly rivals, and you didn't get any second prizes. So we made our way in and set up. I had a huge big lens with me. I tied it on to a mangrove tree to try and keep it steady. And within minutes Diana appeared on the beach with Lord Romsey, and she was wearing an overdress, which she immediately took off, and revealed a bikini underneath. She was about four months pregnant so she had a little tummy. By this time I was halfway through my first roll of film – pictures of her walking down to the beach, paddling, giggling and laughing. Anyway, after I'd got the first two rolls of film I gave them to James and he disappeared off into the jungle to make his way back. Then Prince Charles arrived and I shot more film. They went into the water, kissed each other, just bobbing heads in the water. They came out of the water. He carried her out of the water. She threw a towel over his head. Raced up in the sand. So, to all intents and purposes, a very happy couple together, having a beach holiday. I thought I had the best set of pictures ever.

About an hour into this, I heard some crashing in the jungle beside me, and I thought, Oh God, it's the cops. So I pulled my lens off the tree and disappeared. Sat in the bushes being eaten by insects. But then I heard the dulcet tones of Harry Arnold saying, 'You're wrong, Arthur, they haven't made it. They haven't made it. They never got here.' And Arthur was muttering, 'Yeah, yeah, they'll be here someplace.' So I said, 'Hi, guys, how are you?' 'Where's James?' they asked. I said, 'He's gone off to wire the pictures.' Well, Arthur turned chalk white, because time had run out for him basically, and he was unlikely to get anything in the paper, but he thought he had to try anyway. So he cursed me upside down and he disappeared off with Harry, and I stayed behind and shot another two hours of film.

The next morning, as soon as I woke up, I phoned London. I spoke to the picture editor and he said, 'For God's sake don't wire any more of these pictures. The shit has hit the fan.'

To the Palace, Lennox's photographs constituted a flagrant breach of the understanding they thought they had negotiated with the press, but the pictures were fairly tame. They showed Charles and Diana happy, having fun, kissing. They proved, to anyone who might have begun to wonder, that the marriage was not all misery. The Palace said that Princess Diana was extremely upset about this invasion of her privacy, but Lennox has convinced himself that she was not:

> I met Diana in Wales much later with Arthur and she called us the Eleuthera Two – you know, at that time it was the Guildford Four, the Birmingham Six and all the various people being released from prison. So Diana christened Arthur and I the Eleuthera Two and thought it was a great giggle. She thought it was funny that we were in such trouble, because as you know Diana had no hang-ups about being photographed in a bikini.

Ken Lennox often thought back to his unpublished photographs of a happy couple frolicking in the waves. In the early 1990s, when the media echo chamber was reverberating to the distorted sound of 'You never loved me' and 'You were raving mad', as he waded through the Dimblebys and the Mortons, the photographer would ask himself: 'Did my camera lie?'

On their return from holiday, Diana and Charles retired to Highgrove, where the garden was developing under Charles's guidance while the Princess was decorating the interior. But the newspaper editors no longer had their telephoto lenses trained on the royal couple. They could do better than that. They had a war. On 2 April 1982, Argentina invaded the Falkland Islands. Britain mustered an invasion fleet to drive the 'Argies' out again. Friends and colleagues of the Royal Family would be in danger. And not just friends and colleagues: as a naval helicopter pilot, Prince Andrew was going into action.

During the war, and as Diana's pregnancy advanced, bad feelings remained. Jonathan Dimbleby's book provides a striking example:

> The Princess also seemed extraordinarily self-absorbed . . . Even the Falklands campaign – which preoccupied her husband in his role as heir to the throne, as Colonel-in-Chief of two regiments fighting in the South Atlantic, and as the brother of Prince Andrew who was there as a helicopter pilot – failed to arouse her curiosity or to distract her from her own concerns. Some of those who bore witness to her disconcerting detachment were also perplexed by the fact that she seemed to resent the interest being shown in the Falklands rather than in her.

Did Charles' friends really believe that Britain's future Queen put concern about her newspaper image above a national emergency and the potential deaths of her future subjects? And *resented* attention being paid to them?

It was a marriage. There were good times and bad: deciding one sunny morning to make the best of things; shouting one rainy afternoon about how awful everything was. It was only *later* that a pattern was made, when one side or another decided that the moment had come to strike. Then the nastiness came out, the exaggerated nastiness that fills the front pages and the royal blockbusters. 'He was *always* on the phone to her, I even found some letters', 'You remember during the Falklands, *she* was more concerned about her hairstyle.'

Diana visited a home for the blind near Leatherhead in Surrey – part of a routine 'awayday' as she had now learned to call them: a few detectives, a lady-in-waiting, the local papers.

But someone with her remembers an incident that was anything but routine. An old man was sitting near the Princess. He was clearly upset. She moved towards him, crouching low. 'What's wrong?' 'I'm sad that I can't look at you.' Without a thought, she took his hand and placed it full against her face and held it there, looking at him intently as he smiled in sudden delight.

It's a poignant story, but a little unsettling. Diana unembarrassed and instinctive as she would often be. Reminiscent of her teenage wheelchair technique, the one that allowed Darenth Park patients to see her as she pulled them around the floor.

It's hard to imagine other public figures encouraging such fingertip intimacy, then or now. But, as the witness remembers wondering at the time: who took the most pleasure from the contact, the old blind man or the beautiful young Princess?

At last Kensington Palace was ready. A graceful building on the western fringe of Hyde Park, 'KP', as they soon came to call it, had been damaged by incendiary bombs during the London Blitz. The restoration of the apartments intended for Charles and Diana had been painfully slow. If, as intended, the couple had been able to move in immediately after the wedding, it would surely have made some difference to their first eight difficult months. As it was the Department of the Environment finished the work only five weeks before William's birth, when the royal couple took up residence in apartments 8 and 9. Finally Diana had escaped from Buckingham Palace and had her own London home.

One day after the end of the Falklands War, at 9.03 p.m. on 21 June 1982, Diana gave birth to William in St Mary's Hospital, Paddington. He was two weeks early. Prince Charles watched the birth, the first royal father to do so. Whatever the bad feelings of the past few months, this was an undeniably happy and bonding moment, even a funny one, as Janet Filderman recalls:

> I said, 'Oh God, I couldn't do that, I just could not give birth with my husband there.' And she said, 'When Prince Charles came I kept saying, "Charles, come here and hold my hand, hold my hand." But he kept wanting to go to the front of the

engine instead.' Now I think that was very funny. It was said so nicely and with such a lot of laughter too. She loved jokes like that.

The Queen visited the following day and laughingly said, 'Thank goodness he hasn't got ears like his father.' 'Rejoice!' Margaret Thatcher had ordered. Now the nation had two reasons to celebrate – victory in a war and the birth of an heir to the heir to the throne.

After the birth of William, Diana appeared little in public for two months as she and Charles both focused on their baby. Charles cleared his diary to spend more time at home. Princess Margaret and the Duke and Duchess of Gloucester also lived in Kensington Palace, while Diana's sister Jane and Robert Fellowes lived in the Old Barracks near by. There were impromptu visits, coffee mornings and plenty of supportive chat. This, at last, was Diana's idea of proper family life. She breast-fed William for a short period and carried out most of his early changing and bathing. After ten weeks she hired an experienced nanny, Barbara Barnes, as back-up. Charles and the nanny both got bossed about a bit, but it was clear to all that Diana was both capable and loving.

The christening was arranged in a spirit of co-operation. The choice of name was Diana's (she later said that Charles had wanted Arthur), but having got her way Diana let Charles choose the godparents: King Constantine, Lord Romsey, Sir Laurens van der Post, Princess Alexandra, Lady Susan Hussey and the Duchess of Westminster. But by the time of the christening Diana was suffering severe postnatal depression. Within three months the media noticed that she was looking thin and gaunt again. Janet Filderman gave her beauty treatment during this difficult period:

> I know that around the time of Prince William's birth and just afterwards her hormones were up and down and in and out and I think that caused her a little bit of a difficulty – but no more than any other woman would have, having a new baby and being

young. . . . I certainly don't think that they understood how much postnatal depression she was under. And if you think about it, she married at what, nineteen or so, and immediately became pregnant. And that in addition to all the excitement of the wedding and the after-effects and the media chasing her must have been quite a hard time and one has to recognise that. I am not saying that she might not have been difficult to live with because people are when they are going through a depressive stage but I don't think it was to do with her personality, I think it was to do with hormones. Anybody can have that.

In September 1982, while they were at Balmoral, the Royal Family received news that Princess Grace of Monaco had died in a car accident. The question of who should attend the funeral had to be settled. Princess Grace had met and calmed a very nervous Diana on her first public appearance eighteen months previously. Diana had liked her and wanted to go. The Queen said that Charles should go but he did not want to. Eventually, Diana was allowed to represent the family on her own.

The funeral was chaotic, seething with press people, not least because both Diana and Nancy Reagan had chosen to attend. It was a blazing hot Mediterranean late-summer day, the Rolls-Royce broke down and the royal party got stuck in a lift. Under these difficult circumstances Diana behaved impeccably and impressed all those around her.

On the plane home, Diana burst into tears with exhaustion. As they approached Scotland, she asked whether Charles was coming to meet her. Staff said it was unlikely because Prince Andrew was due back from the Falklands.

> We looked at her big eyes looking out of the window in expectation. She said, 'There's one police car.' She didn't know what that meant – no Charles. She was very upset. She got into the police car and disappeared.

The next morning Diana got an excellent write-up in the press. She called a courtier to discuss the trip.

> She rang up and asked, 'How did I do? How did I do?' 'Have you seen the papers?' I said. 'You were absolutely brilliant.' She said, 'Thanks for saying that because nobody here has mentioned that.'

Having got married, Prince Charles was wondering what to do next. Years of being Prince of Wales yawned ahead but what *did* a Prince of Wales do? Available answers were usually expressed in negatives: a Prince of Wales did *not* get involved in politics, for instance. But Charles was determined to have his say in public life, believing that he could do some good.

At Cambridge, and during a term that he very much enjoyed in Australia, Charles had met young people from backgrounds very different to his own. One friend with whom Charles shared a kitchen at Trinity College was a Labour-voting coal miner's son from South Wales. This helped generate in Charles a desire to intervene in social and cultural issues. Not all of his interests and initiatives were approved of by the men who served him at the Palace. Referring to enthusiasms that brought them work of a kind they did not relish, they would whisper, 'What toys are coming out of the box today?' as their master approached his office.

In December 1982 Charles spoke out to the British Medical Association in favour of alternative treatments, and against the influence of the drugs industry. His intervention sparked an acrimonious debate in which the Prince was widely ridiculed for being gulled by quacks. Twenty years later his attitudes seem less extraordinary. He continued his campaign for serious consideration of the issues by the medical establishment over the next year. Then he spoke out in favour of organic food production in an assault on modern farming methods that outraged another well-entrenched lobby, together with the agrochemical industry. Again, twenty years later he has widespread support. At the time he laid himself open to derision and was duly mocked in the tabloids as the 'loony prince'. And when newspapers said that the causes the Prince was choosing to back were eccentric, the Buckingham Palace hierarchy was inclined to agree.

In the autumn of 1982 Charles suggested that Diana see a psychiatrist. She resisted, but in the end they both saw Dr Allan McGlashan, a dream analyst who was recommended by Laurens van der Post. Although Charles continued to see him, Diana was unreceptive. Instead she agreed to see Dr David Mitchell, a cognitive therapist.

Later, according to a senior member of the royal household, the courtiers surrounding Prince Charles discussed the possibility that Diana suffered from BPD – Borderline Personality Disorder. How this diagnosis was arrived at has never before been made clear, but it made its way into many books and television programmes in the mid-1990s. BPD describes people who are fitfully needy and aggressive, frequently retreating into paranoia. It covers feelings of panic, binge-eating and self-harm. One or another of its manifestations could probably be diagnosed in half the population.

We wanted to discover where the Borderline Personality story came from. Penny Junor, one of the first to specify it in print, told us that:

> Dimbleby helped me come to the syndrome – there were several people actually who had mentioned Borderline Personality Disorder, Dimbleby was one of them. And when I then researched the subject further I discovered that it was absolutely spot on for the kind of behaviour that Diana exhibited.

In the months after the couple separated, Prince Charles's friends spoke at length to Jonathan Dimbleby about Diana's mental state. They told him many shocking stories about the early months of the marriage: Diana listening at doors and steaming open letters; Diana screaming at them and running out of the room; Diana's intense possessiveness and jealousy; Diana's endless suspicions about Camilla.

Dimbleby consulted the medical textbooks. He told us:

> I stumbled across the term BPD in a variety of psychiatric journals while researching the symptoms of the Princess's self-acknowledged condition, bulimia. I discovered that the two disorders are often associated with each other.

We understand that Dimbleby also took his interview notes and shared them with at least two professional psychiatrists. Dimbleby did not reveal to the psychiatrists the identity of the person whose symptoms he was describing, but given that he was known to be working on a biography of Prince Charles they must have guessed fairly quickly.

Conversations with these experts, and close study of the academic journals they recommended, led the author to feel confident enough in the diagnosis to draft an entire chapter about Diana and BDP. But it never reached the printers. Dimbleby told us that he 'came to the conclusion that any conceivable link between bulimia and BPD was too speculative'. We understand that when Prince Charles read the draft chapter he also asked for it to be dropped. Dimbleby concludes that

> The Prince of Wales was concerned throughout to avoid causing distress to the Princess . . . I exercised self-restraint for a range of reasons, among which was a concern to avoid causing unnecessary pain to the family – as I indicated in the foreword to *The Prince of Wales*.

Dimbleby dropped most of his BPD chapter, and excised any direct reference to the disorder from his pages. But the results of his psychiatric research did not entirely disappear. One section about Diana's behaviour that made it on to the page reads

> . . . there appeared to be a terrible conflict inside her that would suddenly erupt in anger or grief. As her public prestige soared, she grew correspondingly anguished in private. She . . . scoured the newspapers for photographs of herself with an eagerness unalloyed by familiarity. Not for the first time, it seemed to their friends that she was searching for her own identity in the image of a princess that smiled back at her from every front page.
>
> Whatever clinical or psychiatric label was appropriate to the Princess's distress, its effect on her marriage to the Prince could hardly be in doubt.

Dimbleby had stumbled upon a huge story, perhaps the key to understanding the evidence gathered for the abandoned chapter. It is easy to understand why he would share his insight, although he was clearly not Penny Junor's only source. Columnist Nigel Dempster wrote about BPD in 1995 and since Diana's death several other writers have alleged that she suffered from it. The result of all this is a now widely reported 'Mad Diana' story.

One of *Diana's* closest friends in the late 1990s was Lana Marks. Her English-born husband Neville, a member of the Royal College of Psychiatrists and former professor of psychiatry at the University of Miami, met Diana several times.

> Borderline personality disorder is a very serious personality problem. The person with this problem has difficulty in all areas of their life and thinks and behaves in ways that are not normal for their culture. In my thirty-two years experience as a consultant psychiatrist, I have treated many people with this condition. Classically it comes on as a young adolescent and then it's pervasive and it lasts their whole lifetime.
>
> I met Princess Diana and I spoke to her, and someone with her responsibilities would not have been able to cope with the pressures of her job, travelling around the world, meeting world leaders, the brightest intellects in the world. She coped with these very stressful, important roles. What she couldn't cope

> with was a more personal emotional role – being rejected by her husband and not knowing how to deal with that.
>
> If she had had a borderline personality disorder she would not have been able to cope with any area of her life. She would have had difficulties that would have been apparent to the world from the day the world first knew about her, right through her life. This is the characteristic of a borderline personality disorder, it's a lifelong condition, it's a serious difficulty with emotions, with thoughts and with controlling one's impulsive behaviour.

Dr Marks is the husband of one of Diana's allies and he would be the first to stress that his opinion was not formed under clinical conditions. But he does, of course, combine professional experience of BPD with a personal acquaintance with the Princess of Wales.

It is interesting to note that back in the early 1980s, long before anyone had heard of a royal case of Borderline Personality Disorder, Buckingham Palace issued a statement about newspaper attempts to psychoanalyse Diana:

> 'Rubbish', a spokesman said. 'This is pretty bloody stupid. No one would give a medical opinion on someone he has never met and is never likely to.'

If Diana was suffering from mood swings in the autumn of 1982, so was the press. James Whitaker, now writing for the *Mirror*, reported in October that Diana and Charles returned from Balmoral after two weeks of sulking followed by a blazing row. Andrew Morton followed suit in the *Daily Star*. Richard Stott of the *Mirror* remembers:

> a picture of her and Charles which was taken by Kent Gavin, the *Mirror* photographer, and she looked haunted. So much so

> that the *Mirror* didn't run it because there were worries being expressed that her health was being affected.

This charitable mood did not last. On 13 November 1982 Diana had a semi-public argument with Charles when, at the last minute, she decided she was not going to the British Legion Remembrance Service at the Albert Hall. Charles left without her and then Diana had a change of heart. Ignoring her staff, who told her it was too late, she followed, arriving ten minutes after the Queen and after Charles had already apologised for her absence. Richard Stott recalls:

> suddenly she arrived, in a rush, through the back door. Something clearly odd had happened. And I think that was the first example of something tangible being shown, that there might be something wrong.

'No one, but no one, is EVER late for the Queen,' proclaimed James Whitaker the next day, noting the thin and strained appearance of the Princess. On 15 November the *Mirror* asked, 'Is it all getting too much for Diana?' Harry Arnold, in the *Sun*, reported that Charles was 'seriously concerned' and had 'taken top medical advice'. The tabloids were not clear what the problem was but they were speculating that Diana, like her sister Sarah, had fallen prey to anorexia.

These stories were immediately denied in other newspapers with Palace spokesmen proclaiming Diana fit and well. Nigel Dempster criticised the *Sun* and the *Mirror* for exaggerating the 'inevitable stresses' of a public marriage and then listed several signs of Diana's stress himself. He quoted a member of the 'inner circle' to the effect that 'quite simply she has freaked out'. At the beginning of December, *Private Eye*'s Grovel reported:

> So badly is the Princess of Wales treating husband Brian – Kensington Palace and Highgrove reverberate daily to her tantrums and staff are complaining that her language when dressing down the Heir to the Throne is full of expletive deleteds

> – that former 'mentor' Camilla Parker Bowles may soon find HRH calling again at her Gloucestershire mansion.
>
> Regular readers will remember that Camilla, along with Aussie harpie Lady (Dale) Tryon, used to attend to Brian's therapeutic needs until they were banished from the inner circle following the marriage to Diana . . .

Dempster topped this in December 1982 when he announced on ABC's *Good Morning America* that Diana was a 'fiend' and a 'monster' and that 'Charles is desperately unhappy . . . because Fleet Street forced him into this marriage'. He claimed to have obtained this information from one of Prince Charles's staff. Dempster was denounced by his rivals. Judy Wade of the *Sun* remembers:

> I was asked to write a story counterbalancing that saying, 'No, no, no, these wild accusations in America, they're totally untrue. Diana is a wonderful wife and mother, and she's helped her husband all the time, and they're planning their garden at Highgrove together.' And I wrote all this tosh because editors believed that the public wanted the fairytale, and that you have to give a young couple a chance. You can't say, 'Oh dear, the marriage is in trouble' so soon. I mean, everybody goes through rough patches.

But the denials were not convincing. *Private Eye* commented quizzically: 'If the *Daily Mail*'s Reptile in Residence is to be believed, the beautiful, demure Diana is a tortured fiend who has to be tied to her bedposts every night.' In early 1983 the *News of the World* was reporting that Diana was 'near to tears much of the time . . . and her quick temper never far from the surface'. She could not handle being left alone and 'might well be heading for some kind of breakdown'.

For Diana, who read the papers and took what they said seriously, the accuracy of the reports must have been unsettling. It was ever more clear that there were leaks, and it appeared that some of them were coming not from chambermaids but from senior staff. Were they ganging up on her? Who could she trust? And what about the *Eye*'s speculations about Camilla?

Meanwhile, evidence of friction within the marriage was piling up. Judy Wade recalls an occasion when

> A photographer was called to Kensington Palace to do some pictures, which would be issued when Charles and Diana went on their first tour abroad to Australia and New Zealand. And when he arrived at the Palace a fairly highly placed official said to him, 'Now look, if they start to fight and row in front of you, please try to ignore it.' He was talking about it as if it was a regular occurrence – as if you can expect them to fight in front of you.

The tour that began in March 1983 came as a blessed escape from domestic tension. No one was left at home this time – William travelled with them. Royal officials had not been slow to recognise the value to the monarchy and to the country of the enormously popular couple. The Charles and Diana show was a gilt-edged opportunity to reinforce the popularity of the British Crown in the far-flung states of the Commonwealth. An affable Canadian, Victor Chapman, was appointed as press officer to beef up the razzmatazz of royal tours and get the most out of the new asset. He did not have to try hard. The public reaction to Diana was extraordinary. Robert Spencer remembers:

> She suddenly became a sort of star, complete star, and I remember going to Australia in January 1983 and being pestered by everybody saying, 'You are related to Diana, this perfect being.' I mean, she was almost a goddess at that stage.

During the seventies the media had lost interest in such tours, but suddenly they were big news again. Instead of five or six reporters tagging along, there were nearer eighty. When the new star turned up in Australia, the scenes were unlike anything seen before.

Arthur Edwards recalls:

> There were just thousands, hundreds of thousands of people just come to see this lady. And I mean it was no secret that she loved it, she absolutely loved it. At the Sydney Opera House she was the star in this open-top car, she was arriving like she was already the Queen, you know. The crowd was screaming for her: 'Diana! Diana!'

The Prince was a veteran of fifty royal tours and had made sure that he would get his moments of privacy. Six visits to a hideaway in Woomargama, New South Wales, were written into the schedule. Charles wrote home about how music and reading 'help to preserve my sanity and my faith when all is chaos, crowds, cameras, politicians, cynicism, sarcasm, and intense scrutiny outside'.

Diana stopped traffic. In Brisbane the city came to a grinding halt. Half a million people turned out on the street in one section of the town just to catch a glimpse of her. And she was so overwhelmed by the crowd that they had to take her into the town hall and give her a drink of water and sit her down.

The royal scrutineers noted that Charles did his best to help and support Diana. Arthur Edwards saw that:

> He was always touching her hand or holding her arm. And they seemed to be very much together. And I remember when they looked at each other they looked like they wanted to rip the clothes off each other, they looked so much in love. . . . And there was all these big gaps in the programme where they would go off for two or three days. Because it was a long tour. And it was obvious that they were looking forward to those wonderful weekends and so they really did seem to be very much in love. I am convinced of it to this day.

Diana was elated, and entered one of her forgive-and-forget moods. She wrote a letter to a friend from Australia that said that she was ashamed of her behaviour in London, proud of the

Prince and grateful for his support and guidance on the tour. To crown it all, William crawled for the first time in Government House.

Before his marriage Charles had expressed some decidedly old-fashioned views about the role of a royal wife, telling Alistair Cooke in 1976:

> whoever I choose is going to have a jolly hard job, always in my shadow, having to walk a few steps behind me, all that sort of thing.

But now the spotlight was being continuously beamed away from the heir to the throne and on to his dazzling wife. Once again the crowds cheered if they were on her side of the road and groaned if they were on his, once again he laughed it off, saying he needed two wives to cover both sides of the street. When the couple did things separately all the press went with Diana. For Judy Wade she was the story:

> Their press officer, Vic Chapman, would come to us and say, 'For God's sake, can't some of you walk with the Prince?' We were all surrounding Diana. We were only interested in Diana because she was so pretty; she had such a great way with the crowds and she was so naïve she'd open her mouth and say amazing things that made good copy.

Even within her own family, traditionalists like Robert Spencer looked at Diana's sudden fame with mixed feelings.

> There was this girl trying to establish herself as the wife of the Prince of Wales, or that's what she should be doing. Instead of which she was inundated with praise and she was on the front of every magazine. She was just unable to get on really with settling down as the wife and mother that she should have been and I think that's where the problem started.

Earlier that year *Time* magazine had posed the question: 'What is a Princess? What is one for?' The answer, it concluded, was simple: to be photographed. But this was not how Prince Charles, with his restless desire to make a real contribution to public life, would have answered the question.

It was wet in New Zealand, but Diana's new informal style was an equally huge success. 'Princess thrills 35,000 children,' proclaimed the *Auckland Star* over a picture of Diana rubbing noses with a Maori girl. 'Red Tape Cut As Royal Couple Warm to Crowd,' thrilled the *New Zealand Herald* on 18 April. Charles seemed to enjoy being paddled by eighty painted Maoris on the historic Nga Toki Matawhaorua canoe at Waitangi, but this was one of the few occasions when the Kiwi press took any notice of him. 'Diana's spontaneous manner in making sure as many as possible of the throngs of school children, the elderly, the handicapped, and the crowds at large were able to meet her first hand ensured her of a lasting place in the memories of the Northland people,' reported the *Northern Advocate*. The unprecedented intensity of the enthusiasm, especially in the British press, alarmed Prince Charles in a way that could not simply be attributed to envy of his wife. Experience had left him with a weary understanding of the ways of journalists:

> The terrifying part, as always in this kind of thing, is that they construct the pedestal; they put you on top of it, they expect you to balance on the beastly thing without ever losing your footing, and because they have engineered the pedestal along come the demolition experts amongst them who are of the breed that enjoy breaking things down. And it is all done for a sort of vicarious entertainment . . . Maybe the wedding, because it was so well done and because it made such a wonderful, almost Hollywood-style, film, has distorted people's view of things? Whatever the case it frightens me.

7
Radiant

> He didn't change his bachelor ways. She wanted him to stay at home with her and the children. There were tantrums and hysterics. She challenged him – it was the first time he had been challenged. It was the first time he had met his equal – he was surrounded by yes-men. Diana accused Charles's friends of being sycophants, but she was her own worst enemy too.
>
> Senior Buckingham Palace official

In the autumn of 1983 local journalists alleged that Charles was again seen riding to hounds with Camilla Parker Bowles. Diana later told Anthony Holden that she pressed the 'redial' button on the phone in Charles's Highgrove study. A servant at Camilla's country home answered. She said that she implored Charles not to go hunting that weekend, but he did.

One of Diana's greatest qualities was her ability to sense and connect with the mood of strangers. It was how she had first caught Charles's attention on the hay bale. This empathy, later deployed at a thousand hospital bedsides, was also deployed at her own. She just *knew* that Charles wasn't happy with her, just *knew* that he pined for Camilla. Given the state of his marriage, he probably did have these feelings, but that did *not* mean he was being unfaithful.

Diana began to deal with the continuing leaks and the rival claims on her husband's time. She pressed Charles to see less of old and faithful supporters such as the van Cutsems, Romseys, Palmer-Tomkinsons and Nicholas Soames. Diana was convinced that they were facilitating secret meetings between him and Camilla. *His* friends all insist that there were no one-on-one meetings between Charles and Camilla until 1985, and no affair until 1986.

Apart from her intuition, Diana's only evidence that the affair resumed years before this date were Charles's frequent absences from her bed. We know that Diana did spend many nights alone at this time, because she would call up her friends and tell them so. After a busy and exciting day, she wanted someone with whom to share her news. Janet Filderman received dozens of such late-night phone calls.

> She would phone up in the evenings, probably nine o'clock or something like that, or later, saying 'Hi, I am sitting in bed with Wills and we are watching telly.' If it was later she was always on her own, but she would just have a little chit-chat. I suppose it was the mother/daughtery thing.
>
> . . . for her the joy would have been to come home and have a conversation with her husband about what her day had been like. Now she could have spoken to him on the telephone for all I was aware, but it would appear that this didn't happen very often because she phoned me or she phoned some other friend to talk to about it.
>
> She talked to me about Camilla and I did the best I could to calm her down, to make her put her energies into constructive things like her work, like her friends.

Diana could be hard on those who had to work alongside her. Oliver Everett, her unofficial private secretary, was drawn deep into her confidence and then suddenly became a non-person. He was not called to meetings, his memos and phone calls were unanswered, his presence in the room was ignored. This lasted for months. What had caused Diana's displeasure was never explained to him, but in December 1983 he resigned. Charles intervened to get Everett another job in the royal household, and was angry at the waste of his talent.

Michael Colborne had been at Charles's side for almost a decade and had enjoyed an unusually frank and informal relationship with him. Now he found himself stretched between Prince and Princess and took the brunt of Charles's occasional outbursts of temper, notably in Canada in 1983 when he was accused of spending too much time with Diana. Colborne said that he thought Charles wanted him to offer her advice and support. What followed was one of the most harrowing scenes of the marriage. Charles screamed at his friend, stomped around the room and kicked the furniture. Then, as he angrily wrenched open the door, he discovered Diana crouched outside, listening and sobbing. Charles calmed down and took her in his arms. For Colborne it was one trauma too many, and he decided to leave royal service.

Diana's mental stability has been the subject of many briefings, and has been written about at great length. Less attention has been paid to her husband's own unpredictable behaviour. While there has never been any suggestion that he physically threatened her, there could at times be a brooding menace in the Prince, as many who were close to him have remarked. Patrick Jephson, Diana's future private secretary, 'learned that, among other feelings he stirred in her, many of them warm and affectionate, the Princess also felt fear . . . When she felt herself to be on the receiving end of his anger, before her characteristic defiance set in, I often saw a look of trepidation cross her face, as if she were once again a small girl in trouble with the grown-ups.'

Jayne Fincher was still taking photographs of every royal event. She saw a real difference in Diana when Charles was not around.

> When she was with him, the protocol was a lot more formal. When he wasn't there she was very flirty, would giggle like mad, particularly if she went on visits with the military. She

> loved all the soldiers, and she'd giggle her head off and flutter her eyelashes and be completely silly.

Diana became pregnant again at New Year, and during 1984 Charles reduced his engagements once again. The marriage still clearly had its moments, but over time there were steadily less making-the-best-of-it mornings, and rather more you-never-loved-me afternoons. Michael Colborne tendered his resignation in the spring of 1984, but stayed to the end of the year. Charles was particularly shaken at Colborne's departure, which brought home to him how much the bad state of his marriage was affecting his own behaviour.

Henry Charles Albert David was born on Saturday, 15 September 1984 in the Lindo Wing of St Mary's Hospital, Paddington. He weighed 6lb 14oz. According to Diana, the birth of her second son marked the end of any hope for her marriage. Charles had been wanting a girl, was disappointed with Harry's auburn hair colour, and left the maternity hospital for the polo field in unseemly haste. Such lack of feeling from a husband devoted to both his sons does not sound credible, but it's what she told Andrew Morton seven years later: 'as Harry was born it just went bang, our marriage, the whole thing went down the drain . . . By then I knew he had gone back to his lady but somehow we'd managed to have Harry.'

During Diana's second pregnancy Charles made a speech that changed several people's lives. On 30 May 1984, at an anniversary celebration for the Royal Institute of British Architects, he gave vent to his dislike for the introduction of steel and glass into familiar neoclassical London landscapes. He pointed to a lack of communication between planners and the recipients of their efforts, and argued in favour of community architecture. So far, so uncontroversial: large sections of the public shared his horror at the urban planning of the sixties and seventies. But then he specifically attacked the current proposal for the extension to the National Gallery in Trafalgar Square, calling it a 'monstrous carbuncle on the face of a much loved and elegant friend'. Although his remarks brought letters of support from the public, they outraged many in the architectural profession, and damaged the career of the architect responsible, Peter Ahrends. Ahrends, whose design was doomed the moment the Prince spoke out against it, tried to point out that it had resulted from long consultations with the gallery's trustees. He called the Prince's remarks 'offensive, reactionary and ill-considered . . . if he holds such strong views, I'm surprised that he did not take the opportunity offered by the public inquiry to express them'.

Edward Adeane had spent days trying to persuade Charles not to make the speech, fearing that it would drag the Prince into a nasty public row with a profession he knew little about. It did. Within six months, Charles's private secretary was gone too.

Ever since his first, upbeat biography in 1979, Anthony Holden had written and broadcast widely about the Prince. Charles valued the support of someone from a newspaper like the *Sunday Times*, and various of his friends provided Holden with briefings and insights into the Royal Family.

In 1979 Holden had seen Charles as a breath of fresh air. He had described him as a 'self-conscious, deeply vulnerable, desperately well-meaning man . . . proud, ambitious, romantic and anxious to carve himself a place in history'. Holden had been impressed by Charles's determination to involve himself in the core issues of modern Britain. But he had warned that:

> He will need to prove himself more in touch with the progressive thinking and relaxed life-style of a large proportion of his own age group, who approach the seats of power quite as remorselessly as he approaches the throne.

The architecture speech convinced Holden that Charles had failed the test. His next book would be much less kind, calling

Charles 'a tortured, self-doubting, almost monkish introvert . . . born in a century which he increasingly mistrusted'. Warming to his wife's more easy-going style, Holden would become one of Diana's great champions in the years that followed, one of many who came to identify her with the spirit of the times, and Charles with the past.

Diana was also developing a new image for herself – as the British fashion industry's most influential model. It was an interesting twist on the role originally allotted to her by the press. As soon as Diana had appeared she had become the subject of an intense style critique. Judy Wade accepts responsibility:

> It was the women's pages that really went to town on Diana. I was writing endless features about the wonderful ruffled romantic clothes she wore. I wrote reams and reams about her wardrobe, her weight-watching, her diet secrets. The Palace thought that we were trivialising the monarchy by writing all this tosh about Diana's frocks, her hairdo. I remember once [November 1984] she attended the State Opening of Parliament, and for the very first time she wore her hair up, and she totally pushed the Queen off the front pages that day.

Lookalike competitions took place in clubs and pubs across the world. Everything she wore was copied: the lamb sweater, the ruffled collars, the wondergirl headband, the chokers, the off-the-shoulder dresses. She brought glamour to the Royal Family at a time when glamour was the new big thing. More and more celebrity and style magazines appeared, and Diana featured in them all. Magazines were launched that were entirely devoted to the British Royal Family. They tended to avoid stories about community architecture, instead going to town on endless photographs of Diana and her children, Diana and her shoes, Diana and her beauty routine. They sold well, and they sold way beyond the old British and Commonwealth heartlands of royal

Look at me!

What Diana wrote in a cupboard at West Heath school

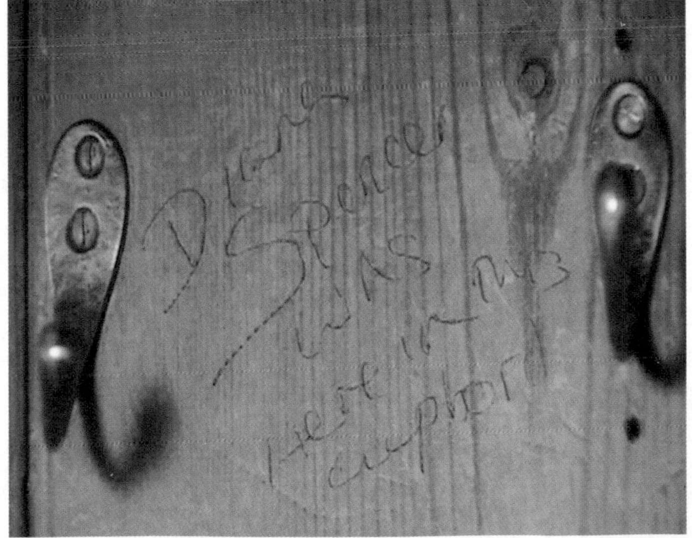

Outside the Young England kindergarten, Pimlico, September 1980, taken by Arthur Edwards

Jayne Fincher's first photograph of Diana, taken after Princess Margaret's birthday party, November 1980

Diana enters St Paul's Cathedral with Earl Spencer, July 1981

On honeymoon at the Braemar Highland Games, September 1981

Diana in Brecon, November 1981

Ken Lennox's long-lens shots of Charles and Diana in the Bahamas, February 1982

Australia's new princess – with Anne Beckwith-Smith (behind her wearing hat) at the Sydney Opera House, spring 1983

With John Travolta at the White House, November 1985

The puppet from the television series *Spitting Image* with American tour headlines, November 1985

A family day out at the Guards Polo Club, Windsor, May 1987

Diana presents the Captains and Subalterns Cup to James Hewitt at Tidworth, summer 1988

Her favourite photograph, autumn 1991:
Diana greets the children on *Britannia* in Canada; and the picture the public never saw – Charles hugging them too

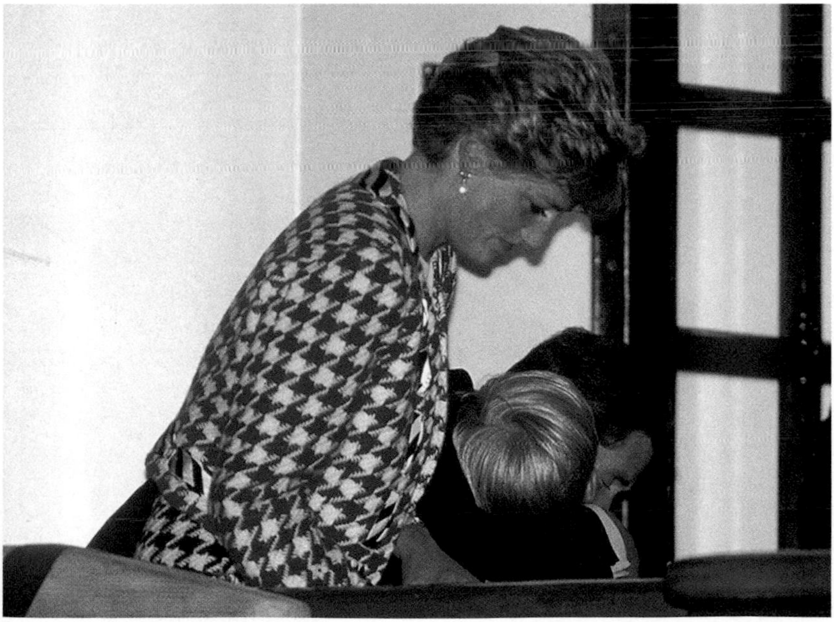

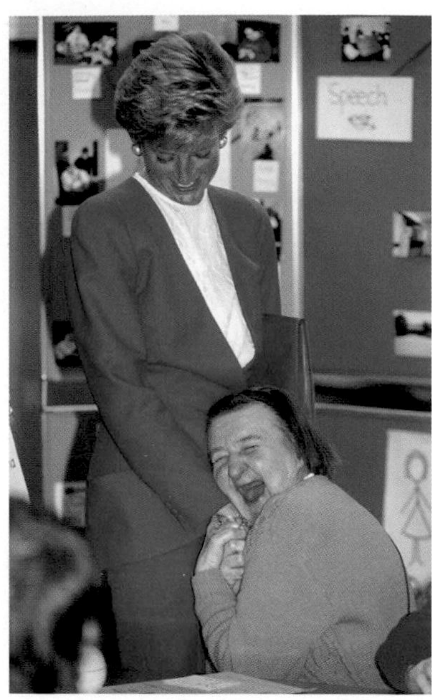

To touch is important: the Six Acres day centre, Taunton, Somerset, April 1991

Working alone on her tenth wedding anniversary at RAF Cranwell, July 1991

The winner's kiss: polo in India, Valentine's Eve, February 1992

Mental acuity diminishes in the absence of ongoing intellectual challenge.

FRIDAY APRIL 15

Notes

enthusiasm, stocking news-stands in New York, Paris and Madrid.

Her dress sense had started out as frumpy and unadventurous, but it soon became genuinely and impressively stylish as she took to wearing the very best of British design. Her original fashion adviser, Anna Harvey, introduced her to Caroline Charles, Jasper Conran and Bruce Oldfield. Henceforth Diana became the standard-bearer for an entire industry, catapulting it out of the doldrums to worldwide acclaim.

Jayne Fincher, who still remembered her first encounter with Diana's green woolly coat, was astonished:

> It happened before our very eyes, the transformation from this shy teenager, who hid beneath big hats, and hung her head, into the self-assured woman and mother, confident in her beauty. It never struck me that she was conceited about this, I think she just enjoyed being who she was, and I'm sure too, *grateful* for being as beautiful as she was. I really saw no evidence of vanity in her, and sometimes I looked pretty hard, because I thought – come on, nobody can really take all this without maybe their head getting turned a bit.

Arthur Edwards recalls royal tours from this period:

> When she got off the plane in a different country you were given a slip of paper: 'The Princess is wearing a dress of blue silk made by so-and-so, and the hat is made by so-and-so in matching colours.' It was quite amazing. I mean, we never got given a piece of paper with 'and Prince Charles is wearing a suit made in Savile Row' or anything like that.

On the tour to Italy in the spring of 1985 Diana wore dozens of different outfits, all striking and stylish. She looked fantastic descending from the plane at Olbia airport in a lavender-coloured suit by Jan van Velden. At La Spezia she sported a white pin stripe with a white nautical hat in a tribute to her hosts, the Italian Navy. She appeared in a black and bright blue dress with shimmering silver and blue stars by Jacques Azagury at the Palazzo Vecchio in Florence. At lunch with the President of Italy she wore a silk seersucker by Bruce Oldfield; in Sicily, a candy-striped silk dress. Being in favour with Diana became important for top fashion designers. The Emanuels were frozen out for years after a dispute. In a gondola in Venice she signalled her forgiveness by wearing a green coat-dress that they had designed.

Diana was irritated when it was reported that for the Italian tour she had spent £100,000 on her wardrobe. She was particularly cross that the leak came from Andrew Morton, one of her favourites in the press corps. Ken Lennox remembers the moment: 'Diana marched right up to him and said, "Mr Morton, don't you know the difference between a lira sign and a pound sign? They are very close but even you should be able to spot that."' Tall and bespectacled, with a modest manner, Morton bore a marked resemblance to Clark Kent, the journalist alter ego of Superman as played by Christopher Reeve. 'Superman' was his nickname in the press corps. Lennox notes that this was just one in a series of flirtatious encounters between Diana and the best looking of the royal pressmen. 'The two of them used to have this little sort of blushing routine between them. She used to complain about his terrible ties, and Andrew used to blush and we always used to look at him and say, "You great big silly sausage, you."' Judy Wade says:

> I vividly remember the first time Diana and Andrew Morton met. It was at a cocktail party and Diana immediately seemed to be interested in him. She was toying with his tie and making comments about what a bright pattern it was. From then on Andrew always wore loudly patterned ties when Diana was around and she always made comments about them. It gave her an excuse to get close to him. Once she picked up his tie and pulled him towards her and we were all standing back amazed, gobsmacked, and the press officer who was standing

near by said, 'God, I think I'll have to get a bucket of water and throw it over them.'

In a decade of celebrity came one of the great celebrity events. In July 1985, Bob Geldof masterminded a sixteen-hour live concert held simultaneously at Wembley Stadium in London and JFK Stadium in Philadelphia to raise money to help the starving population of Ethiopia. As the hours passed and Geldof demanded 'give us your fucking money', phone lines were jammed as millions put donations on their credit cards. The concert was watched by 1.5 billion people worldwide and raised $40 million.

The complicated relationship between glamour and good causes would be an important part of Diana's future. In 1985 many established charity workers were cynical about the intervention of pop stars and fashion models. They expected it all to go wrong, and that Geldof would take money that would otherwise have gone elsewhere. Instead he introduced huge numbers of young people to the concept of helping others. What had been a matter of fusty old collection boxes wielded by pensioners suddenly became part of their world. Compassion and cool were a heady combination, charity made sexy and immediate by the involvement of superstars like Madonna, David Bowie and Paul McCartney and live television pictures that made suffering real in every home. The royal couple attended. Diana jigged along to the music, Charles looked uncomfortable in a suit. Afterwards, in private, he sought to befriend Geldof, telling him how much he admired his initiative. But in public Diana looked in tune with the times, he did not.

The balance of power was altering. Diana, 'fashion Queen', appeared self-assured, whereas Charles, 'loony Prince', looked wayward in his judgment. Most of the tabloids delighted in mocking him. But in early February 1985 Andrew Morton, billed as 'the man who really knows the Royals', wrote an odd piece in the *Daily Star* in the wake of a public argument between the royal couple on the ski slopes in Liechtenstein. Diana had stalked away rather than talk to the press, leaving Charles standing there looking foolish. 'Now I'll get it in the neck,' he said. Morton's article presented a stormy but loving marriage of two strong characters with Charles willingly colluding in Diana's modern ideas on child rearing. He ended by explaining that while Charles might be a mouse, if pushed too far he was a mouse that roared. On the same page the *Star* reported Diana's sacking of her hairdresser, Kevin Shanley, and the alleged fury of Prince Philip that her new hairstyle, worn to the opening of Parliament the previous November, had forced the Queen's Speech out of the news.

In October 1985, just before the couple arrived for a much-trumpeted tour of the United States, Morton's 'mouse that roars' phrase was recast, along with some of his ideas, by Tina Brown for *Vanity Fair*. Prince Charles's former ally, Anthony Holden helped Brown research what was a perceptive and prescient analysis of the royal relationship. Brown spelled out the role reversal. She spoke of reports that the Prince was 'pussy whipped from here to eternity'. Diana had transformed herself from a mouse to a royal Alexis Carrington (the power-dressing anti-heroine of *Dynasty*), the Prince from an action man to a shabby gardener. Each was reacting badly to the changes in the other. Brown spoke with approval of Diana's charisma, but noted that the ascension to stardom had affected her as it affected everyone: 'she is in that adversary mood towards the press that is the first stage in the removal from life that fame inflicts. The second stage is "Graceland", when the real world melts away altogether.'

Brown and Holden's article also made a daring reference to Camilla Parker Bowles's supposed role in helping Charles choose a submissive, controllable wife, and pointed out that the result was far from what Camilla might have intended.

A trip to Brunei generated a letter from Charles that made clear how disenchanted he had become:

> As always on these occasions I heard myself twittering away reproducing the most nonsensical rubbish while small gentlemen in white uniforms crawled about on their knees in front of us, pouring out cups of tea and offering plates of sticky cakes.

Charles had a keen sense of the absurd. *The Goon Show*, a gently subversive BBC radio comedy series from the 1950s, was an abiding passion from childhood. The Goons specialised in making fun of the pompous and the proud. Classic British authority figures, generals and bishops, were undermined with a loud, wet raspberry or the falsetto rendition of their trademark 'Ying Tong, Ying Tong' song. From early youth Charles had a satirist's eye for the silliness of much of what he did: the meaningless meetings with self-important local dignitaries, the tuneless national anthems played in dusty foreign airports, the endless handshaking insincerities ('And what do you do?') at the garden party and the fête. In the mid-1980s his disenchantment – fuelled by unhappiness at home and the disappointing reception given to his initiatives – was at an all-time high. Another 1984 excursion amid presidents, generals, tycoons and arms dealers found Charles fighting 'the urge to say something provocative and outrageous'. As ever, he wanted to escape from the national anthems and the sticky cakes and do something serious. A toe-curling story in Brown's *Vanity Fair* article illustrates the point. Brown recalls being introduced to the Prince alongside the celebrated playwright Tom Stoppard:

> 'I've thought of a good idea for a play,' he told Tom Stoppard. 'It's about a hotel which caters entirely for people with phobias.

It was a small item in *The Times*.' 'We'll go halves on the take, sir,' Stoppard said kindly. 'Actually I thought it was so amusing,' Prince Charles persisted, 'I telephoned Spike Milligan [the *Goon Show* writer] and told him. It's a frightfully funny idea, don't you think?' His words conjured up a poignant picture: Prince Charles asking his secretary to put through a call to Milligan who, after conquering his astonishment, had to listen politely and humour the royal desire to throw out a spark that might ignite somewhere.

'Royal marriage on the rocks' stories had become commonplace. The Palace press office had, for some time, been planning a damage limitation exercise via television. The Queen's press secretary, Michael Shea, approached ITN's Editor, Sir David Nicholas, with the offer of an exclusive interview with the royal couple in exchange for £1 million for the Prince's Trust. In the *Sunday Mirror* on 20 October, ITN executive Bill Hodgson promised that 'the public will be surprised by their Royal Highnesses' remarkable honesty'.

Coached by Sir Richard Attenborough, Diana turned in a polished performance under what turned out to be some unctuously gentle questioning from Sir Alastair Burnet. She denied that she argued with her husband and made light of her petulance on the ski slopes. She also denied that she had tried to change the Prince or that she was a domineering wife. She was not a shopaholic or a perfectionist, and there had been no rift with Princess Anne over Prince Harry's christening, as rumoured in the press. Altogether, she complained, there was too much about her in the newspapers. Charles agreed. For his own part he defended his views on architecture robustly and emphatically denied stories that he had been using a ouija board to contact his great-uncle Mountbatten.

The interview was associated with a documentary and a book

that followed the royal couple through the best part of a year. The programme-makers saw Diana and Charles barnstorm Australia again, and once more the Princess pulled in vast crowds. The fly on the royal wall came from a particularly respectful species. The ITN crew were soon aware of the tension between the couple they were filming, but nothing of that ever made the screen. In theory, the Royal Family had given access to a group of independent journalists; in practice they retained a good measure of editorial control, and even today restrict access to what was filmed.

Only with the help of the rewind button does the viewer, in a single two-second gesture, get a sense of how brittle this relationship had become. It's the twice-yearly planning meeting. Charles and Diana have different ideas for a particular date. Charles tries to make a joke out of it, poking his wife softly and playfully in the ribs. She reacts as if stabbed, arching and twisting her back away from his touch, a look of anger clouding her face. Anne Beckwith-Smith stares, for a second palpably worried about what might happen next. Then the director cuts away.

Elsewhere in the documentary the couple are seen to touch only once with anything approaching warmth. A meeting on the royal plane after a week apart produces a pair of weak smiles and a quick peck on the cheek.

From Australia, Diana and Charles flew to Washington to open the Treasure Houses of Britain exhibition, a celebration of British country-house culture. For J. Carter Brown, director of Washington's National Gallery, who organised the show, the Waleses were the perfect couple to open this British cultural promotion: 'It was romance. It was fairytale. They were both wonderful looking, and represented everything that everybody wanted to be.' The opening would be attended by a substantial proportion of the British aristocracy in their capacity as lenders to the exhibition.

Carter Brown had not anticipated how great a draw the couple would prove. *Time* magazine put Charles and Diana on the front cover with the headline 'Here They Come'. Inside, ten pages were devoted to the world's most glamorous couple. Washington socialites were so desperate to be invited to the opening ceremony that they were offering money.

The tour began with a visit to the White House, a glitzy White House ball. At dinner Diana was seated between the President and the dancer Mikhail Barishnikov, who was in awe of the Princess and nervous when it came to passing the menu to her for her signature, as custom required. 'Why? What's wrong? I've got your autograph,' she teased, and then explained that as a teenager she had stood outside the Covent Garden stage door in the rain to collect his signature. Carter Brown thought that she was as excited to meet the movie stars as they were to meet her. That night she danced with John Travolta and President Reagan. Another dance partner, Clint Eastwood, pronounced to waiting news crews that 'she made my day'. Carter Brown cheerfully admits that he had 'a mad crush on her' himself. He was dying for a dance with the Princess, 'since I did feel it was I who'd gotten her over here, but I couldn't compete with John Travolta, and her dinner partner was Barishnikov, who presumably knows how to dance, and so I was about to see if I could finagle a dance when Cinderella's coach appeared and she was whisked away. I was steaming.'

The next day jet-lag took its toll. As they boarded a helicopter borrowed from the President to go to lunch with multimillionaire art collector Paul Mellon, Diana kicked her shoes off and wilted. She was tired and nervous and had little to say. 'My role is about eighty per cent slog, twenty per cent fantastic,' she told Carter Brown. She was visibly bored by the hours of discussion of fine horses and fine art that followed. She was equally bored, or jet-lagged, or both, during Charles's speech to open the exhibition.

> Well, we had a press conference which was the opportunity for the Prince to sing for his supper. This trip was on behalf of a national cause, and he was being very serious and good and promoting the British country houses as a tourist destination. So, here is the Prince trying to do his job and put the right spin on this show and all these good things, and then the very first question from the press had to do with how the Princess enjoyed dancing with John Travolta. And so when they asked the Prince, he just threw it over to her and said, 'I'm not a glove puppet.'

'Disco Queen Diana Upstages John Travolta,' the *Daily Mirror* duly reported on Monday, 11 November, above pictures of Diana with various stars. The *London Evening Standard* did mention treasure houses: it reported Charles's joke that the exhibition proved that much art remained in Britain despite 'endless raiding parties from the USA'. But it concentrated on another aspect of his speech:

> A gentleman of the press asked me rather tactlessly why the crowds in Washington were bigger than when I came a few years ago as a bachelor. I can tell you why the crowds are bigger. They have all turned out to see my new clothes. All those suits and shoes and ties and everything which have been chosen for me.

If the Princess detected a note of tetchiness directed at her in Charles's wry humour, she did not show it. Instead she looked on impassively from her seat next to Vice-President George Bush, wearing, as the press reported next day, a 'cream coloured evening dress by Murray Arbeid with lace bodice and taffeta skirt cut low in the back'.

To the American press all was sweetness and light, and the British press was just as full of Diana's star quality. But not every journalist ran with the herd. The republican Christopher Hitchens, who had earlier regretted the conservatism of Charles wedding a blue-blooded aristocrat, was invited to a reception at the British embassy:

> I attended with my earlier misgivings intact. Well, if I hadn't had those earlier misgivings then, I assure you, I would have developed them on the spot, because down the steps came this couple who looked as if they had just finished having a really nasty, bitter, pointless row. He looked bored and sickened, as if the whole routine was a trial to him. And she – this is what struck me much more – looked just plain ill, terribly thin, pale, pasty, no tone to her at all, no aura of any kind, plain and sick. And I take my oath, I went home and said to my wife, 'I think she's got terrible anorexia or frightful anaemia or something.' I said, 'She's sick, she's ill and miserable with it.'
>
> Well, I had to read as well as write some of the coverage the next day, and I knew the people who were writing it and I knew they'd been in the room and seen what I'd seen. And the next day there was the word 'radiant' just where it always was in the first phrase of the first sentence of every story. I think the word must have been mandatory in those days. Or, if not, it was lurking in the keyboard, so if you just brushed it with your finger, the word would leap on to the page.
>
> The principle of celebrity coverage is that your actions are judged by your reputation, not your reputation by your actions. In other words, if you are a radiant princess then that's what they'll say you are no matter what you look like or what you do or say.

Neither the royal machine nor the press, nor indeed the public, wanted to admit that the fairytale might not be all it had promised. They all wanted it to continue, and wanted to see radiance where, to the more critical eye, the light had already dimmed.

Diana the fledgling celebrity insisted on a meeting with Mary Robertson:

> I couldn't believe that in five short years my shy, quiet, plump little nanny had turned into this icon. Apparently her schedule was absolutely jammed full already, but we learned later that she had put her foot down and said that she absolutely insisted on having a lengthy visit with Patrick and his mother.
>
> Diana was just herself, she rushed across the floor, didn't give us a chance to curtsy or bow, and again that wonderful big hug, 'How are you?', 'How wonderful to come all this way.' Just Diana, again, no formality. I sat across from them, and they looked very happy to me, they even joked, I'd had my daughter by then, they were even joking with each other that next time they would have a girl. It was very convincing, I had no idea there was anything wrong.

The last leg of the tour was a visit to Palm Beach where Prince Charles would play polo and the millionaire chairman of Occidental Petroleum, Armand Hammer, would chair a dinner and ball for the benefit of one of Charles's causes. Carter Brown tagged along. He still had not had his dance.

> Armand flew us down in his huge plane and we sat with the Princess watching the polo game and Gregory Peck was right near, but was rather shy about talking with her. At the dance afterwards I went through the line, I wasn't gonna be left out this time. So I said to her, 'Well, what does it take to get to dance with you?' She said, 'Oh, no problem, that would be great.' And so the equerry came up at a certain moment and said, 'All right, Mr Carter Brown, it's time for you to cut in.' So I went over, and who was she dancing with but Gregory Peck? The two of them looked daggers. Neither one of them wanted to be interrupted. So, huh, what else is new?

The tour was declared a complete triumph, but even Carter Brown was struck by the way that it was received by the press. He remembered one particular incident:

> When she came out of the exhibition she'd been wearing a hat, which I think was designed to shade her eyes so that the cameras wouldn't see the circles under them. But, at any rate, out she came and it was a blustery, autumn day, and this wind took the hat which was the shape of a flying saucer and therefore developed aerodynamic lift, and it became a flying saucer and it went soaring up into the sky. And luckily my wife, who used to play basketball, made this heroic leap and caught it, and there were so many photographers that that shot was on the front page of newspapers all around the world. I thought, Boy, you work seven years on an art exhibition and what do people remember? It's the Princess's hat.

Mary Robertson was struck by something more personal. Six days after her trip to Washington she was still glowing from her royal encounter when she received a slightly disturbing letter from Kensington Place. Diana, with the world at her feet, was once again being strangely grateful for the kindness of a friend.

> I hadn't even written a thank-you note to her yet, but Diana wrote immediately to me, which in itself is strange, and she said it was wonderful seeing Patrick and me, because it reminded her of such a happy time in her life and it was wonderful to get back in touch with people she had known when her life was simpler, and happier, and she said to us that the meeting with us had been the high point of her trip.

8
Julia from Low Wood

Sarah Ferguson and Diana had lunch once a week, an arrangement dating from before Diana's marriage. In June 1985 Sarah was invited to Windsor for Royal Ascot. There she made a great impression on Prince Andrew, who asked her to come to Balmoral as his guest that summer. In December, when Andrew's ship visited the Port of London, Diana persuaded Sarah to go with her to visit him. Inevitably the two girls drew the attention of the press. 'Just keep smiling,' Diana advised her friend. She did. Her continual smiles and cheerful high spirits endeared her to the press and to the rest of Prince Andrew's family. At Sandringham on 1 January 1986 Andrew told Sarah that he loved her. In February Sarah went skiing with Charles and Diana to Klosters. After one of their now habitual frosty exchanges, Charles asked Diana: 'Why can't you be more like Fergie?'

Diana had been trying to please him. That winter she had spent weeks secretly preparing a routine with the ballet dancer Wayne Sleep. It was meant to be a surprise present for her husband, who was due to attend a Royal Gala performance at Covent Garden. Two numbers before the end of the show, Diana left Charles's side in the royal box and slipped on stage with Sleep to perform a dance to Billy Joel's pop song 'Uptown Girl'. Diana was lithe, sexy and confident, and the audience loved it, demanding eight curtain calls. In public Charles said that he was 'absolutely amazed'. In private he was embarrassed by the undignified show and told her so. A pattern was setting in. Whenever one made a conciliatory gesture the other rebuffed it.

The same pattern was visible to staff at Highgrove. According to housekeeper Wendy Berry, the couple spent happy days together with their children, both active, warm and enthusiastic parents. And she recalls seeing Diana, when the boys were asleep, putting her arms around her husband, only to have her affection shrugged off, as if its recipient was too embarrassed to accept it.

Diana, whose voice could be piercingly loud, was frequently heard berating Charles for some supposedly selfish act, for refusing to cancel this or that arrangement, for staying too late at polo or a hunt meeting without calling home, for not thinking enough about his wife and family. But by 1986 the Prince was growing indifferent to her complaints. His heavily sarcastic 'What is it now, Diana? What have I done to make you cry?' – as if delivered to a moody child – was a common rejoinder. According to Berry, several members of the Highgrove staff believed that Charles was habitually aloof and uncaring towards Diana, although one, his groom Paddy Whiteland, took the Prince's side in the below-stairs discussions, blaming Diana for finding fault with everything Charles tried to do for her.

Arguments could break out at any time. Afterwards Charles carried on in front of the staff as if nothing had happened, while Diana would run to her room, demand dinner on a tray and turn to the telephone for company until the next morning. Charles now rarely made the effort to tempt her back downstairs. Instead, his face betraying not the slightest hint of anxiety, he would announce to his guests that his wife had a headache and regretted that she could not join them that evening.

One day Berry came across Diana crying on the staircase. 'Everything is such a mess and so complicated. I just don't know what to do,' she said.

Sarah's continuing romance with Prince Andrew pushed Diana off the front pages. Andrew proposed in late February.

Once again the Palace got into gear for a royal celebration. One day, as Diana slipped into a side entrance to the Palace, she bumped into James Hewitt, a twenty-eight-year-old captain in the Life Guards. It was the first time he had encountered her since a casual introduction when he had played polo against Prince Charles before her wedding. It was a hot day and he was wearing dismounted review order – quilted red jacket, boots and spurs.

> I'd just come out of a meeting with one of the equerries, Tim Lawrence, to discuss arrangements for the wedding of Sarah and Andrew and get the details sorted out. I came out of that meeting and encountered Diana on the steps near one of the side entrances. I was wearing uniform – she said something like, 'Where are you going, dressed up like a dog's dinner?' It was quite sweet, but it threw one off a bit.

Red-faced, he explained what he was doing and strode off, spurs jingling.

Diana saw Sarah as a potential ally in the family and a friend to have some fun with. Fergie's idea of fun was rather boisterous. Together they dressed up as policewomen in a vain attempt to gatecrash Prince Andrew's stag night. They were arrested for causing a scene outside Buckingham Palace, and bundled into a police van before they were recognised. Allowed out at Annabel's nightclub, they drank champagne before returning to Buckingham Palace, where they ambushed Prince Andrew's car.

During the 1980s magazines, newspapers and television zoomed in on the lives of the rich and famous. The top soap operas were *Dallas*, playing to 300 million viewers in fifty-five countries, and *Dynasty*, both about fabulously wealthy people, power, greed, glamour and lust. New magazines celebrated the lifestyles of the real-life rich. In America the Jazz Age style magazine *Vanity Fair* was revived in 1982.

Top sportsmen and women were pursued by cameras, their private lives analysed to a new degree. Pop stars lived like aristocracy. Models became supermodels. Fashion designers got personalities and became stars in their own right too, mixing with the musicians, the models and the actresses. The 'Charles and Di' story became a staple of this booming TV and magazine culture, she presented as vital and warm, he as distant and disenchanted. All this was parodied in the British satirical puppet show *Spitting Image*, where the dithering wimp Charles talked to plants and fought with his diamond-hard, high-fashion Princess. Graydon Carter is the editor of *Vanity Fair*.

> Diana was an icon, an international symbol the likes of which you get maybe three or four times a century. She lived her life in such a public way. And she sold. Like Madonna sells. These women are unique in their own ways, through circumstance and talent and drive, and people either love them or hate them, but either way they're fascinated by them.

The world felt it had a right to know about this couple. It had attended their wedding, cooed over their baby pictures, and then watched the body language change. The next plot twist was inevitable.

Andrew and Camilla Parker Bowles moved house in the summer of 1986. Diana's rival's new home, Middlewich House, was even closer to Highgrove than her last, a mere twenty minutes by car. Diana could time the distance herself, because Charles took her to the Parker Bowles's house-warming party.

Whatever Diana did was news, whoever she saw was news, whatever she wore was news. In Tokyo, in May 1986, 100,000 people had lined the streets to watch her drive past standing in an open Rolls. And yet, as she complained during those long evening phone conversations from Highgrove, it was the man cheerfully passing around drinks downstairs that she wanted to love her, and he patently did not. She may have played a large part in driving him away – the precise share of responsibility can never be calculated. But the twenty-five-year-old beauty was not getting what she wanted.

Diana grew close to her personal protection officer, Barry Mannakee. She had first met him as a back-up officer in 1984. The next year he was promoted to look after the children, and finally to look after Diana. Protection officers travel everywhere with their allotted VIPs and the relationship is inevitably intimate. He was calm, unflappable and supportive. Mannakee and Diana got on very well, and she sought his advice on clothes, modelling dresses for him from time to time. After a few months they would disappear on long drives together.

Diana certainly exchanged flirtatious banter with Mannakee – teasing him, for example, in the following: 'Barry, how do I look?' 'Sensational, as you know you do. I could quite fancy you myself.' 'But you do already, don't you? Escort me to my car, if you please.' Wendy Berry, the Highgrove housekeeper, recalled Mannakee telling her that he felt obliged to listen to the Princess's problems and, at times, hug her when she was crying in front of him.

Rumours about their relationship did the round of the various palaces. The senior royal protection officer, Colin Trimming, who was also Prince Charles's bodyguard, warned Mannakee that he was getting too close, and he was made Prince Charles's bodyguard. But the warm friendship with the Princess continued. Finally, in July 1986, he was transferred to other duties in the Diplomatic Protection Squad. In July 1987 Mannakee died in a road accident. When she heard about his death Diana was utterly distraught. For a while she believed that he had been murdered. In fact he was hit by a teenage learner driver while riding as a passenger on a motorbike.

Maybe it was all down to what Nicholas Soames would one day describe as her paranoia, but because Diana felt she was being undermined and criticised by so many of the people around her, she could turn on them. Courtiers like Everett had already felt the icy edge of her displeasure, but some lower down the royal pecking order – like her dresser Evelyn Dagley – received a hotter variety.

> Look at this fucking shirt, Evelyn, look at it you idiot, it's rubbish, rubbish, rubbish – what is it Evelyn? Rubbish . . . Get out of my sight.

Wendy Berry relates that inside Highgrove the servants would mutter that Diana, so sweet and so tender to the outside world, frequently seemed spoilt and contrary. There is a strong savour of class war in Wendy Berry's memoir. She thought Charles was haughty and didn't take to Andrew and Sarah's offhand ways at all. Up to a point she fits Diana into a general thesis about 'them' and 'us'. But this raises an interesting issue. A large part of Diana's appeal was based on the sense that she was somehow not quite 'one of them' at all, that she was the anti-establishment princess – a 'fifth columnist', in constitutional historian Ben Pimlott's phrase. There's no doubt that Diana *did* become strongly anti-Windsor, but throughout her life she was an aristocrat to her fingertips.

Yet the same staff who have told us that Diana could be a difficult woman to serve also say that she was frequently the pick of their royal employers. She was the one who would kick off her shoes, sit and chat in the kitchen, join in at the annual staff dance. A former royal butler told us how refreshing it was to have someone come through 'the green baize door' that separated the servants from their masters and ask them questions about their lives, mark their birthdays with thoughtful presents and turn up at their drinks parties.

Charles's friends were closing ranks around their Prince. Seeing him so despondent, listless and irritable, they decided that he needed Camilla. If Charles and Camilla did recommence their affair at this date, and not years before as Diana always believed, the story – as told to Penny Junor – goes as follows.

> He went back to Camilla in '85, '85 and '86. Friends brought them together, friends who were desperately worried about the Prince. He was on the brink of real despair. Suicidal is perhaps being overdramatic, but he was in a very, very bad way and friends thought that he needed someone to talk to. They knew that he had always got on very well with Camilla. She'd always been very good with him. They knew that she was pretty unhappy because she was in a fairly dud marriage herself and so they brought them together again . . . I think that Camilla brought him back from the brink, and I think that Camilla has a very, very good effect on him. I'm not saying they immediately began an affair once they got together again but they started to talk and he desperately needed someone to talk to. Throughout the years, the black, black years of his marriage, he never said anything to anyone, he didn't complain about Diana ever.

It was Patti Palmer Tomkinson who took the initiative, putting the two in postal contact and then, some time in 1986, inviting them to meet at her house. The date at which the relationship is said to have resumed (having been denied *completely* until the Camillagate tapes were played in 1992) is now around the time of Diana's first confirmed affair.

In the summer of 1986 James Hewitt received an invitation to a Buckingham Palace drinks party. It clashed with a dinner engagement and he almost didn't go.

> One of her ladies-in-waiting – a lady called Hazel West – had a drinks party to which we were both invited, and I spent most

> of the time talking to Diana. It made the drinks party more bearable – I mean, that sounds rude, but you know drinks parties can be a bit difficult when you've got to make small talk and be polite, particularly in that environment. But that wasn't the case talking to her, it was very easy and natural. I think she was trying to find out more about me and what I did and she learned that I was a riding instructor, and that's really how we started. She said she would like to learn to ride again. She had hurt herself as a young child falling off, and lost her nerve, and wanted to get her nerve back again. So I said I would be able to help, and so it was arranged.

The previous year Hewitt had given riding lessons to Princess Michael, Diana's neighbour at Kensington Palace. As a polo player he also had a nodding acquaintance with Prince Charles. There was nothing particularly unusual about Diana's request and the lessons were easy to arrange. Hewitt knew the colonel at Hyde Park barracks and got his permission. Other members of the Royal Family rode from the barracks already. Hewitt was an experienced instructor and the lessons quickly fell into a pattern:

> Once I'd established what she knew and she'd got a little bit of confidence in her horse we went outside, and then there were three of us, Diana, Hazel [West] and myself, and a few police cars, and a few bodyguards wandering around. They were great fun. Other people would join our little ride. A terribly nice major-general [Sir Christopher Airy] would come riding with us, and we would see various other people out and about, like the Duke of Luxembourg – particularly around the time of the Queen's birthday parade when they suddenly feel it's time to get back on a horse and practise for Trooping the Colour.

The lessons took place two or three times a week and they both enjoyed them.

> It soon became very obvious to me that she got a great deal of pleasure from doing it. And it was something that she looked forward to, away from her normal routine and existence.
>
> We'd discuss minor politics or people, or events that were going on in the news, or where she had been. Occasionally she'd point someone out and talk about them or what they were wearing, in an idle sort of chit-chat way. We'd stop and talk to the tramps who were sleeping on the benches. 'What are you doing there?' I know it sounds a bit ridiculous, sort of staring down, but – it was meant in a kind way and I think it was received in the way that it was meant.

As they got to know each other, Diana started to ask for his advice:

> What do you think I should wear to this engagement or that engagement? Or did you see me on television the other day, do you think I looked all right? I suppose she wanted to build up her confidence, not only on a horse but also in her life as well. I think she wanted recognition from someone.

When she rang him to arrange a lesson, they would talk on the phone for an hour or more. In late autumn, he was promoted to acting major, and took charge of Headquarters Squadron at Combermere Barracks in Windsor. He was delighted that Diana decided to continue to ride with him there. But the last thing he expected was that his increasing devotion to her might be reciprocated.

> It's something that I wasn't expecting or wanted to happen. I mean, sometimes when you don't expect something you don't see it until it hits you in the face. I left London and was posted back to the regiment at Windsor and she made the effort to come down to Windsor to continue to ride, which was a big effort. Then there were less bodyguards about, less police. Windsor Great Park's a big place, a great place to go riding. You can get lost in there. She said, 'I wish we could be alone.'

> We weren't being stupid about it, because there was a very real risk of some madman trying to kill her. So I was always in touch by radio and always had security in the back of my mind. I enjoyed her company, we enjoyed each other's company, and the more time we could spend together, the more we'd enjoy our week.
>
> We were sitting in the anteroom of the officers' mess at Windsor and we'd been riding. It was quite crisp and cold outside and we were having coffee and biscuits. I think she'd had a hard week and she just poured out all her problems to me, which was extraordinary because that was the first time I realised how dreadfully unhappy she was in her life.
>
> She explained that underneath the veneer of calmness meeting big crowds of people would really make her very nervous. She explained what bulimia was to me, which is the first time I'd ever heard of it. She said she wasn't appreciated as much as she should be by those who were asking her to go and meet the crowds and go and be a public figure and go and work for the firm, the firm being the Royal Family.
>
> She was in a tearful state – she apologised for that afterwards – she was in a tearful state and I remember she was sitting on the back of one of those leather chesterfield sofas with her boots on the cushion and I was sitting in the middle, sort of looking up. She was very tearful at that stage, so she came and sat next to me and we hugged each other.

When Diana phoned that evening, when Hewitt could have told her that their relationship was impossible, he didn't. She invited him for dinner alone at Kensington Palace and he stayed the night. From then on they continued to ride in Windsor Great Park, but about twice a week Hewitt would visit Kensington Palace and leave in the small hours. Occasionally he met friends such as Harry Herbert, Kate Menzies or Carolyn Bartholomew there, but normally they were alone. Sometimes they went out to dinner – usually at San Lorenzo in Knightsbridge – with cover provided by Carolyn Bartholomew and another girlfriend. There were trips to the opera, Mozart, champagne, secretly holding hands in the dark. Bartholomew told Hewitt that he was good for Diana, 'the one light in her life'.

Diana felt desired. This was the relationship she had wanted: love poems, secret gifts, shared confidences. One day Hewitt sent her a handwritten copy of Shakespeare's love sonnet 'Shall I compare thee to a summer's day'. That same afternoon she heard it recited at a school she was visiting. It was fate, she declared; they were fated to be together.

> It was important for both of us. I became deeply in love with her, and that's a great thing to happen. It's a great thing to be in love with someone. And if they're in love with you, I mean, you know, it makes you want to sing and walk with a bounce in your step. And all the things that you can do, you can achieve, if you've got those feelings. I mean, she told me time and time again how much she loved me, and what our relationship meant to her.

In 1987 Prince Edward asked the Duchess of York to join him in *It's a Royal Knockout!*, a game show he had organised for BBC Television. She agreed, as did Andrew and Anne. Charles and Diana declined. Fergie received most of the blame when, after much costumed whooping and cavorting, the programme was deemed a vulgar embarrassment. The tabloid Glenda Slagg, who had so praised the Duchess a few months before, now leapt on any example of bad taste, fluctuating weight or exuberant holiday fun. Soon she was 'Freebie Fergie' and the 'Duchess of Pork'.

The Royal Family was under pressure. At the end of *Knockout*, Prince Edward stormed out of a press conference after criticising the watching journalists for their lack of enthusiasm. His petulance was mirrored by Charles's own behaviour on

Radio 4's *Today* programme. When pressed about some of his more controversial public statements, he snapped, 'There is no need for me to do all this . . . If they'd rather I did nothing, I'll go off somewhere else.' Charles was similarly stressed when he met the editors of *The Times*, the *Sunday Telegraph* and the *Economist*. He spoke with 'frightening intensity' as he complained that his family were being reported as a soap opera. 'I have been brought up to have an active role. I am determined not to be confined to cutting ribbons.'

When Diana returned to Kensington Palace after a hard day's ribbon-cutting, winding down from another performance in front of the cameras, she no longer had to face a flat that was empty, or empty save for sleeping children and servants.

> She'd come in still fairly hyped up and bubbly and excited by it, because she would have had to get herself into that kind of attitude, and before she could continue the evening, she'd need to completely unwind.
>
> I would stand up when she came, and she'd just come bouncing into the room, and the whole place would light up and change and she'd come over and hug and her whole energy would be very evident. She'd say, 'I can see you've started on the whisky already,' or something like that. And there was always a joke and a laugh and a kiss and – and it was just wonderful, I mean, it was just a wonderful existence. And then she would talk about her day, her trials and tribulations or if it had gone well what she enjoyed about it, and then relax. And then you could see the sort of flow of exhaustion come across her. You know, it was very evident to see how much a day of public engagements can take out of you.

Now Diana began to talk more intimately about the problems in her life. As she explained it to Hewitt:

She felt that she was in an unloving marriage, but I think that can be survived. So it ran deeper in that she sincerely believed that she wasn't being appreciated. Everything she did or tried to achieve she felt she was being criticised for, and there was very little support.

When she was speaking to me she tended not to refer to individuals. And when she was being critical it was 'they' or 'the firm'. There were times when she was so frustrated that she would become unguarded in her criticism, for example towards the Queen. Any of us can get in a bit of a paddy about something and say something that we later regret. She would say, 'The Queen doesn't appreciate what I'm doing. I try to do my job. She's not helping me.' But then she would temper that with always sort of trying to show that she was respectful of Her Majesty, which was rather nice and touching, actually.

She would have much preferred to be involved and supported, and seen to be supporting the Royal Family – very much so. I believe that she'd have been a power to be reckoned with. I think there was a really big mistake – she wasn't a rebel, you know. It was her choice to get married to Prince Charles. She knew what she was getting into – the wider implications – she knew the importance of the monarchy. And let's face it, her son was going to be a king one day. There's no doubt in my mind that she would have loved to have been there supporting, and would have loved the outcome to have been completely different.

When she told me, 'I think they're jealous because I seem to be more popular,' this complete expression of disbelief must have come across my face because, you know, I just didn't think that people could be so petty about that.

Hewitt used to play with William and Harry, and even read them bedtime stories. A visit was organised to his regiment, and Hewitt had uniforms made for them. By the summer of 1987 Diana would go with Hewitt to his mother's house in Devon. One day Shirley Hewitt answered the phone:

> There was a girl the other end. A voice said could she speak to James? And I said, 'Yes, just hold on a moment, I'll see if I can find him for you. Who is it?' And this pseudo sort of cockney voice said she was Julia and she wanted to speak to James. So I trotted off to find James and I said, 'James, there's a girl on the telephone for you. She's called Julia.' I probably said it rather scathingly. And his eyes lit up, 'God, I know who that is!' And, of course, he told me who it was, and the name stuck. She had to be Julia from there on in. So Diana became Julia and to complement that Highgrove became Low Wood, so it was Julia from Low Wood.

Before 'Julia''s first visit a detective came down to check that the Hewitt house was sufficiently private and secure. Anxious that all should go well, Mrs Hewitt gave the girls who worked at her riding school the day off. But she soon realised that there was no need to and that Diana's presence could be quite inconspicuous. Her visits were meticulously organised, as James Hewitt explains:

> If she said she was going to be there at seven o'clock, she was there at seven o'clock. I think that the Jaguar might have exceeded the speed limit occasionally. We'd be sitting in the sitting room and she'd arrive and I'd go to the front door and let her in the hall and she'd come bouncing in, in an excited mood, and hug my mother and say hello, probably half knocking her over because my mother hadn't quite got up from her curtsy yet – my mother's not a tall person and Diana was tall. So she'd arrive and the whole place would come alive and be fun and carefree and jolly.
>
> She'd arrive on a Friday evening and we'd have a dinner party. My mother was about, or my sisters – we generally kept it to family and the personal bodyguard. And they were all great people. So it was a big party atmosphere. Everyone mucking in in the kitchen and helping with the washing up. I mean, she wouldn't cook but she'd wash up – great laughing times. And

then you'd get up and have breakfast and go for a walk or go for a ride, and another dinner party on Saturday night and then get up late on a Sunday morning and read the Sunday papers and either go back on Sunday night or Monday morning. So they were good long periods of relaxation and fun.

I don't know where people imagined she was. Somebody must be responsible for knowing where a member of the Royal Family is and you can't just disappear for three, four days – anything could happen to you. So somebody would have known and I remember on more than one occasion she asked my mother if she could use the phone in order to ring Balmoral – which I think is quite amusing. It made me giggle.

It seems unbelievable now that we weren't found out for a long time – although I think that's a bit misleading because I think we were known about by those whose business it is to know about these things: the police and the security forces that support the police behind the scenes. It would have been their job to know about it. Also, in the initial stages, for example, going down to Devon: the first time she came down in her Jaguar with a back-up car following and a police car following that. And every time they passed from one police authority area of responsibility to another they'd pick up a different police car. That happened quite a few times till we thought, well, actually that's rather silly.

Ken Wharfe, Diana's new protection officer, would sit up late playing poker with Hewitt, then sleep on the couch while his royal boss spent the night with her riding instructor. Hewitt saw all the official back-up and concluded that the relationship was sanctioned at the highest level.

Meanwhile, Diana's friendship with banker Philip Dunne attracted much speculation. He invited her to join a weekend house party at his parents' home in Herefordshire. In June 1987 they met again when Charles and Diana attended the wedding of the Marquis of Worcester and the actress Tracy Ward. Charles danced with Anna Wallace and talked to Camilla Parker Bowles. Diana danced flamboyantly with Dunne late into the night. The press seized on what may have been no more than a cleverly laid trail leading away from James Hewitt, who was the main and probably the only significant love interest in Diana's life for several years to come.

With new self-confidence, Diana was trying to change her public image. Determined to play a more significant part in royal business, she increased the number and seriousness of her solo engagements. One suggestion that came her way was that she should identify herself with the plight of AIDS victims.

The first British AIDS ward was being opened at London's Middlesex Hospital. Dr Mike Adler, the clinician in charge, remembered that:

> A letter was written to the Palace asking whether a member of the Royal Family would be prepared to open the ward, and I think we actually expressed a preference for Prince Charles. And we got a letter back saying no, he was too busy, but would we consider the Princess of Wales, and we jumped at it.

Many were terrified of AIDS, widely known as 'the gay plague'. Few understood how the disease was caught, and there was great distrust of anyone who had it. Mike Adler suggested to the Palace that it would do a great deal to ease public anxiety, and remove the stigma attached to AIDS sufferers, if Diana was seen to shake hands with a patient. The Palace initially asked whether the Princess should wear gloves to protect herself. The question may sound ridiculous now, but it is a sign of how bad the situation was. It is to the great credit of the Princess and her advisers that she agreed to the gloveless handshake.

Adler had not met Diana. He hadn't thought of asking her initially because he assumed she would not be interested in such a serious subject. But, once she agreed, he was quick to realise the potential. He assiduously briefed the media for weeks before the opening. The Middlesex Hospital was combed by Special Branch. Then the day came.

> She was clearly nervous when she came in. We did a very short seminar for her and then we took her into the ward. But the moment she started meeting patients she relaxed. And, of course, there was that very famous photograph of her shaking hands with a patient who had AIDS. That was wired all over the world. It made a tremendous impact, just a member of the Royal Family *touching* someone. It was a colossal impact. It shouldn't have been but it was.

Shortly afterwards, Diana met Margaret Jay, the head of the National Aids Trust. Soon Diana was Jay's most valuable asset:

> She used to come to Scotland – where there was an enormous problem with AIDS and HIV related to drugs misuse. And she was very good at talking, particularly to young women. I have a mental picture of her kind of sitting on the floor, drinking Nescafé out of mugs and chatting to them about the sort of concerns that they had in their lives. They didn't feel, in any sense, that this was some figure from a completely different planet who was talking to them, or patronising them in any way.

Diana derived great satisfaction from these personal encounters with suffering, encounters that soon became a feature of all her tours and visits. She later spoke in almost religious terms of the deep serenity she felt as she shared quiet hand-holding moments with the terminally sick, simply sitting, smiling and listening to them speak about their feelings. She said on numerous occasions that she felt strangely happy at times like this and hated being made to break away.

Sunday evenings at Highgrove settled into a pattern. Diana would leave with the children in the late afternoon. Soon the hot-water pipes would rumble, and around eight Charles would appear dressed in smart jacket, shirt and cravat, and smelling of cologne. One of the detectives would then drive him to Middlewich House.

The most embarrassing part was Diana's phone calls. Wendy Berry recalls having to lie to the Princess when she asked where her husband was, and then cope with her alternate sadness and fury at the other end of the line. Sometimes Diana would phone Charles while he was in his car on his way to a meeting with Camilla. The conversations were heated, but the car never once turned back. Diana had always believed that Charles was seeing his lover secretly and occasionally, but these new, regular and semi-public assignations carried out in front of people who worked for them both struck her as the keenest humiliation.

But Diana had her riding instructor now, and Charles had made no fuss about it. So why should she get so exercised about Camilla? The answer – as Diana told Hewitt and several other friends – was precisely because it *was* Camilla, the woman who'd ruined her engagement, her honeymoon, the woman who'd blighted her life. If Charles had chosen to find some extramarital diversion elsewhere, she said she would not have minded. It's hard to believe that Diana could ever have been comfortable with Charles seeing another woman, but a lower-level fling or two would certainly not have hurt her as much as this.

However much she was worshipped in Tokyo or Ottawa, in the Middlesex Hospital or the *Daily Mirror*, the people that mattered – her peer group, his peer group – all knew that the Prince of Wales had finally, definitively, turned her down. And no one could help her get him back. Diana told Hewitt that she had made a special visit to the Queen to ask whether she could stop her son seeing Camilla, but she had refused to intervene.

Wendy Berry saw no more attempted hugs in the garden. The

two shouted less often, but their remarks were ever more sarcastic and disdainful. Charles read the papers one day and announced: '"Difficult Di causes Malice at the Palace" – sounds about right to me.' Diana asked him one morning, 'Who is getting the benefit of your wisdom today? The sheep or the raspberry bushes?' She invented last-minute excuses to stop the children watching Charles play polo, excursions both they and he looked forward to.

In the autumn of 1987 newspapers calculated that Charles and Diana had not spent the night under the same roof for over five weeks. Their mutual friend Jimmy Savile urged them to visit South Wales together to inspect the after-effects of recent flooding. The *News of the World* hired an expert in body language to study them that day. He noted an aversion to physical contact, finding them nervous, uncomfortable or anxious. 'The emotional temperature is very, very cold,' he pronounced. After the tour, Charles went to Balmoral and Diana returned to London. By November 1987 there had been enough leaks for the American magazine *Time*, summing up British press opinion, to assert with confidence that Charles and Diana were living separate lives.

It quoted the *Sunday Times* to the effect that 'It has been impossible to disguise the differences between the Royal couple, and certainly in recent months they appear to have given up even trying.' The usual flock of royal commentators offered their opinions on the reasons for the disintegrating marriage. 'A former flatmate of Di's' was quoted to the effect that 'Diana never had a growing-up period of flirtations that most teenage girls have. Diana is now going through that stage, which is something Charles can't cope with.' It is easy to forget that Diana was still only just twenty-six. *Time* concurred with the verdict of the *Sunday Times*: 'The fairy-tale romance peddled so avidly by the world's media has gone. In its place, after all the hubbub has died down, is a marriage demystified and much like any other – vulnerable.'

Nevertheless, *Time* predicted that they would preserve their marriage together. In a remark that was typical of the bitchier tones in Buckingham Palace, 'one palace source' told them that 'Diana wanted to be Charles's wife from the age of 15 and will do nothing to jeopardise this now'. They had, it appeared, come to a typical aristocratic arrangement.

By 1988 an understanding *was* developing – a largely unspoken understanding, and one with which the Princess was only sometimes minded to comply. Nevertheless, both partners were happier than they had been. Charles and Diana were together at Highgrove in February and outwardly much calmer. Then came a skiing accident at Klosters. Equerry Major Hugh Lindsay was killed in an avalanche after Charles's party had skied down a dangerous off-piste slope. Patti Palmer-Tomkinson was seriously injured and Charles was only yards from death himself. Diana – who had stayed indoors that day – was widely praised inside and outside the family for the way she handled a very shocked and guilt-stricken husband, stopping him from skiing again the following day as, in his disturbed state, he had first wanted to do.

During this 'truce of equal indifference', weekdays were spent on separate royal duties, and Charles was rarely seen at Kensington Palace. Highgrove was effectively shared, one weekend his, one weekend hers. Staff there witnessed frequent visits from Hewitt and noticed an 'air of relaxed domesticity between Diana and James'. Hewitt chased the children around the garden and joined in pillow fights with protection officer Ken Wharfe. He found it

> quite weird being at Highgrove because it didn't seem very homely. It was far harder to relax there than in Devon because there was staff there with all that that entails. When you walked around the gardens the security camera followed you. The

camera watched you having a swim in the swimming pool. Inside the house it was a little more relaxed. Occasionally my mother stayed as a guest at Highgrove and my sister, and on occasions other friends of Diana's came, such as Carolyn Bartholomew. So that was nice as well.

In my experience Diana enjoyed it there. She liked the place. The reports that she was a London girl, she only liked Kensington Palace and that she hated to go down to Highgrove, were totally inaccurate. I suppose at times it was difficult for her. I don't think she liked to be there alone. But she loved the countryside, she loved her riding, although she never really got over her fear, she liked shooting, and the whole way of life, of countryside pursuits and living in the country. In my experience she loved that.

When it was Charles's turn to have the house he would go out for dinner and return very late. On other weekends Diana would go to Devon to stay with Hewitt's mother and sister. There she enjoyed something resembling normal life.

We'd go for a walk along the beach at Budleigh Salterton, along the pebbled beach there. I was quite happy staying at home but she would suggest that it would be nice to go for a walk or go out and, you know, walk off lunch or whatever. Budleigh Salterton by the seaside was a favourite. She'd put on a hat or, I mean we weren't trying to sort of flaunt anything, so a disguise of sorts was used – just a hat. We passed people and you would wonder whether she'd be recognised. But people don't pay much attention. So it worked – we were able to do that. And we'd walk across Woodbury Common, which was fairly wild and open – it's like a moor – which was great, but again there was a danger of bumping into people. We would try and avoid crowds – if we saw too many cars parked in the carpark we'd move somewhere quieter – you're able to do that in Devon. Then we'd ride in the riding school at home and in the fields and up the lanes. So as near as damn it, it was a normal existence. Of course, when we went walking either Ken, Allan or Peter [the royal protection officers] would be in close attendance or within range for me to contact them by radio. So we weren't being stupid.

But being away from the pressure of work, the pressure of London, the pressure of life and of living in a glass bowl and being married to a future king – that was where there was a relief valve.

In Devon even the detectives relaxed. Shirley Hewitt recalls:

one in particular was a very good chef, and he said he'd cook dinner for us one night. So having got all the necessary ingredients for him I thought, 'That's marvellous I can go and sit down and I can enjoy James and Diana's company and be a guest in my own house.' And dishes were clattering away and suddenly he burst forth into some operatic aria and it was just so wonderful to hear it because he had quite a good voice as well.

Whenever Diana came to stay she brought a little gift.

they were never over the top they were the sort of gifts that one would perhaps give oneself when going away. Then she discovered that we liked a little tipple after our dinner at night and so she nicked a bottle of orange vodka from the cellar – I think it was made at Highgrove by their cook – and it was excellent. Thereafter, each time she came down she managed to smuggle a bottle. I should think Prince Charles must've thought he had a secret drinker in the house.

Shirley Hewitt remembers above all one particularly idyllic hot summer night when they all ate out under the stars:

we were on the terrace having supper and she sat back in the chair and looked up and looked around and she said, 'Christ, this is such a lovely place!' I've always remembered that actually. She seemed to be so, you know, this is just heaven. It was merely an ordinary supper, but it was a lovely night.

Diana and Hewitt shared a fantasy future together: peering through estate agents' brochures and picking out country houses in which they would live; daydreaming about walks along country lanes, their future children riding ponies in the paddock.

She would say that she wanted a quieter life and a different existence. She would say it would be great to just be an army wife. I expect a lot of army wives would disagree with that, but that's what she wanted. That's what she said she wanted. To find some small, cottagey-type longhouse in Devon – nothing big, grand or majestic but somewhere that's cosy and comfortable. A bit of a sort of dream cottage. We spoke about that at length quite often.

The love affair was evidently precious to Diana but in Devon she had also found something else that she craved – a relaxed and informal family life of a kind that was just not available where your husband was the future King. She enjoyed being with Hewitt's mother and sisters and kept in touch with them when she was away on tour.

One would be sitting at the kitchen table having a supper, probably quite tired at the end of the day, and the phone might go and it would be Diana ringing from some outlandish place where she'd escaped to her bedroom just ringing to see how we all were. And it wasn't just a three-minute hello how are you, I'm here in such and such a country but she would want to know what one had been doing and she'd chat away . . .

By now Hewitt was more relaxed about the treasonous aspect of his relationship with the Princess of Wales.

I don't think I'd be far wrong suggesting that it was authorised by those who may be making executive decisions from on high – I don't know if it's done by committee or what, but quite

> clearly it was known about and presumably – you know, it could have been stopped.
>
> Charles knew about the extent of our relationship, in the same way that Diana told me the extent of the relationship between Mrs Parker Bowles and Prince Charles. But also he would have been briefed about it by the firm, on two fronts really, politically speaking and for security reasons.
>
> Diana told me that she had discussed our relationship with her husband. I don't know what was said – they discussed all sorts of personal things that I didn't really want to know about. It was a tacit understanding between Diana and Charles that I was a part of her life in the same way that Mrs Parker Bowles was part of Prince Charles's life. Not only that – I'm suggesting that it was understood by those who are in political authority over us, and security, and by the royal household. You know, those three factions knew about the extent of the relationship yet nothing was done, no approach was made to stop it.

People who joined the royal household about this time tell us that they were discreetly informed about the difficulties in the marriage and the joint affairs, and confirm that Charles and Diana and the royal household had reached a tacit understanding about them. But the courtiers were worried about the strength of Diana's commitment to the pact:

> When I arrived at Buckingham Palace, I was told the problems, that they could occasionally bear to be together in public, but couldn't bear to be alone together. There was an accommodation for a couple of years, Charles and Camilla, Diana and Hewitt. The problem was she couldn't stick to it. This was a girl who had no stability, didn't have the intellectual rigour or the concentration, or the sense of duty to stick it out.

Hewitt's confidence that his role in Diana's life was being tacitly encouraged by the Prince of Wales was made even firmer when he was invited to Charles's fortieth birthday party in November

1988. Hewitt took great satisfaction from the evident fact that Diana was much happier and more relaxed than when they had met. With him she might have been, but there were still angry late-night phone calls to her other friends, during which Diana would complain of the unfairness of her life. Whatever she got from Hewitt, and however many dreams she shared with him, it was never quite enough to forget or forgive the wrongs that she believed had been done to her by her husband, 'that woman' and the firm.

Diana's continued isolation and need for emotional support shine through many of the letters she wrote at this time. They are warm, affectionate and yet faintly sad, accompanied by numerous teenagerish exclamation marks and little smiley faces down the side. One regular correspondent was former boss Kay Seth-Smith.

> She was a remarkable letter-writer. I sent her a birthday card and was very surprised to receive a letter thanking me, for the card. I mean a thank-you letter for a birthday card in itself was fairly remarkable, but the fact that it actually had been written on the day of her birthday I found rather sad, because I felt she should have been doing other things than sitting there writing thank-you letters for birthday cards.

There were periods when Diana was with the Royal Family or working, and she could not see Hewitt. They invented a little sign system to communicate secretly:

> She said, for example, 'I'll play with my ear or flick my nose when I'm on television, which means I'm thinking about you.' I said, 'Well, I'll watch out for it, then.'

They bought each other presents and made little pacts:

> She had quite badly bitten nails when I first met her and I just think that, you know, nicely manicured hands are quite

attractive and so I said, 'Look, how can I bribe you to stop biting your nails?' She said, 'Well, I'd like a pair of earrings,' and I said, 'OK, well, if you stop biting your nails then I'll buy you a pair of earrings. What sort of earrings would you like?' And she said, 'Emerald, so they are quite difficult to find.' So I sold a horse and bought her the earrings.

As time went by Diana became bolder and more determined to spend as much time as possible with Hewitt. One day in the late summer of 1988 they were working out when they could next meet. Diana invited Hewitt to Highgrove for the weekend, but he had to excuse himself because the regimental polo team had reached the final of the hotly contested Captains and Subalterns Cup.

I said, 'No, I'm afraid I can't. I've got to play in a match on Saturday in Tidworth.' And she said, 'Oh dear! Well, can I come and watch?' I said, 'Well, that's going to be very difficult, isn't it? I'd love you to, but I mean that's going to be really obvious.' She said, 'Oh, I suppose so, you're right.' She said, 'Who are you playing?' And I said, 'We're playing the 13/18th Royal Hussars.' And you could see her face light up, and a twinkle in her eye and she immediately got a plan together in her mind. She said, 'I'm Colonel of the 13/18th.' So she rang up the commanding officer and said, 'I understand that your regimental Captains and Subalterns polo team are playing on Saturday.' And he said, 'Oh yes, ma'am.' And she said, 'Oh, well, can I come and watch?' And they were surprised and delighted, of course.

We took a picnic – the Life Guards team which was myself, Rupert Mackenzie-Hill, Milo Watson, Giles Stibbe and a chap called Christopher Mitford Slade. My mother and my sisters and a few other friends came to support and watch and it was a lovely day, I remember, a sunny day, and Tidworth Ground is wonderful, so it lends itself to a nice picnic before the match. So we were sitting behind the cars, the boot of the car open, with a picnic on our dirty old horse blanket, and she had to attend lunch in the officers' mess. I think she was in the pavilion near by. She had told the commanding officer to keep it a bit low key, but of course he had organised lunch to which she went. Then she just cut away from that and came and joined us at our picnic, which must have seemed very strange to the poor commanding officer of the 13/18th.

I obviously knew exactly what was happening. I told the rest of the team – I was captain of the team. I said, 'Keep it to yourselves, chaps, but Diana's coming. She's Colonel of the opposition.' Anyway, we arrived and got our picnic gear out and the commanding officer of the 13/18th came over to me and said, 'James, I think you ought to know, just keep this to yourself, but the Princess of Wales is coming to support us. You may just want to be aware so you can follow the right protocol and all that.' I said, 'Oh, thank you very much indeed, Colonel, for letting me know that.' He was oblivious to the fact that I already knew that, and the rest of the details, and the reasons why, or the real reasons. It was a lovely, lovely day.

She came over and just plonked herself down and I said, 'Well, what are you doing?' She said, 'Oh, there's a stuffy lunch going on, or something.' I said, 'Well, you ought to be there.' And she said, 'No, I said I was just coming over to give the opposition a bit of encouragement. They looked as though they were suffering a bit having their curled-up sandwiches instead of this smoked salmon.'

And I think we won by a good margin of six, seven goals probably. I'm not quite sure when she was asked to present the cup – I suppose she might have been asked at lunch by the commanding officer if she'd be kind enough to present the winners with the Captains and Subalterns Cup, which was huge. It's a wonderful piece of silver. Anyway, she said she would.

It was just wonderful to go up and receive the cup from her. And that small memento, a bottle of champagne for each

> person. So you go up and bow. It was quite amusing. I don't think she could speak, other than saying well done. I think she was about to get the giggles and she didn't really say very much to me at all. But she looked at me and I looked at her and we didn't really need to say anything and I could see that she was about to get the giggles so I said thank you very much and walked back as quickly as I could. And then she actually held the others in conversation, putting on a wonderful show. She said to Rupert Mackenzie, 'Oh, wonderful, I've heard so much about you.' She was just having great fun.

So carefree was Diana about her relationship with James Hewitt that her new equerry, Patrick Jephson, feared credible evidence of it would soon emerge.

> That anxiety was heightened by the kind of effort at innocent social contact which gives illicit lovers such a thrill but fools practically nobody. I imagine a similar anxiety existed among the Prince's staff as they quietly accommodated his need for Mrs Parker Bowles.

Diana gave James Hewitt a gold cross with the inscription 'I will love you forever'. Hewitt and Charles still occasionally met at polo matches.

> We saw each other from time to time at polo – weren't, you know, closest buddies but knew each other to say hello and how are you and how's it going. He played occasionally on the same team as me as well as against me. Actually on this particular occasion we were on the same team and so he came over and said hello, how are things and how's the riding instruction going? How's my wife getting on? And I said, 'Actually, very well – we'll soon have her in the hunting field, sir.' And then I think he looked rather sideways at me at that suggestion, I think he thought I might have been serious, but there we are.

Hewitt also saw Andrew Parker Bowles from time to time in his regiment's officers' mess. He was now the Colonel Commanding the Household Cavalry, and thus Hewitt's commanding officer. From time to time Hewitt exchanged pleasantries with the husband of his lover's husband's mistress. He marvelled at the finesse of it all. All the parties knew exactly what all the others were doing, and so did some others in the mess, but no one ever referred to it. All very civilised, all very grown-up.

But Diana was not always prepared to play the game. In February 1989 she went to a party at Lady Annabel Goldsmith's house on Ham Common. She knew that Camilla would be present, but she had been encouraged by Hewitt to hold her head up high.

> I said: 'Camilla, I would just like you to know that I know exactly what is going on between you and Charles, I wasn't born yesterday . . . I'm sorry I'm in the way, I obviously am in the way and it must be hell for both of you but I do know what is going on. Don't treat me like an idiot.' . . . In the car on the way back my husband was over me like a bad rash and I cried like I have never cried before – it was anger, it was seven years' pent up anger coming out.

After so many months of the civilised, grown-up approach, Camilla must have been confused. Surely Diana had now accepted her place in Charles's life? But she said nothing to provoke her future Queen, limiting herself to a deep and over-elaborate curtsy as Diana swept out of the room.

In the autumn of 1989 Hewitt was given a two-year posting to Germany. He had originally agreed to the ceremonial duties and the period at headquarters on the basis that he would then be given charge of a combat squadron. Now he was offered the role that he had wanted, which was an important stage on the road to promotion. Moreover, there was trouble in the East and the British Army was in a state of high alert. It was possible that Soviet tanks would come to the aid of the embattled East German government, and the situation was highly unstable and tense.

He could not bring himself to tell Diana until the last moment – the posting would reduce their time together to rare weekends. She wanted to pull some strings to keep him close. When he forbade her, she felt let down.

> It was a shock but there was a way around it. I mean, the idea of being in Germany wasn't as horrific as it may first appear because, let's face it, it wasn't as though we were living together. We were seeing each other two, three times a week, perhaps once a week, and that pattern could have continued in Germany as long as I wasn't on exercise. But actually the pace of life in the army in Germany is a bit quicker and you are quite busy – particularly at that time when it wasn't necessarily a case of *if* the Russians come over the border, it was *when* are they going to?
>
> In reality I wasn't able to get back, certainly during the initial stages. It was a very busy period – the transition and retraining, going from armoured cars on to tanks. And, you know, I had quite a responsibility to train the men and to retrain myself and to be there.
>
> After a while it just sort of petered out. I think she felt that I let her down badly by doing that, and I think she needed someone around her and I wasn't there to be around her.

They hardly spoke for the rest of the year. Hewitt trained his tank crews and watched the news coverage as, in Berlin, youths tore down the Wall from both sides. The Russians did not come to the support of the East German regime. The Cold War was ending. The old established boundaries were being torn down and nobody knew what would follow.

9
Miracle on Henry Street

'Verona, guess what? I just got a call from the mayor's office. Now sit down before I tell you this.'

Verona Middleton-Jeter's first thought was that the programme had lost its funding. The threat had been hanging over them for some time. She leaned against the window and for a moment looked out over Baruch Place. Under her breath she whispered, 'Oh no.' But her boss, Danny Kronenfeld, had different news. 'You'll never imagine who wants to come to Henry Street . . . Princess Di.'

Not the money – good. But Verona's first reaction was far from positive. 'Now what do I have to do, take time for this? How's she going to help us, Danny, she's not even from this country. How's she going to help the homeless people in New York City?'

'Verona, don't you get it?'

Verona had taught on a pioneering programme in Atlanta and brought one of her favourite students, Frances Drayton, up to New York to help her manage the Henry Street shelter for the homeless and for battered women in Manhattan's tough, poor Lower East Side. Here, amid the crumbling high-rise housing projects strung out along the edge of the East River Drive, the two women supervised dormitories, nurseries, resettlement and training programmes and generally sought to improve the lives of several hundred temporary and permanent residents. Many had been down as far as it's possible to go: sleeping rough, beaten by their partners, addicted to drugs, selling their bodies.

Henry Street was one of the best-managed social welfare programmes in America, widely praised for its policy of employing the formerly homeless and battered to help others in similar situations. Lives were changed by Henry Street, dozens every year. To achieve that needed the dedication of Frances and the other workers. It also needed money, and in New York money follows publicity, which is why Danny Kronenfeld was so excited about this English princess.

> Danny said, 'We need to get our message out. The way we approach families, the fact that we insist on being respectful, insist on helping people to help themselves, rather than doing it all for them.'

Danny told Verona that even if Princess Diana could do little herself to help she'd get Henry Street's name out. Verona talked it through with Frances. They were both unsure. There had been a lot of celebrity visits in the past and both women had grown tired of 'rich folks coming downtown to do some charity'. In recent years several high-profile people had asked to come by and been told politely 'no'.

> I felt like they might be on a guilt trip, like they were not really concerned about what's really going on but more 'it'll be in the newspaper on the society page'.

Shirley Reese had been homeless herself, and was now working in the self-help support group. She was juggling that with trying to raise her eight children in a new apartment near by. But, as she says, 'Henry Street has a way of bringing out the best.' When she heard that Diana was coming, Shirley had none of Verona or Frances's reservations and questions, but she did have one of her own: what do you wear to meet a princess?

There was nothing haphazard about Diana's request to see Henry Street. The visit to New York in February 1989 – during her affair with James Hewitt – was her first solo tour abroad. Her new equerry, Patrick Jephson, and her lady-in-waiting cum private secretary, Anne Beckwith-Smith, had organised the trip to promote her as hard-working, caring and fearless. No more shopping and fashion parades – well, maybe a few, but carefully balanced against other events and interests.

The call to Henry Street was the result of a series of transatlantic exchanges. Diana, Beckwith-Smith and Jephson decided the shape of the tour and the kind of visits it should include. The British embassy in Washington worked with the British consul in New York and the City Hall to draw up a list of likely institutions. Diana personally vetted this before anyone approached the men and women on the ground.

When it was all announced in Britain, *Today* newspaper reported:

> Princess Diana has asked to spend most of her first trip to New York touring its notorious ghettos.
>
> She will tour a run-down hospital for child AIDS victims and drug-ravaged, violence-ridden districts that are considered 'no go areas' for tourists.
>
> At Harlem Hospital caring Di will see eight babies doomed to die of AIDS before their first birthdays.

Verona Middleton-Jeter was still not sure whether she was excited or suspicious about meeting Princess Diana, but the staff at her public library were thrilled on her behalf. She'd gone in there looking for a book about royal etiquette.

> The Princess Diana people said they would send us something on protocol, but we couldn't wait. So I went to the library to make sure, because we don't wanna look like we don't know what we're doing. And I said, 'Oh, I'd like some information

on protocol, for when the Princess comes to visit us.' And this woman said, 'What princess?' I said, 'Oh, Princess Di's supposed to come to my work.' And she's just screaming and singing all over the library. 'She's gonna see the Princess! She's gonna see the Princess!' So then later she got me some material, about what we should do, and what we shouldn't do. And she said, 'You don't seem so excited.' I said, 'Yeah, well, you know.'

Anne Beckwith-Smith came to Henry Street a few weeks before the visit to plan the itinerary. Verona was impressed.

It wasn't, 'Oh, well, we just wanna talk to the directors, and the governor's wife, and maybe the mayor's wife.' It included her opportunity really to interact with clients. They wanted to know could she visit with a family. And I thought, Now that's really down to earth. And so we said, 'I'm sure we would find a family that would be interested in doing that.' And we had a lot of other ideas about what she could see, and she definitely wanted to see the nursery programme, because she had a special interest in kids, and so they set up an itinerary that made her touch people.

Then we talked about the self-help programme, which Shirley was a part of, and so they decided, OK, these were the places that she would visit. And by now I'm still sceptical and doing what my boss told me to do . . . but I'm beginning to say, 'Maybe this is a little different.'

Meanwhile the library had come up with another book on British royal protocol. In between dealing with the day-to-day work of the shelter, the women practised etiquette in their office. 'We were all clear. We should not curtsy, we should not try to shake her hand, if she didn't reach for our hand. We'd have to call her "Your Royal Highness" first then "Ma'am". It was funny.'

Shirley Reese had tried and rejected half a dozen outfits. Verona and Frances teased her about the ordeal to come.

We gave the book on etiquette to Shirley and told her to read it three times . . . We kept asking her if she'd read it because we wanna make sure everything is just right. We had to figure how we're gonna contain her excitement and make sure we're not all acting like real fools in front of this Princess.

Patrick Jephson had recently joined the Palace staff from the navy. He relished foreign travel and good food and drink, and a period of royal duty offered these in great style and abundance. His study of politics at Cambridge University was a further recommendation for royal service. His first two royal engagements abroad were the New York trip and a joint royal visit to the Gulf States, on which Jephson was able to observe the Prince and Princess together. At one stage their host asked Diana what she was planning to do. Before she had the chance to mention the many serious projects that Jephson had arranged for her, Charles leaned forward and said, 'Shopping, isn't it, Darling?' Diana coloured and looked at the floor.

On her own, Jephson found Diana an altogether different proposition. Inside the limousine or the helicopter the woman in the Catherine Walker suit and the designer sunglasses would be a riot of giggles and dirty jokes, gossip and restless energy. Looking out at the crowds: 'Oh, look, he's a bit dishy, hope I'm meeting him later.' A mobile telephone in one hand, today's schedule in the other: 'Oh, do turn that up, it's my favourite.' More indiscreet chatter. The other royals were 'the Germans', her husband 'the boy wonder', his father 'Stavros'. 'Patrick, what do you get if you cross an apple with a nun?' 'I don't know, ma'am.' 'A computer that won't go down on you.'

At the hospital or the old-people's home the one-liners would keep flowing. Diana's enthusiasm about the people she met was spontaneous, unforced, her talent for undercutting the everyday pomposity of life instinctive. 'Oh, I have Capital Radio on too.' 'Does your boss always go on like this?'

Later Jephson would detect cynicism in the way Diana went among her people, 'cherry-picking' the most appealing photo opportunities. But the inherent compassion would always remain and would always impress – what Jephson called her 'erratic but genuine kindness'.

Jephson and others saw Diana switch effortlessly between silliness and solicitude, walking without a trace of self-consciousness into cancer wards and leper colonies. If Diana did have something like Borderline Personality Disorder then it was well named for her, for she respected few of the emotional borders that hold most people back – feeling embarrassed, not wanting to appear crass, not knowing what to say.

There's a beautiful passage in Jephson's book, recalling a scene from the late 1980s.

> As I watched her at a dying child's bedside, holding the girl's newly cold hand, and comforting the stricken parents, she seemed to share their grief. Not self-consciously like a stranger, not distantly like a counsellor, not even through any special experience or deep insight. Instead it just seemed that a tranquillity gathered around her. Into this stillness the weeping mother and heartbroken father poured their sorrow and there, somehow it was safe.

And suddenly they're back in the helicopter. 'Watch my hat someone. Pass me over the *Mail*, would you. Oooh, hold on to your hats. Wonder what Dempster's written today, something juicy about the Germans I hope. Anyone got any chocolate?'

The visit to Henry Street was combined with high art and high society: a performance of the opera *Falstaff* and a $1,000-a-seat gala dinner afterwards. Tuxedos and incubators, battered wives and canapés, overtures and AIDS: it was a mixture Diana was making all her own, while traditionalists represented by Harold Brooks-Baker, editor of *Burke's Peerage*, fumed about commercial exploitation of the Royal Family.

New York rose to Diana – every magazine, every radio station, every society hostess. This was Jackie O with an English accent, all the glamour of real-life royalty but none of the stuffiness. Even the Irish-American demonstrators, who normally dogged high-profile British visitors to this least respectful of American cities, were thin on the ground, their jeers drowned out by the tens of thousands who stood behind the NYPD's blue crush barriers to try to get a look.

The same barriers were lining Baruch Place and, when Diana's limo turned the corner, Verona Middleton-Jeter was surprised to find that she could hardly swallow. Her knees were beginning to feel weak too. There were security people running around talking into their collars and, for a hundred yards down East Houston Street, people were waving flags and hand-made posters. Inside the shelter, Shirley Reese was being fussed over by her friends.

> I'm probably overdressed, and I get to the place and they have to tone me down because I wore too fancy a dress, so they put a jacket on me. Oh my God. I'd forgotten it all. I didn't know what to do any more. They were telling me, you know, 'do's and don'ts', you know, should we curtsy, when should we?

Verona was still waiting in the courtyard.

> She got to the kerb, and someone said, 'Well, who is gonna greet her?' And so Danny said, 'You, Verona. It's you, Verona.' And I was like, 'Oh!'
>
> So then I walked over to the kerb, the car was already there . . . I guess I knew it was happening, but I – the excitement and all around us – I was in a daze. And I rushed over to the kerb, the car had driven up, and they opened the door, and this very tall, thin woman got out. And I reached my hand, and I jerked it straight back because . . . I don't know, I was doing exactly what we knew Shirley would do . . . And I jerked it back – it was nerves – and then she got out, and she reached

> straight for my hand and she's shaking it, and she's saying, 'Oh, hi.'
>
> Then she says, 'Hey, we're wearing the same colours.' And then we went and we introduced her to the family. And the next thing I know she was in this kid's bedroom, the little boy, and they had pictures on the wall, Michael Jordan, and right away she's into basketball with this kid, and they're talking and chatting, and talking about what's on the wall. And she really took time and talked with that kid, and she came back out, and talked with the mother, and all along I'm standing there thinking to myself, Wow, she is *really* nice.

Then Shirley's big moment finally came.

> We're sitting in this huge room with everybody in a circle, and I'm just looking at this woman, like. I can't believe it, it's real, she's here. And then I want to say something so bad, but I don't want to be, you know, rude or out of place. And I'm trying to compose myself, and I just burst out, 'Listen, I just got to say it, I don't know if I should say it or not, but oh my God, your skin is so pretty!'

Verona threw her head back and laughed. The picture made all the New York papers.

VERONA: People always ask about that picture where I show all my teeth, but it really started with Shirley. Because everybody's focus was to keep Shirley in line. This was not her Hollywood debut, and we wanted her to be just right on target. We had already put a jacket on Shirley so as to tone her outfit down, and Shirley was trying to contain herself. And the Princess, she had a way of kinda looking down when she spoke – and she's tall too – so we were kinda looking up at her and I saw Shirley go, and I thought, 'Oh-oh, Shirley's gonna talk . . .' And Shirley said, 'Oooh! God, you're so preeety!' And we were like, 'Oh-oh! There it is. Shirley's done it.'

By now people are lined up out on the street, and so somebody's like, 'We've gotta take that walk.' And so by now, you know, we're like old buddies. And there was a kid with some tulips, and she just broke away from us and went over to that kid and she starts shaking hands with everybody behind the barricade. And again, it was like, 'Wow! Just look at her!'

And all along she would shake hands, all the way over to the family school, and we just talked and we strode along, and when we got in there, there were the kids . . . and you can see her lighten up.

SHIRLEY: Started tying shoes, and . . .

VERONA: Yeah, right away she – she was clearly a mother.

SHIRLEY: Yeah.

FRANCES: I was sitting right beside her, and the suit I had on, one of the buttons popped off, and she beat me to it, picked it right up, and she said to me, 'We have to keep up with these little things.' It was really nice. And then her conversation was just genuine. She wasn't just asking questions, she was *there* with us. Really concerned about what the situation was with the homeless, with our population, with the battered women, with – talking a lot about the shelters, the services that we have, and it was really exciting.

VERONA: She helped Frances with her button, but it wasn't again like, 'Oh well, you know, that kid's shoe is untied, maybe one of you teachers should tie it.' She got down there, and she's tying the kid's shoes. She's relating to the kids, she's talking to them, in such a very natural way. And once the visit was over, I really was happy that we did it.

We went to Henry Street twice. We walked around the projects, talking about Diana and trying to make sense of it all – for someone like her to come somewhere like this, and for it to mean something; this girl from the English country house and the Swiss finishing school. What they call the family school is a basement of one of the high-rise blocks. The teachers have to duck their heads to avoid the pipework. But there's a lovely atmosphere – children's pictures on the freshly painted walls, a sandpit, a slide, everything clean and organised. A lot of these children come from extremely deprived backgrounds. Most have been starved of opportunities, and some have been starved of love. One little boy grabs the hand of any visitor and tries to hug them. A teacher discreetly explains that he had been abused by his father before his mother got up the courage to bring her family to the shelter.

When we recorded our interviews we did everything we could to get Verona, Shirley and Frances to criticise Diana. 'How could she understand the children of Henry Street?' we asked. 'Wasn't she just using you as a photo op before getting in the limo and heading back uptown?' But all three were entirely won over by her, despite their initial scepticism. There was something about this woman that, eleven years later, made them feel blessed – and that is not too strong a word – to have spent half a day in her company. Frances Drayton says:

> They come, you know, high-ups, to meet us and you right away think, What can we offer you? What are you getting out of coming to us? But with her it was a different feel. The questions she asked, the way she asked them, her concern about not even asking questions until the press people left, was all out of respect for who we were. I don't say that because a person is blessed to have a silver and a gold spoon in their mouth that they cannot have empathy for something that another person might have. Because that's why communication is so important.
>
> We had a big sign that said 'Welcome, Princess Di'. The families did that and we put it out front for her. It was nothing that we bought, we didn't have to go out to shop to impress, we just did what we usually do, had all the children's pictures, as you saw this morning in the community room. Everything

was just genuine and she just fit right in. Such a beautiful person.

Two days earlier we had filmed our interview with Christopher Hitchens, Diana's sternest public critic, then and now.

'Christopher, don't you get it?'

Well, when it's said to me, 'What about the magical element, the element of happiness and fairy dust?' I can't think of it as actually an argument . . .

Look, no one can stop anyone forming a fan club for Barry Manilow, for example. I don't know why they do it, but I don't *have* to know. But if it is said that people could not *live* without this as part of their system then I say that is an insult to people. It *could* be outgrown, it could *easily* be lived without. We're not all children. But it's exacted from us, whether we wish it or not.

Where was Madame Ceausescu ever photographed except in an orphanage? Anyone who has even the slightest knowledge of the arts of political manipulation knows that's what you do . . . And it worked on many people who thought, You may say what you like about the Ceausescus, but that Eleanor, she really does her charity work.

Sometimes it can be done charismatically – as in the case of the Perón regime in Argentina. Now Juan Perón on his own would hardly have passed muster in a convention of lounge lizards, but his wife – little Eva – did have the common touch and people really wept hot tears when she died and felt that they'd lost someone who could *intercede* for them. And the choice of word, by the way, is deliberate, because the suggestion is that this is approaching sainthood or canonisation. It's unhealthy, it's dangerous and to justify it on the grounds that it's popular is missing the point completely.

I've studied a number of reprobate politicians who've gone

the charity route to enhance their reputations, and over the even medium run it's indissolubly related to cynicism. Certainly in New York there's every sign of people being very competitive. You know, 'I saw that leper first, that's my charity! I'm going to send out the fund-raising letter for this! And Bono said he's coming to my thing and I'll bet he's not coming to yours.' And the scope for coarsening is very great, and there's every evidence that she, Diana, began to succumb to it.

By the end one got the distinct impression that it was part of her accessorisation, that these were accessory charities, that it was part of the appurtenance of any properly turned-out celeb.

Hitchens is deadly accurate about the cynicism behind some charity work, but is he right about Diana?

If you want the world to love you – if you *need* the world to love you – then you do go the charity route. It stands to reason. And once you go to the orphanage or the hostel you also make sure that you stay around for a while after the cameras have been put away, so that people can report that fact too. All these things Diana did, consciously or not.

If there's an answer to all this then it probably lies down Henry Street. You could not meet more sincere and dedicated people than Verona, Frances and Shirley. Real people, real humanitarians, the ones who should be receiving the awards and wearing the nice dresses. They had looked at Diana with a cold eye and they had pronounced her the real deal.

Patrick Jephson spent a lot of his time puzzling over the contradiction between the motives for these visits and the impact that they had. He knew that sometimes – and by the end, quite often – they were weapons in the Princess's armoury, used, with the utmost calculation, to win her public support. But Jephson saw a difference between the motive and the act, and it was in the act that Diana excelled. For whatever inner reasons, once she went among the halt and the lame something shone through her that, if it wasn't sincerity, came as close to it as to make little difference. Frances, Verona and Shirley certainly thought so, and they have seen a number of fakes in their time.

Margaret Jay of Britain's National Aids Trust grew short-tempered when we pressed her on this subject.

> Look, it doesn't really matter to me why she wanted to do this kind of thing. We live in a world in which celebrities have a huge power to help organisations like mine. This one chose to and I'm grateful. End of story. And she didn't have to. Or at least she didn't have to quite as much and quite as well as she did.

AUTHOR: It's a shame that she gets an award for doing humanitarian work, and you guys don't.

FRANCES: I don't know if she got a reward, I think she got what she needed here. She really probably came to see and to share. I think it was an even exchange almost. She was honoured to meet us. That's the way she came. She was happy to be here, you could tell. She's still here, a piece of her. She left that here. She's a magical type of person.

In 1923 Marc Bloch published the classic history of the 'royal touch', the ancient belief that the King's hand could cure. Bloch wanted to explain 'the trick' of royal healing, its manipulation of the common people's superstitions, the part it played in keeping them in their place. But he was also interested in the reason why ordinary people wanted to believe this kind of thing, at times seemed to demand that the trick be played upon them.

> If an institution marked out for particular ends chosen by an individual will is to take hold upon an entire nation, it must

also be borne along by the deeper currents of the collective consciousness.

For centuries in Britain royal healing was held as a proof of the Divine Right of Kings. 'Countless witnesses have testified to it, and its fame died out only after seven centuries of sustained popularity and almost unclouded glory.' The touching was sanctioned by the Church and accompanied by a special liturgy. The monarch remained seated, a cleric brought the sick to him one by one, and he laid his bare hands on them, then they came back again, one at a time, for him to make the sign of the Cross over their sores and hang a gold coin on a ribbon round their necks.

Why did the custom of touching last so long when people could plainly see that usually it didn't work? Bloch's answer was the enduring power of collective illusion: 'Public opinion was unanimous in affirming that great numbers of sufferers . . . had been healed by the King. The age of faith . . . did not demand that wonder-workers should always display an unvarying efficiency. As for the numerous cases where the disease resisted the touch of the august hands, they were soon forgotten. Such is the happy optimism of believing souls.'

We no longer believe that touching by a king or princess can heal. Or do we? Most assume without question that a visit from a famous person can make a hospital patient feel better, or that the sound of a favourite pop star's voice might rouse a child from a coma. The actor-singer David Soul says that when he was a star in the mid-1970s he was frequently asked to appear at the bedsides of dying children, or simply speak to them on the telephone. It is an unsettling request that's familiar to many celebrities. Unlike Diana, most won't do it, feeling embarrassed, not knowing what to say. But ever since Darenth Park, ever since she'd held the blind man's hand against her face, Diana could connect to strangers and, somehow, make a difference.

Nobody in a terminal ward expected to be cured by Diana. Nobody in a battered women's shelter expected her to find them a new apartment. But most claim to have felt better for her presence and some, like Frances Drayton, say they still feel positively joyous to have spent a few moments in the intimate and understanding stillness she carried around with her. Few, if any, have ever said they wanted her to go away and not bother them.

Some people get it and some people don't. If royal healing worked at all it did so because a moment's proximity to greatness lifted the sufferer's morale. In this respect there is a plausible connection to Diana's dazzling arrival in the ward or the shelter.

And are we truly as far removed from Bloch's 'age of faith' as we like to suppose? When she died, Diana was taken by many to represent human nature at its caring best. And she did have an instinct for popular spirituality – the way people feel at their children's carol concerts, the way they support each other at a funeral or a hospital bedside. Her friend Rosa Monckton was convinced she could see God in her actions.

Miracle, manipulation, or both?

10
Secret Squirrel

For both Charles and Diana, with their busy, peripatetic lifestyles, the mobile phone was a dream accessory. They kept themselves equipped with the latest models. But mobile telecommunication was still a new technology and at this time it had one serious drawback. For a few hundred pounds a portable 'scanner', long used by amateur radio enthusiasts to eavesdrop on the police or air traffic control, could be retuned to pick up nearby cellphone signals. People began to amuse themselves by listening in to the conversations of strangers, hoping to hear something illicit, salacious or just plain silly. By the end of 1989 two men had recorded royal conversations with all these qualities.

In January 1990 a radio ham named Cyril Reenan approached the *Sun* with tapes of a conversation between Diana and an unknown man made the previous New Year's Eve. Stuart Higgins, one of its royal correspondents, travelled to Oxfordshire to meet him.

> We went to Didcot railway station and he came and sat in our car. We put the cassette in and listened to it almost mesmerised for twenty minutes. My gut instinct was that it was absolutely her. The content was explosive and we knew we had a major, major story.

Higgins heard Diana complain that the Queen Mother looked at her with 'sort of interest and pity mixed all in one'. He heard resentful remarks about all she had done for 'this fucking family', also long exchanges of endearments, bits of news and television programme updates. Diana was speaking to someone called

'James', who kept referring to her as 'darling', 'honey' and 'squidgy', and looked forward to wrapping her in his protective arms in a couple of days' time. She even said that she was anxious not to get pregnant. Higgins was aware of rumours about Diana and an army officer called James Hewitt. But this must be a different James, because at one point Diana complained that she had dressed Hewitt from head to foot. The man said that he had been obsessed with her for only three months. Higgins set out to check the tape for fraud and to find out the identity of the mysterious James.

> Eventually we managed to pin down the man who called the Princess 'squidgy'. It was James Gilbey. He lived in Lennox Gardens and we went to his house early one morning and confronted him when he was just about to go to work. We told him face to face, fairly aggressively, because we wanted to be provocative, 'We have got a tape which we believe contains private conversation between you and the Princess of Wales in which you repeatedly call her "squidgy" and it is a fairly intimate conversation.' At which point he went completely white, got in his car and drove off. That doesn't amount to him signing a piece of paper saying, 'Yes, it is my voice on the tape,' but clearly we had the right man.

As Higgins expected, the first thing Gilbey did was tell Diana about the danger they faced. All they knew was that a conversation had been recorded. But which one? It's possible that the couple had exchanged remarks even more embarrassing than those played in Stuart Higgins's car. It's easy to imagine their anxiety. By chance, perhaps, the *Sun*'s sister paper, the *News of the World*, soon began to receive blackmail-style cut-and-paste notes alleging an affair between Charles and Camilla.

Had it been an incriminating tape of a TV quizmaster or a football star then there would have been no question. Its contents would have been splashed all over the first available front page. But this was the Princess of Wales. At News International's offices in Wapping the editors and royal correspondents wanted to run the story, the scoop of their careers, but the management was not so sure. After months of discussions, the *Sun* decided to sit on the tape for the time being. Andrew Knight was Chairman of News, Rupert Murdoch's man in charge in London.

> Everybody knew that all was not right [in the royal marriage] and had known for quite some time, and in fact felt that they were unable to report things which were in general currency among the journalistic community.
>
> The royal institution was important and it [the tape] would have rocked it. It just didn't seem right or proper to carry it. The feeling of myself, and I'd always been a royalist and remain one, and also of Rupert Murdoch, was simply that these stories were too explosive to carry.
>
> The irony is that by the time these events started coming out Mr Murdoch had come to the belief that the Royal Family, although it was the pinnacle of a system of snobbery that he didn't relish, nevertheless on balance was a good thing, and he was reluctant to see it undermined. I don't think that's ever been believed . . . but it's true. He knew that Middle Britain, the sort of stalwart core of Britain, is pro-royalist and it wasn't his job to undermine it.

The *Sun* paid their source and hid the tape in a safe. From time to time Stuart Higgins would play it at dinner parties to amaze his friends. He grew resigned to having 'the scoop that got away'.

But Diana knew nothing of the conversations in Wapping. For months she expected the phone to ring at any moment with news of headlines that might destroy her reputation, opening the way for a divorce very much on her husband's terms.

Since the start of her affair with James Hewitt, Diana had been following a rigorous regime of clean living and self-improvement. There were exercise classes, morning swims, fancy diets, reflexology and aromatherapy, evening swims, massage, colonic irrigation and speech coaching. A procession of therapists and healers came in and out of Kensington Palace as the diary was cleared for 'pamper Diana days'. She worked out at least twice a week, toning her body into its best shape for years. Carolan Brown started work as a personal fitness trainer in 1990:

> She was always game for a laugh . . . she thought it was very funny to be parading around in a thong leotard, and would sometimes wait for the butler to be walking by, or to come into the room, and she thought that was all great fun to shock him. And I think it was just to break through the stuffiness. And she was a fun, fun person. We would have some riots on the good days.
>
> But, quite quickly after I'd been training her, I did see a sadness in her. She was a very young and naïve person. I almost felt in some ways she was too young to have children. And there was something in her, a sadness that I could see within her.

For all her new-found vitality, Diana without Hewitt needed frequent reassurance. Peter, Lord Palumbo, who had known her since her marriage, was one who tried to offer it.

> Well, she could be in a great deal of distress but then pull herself together and go out to a public function and be absolutely wonderful and receive tremendous applause and affection. And with that ringing in her ears she would go back to Kensington Palace, very often alone and being served dinner on a tray in her room. And watching television. And it was that, I think, that she found disturbing: the adulation on the one hand and the loneliness on the other.

Carolan Brown also tried to help.

> I would constantly be telling her, 'You look great! Go on, get out there, do your thing and feel confident about yourself

because you're doing a really great job.' And she'd sometimes come back after a hard day and say, 'Oh, is it all worth it? Do people really appreciate what I do?' And I'd say, 'Yes, people really, really do appreciate you. You don't know how much they appreciate it.'

In December 1989 *Vanity Fair* had reported on Diana's latest evolution. First Demure Di, then Disco Di, next Dynasty Di, now Dedicated Di. 'Some people are even beginning to talk about her as a saint.' Their article echoed the *Sun*'s recent appeal:

> DID CARING PRINCESS DI RAISE YOUR SPIRITS AND HELP YOU IN YOUR TIME OF NEED? Has any royal made your life a little happier when you needed some support and encouragement? If so, share your experience with fellow readers. Write to ANGEL DI, The Sun, London E1 9XP.

Diana worked with the marriage guidance service, Relate. In a photomessage as blunt as any she ever sent, she sat in on Relate's sex therapy sessions and publicly said that she would like to work with couples whose marriages had gone wrong. She even let it be known that she kept a copy of the *Relate Guide to Marital Problems* on her bedside table.

Diana, long seen by the public as the most compassionate member of the Royal Family, now went out of her way to identify herself with groups on the fringes of society and with victims. Her new agenda owed much to another figure from her past who had recently re-entered her life, and would play a decisive role in shaping the rest of it. Dr James Colthurst, a member of Diana's old Sloane set, had been a high-spirited Old Etonian, the Martin Luther King impersonator on her 1979 skiing holiday. Outside her circle after 1981, Colthurst witnessed Diana's metamorphosis from the jumper-wearing, snowball-throwing girl he had known into the glamorous but nervous princess of the early 1980s, and then into something more interesting – the Princess of Henry Street.

Colthurst, like Diana, had grown more serious. Having trained as a surgeon, he grew to distrust high-technology medicine and turned towards homoeopathy. As his clinical interests changed, so did his politics. By the late 1980s Colthurst believed that Britain laboured under a suffocating system of class privilege that had little relevance to the lives of most of its people. It was the society he had grown up in, driven by snobbery, inheritance and mediocrity. And he believed that much of what was bad was embodied in the family into which his old friend had married.

When Diana decided to create a stronger role for herself in public life, she no longer trusted the official apparatus around her. It was obvious that it owed its principal allegiance to the Crown. Seeking intelligent but independent sources of advice, she turned to Colthurst and got him to draft some of her more serious public speeches. Felix Lyle was one of Colthurst's closest friends at the time and soon came to advise Diana too.

> I think she hadn't thought beyond having children and producing heirs, initially. But she felt completely abandoned as far as the Royal Family was concerned. She felt they were stuck up and really self-serving. They were just interested in protecting their own territory, their own rights, protecting them from the advance of the modern age. She had something that she couldn't really define, but it challenged the authorities, and challenged the established way of doing things in this country. She wanted to show that a royal family can play a participatory role in a democracy, can participate with the people. She showed our existing monarchy up for what it was, a stultified, obfuscated, rotting institution, completely out of touch with the people.

As he grew closer to her, Colthurst found that Diana needed more than political advice, as he explained to Felix.

> James is a doctor and he also has a bit of a mission to save the world. He's very driven to make people better. And I think Diana was irresistible from that point of view. I mean, let's make it clear, it's *that* point of view only. She was a maiden in distress and James offered to help. The intention being for her to win a measure of composure and self-determination – that she could then start to live her life for herself. Because she really had slipped that low, at that stage. He told me at length that he'd been helping her, and that she had deep psychological problems, and that he'd been drawn in quite heavily. It was a lot of counselling. I don't know if any medicines were involved but there was a lot of hand-holding. And he also wrote speeches of hers and helped her through that.
>
> He put himself at her disposal, pretty much on a twenty-four-hour basis at one stage, and she was phoning up all the time, asking, 'What can I do? Help me' basically.

As Diana was growing to depend upon Colthurst's advice, Patrick Jephson was becoming worried about unofficial rivals and their influence on her public speeches.

> Long and sometimes incoherent drafts would appear . . . haphazardly typed on unfamiliar paper. Some seemed to have been written by the current therapist . . . Others, on medical subjects, I guessed came from her close friend . . . Dr James Coldhurst [sic].

Colthurst learned every detail of Diana's troubled marriage. He came to believe that her international success was perceived as a threat to Charles's position as future head of the Windsor family. Whether he knew about the Gilbey tape is not clear but, like Diana, Colthurst felt that the Princess's enemies were determined to discredit her and might move at any moment.

As Diana worried that her private life was about to become public knowledge, other forces were moving to pull her marriage apart. In late January 1990 Anne Beckwith-Smith was deposed as Diana's private secretary, although she continued for a while to be her chief lady-in-waiting. Patrick Jephson succeeded her with the title assistant private secretary. Instead of returning to the navy after his two-year secondment, Jephson now became a career courtier with perks that included a small house in fashionable Notting Hill.

Meanwhile, Jephson's erstwhile friend in the Prince's office, Richard Aylard, made the same career choice. For some time he had been an assistant private secretary and comptroller of the household. There were two more assistant private secretaries – Peter Westmacott from the Foreign Office and Guy Salter. At the head of this enlarged establishment was Sir Christopher Airy, the Prince's new private secretary (and the friendly old major-general who had joined in Diana's early horse-back rides with Hewitt). Increasingly he seemed little more than a figure-head. Aylard was the driving force in Charles's office. He and Jephson, the two rival assistants, played a full part in the growing animosity between the separate halves of the office.

Beckwith-Smith and the civilised Sir John Riddell, Airy's predecessor, had been restraining influences on Diana, gently persuading her to do things the Buckingham Palace way. But Jephson was her man, willing to fall in with her way of doing things and determined to support her initiatives, especially if it meant upsetting what he saw as an insensitive and maladroit old guard in the Palace. He found the Prince's people particularly unctuous and condescending.

Jephson was determined to complete the job of recasting his Princess as a dynamic modern royal performer, the task begun with the opening of the AIDS ward in 1987 and strengthened with the solo trip to New York in 1989. And Diana was growing into the role. She did particularly well during a visit to a leprosy hospital at Sitanala near Jakarta. Before departure the press warned her not to let the royal hand even brush against a leper. Jephson took care to check that the horrible consequences imagined by the tabloids would not ensue, and once again the world saw his Princess touching the untouchable.

Diana was now actively planning a future outside the Royal Family and took various secret initiatives with this in mind. One was an escalating series of press briefings. Another was to appoint Joseph Sanders to look after her financial affairs.

> I was introduced to Diana in May 1990 by one of my clients who I'd made a lot of money for and done very well for. And she phoned me up and she said, 'I want you to meet a friend of mine.' And I said, 'Who do you want me to meet?' She said, 'I can't say, it's all secret squirrel.'
>
> So I went and I met this new client and I was absolutely amazed. It was Princess Diana! And she was just so charming and so nice, and she said, 'Joseph, I've heard a lot about you. I'd like you to look after my financial affairs. I'd like to make a break from the Royal Family. I'd like to set up life on my own. I might move abroad. I could get married later on, I could have a couple of children.' She didn't really know what she wanted to do but she knew that she wanted to make a break from the Royal Family . . . She was in a difficult situation. I think she needed help. She felt she could trust very few people.
>
> Diana planned to get a divorce in 1990. Um . . . it took her a few years to get there. But she planned it. She wanted to look as if she was the goody and the Royal Family were the baddies.

On 28 June 1990 the Prince broke his arm playing polo. In severe pain, he was taken to hospital at Cirencester, where doctors decided to reset the double fracture without pinning it. On leaving hospital he posed for pictures with Diana before she drove him back to Highgrove. Minutes after she dropped him off, she left again for Kensington Palace. Camilla Parker Bowles then arrived to care for him. Janet Filderman was still very close to Diana. She says that the broken-arm incident was an insult too far.

> She said to me that she wanted to go down to Highgrove to nurse him. Prince Charles didn't want to be nursed and after then I saw a change in Diana. I don't think she was prepared to work at the marriage any more.

Housekeeper Wendy Berry saw a lot of Camilla around Highgrove at this time. The passionately anti-smoking Prince even allowed her to light up in the drawing rooms.

It is possible that Diana wanted to look after Charles. Certainly she wanted to be seen to want to. Charles, his temper worsened by continuous pain throughout July and August, was not at his most accommodating. His friends gave their advice. Patti Palmer-Tomkinson recommended the doctor who had helped her recover from the skiing accident. The new doctor insisted that Charles's arm was not healing properly and that surgery was imperative. His opinion eventually prevailed, and the Prince was booked into the Queen's Medical Centre, Nottingham, for early September.

While waiting for his operation, Charles joined his friends the Romseys in Majorca. Diana and the children arrived a little after the ratpack. The tabloids were seizing every opportunity to make him look unpleasant. It was bad enough when they put two and two together and made four, but it was worse when they made forty. 16 August was not one of the *Sun*'s most inspired days: 16 August 1990 – 'Charles hugs his old flame', with a picture of a 'lingering, warm embrace' between Charles and 'former escort' Penny Romsey; 17 August 1990 – 'Tragic Secret behind Charles's Embrace: Lady Romsey told him her girl, 4, had cancer'.

After the *Sun* had grovelled for a day, the long-suffering heir carried his painful arm from Majorca to Balmoral and from

Balmoral to Nottingham. There, to his wife's disgust, his courtiers took up residence too, fussing over him in what the Princess's rebel band saw as an obsequious pantomime.

Rumours that Diana's touch could heal were soon emanating from the very hospital in which her husband's arm was posing such an obstinate problem for conventional medicine. As Diana left Charles's room after one of her visits, she came across a woman crying in the corridor. It was Ivy Woodward. On 30 August 1990 her son Dean had been involved in a serious road accident and was in intensive care. He was in a coma and his chances of recovery were not thought to be good. Dean's wife, Jane, was by his bedside.

> Diana said, 'Do you mind if I come in?' And Dean's mum says, 'No, not at all.' And I was in a state of shock anyway, myself. When she walked in I was like, 'Oh my God!' It's just total disbelief and it's not until after that – you've gone away and thought about it – that, you know, you think back, and think, God, yeah, she was actually there.

Dean later heard Diana's side of the story:

> And then Princess Diana said, 'He'll pull through. I know he'll pull through.' And then she went away – and this is the exact words she's told me, Princess Diana – that bells was ringing, go back and see that lady. So she came to see me mum again and said, 'Can I come and see your son?' And then from that day, every time she visited Charles, she came in to visit me.

The *Sun* quickly took up the story, reporting the day after Charles's operation, 3 September 1990: 'Di Weeps at Bedside of Coma Dad Dean'. The *Sun* quoted Dean's Uncle Terry: 'She had been sent by God as far as I'm concerned. She is an angel.' Terry told reporters that Ivy thought her son's grip had tightened when Diana touched his leg. 'We're all praying for a miracle,' he said.

The miracle arrived. By late autumn Dean Woodward had come out of his coma and was convalescing:

> I was having my dinner in Glendon Lodge, in the grounds of the City Hospital, and the receptionist came out and she said, 'Dean, there's a phone call for you.' I said, 'Who is it?' She said, 'It's Diane.' And I've got a sister Diane. And I said, 'Oh, tell her I'm having me dinner, to call back later.' She went away, she came back and she said, 'Oh, she can't call back.' So I went in – finished, stopped my dinner – went and spoke on the phone and then I said, 'Oh, hello my duck' – I'd had a tracheotomy so I could talk then. And she said, 'Do you know who you're talking to?' I said, 'Yeah, Diane.' And she said, 'No, you're talking to Princess Diana from Kensington Palace.' Unbelievable.
>
> And then she said, 'Are you OK, is the family OK?' And before she went she said, 'Is there anything you need?' I said, 'Yeah, there is. When you visited me I was unconscious, but now I'm conscious can you come and visit me?' And she said, 'Yeah, I'll come and visit you but I don't want no reporters or nothing, just a casual visit.'

She said she would come and visit at New Year.

James Hewitt had been trying to forget Diana and had not spoken to her for more than a year. He was still based in Germany when the decision was made to send British troops to the Gulf, part of a force intended to drive Saddam Hussein out of Kuwait. Hewitt was told that his tank squadron would be travelling to the desert soon.

> She suddenly rang me out of the blue. She was wondering whether I was going. So I said yes I was and she said she'd like

to see me before I went out there, so I said, fine, I'm coming back for my sister's wedding, to which she had got an invitation but she didn't go. I saw her after the wedding, before I flew back out to Germany to get things moving in readiness for going to the Middle East.

Then from Germany I went out to Canada to watch some army manoeuvres because it's very open and apart from it being a prairie it's quite like the desert and they were using the latest tactics. But there was a stopover in England and I stayed the night at Highgrove.

So after quite a lengthy period of being out of touch we took up really where we left off without an 'if' or a 'but'. Again, you know, I didn't want to be questioning. And then this amazing affair was rekindled really.

Diana had invited Hewitt's mother and his sister, so that they could all see him before he left for the Gulf. Not for the first time Mrs Hewitt felt a sense of unreality descend upon her, as a servant parked her car and she was ushered into the Prince of Wales's house. She felt as if she was someone else. But Diana resumed family life with the Hewitts as if there had been no interruption.

During the weekend James Hewitt discovered that Diana was now determined to leave the Royal Family.

I know that Diana did not want to be Queen of England. 'I will never be Queen' – she was quite determined. She wanted to get out of the marriage, so for that reason alone she had no desire to be Queen.

Hewitt flew out to Saudi Arabia on Boxing Day, 1990.

She wrote to me every day I was out there, sometimes twice a day. And very occasionally I was able to speak to her. But on the satellite phone. At that stage we didn't know how 'the mother of all wars' was going to turn out. So we were worried that it could have been a fairly bloody and nasty situation.

> She said, 'I know you'll be fantastic.' She was trying to be supportive in everything she said and she was obviously concerned that I might die. But we didn't speak about that – at great length, anyway. She was terribly interested in what morale was like and what was happening – what life was like being stuck in the desert. She wanted to know what I needed – not necessarily needed but what would make life a little more comfortable and bearable out there. So she immediately sent me bottles of whisky and hampers from Fortnum and Mason, which were well received and shared among my men. And little things like a jumper to keep warm at night because it could get very cold out there.
>
> She went down and saw my sisters and my mother, and stayed down there on one occasion. I suppose it was a time when my mother was sort of worried and she thought I might not come back, so she was being supportive. She liked to reciprocate that kind of thing.
>
> The letters kept me going. It's amazing until you've been in that situation, you don't realise the importance of correspondence and hearing from people at home and getting their support.

Diana also remained in constant touch with Hewitt's family, usually by telephone but Shirley Hewitt remembers that:

> sometimes if she couldn't stand the stress any more she would leap into a car, sometimes accompanied by her sons, or one of them, and she would drive down just for the day. Whether anybody knew that she had taken it upon herself to do that I don't know, but it was good to feel that she felt she could, that she had somewhere to come and discuss what was going on.
>
> I wasn't always there and she would come down and perhaps spend the day with James's two sisters. They used to do the usual girly things, jokes and things, and pull each other's legs and they got on frightfully well. Obviously it helped with the anguish of James being away and being in the situation that he was – it helped, it lightened it a little bit, and yes it was

always a breath of fresh air when she came down, it was good to see her.

Hewitt used to send his letters to Diana via his mother in Devon.

And on one occasion there'd probably been a hold up with the mail – she probably hadn't heard for a couple of days, and she rang me and I said, 'Yes, the letters came this morning.' 'Oh, oh can you please read it to me? Will you read them to me?' I said, 'I can't do that! I can't! They're your letters.' 'Oh please, please, please!' She pleaded with me to read these letters. And so I had to – I duly opened them and read them to her. I mean I thought that was a bit much really, to read those sort of, well, endearing letters between two people and me being the outsider really. But I did and she was happy and she said, 'Now please, please will you post them today.' I said, 'Of course I will.' Which I did.

Letters were not all that Diana sent to the Gulf in return:

She sent out a parcel of *Playboy* magazines, which was amazing actually. I mean, occasionally we got a newspaper out there and if there was a picture of a woman in a skirt it would have been blacked out by the Arab authorities. So it was quite a coup getting *Playboy* and *Mayfair* and *Penthouse* sent out uncensored. I just gave them to the chaps and said, 'I have contacts in high places.'

On 2 January 1991 Diana left Sandringham, where the day before she had been pictured walking unhappily alone on Snettisham beach, and drove the hundred miles to Dean Woodward's parents' home. Jane Woodward couldn't believe it.

JANE: In the morning, Dean's uncle picked us up and I thought, No, this is a wind-up. I thought, This is a Jeremy Beadle thing. We got to the house, and I thought, No, it's still no. And we must've been at the house ten minutes and a car pulled up and that's when it hit me – I thought, God, she's really coming to the house!

DEAN: I looked out the window and I could see her get out of the Jaguar and she came down the drive and came in, with her arms open, gave my mum a hug and 'Hello, Ivy' – first-name terms. And 'Hello, John' to me dad. And then she said, 'Oh, I'm sorry I'm late.' And then she said, 'Where is he I've come to see?' And she looked across the room, she said, 'Oh, hello, Dean,' arms open, kissed me on the cheek.

JANE: And she says to Dean, 'Oh, it's nice to see you now you've got your clothes on!' So we all had a laugh about that. She broke the ice, she didn't make you feel uncomfortable or anything.

DEAN: Me dad was addressing her as 'Your Highness' and she said, 'No, no – I'm Diana, you're John, we're friends now.' Once she sat next to me, talking to me, I said, 'Well, why've you come to visit me?' And she said, 'It could've been anybody, but it was your mum that was in intensive care.' And then to have the future Queen sitting next to me, having my children on her lap – I couldn't believe it.

She told me, when she rang me, she said, 'No reporters.' But there was people over the road, Joe Public, waving flags, and I thought, Hang on a minute! And she was shocked to see that, because she didn't come for that, she came for me – me and my family. Not papers, not cameras, not public – she came for me and my family.

The following day the *Sun* reported Diana's hundred-mile mercy dash and set it against pictures of Charles riding at Sandringham. As the newspaper printed more and more anti-Charles material, the Gilbey tape continued to lie unpublished in Stuart Higgins's safe.

The War of the Waleses had commenced. Diana was out to get Charles and Camilla, and stories written with her help appeared, naming her rival more and more openly as the 'friend' that Charles preferred to spend his time with. Discreet briefings on behalf of the Prince were starting too. Stuart Higgins received several.

> In public terms there was supposed to be a dignified silence. But quite clearly the friends that the Prince had were very influential, had good contacts with the media across a wide range, and they set about – not with any kind of great strategy – but when they were asked, they took the opportunity to say that this was the Princess's fault. I was told one day that the Princess was clinically mad and needed treatment.

Harry Arnold had the same experience.

> One extreme story being planted at the time, by Charles's friends, is that Diana was mentally unbalanced, that she ought to be locked up in a lunatic asylum – which was certainly going over the top.

And so did Ken Lennox.

> There were not open briefings, not big briefings, two hundred people sitting down, and them saying that the Princess of Wales is mad. It doesn't work like that, it's one to one – 'Whisper, whisper, and of course you can't quote that, old boy, but we're just setting the record straight.'

Max Hastings was the editor of the *Daily Telegraph*, staunch defender of the establishment.

> Once there started to be leaks from the Princess's side about troubles in the marriage, some of the Prince of Wales's friends did start to suggest to me that we might carry 'his side of the story'. Privately I told them that this was madness.

Dating these anti-Diana briefings is difficult because the papers did not print stories saying that the Princess was mad – editors were just being warned not to believe everything that they heard from her camp. We have spoken separately to six journalists and editors who say that the serious briefing began around this time, or perhaps even earlier. But it is possible that some of them may be recalling later attacks on Diana.

There's no question that by 1992 the gloves were off, but were they in 1990? Diana and James Colthurst thought they were, and saw their *own* actions as a reaction to a determined assault on her character. Jonathan Dimbleby swears, literally hand on heart, that Charles told everybody close to him at this time *not* to get involved in a war of words with his wife. But it is entirely possible that some of Charles's friends may, quite early on, have begun to speak in his defence without his specific approval.

With her acute concern for what high society thought, it's likely that Diana was just as worried about the accounts of dinner-party conversations that were reaching her ears. She was told that some of her husband's friends had been overheard calling her 'the mad cow' (after the newly discovered cattle disease). Vivienne Parry, another friend on the charity circuit, heard such stories and talked to Diana about them. She says that the Princess was convinced a whispering campaign was questioning both her sanity and her fitness to remain in public life.

Whoever started it, the pace was quickening. In February 1991 Nigel Dempster wrote that Diana had cause for concern because her friend James Hewitt was serving in the Gulf, where the ground war threatened to start at any moment.

As preparations for the assault began, Diana was increasingly anxious for her friends in the front line. Hewitt was leading a squadron of tanks, and Diana knew several of his men. She was glued to the television, and tried repeatedly to get out to the Gulf but was refused permission. Instead she talked to the wives of the other soldiers. One of the senior courtiers was asked to 'have a word' with Diana about the large number of letters and packages leaving Kensington Palace. He told us:

> She was very concerned that there would be a lot of bloodshed. I said to her that it wasn't a good idea to write letters to James Hewitt. She got upset and cross.

Richard Kay, a reporter on the *Daily Mail*, went out to write about Hewitt's squadron. He was there when the news came through that the ground war was imminent and offered Hewitt the use of his satellite link to phone home. Hewitt phoned his mother and then Diana. Then, on 24 February 1991, the attack began. Diana refused to go on the regularly scheduled family holiday to Klosters because there was a war on ('Grumpy Charles Mopes on the Slopes,' reported the *Sun* on 28 February). But later that week Saddam Hussein withdrew from Kuwait.

In early March a former girlfriend of Hewitt provided the excuse for the *News of the World* to break the story of Diana and James. It stopped just short of saying they were lovers, and the following day the *Sun* produced a disarmingly innocent account of 'How flirty Di captures all the fellas' hearts' alongside a photograph of Diana handing Hewitt the Captains and Subalterns polo cup. It was clear that from now on Hewitt would be watched.

> It was after the war had finished, but we were still stuck out in the desert. I came back into regimental headquarters and there were some English papers, Sunday papers. And the news was there. I can't remember exactly what it said but words to the effect that Diana's hero in the desert was more than just her riding instructor. Previous to that there had been little snippets in gossip columns, but this was basically saying we know about it.
>
> It was a hell of a shock. The first I knew about it was somebody handing it to me and saying look at this. And I said, 'Oh my goodness.' I had a system called Ptarmigan, which was

a field telephone. In the middle of the desert I used the army phone to ring her up and say, have you seen what's in the papers? And she obviously had, and she was very cool and laid back about it. She said, 'Don't worry.' Don't worry! I mean, it's easier said than done. She said, 'Everyone's cool about it here.' It was extraordinary.

Diana was photographed at Thorpe Park with her sons on the water slide. 'Charles the Absent Royal Father' was castigated in the *Mail*. In stark contrast to the way Charles was raised, Diana's sons were surrounded by maternal affection, dressed informally, taken to mingle with the people, and introduced into Diana's charity work. She was undoubtedly deeply attached to her children and determined that they should not be as removed from real life as other royal children had been. So was her husband, although you would not have known it from the press reports.

With Jephson's help, Diana attempted to upstage Charles as often as possible. Jephson took some pleasure in outwitting Richard Aylard, his opposite number in the Prince's office. In March Aylard discovered that Diana had arranged to take William to Wales on St David's Day without mentioning it to her husband. Aylard was forced to change all of Charles's engagements on that day to spare him more critical press attention of the 'Where Was Charles?' variety.

In May 1991, following the departure of the joint private secretary, Sir Christopher Airy, Richard Aylard took over. If the loss of the amenable Airy was a disappointment to Diana, the idea of Richard Aylard as replacement was totally unacceptable. So the offices of the Prince and Princess of Wales finally split, and Diana formally acquired her own private secretary, Patrick Jephson. The offices, like their bosses, took ever more divergent paths. A member of the royal household told us about her first-hand experiences of this:

> The sadness was that immediate staff would have to choose, either go with one side or the other. It was Jephson versus Aylard. The rest were piggies in the middle.

Diana's side was clearly winning. With some dexterity, Jephson constructed an ever more positive image of the Princess. Also working just about full time for Diana were various friends, notably James Colthurst. They pointed out to Diana that Andrew Morton was writing pieces that were sympathetic to her. Morton received more and more information from 'friends of Diana'. In late May in the *Sun* he was the first to write explicitly about Diana's unhappiness at the role of Camilla Parker Bowles in her husband's life. Camilla was hosting dinner parties at Highgrove, his story claimed.

On 3 June 1991, William was injured by a golf club. The story has been told two ways, each slotting neatly into the prejudices of one party or the other.

The Princess was lunching with a girlfriend at San Lorenzo when her bodyguard broke the news that William had been involved in an accident at Ludgrove School in Berkshire. He had been struck a serious blow to the head by a golf club wielded by a friend, and had been taken for tests at the Royal Berkshire Hospital in Reading. When the parents arrived, William was having a CT scan and doctors were advising that he should be

With the Princess at lunch in London, the Prince was at Highgrove when his policeman broke the news to him that William had been hit on the head by a golf club. 'I knew it was something terrible. My heart went cold,' said Charles later. His housekeeper noted that he ran down the stairs, shouting for his coat, his face white with shock. He told his anxious staff that he had been informed that the injury wasn't serious, but that he felt that transferred to the Great Ormond Street Hospital for Sick Children in London. Diana accompanied William in the ambulance while Charles followed in his Aston Martin sports car. Tests confirmed a serious depressed fracture to the skull requiring an immediate operation under general anaesthetic. There was a possibility of brain damage. Typically, the Prince of Wales felt unable to alter his schedule and left to attend a performance of *Tosca* at the Royal Opera House, Covent Garden, with some environmental Eurocrats that he had set his heart on influencing. Diana, quietly furious with him for abandoning his child, held her son's hand as he was wheeled into the operating theatre and waited outside throughout the seventy-five-minute operation. They were, she said, the longest minutes of her life. Then she remained at William's bedside, again clasping his hand, as nurses checked his blood pressure and reflexes every twenty minutes through the night. A rapid rise in blood pressure, she was told, could prove fatal. he must go to the hospital at once. Seconds later his Aston Martin roared down the gravel drive and sped away. Charles drove fast, dreading what he might find when he reached the hospital. To his enormous relief, he found William sitting up in bed chatting away. Nevertheless, the doctors suggested an examination by neurological specialists at the Great Ormond Street Hospital for Sick Children. They explained that it would be advisable for William to undergo an operation to pull the depressed bones out and smooth them off. They explained to both parents that this was a routine operation involving negligible risk and that there was no point both of them waiting in the ward. Diana made it quite clear that she didn't want Charles around and it was obvious that there would be public friction if he stayed. Under the circumstances Charles decided to carry on with his arranged programme – to host the European Environment and Agriculture Commissioners and a group of Brussels officials at a performance of *Tosca* at Covent

Charles slept on the royal train – code for 'he spent the night with a girlfriend' – as he travelled to an environment conference in York. The next morning's papers upset Diana, who was overwrought after a sleepless night, by suggesting that William was epileptic. Charles, who took no notice of what the public thought, was faxed the *Sun*'s front-page headline, 'What Kind of a Dad Are You?', which reminded him that 'a fractured skull is not a trivial matter'. The nation concluded that only the most callous of fathers could dress up in black tie and go to the opera while his son underwent emergency surgery.

Garden. With this engagement completed, the Prince phoned the hospital to be told that the operation had gone well and that William was asleep with the Princess on hand, so the Prince travelled on by train with his European guests and British officials for the morning's visit to the Yorkshire Dales. The next day he returned to London and went straight to the hospital to find that, as promised, William had made a complete recovery.

The version that appeared in the tabloid press was a lot closer to the left hand column than the right. The *Sun* reported under the headlines 'Wills in Brain Scan Scare' and 'Blood Soaked out of his Bandages'. One of Charles's aides told us that 'He thought he had checked out that he [William] was OK with his mother and that she was in charge. She was not furious with him – that was just the press. Day after day the hacks had got into that habit – she the goodie, he the baddie.'

Charles did have a busy schedule, but he set apart as much time as possible for two boys that he loved very much, as everyone who has seen them together testifies. But by now the press had their caricatures, and they were sticking with them.

Later that same year Charles and Diana visited Canada, where they joined their sons, who were already aboard *Britannia*. Jayne Fincher was in Toronto harbour to record the moment.

> At first it was very formal and Charles and Diana were piped aboard by the captain and did all their hand-shaking bit. And suddenly these doors burst open and the two boys came out and they were so excited. They were hopping up and down waiting for their mum and dad to come, and Diana whisked past the hand-shaking people and her whole face lit up, and she took her hat off and she scuttled down the whole length of the yacht as fast as she could and was hugging them and kissing them.

Fincher's photograph is one of the most famous ever taken of Diana, her arms outstretched, William launching himself into her embrace. She asked Fincher for a copy which she displayed in her dressing room at Kensington Palace. But it wasn't the only picture on that roll of film.

> And then a few seconds behind her Prince Charles did the same thing. He came down, he was hugging and kissing the boys too. But the sad thing was that all the pictures that were used were her with her arms out, and nobody ever used a picture of him.
>
> I think he got a bad press with the children at that time. Everybody kept saying, 'Oh, this awful father' and everything, which wasn't true. He's always been a lovely father. But I think he wasn't seen with the children and she was – and in a lot of high-profile places like Thorpe Park. And so people tended to see that and think, Where's he? all the time.

Earlier in the year, Adrian Ward-Jackson, an art dealer and governor of the Royal Ballet, had been presented with a CBE at Buckingham Palace. Nick Serota, Director of the Tate Gallery, held a celebration lunch at the Tate, and Ward-Jackson asked that Diana be invited as a special guest, since he knew her as Patron of the Royal Ballet. It was at that dinner that Diana met Serota's wife Angela, a former ballet dancer and a close friend of Ward-Jackson. He was deputy chairman of the AIDS Crisis Trust, and that was the context in which he had originally met the Princess. Angela Serota was one of the few who knew that Ward-Jackson was himself HIV positive.

In the spring Ward-Jackson's condition deteriorated, and he was confined to his Mount Street apartment. Serota was in constant attendance at his bedside, and Diana made frequent visits too. Ward-Jackson was a good listener, and Diana poured out the story of her life to him. Andrew Knight, chief executive of News International and a close friend of Serota's, was another visitor.

As the couple's tenth wedding anniversary approached, the press clamour against Charles reached a crescendo. In June 1991 the *Daily Mail* announced that he was intending to stay away from Diana's thirtieth birthday party in London. Nigel Dempster was then briefed by a 'friend' to the effect that the Prince had offered Diana a party at Highgrove, but she had refused. Accordingly, he produced a front-page story headlined 'Diana and Charles: cause for concern'. After citing Diana's petulance as the principal problem with the marriage, he concluded that 'close friends' said 'the Prince is being made to look bad through no fault of his own'. Andrew Morton in the *Sun* replied that Diana did not want to spend her birthday with Charles's 'stuffy old friends'.

Instead, she attended a lunch party at the Savoy Hotel in aid of the Rainbow House children's hospice appeal. Sharon Carter, aged twelve and suffering from cystic fibrosis, helped Diana blow out the thirty candles on her birthday cake.

When President Bush and First Lady Barbara Bush visited London in the summer of 1991 Patrick Jephson took the opportunity to confirm to America that Diana's transformation from clothes-horse to workhorse was complete. Diana took Barbara Bush to visit Mike Adler's AIDS unit at the Middlesex Hospital. Adler had only a week's notice:

> This was one week of pandemonium, as you can imagine. It was very much Diana wanting to show Barbara Bush something that she, Diana, was involved in. And it was a terrific visit. I mean, Barbara Bush was terribly well informed. She herself was involved in HIV and AIDS among children and orphans in the States, and came across clearly as a very intelligent woman who, you know, knew a lot about it . . . But the patients loved Diana. She would sit on their beds, she would hold them and the mood after she left would be electric.

As they drove away, Diana said of Barbara Bush, 'I like her a lot, but she hasn't got intuition with these patients. They need lots of TLC.'

In mid-August Diana was at Balmoral with Fergie. The women were in playful mood, irritating the other guests by taking a nocturnal motorbike ride across the nearby golf course, and performing handbrake turns on the royal gravel in the Queen Mother's Daimler. The Duke of Edinburgh told Sarah not to flirt with the staff. Diana and her sister-in-law retreated into their own world of shared confidences, in-jokes about 'the Germans' and daydreams of joint escape. On 19 August, Angela Serota phoned to say that the last rites had been administered to Ward-Jackson. Diana called James Colthurst and asked him to find her an executive jet. After spending hours on the phone, Colthurst managed to persuade someone to help. But Diana had already left by car without asking the customary permission of the Queen. With her detective, she drove 550 miles through the night from north-east Scotland to London so as to share Ward-Jackson's last moments. In the event he clung on to life until the early hours of 23 August.

Diana's relationship with Hewitt had flared briefly when he got back from the Gulf shortly before her thirtieth birthday. She had been telling him in her letters that she wanted to change her life. From what she had written, he once again hoped for a future with her.

> As soon as I got back to England from the desert I went and saw her, went and stayed. And we didn't really speak too much about it [the future]. There was too much else to catch up on. Obviously we touched on the subject of the situation as it now was.

After the *News of the World* story Hewitt was being followed, and meeting Diana in public was now impossible. She explained that things were even more complicated than that. The Yorks' marriage was on the rocks too and Sarah was always on the phone seeking advice.

> And that was it really, that was it. Back to a very strange existence. After a little bit of leave I went back to Germany again. To a terrible, terrible period. For six months or more before I was posted back to London, to Hyde Park.
>
> Publicity killed the relationship. It was impossible to carry on as we had been in that environment. I do think the relationship would have continued had the publicity not been there.

In Germany life was made increasingly difficult for Hewitt. In the autumn of 1991 he sat exams for promotion to major and was told that he had failed each paper by one per cent. It was clear that his career in the army was effectively at an end. He met Diana on a couple of occasions at Kensington Palace but their meetings were furtive now.

Too much had happened and it fizzled out again. In a similar way that it had once before when I first went to Germany. I tried to contact her but as soon as I realised my calls weren't being returned, I knew – been there before, so it was plain to see.

By the end of 1991 it was quite clear to anyone who read the newspapers that there was a great deal wrong with the Waleses' marriage. But there was a consensus that there could be no question of a divorce. All the most damaging articles were accompanied by shorter, calmer pieces saying precisely this. But an enterprise was already under way that would prove them all utterly wrong.

11
A Malign Planet

From mid-1990 onwards, through her financial adviser, Joseph Sanders, and through James Colthurst, Diana had been preparing the way for a separation on her own terms. Then a new opportunity revealed itself. Colthurst learned that Andrew Morton was planning a major new biography of Diana.

James Colthurst had grown to trust Morton, with whom he regularly played squash. Morton was a talented, lively writer, and because he was freelance he was less vulnerable than most journalists to the threat of editorial interference. Following the sacking of Sir Christopher Airy, Morton wrote pieces in the *Sunday Times* that highlighted divisions between the Prince's and Princess's staff. Richard Aylard searched for the identity of the mole providing him with information. Robert Fellowes strongly suspected his sister-in-law's private office. Photographer Arthur Edwards told Morton, 'Watch your phones.' All this cloak-and-dagger excitement made the writer even more attractive to the Princess's circle. Colthurst asked Morton to a meeting far away from the normal royal beat.

> It was over a plate of bacon and eggs in a transport café in North Ruislip, well away from prying eyes. We chatted about Diana's life, and the real despair and despondency she felt, and how some of her friends really felt that she was on the verge of committing suicide. And he mentioned how she suffered from this eating disorder – bulimia – how she was in a bad way, mentally. How she was really finding it hard to cope, how she would run out of the room when Prince Charles arrived in the room. How she couldn't really get to grips with being an

international superstar in the public eye and being treated in such a poor way by both the Royal Family and particularly by Prince Charles.

And the thing which riled her most of all was that she was living a lie in terms of her marriage. Camilla Parker Bowles was effectively the mistress of Highgrove and the mistress of Prince Charles. And that was driving her to despair. She's a jealous woman, she's an obsessive woman, and it was breaking her up. And this astonishing tale poured out, about how she'd made these various failed suicide attempts, how Charles had been consumed with a passion for Camilla Parker Bowles which had – in Diana's eyes – been the cancer at the heart of their marriage. And when I walked away from that café, I remember thinking to myself, this is Walter Mitty land. It can't be true.

Morton and Colthurst discussed whether the story of Diana's marriage could be told with the direct help of the Princess and the on-the-record endorsement of her closest allies. The result could be one of the most sensational bestsellers of all time, but Morton's publisher, Michael O'Mara, was nervous of proceeding without proof that Diana was truly willing to assist. By the time Colthurst met O'Mara, he was able to play some tapes that gave credence to his story. But O'Mara wanted more evidence. Colthurst went back to Diana. She was uncertain about whether to go ahead. Colthurst suggested that she might consult his friend Felix Lyle, an astrologer.

Diana was an avid reader of the star signs at the back of her favourite magazines and considered herself to be a typical Cancerian. For several years she had shared Sarah Ferguson's enthusiasm for society astrologers, previously consulting well-known practitioners such as Penny Thornton. Perhaps the movement of the stars would now guide her to the right decision about Andrew Morton's book. Colthurst invited Lyle to the pub for a drink.

> James approached me out of the blue and said, 'How do you fancy doing an astrological reading for Diana?' And I looked at him and I thought, Hmm, you're winding me up, aren't you? But no, he meant it. Diana was thinking about doing a book, *The Revenge of the Princess*, basically, and she wanted some astrological advice on it. And I thought, Perhaps you need a bit more than astrological advice! But I was very keen to do it.
>
> People have said, if she had astrologers of her own, why did she not go to them? But James felt that I would give her an objective picture of what I saw.

One evening in August, Diana drove to Fulham, parked down a quiet side street, left her detective waiting in the car, and rang the doorbell of James Colthurst's terraced house. Waiting inside was Colthurst, his wife Dominique and a rather tense astrologer.

> I caught myself by surprise by how nervous I was. But she just swooped in and said, 'Hi.' Very effortless and very naturally. James and Dominique scurried off upstairs, and hid themselves away for the duration of the consultation, which lasted about two hours.
>
> In the first consultation the focal point was the book. She asked me what the auguries were for publishing the book.

The strongest message coming back from Diana's chart was perhaps the most predictable:

> I said, 'There's scandal here.' There was Neptune playing quite a devious game in her chart, and also Pluto playing a very strong role, and so there was a complete transformation coming.

Diana was impressed. She then took Felix through the story of her marriage.

> There were real feelings of anger there – it's strong in her chart anyhow. She felt unloved, she felt used, and she felt that there was another person in her husband's heart. Did he have a

> mistress or did he not, and was it acceptable to Diana or was it not? She took the view that he did have one, and that it was unacceptable, and this is not why she married him.

And the future?

> She had serious worries and reservations about the book. And we talked all about that. Pluto in the transformation takes a very long-term approach to things, so as it unravels, you unravel with it. And she said, 'Well, if this is what's happening anyhow, I might as well facilitate it, you know, make it easier.'

As she sat under the Sign of Fulham in the House of Colthurst, what was going through Diana's mind? The path of the *Sun* through the zodiac of Wapping? Hewitt in retrograde motion? The Moon was in Capricorn, Mercury was in Aries and Camilla was still in Highgrove. Scandal and transformation were coming. 'Oh well, I might as well facilitate it, then.' Decision made.

Members of Britain's ruling family have long flirted with the occult. But no seance, no turn of a tarot card and no finger run along a royal palm ever had an impact like this. The future Queen was poised to break the rules of secrecy and loyalty that had sustained the Windsors for generations. And no one could predict the consequences. Although one astrologer did try:

> We talked about the possibilities and the mud-slinging that would come out as a result of it, and the likely reaction of the Royal Family, which isn't exactly tame in the way that it protects interests.
>
> But she wanted revenge – there's no question about that. That was a very strong motivating factor in bringing the book out. She had her story to tell, and she felt that the only way to gain some kind of composure was to hit back. I think at that stage she was bitterly, bitterly hurt, and would see the

> tearing down [of the Royal Family] as a perfectly justifiable end.

Colthurst and his wife could bear the tension no more.

> James and Dominique started making scuffling noises at the top of the stairs, oversized mice noises, and decided that they wanted their house back. We could have carried on for another hour and a half. So they came down, and that was it. We smiled at James and said, 'Well, that's it, then, we're going ahead. The book is going ahead.' And James said something like, 'Well, that's excellent.'

Most of Diana's loyal society friends, like Lord Palumbo, say that had she consulted them they would strongly have advised her against the book. They would have told her that to raise the stakes in this way would be catastrophic.

> If she'd come to somebody like me or others, and said, do you think we should do this, do you think this book is a good idea, we would've all said, 'No' – or I would've done, anyway – and that was not what she wanted to hear. So she went ahead anyway because she was an instinctive creature.

Diana knew what her more conservative friends would say and so she did not ask them. Felix Lyle had one more conversation with Diana over a dinner table, and then Colthurst called him with exciting news.

> 'I've got the whole thing rolling!' The whole thing was rolling. The information was being gathered. She gave the lot. It was a very slick operation because Morton never had to meet her. It's a bizarre thing to write, isn't it, a biography about somebody that you never meet, when she's still alive?
>
> James was the centrepiece, he was the linchpin for the whole thing. It was the contact between James and Diana, James and Andrew Morton. And I was never very clear about whose idea

> it was. I'm not sure that it was hers. I'm pretty certain that it wasn't actually.

Colthurst and Diana made dozens of tape recordings that were passed to Andrew Morton. He would listen and then send supplementary questions back to Diana. At the same time some of Diana's friends were approached for their testimony about her and to act as on-the-record repositories for Diana's own words. In return Diana demanded only one thing from Morton.

> The straightforward deal was that she would always be in the background, that she had total, utter deniability – so that I would take the flak for it, it would be my responsibility. Some of her friends would bear the burden of it as well, and that was it. And she could then say to the Queen, say to Prince Charles, say to the Prime Minister, 'Nothing to do with me.'

As Morton's project got into full swing, high-level steps were being taken to curb the intrusive instincts of the British press. Senior journalists were alarmed that new laws might be directed against them, and so they took action to maintain self-regulation. In January 1991, a new body named the Press Complaints Commission took over from the old Press Council as journalism's governing authority. It promised to take a much firmer line on the invasion of privacy, and all editors and publishers agreed to abide by its code of practice. Lord McGregor was appointed chairman. After a rash of intrusive tabloid stories, the privacy of the Royal Family was at the top of his agenda. McGregor was particularly anxious about the Prince and Princess of Wales.

He had lunch with Sir Robert Fellowes, the Queen's private secretary, and Charles Anson, her new press secretary. Sir Robert later invited Lord McGregor and his PCC colleagues to a lunch at the Palace. The courtiers told them that stories about problems in the royal marriage were all untrue, but McGregor was soon advised otherwise. The *Daily Mail*'s owner, Lord

Rothermere, explained to him that both Diana and Charles had sought to use national newspapers to place their versions of their marital problems before the public.

Thoroughly amused by Colthurst's story of how his project had been authorised, Andrew Morton went to Lyle for a reading too.

> And it became a merry little party. I seem to remember he quotes me in his book as saying something fairly banal like, 'It's gonna be a hard ride.' Well, I don't have to be an astrologer to come up with that kind of observation. And that was it – he went away and wrote it. And I think he wrote it quite quickly because it must've been one of the easier jobs for him because he didn't have to do much of the research!
>
> I did actually make an invoice in the end, and it was agreed that the Morton estate, as it was called, would pay for the consultations. So it makes it look as if it was a bit of a conspiracy, but it wasn't really, it's just that I wanted to be paid, I needed the money.

Some of Diana's friends were contacted by Andrew Morton with messages such as 'I'm doing a book. I know you are very important to Diana. Can I come and talk to you?' All immediately contacted Diana, who said to most, but not all, that she had no objection to them talking. James Hewitt

> received a letter in Germany from Andrew Morton . . . asking me to contribute to a book that he was doing. And I . . . rang up Diana and said, 'What's all this about?' And she was particularly vague about it actually. I hadn't spoken to her for a while. And I said, 'Well, what do you want me to do?' And she said, 'You must do what you feel you must do.' I said, 'Well, that's not very helpful, for heaven's sake.' She said, 'Well, do what you want.' . . . So I wrote back to Mr Morton and said, 'I'm

> sorry, I don't know what good it would do to speak to me and I would have nothing to add to your book about the Princess of Wales.'

While Hewitt refused, most others accepted. James Gilbey and Carolyn Bartholomew were major contributors. Angela Serota consulted a friend in the media, Andrew Knight, the executive chairman of News International.

> I heard from Angela Serota that this book was being written and that she had been asked to co-operate in providing material for it. She was saying, 'Look, you're in newspapers, you know more about this world than I do, what do you think I ought to do? I've been counselled by the Princess of Wales that I should tell all that I know, in as responsible a way as I can, to Andrew Morton – do you think that's right?' I was slightly amazed but I said, 'Well, if that is the case, yes, I think you should.'

Diana visited Angela Serota at home, to give her blessing in the most positive terms. Serota invited Morton over for an interview in which she talked about Adrian Ward-Jackson. Another confidant approached by Morton was Diana's masseur, Stephen Twigg.

> She hoped that other people close to her – her family, the Royal Family, her husband even – would understand more than they seemed to do how she felt and the situation she was in. Because she felt entirely helpless. She felt that she was trapped and she said to me, 'There's no way I can get out of this.' And I told her that, in fact, the Royal Family were stuck with her until *she* decided differently, because you have lots of other options than to stay in the situation that you're in.

Felix Lyle met Diana again.

> She came to Fulham again. She wanted to talk about the meaning of life. She liked the alternative and the occult view. She was looking to turn up stones and looking for answers.
>
> She was particularly mindful of what she called the cruel streak in the Windsors and she said that Charles had shown this to her. . . . And that bothered her. She was concerned for William's development. She really didn't want him to follow in the footsteps of the Royal Family. She wanted him to be different, she wanted him to be a modern monarch. I think she'd put a lot of thought into the upbringing from that perspective. Of all the royals that were around her at that time, she was the only one who really understood the importance of having the public on your side.

As the book was written, draft chapters were sent to Diana. She annotated them and sent them back. To further satisfy Morton's desire for proof, she showed him some of Camilla's recent letters to Charles.

On 15 January 1992 the *Daily Mail* published photographs of Sarah, Duchess of York, with an American named Steve Wyatt. The photographs had been found in Wyatt's Belgravia flat. Sarah believed they had been planted. For two more days the tabloids revelled in the story. After six days of this Sarah told Andrew that she thought they should separate, and the next morning they went to see the Queen. They agreed not to make anything public until after the general election that had been called for April.

In February 1992 Charles and Diana toured India, looking unhappy in each other's company. Many of their engagements were separate. The Prince of Wales dutifully attended meetings on behalf of British business. Diana visited hospitals and met Mother Teresa. The most damaging moment came from an apparently innocent day of tourism. While Charles talked to more industrialists, Diana visited the Taj Mahal. Charles had been there before and did not want to overcrowd his schedule. Inevitably, the press followed Diana. Photographer Jayne Fincher could not believe how clumsily the schedule had been arranged:

> We were told that it would be very bad of us if we all went to the Taj Mahal and nobody went with Prince Charles. I mean, what a stupid thing! . . . When the Princess of Wales, the most photographable woman in the world, is sitting by the Taj Mahal for a photograph, who on earth is going to ever expect any photographers to go and photograph a man in a suit at a business forum?

The officials failed to see the danger. The photo opportunity with Diana sitting sadly alone outside the world's most famous monument to love was laden with ironic potential. But only Diana knew that she was about to publish a tale of cruelty and neglect. Now the woman who had dreamed of marrying a Prince was happy for the world to see that the fairytale had no happy ending. Judy Wade asked her a question:

> I said, 'What do you think of the Taj, ma'am?' And she went into some very cryptic description about it being 'a very healing experience' to be there. And we all got the message that she needed this experience because she was so neglected and abandoned by her husband and that's what made front pages around the world the next day.

Two days later there was a polo match in which Charles would take part. Diana was to present the prizes to the winning team. Not to have done so would have been rude to the magnificent Indian cavalry who were competing. On the boundary, Diana agonised with her staff over what to do if Charles's team won. One of them told us:

> Diana said to me, 'I'm not sure if I can kiss him in public.' She didn't want to maintain the myth. I knew there would be trouble.

They all watched in horror as, from sixty yards out on the boundary, Charles scored one of the luckiest and most spectacular goals of his career. Charles, stoic as ever in public, was also expecting trouble as he walked over to kiss Diana. But it had never occurred to the equerries who had arranged the schedule that to photographers like Jayne Fincher the date was crucial:

> It was the thirteenth of February, the day before Valentine's Day. And everybody wanted a picture of them kissing to run in the paper on Valentine's Day. And Diana always kisses Charles when she presents him with a prize. We used always to get them kissing on the lips at polo and giggling into each other's faces. This one, it was a turned head and a quick peck here [on the neck] and both looked pretty miserable. So we all ran the story that this kiss symbolised the bad marriage.

The opposition was deploying heavy artillery. In London, Richard Aylard let Patrick Jephson know that the lawyer Lord Goodman was now engaged on the Prince's behalf. He took this as an indication that the Prince's side might be looking for a separation. The Princess hired her own lawyers.

Meanwhile, in deepest secrecy, Diana's forces were drawing up their own howitzer. While she was in India, Andrew Morton and Michael O'Mara were trying to sell the newspaper serial rights to his book, now called *Diana: Her True Story*. The *Mail on Sunday* had already bid £300,000 when they approached their favoured target, Andrew Neil, editor of the *Sunday Times*. They pursued Neil because of the credibility that the *Sunday Times* could bring to the book.

Andrew Neil's first instinct was to dismiss it all. The author told Neil that his key sources had all signed statements backing up their contributions to his book. Neil was still not convinced. Then the *Mail* withdrew their offer. Morton feared the worst.

> And we had an awful week, I remember, in February 1992 when David English, the editor of the *Daily Mail*, turned the book down because . . . he didn't think there was enough new information in it – which is a bit like the guy who turned down the Beatles. It looked almost as if we couldn't even get a serialisation for the book in either the *Daily Mail* or the *Sunday Times*.

At this point News International chairman Andrew Knight intervened and told Andrew Neil that he knew the book was authentic because one of the sources, Angela Serota, was a completely reliable friend of his. Neil, a well-known republican, was still not convinced, and Knight found himself having to persuade him:

> So there we were in a rather curious position – me, as a rather soppy royalist, urging Andrew to take seriously a book which he would've been far more likely than me, you would've thought, to want to publish. It was really only when it became more and more evident that the book was likely to be true and explosive that he became very interested in it.
>
> It was 'to end the fairy story', that was the phrase that the Princess of Wales was using over and over again.

Sue Douglas at the *Sunday Times* scrutinised the book's more controversial statements. Knight several times asked Serota to check a fact, and five minutes later she would call him back, having spoken directly to Diana. This, and continued firm support from the other witnesses, slowly convinced Douglas and Neil that Diana truly stood behind the project. The serial deal was signed.

Meanwhile, at the *Sun*, Stuart Higgins was negotiating a secondary interest in the rights:

> I had to go and read the book – sign confidentiality clauses, all that sort of thing. So I was privileged enough to know that there was hot property, massive material in this book that I

> thought was going to blow the whole marriage up in the air and was very, very exciting. I obviously quizzed him [Morton] about the authenticity of it and his words, which will stick with me for ever, were, 'Well, you can treat this book as though she has signed every page of the manuscript!'

Attempts to keep royal scandals out of the newspapers in the run-up to the election failed miserably. Lady Colin Campbell's book *Diana in Private* was serialised in March. But Campbell's stories were knocked aside by a bigger piece of news. On 18 March 1992, three weeks before a general election, the *Daily Mail* broke the story of the separation of the Duke and Duchess of York in an exclusive written by Morton and Richard Kay. The story was supposed to have been kept back and everyone assumed there had been a leak. The lunch-time radio news programme, *The World at One*, announced 'the knives are out for Fergie at the Palace'.

Sarah Ferguson thought the Palace had leaked her unhappy news:

> They also needed to send a warning to Diana, to keep her in the fold and shore up the monarchy. My public vivisection would be a pointed reminder: *This is what happens if you cross us*. (They did indeed scare the daylights out of my sister-in-law, who was now afraid to be seen with me, and I could not blame her.)

After writing the Fergie divorce story, Morton was warned by a trusted contact that the Palace was looking for his source. He was again told to watch his phones. Two weeks later his office was broken into. After this he started using public telephones for any sensitive calls. When he learned that journalists were seeking to obtain an advance copy of Morton's book, so as to run a 'spoiler', Michael O'Mara decided to print his first edition in Finland.

The Princess, who had been on a ballet patronage trip to Hungary, now found it convenient to reverse an earlier decision not to go skiing with the Prince. So on 28 March, Charles, Diana and the boys arrived for a holiday in the Austrian ski resort of Lech. The next day the trip was cut short by the news that Diana's father, Earl Spencer, had died in hospital. Overwrought as she already was, this very sad news caused Diana to break down completely, but she would not accept the Prince's attempts at consolation. He decided to attend his father-in-law's funeral against his wife's wishes, and travelled to Northamptonshire by helicopter while Diana went by car. The press noted that he was not there to comfort her on the journey.

In April, with the election safely out of the way, Princess Anne opened divorce proceedings against Mark Phillips. Three out of three royal marriages were now officially in trouble. In May Diana again left the country for an official visit to Egypt.

As the serialisation of *Her True Story* approached, rival newspapers ran their 'spoilers', although none managed to penetrate Finnish printing security. The articles only served to heighten the excitement about what was coming. At the PCC, Lord McGregor was moving to condemn repeated speculation about the royal marriage. Andrew Neil sold the story aggressively as coming from people close to Diana. Hundreds of posters appeared by major roads and adverts ran on television. Other newspapers were equally certain that the story did *not* have royal authorisation and set out to prove it. Richard Stott, editor of the *Mirror*, thought he was on the firmest possible ground:

> When we knew this book was coming out, we actually asked Diana. Kent Gavin the photographer asked her on her royal trip to Egypt whether she'd co-operated with this and she just said, 'Absolutely not,' in no way had she ever co-operated with it. We should have known then that she had!

Angela Serota spoke to Diana's close Brazilian friend, Lucia Flecha da Lima, about the book, assuming that she already knew about it. The horror with which Flecha da Lima responded to the news unnerved Serota. But it was now far too late to stop. The Wapping presses were rolling and Pluto, the dark unraveller, was about to have his hour.

12
Her True Story?

On Saturday, 6 June 1992 Robert Fellowes called Wapping to ask what the *Sunday Times* was printing. It sounded grim. Richard Aylard decided that the Palace must not stay silent. He drafted a statement condemning the book and insisting that it was inaccurate. Patrick Jephson read it to Diana. She refused to put her name to it.

Charles had the newspaper faxed to him at Highgrove. Then he marched upstairs to confront his wife, who left for London in a hurry. Charles went to play polo at Windsor. In a display of public support for her son, the Queen had invited Andrew and Camilla Parker Bowles to join her in the royal enclosure. Sharp-eyed spectators noticed that Camilla was wearing a suit in Prince of Wales check.

The *Mirror* headline attacked its rival the next morning with Kent Gavin's Diana quote: 'I Have Not Co-operated With This Book In Any Way'. That same day the Press Complaints Commission drafted an angry statement denouncing this 'odious exhibition of journalists dabbling their fingers in the stuff of other people's souls'. Lord McGregor rang Fellowes and asked him to confirm that Diana had nothing to do with the book. Fellowes did so and the PCC released their statement. One of McGregor's colleagues, David Chipp, already had a sinking feeling:

> McGregor thought and was led to understand that there had been no help with this at all, and this was really a piece of pretty unpleasant intrusion. And he concocted, with some of us, a statement in which he used this extraordinary remark by Virginia Woolf about dabbling fingers in people's souls which

made the whole thing look rather ludicrous and made people laugh at us a bit.

Max Hastings from the *Telegraph* was aghast. He went on Radio Four's *Today* programme to argue with Andrew Neil, telling him that royal reporting was what a chap did if he failed to land a job playing piano in a brothel. Neil challenged Hastings to deny the strength of his sources, but on ITN news Andrew Morton was obliged to fulfil his promise to the Princess. He denied that Diana had helped him in any way. The Palace and the PCC appeared to be vindicated, and Morton and the *Sunday Times* were exposed to widespread vilification, their book undermined.

The following day Andrew Knight contacted Lord McGregor.

I did write probably a rather pompous letter to him saying, 'Look, we know that this book is true and moreover we know that it does have the willing sanction of the Princess of Wales.' And he rang me and we had a conversation about it, which he was surprised by. 'Well,' Lord McGregor said, 'I don't believe you, Mr Knight.' So I said to him, 'Well, look, Lord McGregor, if you don't believe me, just look at tomorrow's newspapers, because in tomorrow's newspapers will be reported an event which has not yet happened. Later today the Princess of Wales is going to visit Carolyn Bartholomew, who's one of the sources for the book, and that story will be reported with photographs, and we know about it in advance. It will be reported with photographs in tomorrow's tabloid newspapers.' And he said, 'How extraordinary. I'm amazed.'

Calls were made to the picture desks of various newspapers to tell them of the Princess's imminent visit. Stuart Higgins says, 'I took the call. It was a very, very polite lady.' He says he is not certain who she was. Ken Lennox was at home in Chelsea when he also got a call telling him that the Princess of Wales would be leaving Carolyn Bartholomew's house at precisely nine o'clock:

So I shot round there, got into the street, parked my car at the top of the street and ran down and there was a detective waiting for me who I recognised. And he said, 'Can you do your shots from here, Ken?' Which was forty yards away from the front door. And I said, 'Yes.' So he said, 'I'll leave you here and I'll go back and sit in the car.' The door opened up, sharp on nine o'clock, Diana stepped out, looked up at me, turned round. Carolyn came to the door and out on to the front step carrying her baby, with her husband. Diana kissed Carolyn on both cheeks, kissed the baby and kissed Carolyn's husband, looked up to see if I was shooting, walked to the car, got in the car – the front seat, not the back seat – and looked at me all the way up the street as she drove towards me, giving me a full chance to get more photographs.

It was significant that whoever called me was able to tell me when the Princess of Wales was leaving. Lots of people know when somebody's arriving someplace, but it's very difficult to guess when somebody's leaving.

. . . Well, only I know who phoned me – and I'm not telling you!

The photographs were used in most of the following day's papers. David Chipp felt himself sinking lower:

And McGregor was outraged and furious, livid, because he felt that he had been misled – whether wilfully or not I'm not sure – but he felt he'd been misled by the Palace officials and by those around Diana in suggesting that she had no knowledge of this. And I don't think he was ever quite the same again.

When Robert Fellowes returned from Paris he called Diana into his office. After a severe meeting she flew in the afternoon to Merseyside to visit a hospice. She called Joseph Sanders *en route* and told him that she was anxious about the reaction of the crowds. But when she arrived her audience burst into applause and she burst into tears.

The moment Diana posed for Ken Lennox's camera was the turning point of her life, an act of open defiance. There could be no going back now.

> 'Patrick . . . What do people think of me going to see Carolyn like that? . . .'
>
> 'I think they see you as a very supportive friend.'
>
> 'And the photographers?'
>
> 'Well, they follow you everywhere, don't they?'
>
> 'Yes, they certainly do!'

Patrick Jephson was interrogated by his fellow courtiers: 'Come on, Patrick, we all know that she did it.' Jephson saw Diana by turns proud and anxious, one moment confrontational, the next timid. She told him that 'this family had this book coming to them', but he worried that, while the Royal Family might be damaged, in the long term she would be ruined – cut adrift and vulnerable to 'those whose motives seldom began or ended with her welfare'.

Mary Robertson was visiting England. She had written to Diana asking if they might meet, and Patrick Jephson had replied offering lunch at Kensington Palace on 25 June. The Robertsons arrived just as the serialisation of *Her True Story* began. They read it with alarm, half expecting their lunch to be cancelled, but it was not. They arrived at Kensington Palace uncertain what to expect:

> She was absolutely radiant. She'd been down to William's school to watch him play soccer. Harry had gone with her. She was looking forward to seeing us. It was a very good day for her, although she'd had plenty of bad days. She seemed very much to have gotten it all together. All I did was vaguely allude to what a terrible time she'd had, and ask her if she was all right now. She said, 'Mrs Robertson, I'm absolutely fine now, you don't have to worry about me.'

She was humorous about the Royal Family. She had said that the myth that the Queen Mother had helped her in her first months as Princess was completely untrue. She laughingly referred to the Royal Family as 'that lot', and said, 'They never let you know when you've done something right, but they certainly tell you if you've done something wrong.'

The great headlines in Morton's book came from the Sandringham staircase story and the other 'suicide attempts'. It's clear now that the staircase affair was a simple accident misleadingly described, and the other incidents seem faintly ludicrous. As one of Lady Colin Campbell's interviewees ('a relation of the Prince') asked: 'How do you kill yourself with a lemon slicer? Do you peel yourself to death?' Diana backed away from many of these stories and told later friends that Morton had exaggerated. But she accused him of making up the staircase saga too, although she had recorded it all for him on tape. After all, this was *her* true story, not necessarily *the* true story. A sensational piece of journalism, no question, but more of a divorce petition than a biography, and as one-sided as such documents habitually are.

Morton's first reaction – that he was being invited to take a trip to 'Walter Mitty land' – is echoed in the response of Diana's more sober friends to his book. Most of the people we have spoken to, people who knew Diana as a child, a teenager and even as a young married woman, say that the Gothic doom and gloom of *Her True Story* is not how they remember things. Janet Filderman sums up.

> I know from Diana herself that she wasn't as unhappy as that book purported her to be. It made it seem as though she was a misery all those years, and it wasn't true, because I knew her in those years, very, very closely and very well. It's exactly what would happen in any marriage if you take the wife and the

> husband's side totally separately. You will always go one way or t'other and I think that is what it was all about.

Some of those who had played a major role in the book – like Felix Lyle – were soon having second thoughts.

> I think it satisfied her need for revenge, it undoubtedly showed the Royal Family in a very unfavourable light, and to a lot of people this was long overdue. I just felt it didn't get to the heart of it. I felt it had too much of an axe to grind, to be honest, and part of me felt a little bit ashamed of that actually, and I just felt that maybe I should have rethought my strategy originally.

Andrew Knight looks back with mixed feelings too.

> I had second thoughts when my mother cried when we ran this book, and I realised that we'd hurt her and millions like her. And yet I knew it was true. And for that reason I also felt hurt that good people – because I think the Prince of Wales and the Princess of Wales *are* good people – I felt hurt that they were hurt.

In a report leaked soon afterwards, McGregor managed to improve on soul-dabbling when he accused Diana of 'invading her own privacy'. From now on she could expect little in the way of protection from a Press Complaints Commission led by a very bitter lord.

> I felt as I have always felt, that the protection of the privacy of public persons turns in part on their prudence, and the observance of proper standards of behaviour and partly on their truthfulness. And I felt that in this particular instance, on all those counts, there had been a serious failure.

On 5 July Diana's masseur, Stephen Twigg, told the *Sunday Express*, 'the situation has to end . . . otherwise there will be a tragedy.' Charles read the article over breakfast at Highgrove and casually asked Diana whether there was anyone she knew who was *not* talking to the press on a daily basis?

If Charles couldn't understand Diana's behaviour, it was even harder for his mother, born and raised to the stiff upper lip. How should she handle the beguiling but skittish Princess now? Patrick Jephson felt that the Queen should make one final effort to try to understand his boss and coax the 'nervous thoroughbred' back into the stable. But the only thing that might have made a difference, the banishment of Camilla, was the one thing the Queen had never felt able to ask. And, anyway, Charles had by now made it clear to his own and to his mother's court that Camilla was a non-negotiable part of his life.

A carefully balanced account by Robert Lacey in the August edition of *Life* magazine recognised that this was the end. 'Two emotionally needy people have come together and have discovered they have only demands to make.' Lacey's prediction of the Palace reaction was as accurate as his analysis of the cause of breakdown: 'the Princess's refusal to disavow the book adds up in Royal eyes to a clear case of treason'.

This rebel princess appealed as never before to those Britons who disliked formality and the drab Victorian attitudes commonly thought to be embodied in the Windsor family. The historian David Cannadine described the monarchy as 'passive, philistine, bewildered, anachronistic, obsessed with protocol and tradition, and smothered in a courtly embrace redolent of quarter-deck attitudes and saddle soap'.

The people had never witnessed members of the Royal Family at each other's throats like this before, and many quite enjoyed it. Even monarchists could enjoy a frisson of anti-establishment fervour by backing Diana, because she wasn't necessarily anti-royal, she was just anti-Windsor, anti-'that lot'.

In Nottingham Dean Woodward rallied to her standard.

> The royals want to stay up there, the public down there. I wasn't interested in the royals, but ever since Princess Diana

> did what she did for me and my family, I've not been a royalist but I've definitely been a number-one Dianaist.

The whole world had gone 'Dianaist'. Morton's book was a bestseller everywhere. In America, the edition of *People* magazine that featured it was the all-time most popular. With its unbeatable combination of majesty and mischief, the Charles and Di story was a blockbuster now, with Diana cast firmly in the ever popular soap opera role of the wronged wife who won't take it any more.

According to Jonathan Dimbleby's account, Charles's friends, disgusted by his wife's treachery, contacted Richard Aylard asking for permission to speak or write on Charles's behalf. Diana's allies dismiss this as Palace spin. They say that St James's Palace organised the counter-attack itself and then carefully created the appearance that Charles was being dragged unwillingly to the battlefield.

At first little appeared in direct defence of Charles. Just one account found its way into the *Sunday Times*. Then Lord Romsey spoke to Andrew Knight off the record. Knight passed his comments to Andrew Neil but told him not to link Romsey's name to the story. But Neil did. Then Penny Junor wrote a long essay in *Today* under the headline 'Charles: His True Story'. It was a point-by-point rebuttal of Morton, demanded, the newspaper claimed, by Charles's friends. Junor had been telephoned by one of them after she had appeared on the radio defending Charles against Morton. In *Today* Junor described Diana's conduct as 'irrational, unreasonable and hysterical'. She insisted that Charles and Camilla were just good friends and that Charles was 'not the adulterous kind'. On reading the piece, Diana asked Charles, 'Why don't you save yourself a phone call and ring the papers direct?' Given her own recent contacts with the media, it is easy to imagine his response.

The Romseys and van Cutsems wrote long letters to the Queen, explaining how Charles had suffered in silence throughout his dismal marriage. For the first time, the Queen and Prince Philip raised the question directly with their son. Diana met Prince Philip, and the pair exchanged a series of letters. Diana drafted hers with the help of a lawyer. Her description of Philip's letters as 'wounding' and 'condemnatory' appeared in a later book by Morton. Philip, she said, threatened her with the loss of title and position. Summoning up all her Spencer pride, she replied that she had come into his family with a title of her own and didn't need one of his.

The Queen met Charles and discussed a separation. She instructed the couple to go away together one last time. Diana agreed to what she later described as the 'holiday from hell' on Greek billionaire John Latsis's yacht. She had holidayed on the yacht the previous year, undergoing what the press described as a 'second honeymoon' with relative equanimity. But when, dutifully but implausibly, the papers presented this trip as a 'second honeymoon' yet again, there were no smiles to convince anyone that all was well.

August at Balmoral was not pleasant. As the entire Royal Family gathered for the rest of the summer holiday, further scandals hit both royal wives. The *Mirror* pulled off a huge coup with its pictures of a topless Fergie having her toes sucked by Johnny Bryan, her financial adviser. The Duchess fled from Scotland. Patrick Jephson was on holiday with his family in Devon. Diana had him standing at dawn in a telephone box, reading the morning headlines to her, before she decided whether to go downstairs to face the kippers and the in-laws.

Having assisted Andrew Morton and the *Sunday Times* so publicly, Diana was now regarded by other papers as fair game. The *Sun* had been sitting on the Squidgy tape for two and a half years. The tape was mentioned by the *National Enquirer* in America, and excerpts from it were published there. On 25 August 1992 the whole story was printed in the *Sun* under a huge banner headline, 'My Life is Torture'. Stuart Higgins was acting editor on the day:

> Apart from some of the material at the beginning of the tape, which we thought was rather tasteless and offensive, we published every word of the tape and put it on an 0898 number for people to listen to as well. . . . She had had her say if you like, and clearly part of her aim in writing this book was to dilute or to stop Squidgygate ever appearing if she could.

If so, she had had some success. *Her True Story* had explained the unhappiness and isolation that provided the background to her remarks on the tape. And although she clearly had been enjoying some sort of intimate relationship with James Gilbey, it seemed to most listeners that he was a great deal more besotted with her than she was with him.

Back in the autumn of 1989 a second radio ham had been amusing himself by listening to royal phone calls. He had a tape too. Seeing the Squidgy story in the *Sun*, he took his recording to the *Daily Mirror*'s Manchester office. Soon it was on editor Richard Stott's desk in London:

> I actually thought it was a *Spitting Image* sketch. Not only did Prince Charles sound like his puppet but the conversation sounded as if it was something from *Spitting Image* – although I suspect that they would have paid millions for a script like that! . . . Because it's clearly dynamite. I mean, it was seriously worrying because the monarchy was in such terrible sixes and sevens and in crisis over Morton and then Squidgy. And to have a tape where the Prince of Wales is ruminating about being a Tampax was not something that was going to endear

the monarchy, or indeed the *Daily Mirror*, to the nation as a whole.

One of the first tasks was to check the voices. Stott called in his expert, Harry Arnold, who had recently moved from the *Sun* to the *Mirror*:

> Richard Stott played the tape and said, 'Whose are those voices?' And I said, 'Well, one's the Prince of Wales and the other one's Camilla Parker Bowles.' And he said, 'How can you be so sure?' I said, 'I've heard their voices so many times, I'm sure.' And he said, 'Yes, but if you're wrong I'll be in the dock, not you.' So he gave me the task of proving to him that the tape was genuine and I spent six weeks doing it . . . playing it to phonetics experts. We had other experts examine the tape to make sure it wasn't spliced and cobbled together.
>
> When I first heard the tape I was utterly amazed. Not simply the racy part of it, which was in itself very enlightening, but the degree of intimacy between them, the arrangements they made to meet in private and the secret addresses. . . . One of them used the word 'Bowood' – it meant nothing to me. And then we discovered it was a stately home of one of his friends.

Ken Lennox was given the task of identifying the houses that were mentioned in the tape and establishing whether Prince Charles had been there or not. Someone in the local post office was usually able to help. The phonetics experts confirmed that one voice on the tape was that of Prince Charles and, by recording her answerphone message, Arnold allowed him to identify the other voice as that of Camilla Parker Bowles. He also satisfied himself that the tape had a relatively innocent origin:

> There are a lot of myths about the origins of this tape – MI5 and MI6, all sorts of nonsense. In fact the truth is very, very simple. A radio ham who lived in Cheshire was twiddling with the scanner late one evening and he heard Charles's voice

> reading a speech. Charles used to read his speeches to Camilla for her approval. And she also used to collate them as a form of library. And he'd finished reading the speech to her when this man started recording with a very ordinary second-hand tape. That's why the conversation picks up in the middle of a sentence – he'd just switched it on. He was terrified at first. He thought that if anyone discovered that he'd secretly recorded the heir to the throne he'd be thrown in the Tower.

Having proved to his own satisfaction that the tape was genuine, Stott had to decide what to do next:

> And it was a considerable dilemma because what the *Sun* had done was to just run a whole tape, and my view was that this was such strong meat we couldn't possibly do that. It would've brought a Press Complaints Commission charge of invasion of privacy. Not because we were wrong to be pointing out that Diana had been right and that Charles had been lying, but because it was so shocking . . .

As Stott considered what to do, the royal couple were scheduled to go on a joint visit to Korea. They were barely on speaking terms and Diana did not want to go. Royal officials tried to talk her round. One of them told us, 'Diana said, "It's dishonest, such a sham, making a pretence," then she changed her mind – I thought of her own accord, but it was after she had spoken to the Queen. And not to go would have caused immense offence to the Koreans.'

But having gone, she sulked. In fact they both did. The press called them 'the Glums'. To support this headline some newspapers used a photograph of the couple wearing suitably solemn faces in order to lay a wreath, and then cut the wreath out of the picture. Royal photographer Jayne Fincher remembers it as a thoroughly depressing experience for everyone involved:

> They were visiting a temple and we wanted a picture of them walking down these temple steps together with the temple behind. And they actually both came down a separate staircase. So we had a picture of them, one there and one there. You couldn't get them together. I felt really sad one particular evening when I went to photograph her at the President's banquet. She arrived and she'd obviously been crying. Her eyes were red, she'd put a lot of make-up on her face to cover up her bags and her red, sore eyes. She stood there shaking all these hands and then she went and sat at the banquet table and this huge Union Jack was hanging on the wall behind her, which was very poignant really. She sat there with all her finery on and her tiara and she just stared at the tablecloth.

Photographed at the Cenotaph a few days after her return, Diana appeared to be isolated among the other royal women. Richard Stott decided that he would run the 'Camillagate' story soon.

On 13 November the Princess left for Paris on what Jephson considered her most successful solo trip. It included a forty-minute meeting with President Mitterrand, an honour never previously extended to a lone Princess of Wales. Diana was heartened by *Paris Match*'s cover with its Patrick Demarchelier photograph and 'Courage Princesse!' headline. She glowed in the rapturous attention and performed with flawless composure throughout.

The separation was finally precipitated by Diana's refusal to co-operate with Charles's plan to maintain a united front on the children's next weekend away from school. He had planned a weekend party at Sandringham for the family and sixteen of what Jonathan Dimbleby called 'their friends' ('they're all *his* friends', she complained). When Diana returned from Paris on 15 November she announced that she was not coming, she was taking the boys to Windsor Castle instead. 'Just think Patrick,

Nicholas Soames can eat all the food they'd bought for me,' she joked to her secretary. Charles said that he couldn't cancel his arrangements only days before the weekend. She refused to relent and took the children to Windsor. As it happened the castle proved an unfortunate destination that weekend. On Friday, 20 November fire swept through it. The Prince rushed from Sandringham to comfort his mother and then returned to complete the weekend with his friends.

The fire had started in the private chapel and then spread, causing damage estimated at between £20 and £40 million. The castle was uninsured. Heritage Secretary Peter Brooke's offer to pay the bill brought a storm of protest, supported by opinion polls. For the last two years of deep economic recession the issue of whether the Queen should pay tax had been simmering. Dissatisfaction with the monarchy was now reaching boiling point.

On 24 November, with Windsor Castle still smouldering, the Queen made an anniversary speech at the Guildhall. Instead of delivering the usual platitudes, she spoke about her own recent experience, her voice husky from a head cold exacerbated by time spent among the smoking ruins of her home. '1992 is not a year on which I shall look back with undiluted pleasure,' she said with dry understatement. 'In the words of one of my more sympathetic correspondents, it has turned out to be an *annus horribilis*.' She gave a first indication that things would have to change: 'No institution – City, Monarchy, whatever – should expect to be free from the scrutiny of those who give it their loyalty and support, not to mention those who don't.' On 26 November it was announced that the Queen and the Prince of Wales would pay tax on their private incomes from 1993, and that Civil List payments to five other members of the Royal Family would cease. 'The Queen Pays Tax and it's Victory for People Power,' boasted the *Sun*.

But the '*annus horribilis*' had not ended. Richard Aylard, 'wearing his most important expression', confronted Jephson to demand the name of the Princess's lawyers. On 25 November Prince Charles told Diana he wanted a separation. He removed his effects from Kensington Palace and she removed hers from Highgrove. She told Joseph Sanders that before she left Highgrove for ever she took the opportunity to throw some of her husband's clothes on a garden bonfire.

On 9 December, John Major announced the separation to the House of Commons. There was, he said, no question of a divorce, and in the event of Charles becoming King, Diana would be Queen.

The Queen's twin tormentors had still not finished with her. The Buckingham Palace press office was forced to announce that the Princess of Wales had decided not to spend Christmas with the Royal Family, and two days before it was due to be delivered the *Sun* published the leaked text of the Queen's upcoming Christmas broadcast to the nation.

Diana went skiing in America with Jenny Rivett. Rivett had been one of her personal trainers since 1991. And like Carolan Brown before her, she'd become a friend as well. In December 1992, Diana told Rivett that she was not looking forward to her first Christmas holiday as a separated wife.

> I felt sorry for her because she was dreading that time between Christmas and New Year when she was going to be on her own. And out of the blue I just suggested that we would go skiing together in Vail, Colorado, because I used to live there. I never expected in a million years that she would say, 'Well, I'd love to, Jenny.'

Rivett organised a fantastic holiday for Diana at the large, secluded home of a friend.

> She had a wonderful, wonderful time and I saw a different side completely. She was just totally relaxed and she said to me that

it had been one of the best holidays that she had been on. And I saw a side to her that was just so much fun.

I remember her shrieking up the mountain to me when I was skiing behind her. I just remember her saying, 'Jenny, Jenny,' and she was doubled over laughing at some lady who was skiing with her poles up in the air. She just found everything amusing.

[At night] we just stayed in and everybody mucked in with cooking and cleaning. It was just like going away with a group of friends.

I remember a certain guy who was trying to introduce himself to her and he had obviously prepared a speech in the mirror that morning. And she just looked at him, and before he could get his speech out she just became completely hysterical and laughed and looked at me and I started to laugh and she fell back in the snow and was just laughing so hard.

Diana at thirty-one, happy in the snow. It's an arresting image of the kind of life that could now have been her fate – wealthy friends, lots of time abroad, a low profile. But although she could have moved easily into this world, she told her friends that she had a different sense of her future. She still wanted to play a part in public life, and she wasn't going to hand over control of her children to the Royal Family.

13
What Men Are Like

In January 1993, Harry Arnold was finally writing up 'Camillagate', the scoop of his life. His first draft paragraph read: 'The heir to the throne has been conducting an adulterous affair with the wife of one of his closest friends before and during his marriage to the Princess of Wales.' Richard Stott swallowed hard and said, 'Try again, Harry.' After several long sessions with the lawyers, Arnold's fifth version of the story was published. It revealed a sleepy, funny and loving late-night conversation. Charles made self-mocking jokes, Camilla was supportive. They talked about his speech. They missed and wanted each other very badly. The sex talk was intense. The details of how they organised their meetings were embarrassing.

Despite all the denials that had followed Morton's book, the tape proved that Charles and Camilla had been lovers. Not, perhaps, throughout his marriage, but certainly by 1989. And given their obvious dependence on each other, many listeners assumed that the relationship was well established by this date.

The day after the story ran, Buckingham Palace was besieged by reporters. Charles Anson and Sir Robert Fellowes offered 'no comment'. Cartoonists had Charles talking dirty to his plants and Diana's legal team had solid evidence to support a cross-petition for adultery should they need one.

Camillagate reinforced Diana's image as the world's foremost female victim. In the battle for hearts and minds she was already doing especially well with women, as poll after poll attested. At the Chiswick Family Refuge in March she said to great applause, 'Well ladies! We all know what men are like, don't we?'

Writers such as Suzanne Moore and Camille Paglia praised her as a woman who refused to accept the roles and limitations set down for her by society. In June, as patron of Turning Point, a mental health charity for women, Diana announced to huge cheers that 'Sisters are doing it for themselves!' In the middle of a thoughtful speech, she said: 'It can take enormous courage for women to admit that they cannot cope . . . as their world closes in on them, their self-esteem evaporates into a haze of loneliness and desperation.' To warm applause, Libby Purves, chairing the meeting, claimed that Diana 'is one of us, a wife, a mother, a daughter, who has known problems in her own life and who has courageously used these experiences to comfort other people'.

Judy Wade watched and was impressed.

> She was courageous enough to stand up to the most powerful people in Britain, and give them a two-fingered salute. She said, 'I'm not going to be the quiet, long-suffering little wife and put up with what other royal wives have put up with for centuries.'
>
> And the whole mental health thing was so sexist anyway. Prince Charles had gone to psychiatrists and *he* was seen by the establishment as somebody who wisely sought help when he needed it. But Diana, when *she* talked about her depressions, she was called an hysteric, somebody that should be locked up. A lot of women have experienced that kind of double standard.

In February 1993 Anthony Holden had written a cover story for *Vanity Fair* entitled 'Di's Palace Coup'. 'There is a new bounce in her step, a cheekier smile on her face, a new gleam in those flirtatious blue eyes . . . at long last the sham is over.' Since falling out with the Prince, Holden had written extensively against him and had been attacked in turn by Charles's supporters. He soon discovered how grateful Diana was for his words:

I got a phone call from a friend saying, 'Be at San Lorenzo at 12.40 p.m. next Wednesday.' I met him and we noticed that the table next to us was the only one with flowers on it. At one o'clock in she came with the boys and a nanny and she saw us and said, 'Oh, what are you two doing here, why don't you join us?' And this was the beginning of a process that recurred quite a lot over the rest of her life. And the gist of it was that she was saying thank you to me for being supportive in what I'd written in *Vanity Fair*. And I have to say I thought, Well, this is some measure of the difference between them as human beings. Because for at least ten years I thought I was a better PR man for Prince Charles than the ones he actually paid – for most of the eighties in fact – and there wasn't the slightest note of thanks from him.

She was very funny, very smart, very good company. OK, she wasn't going to win the Nobel prize, she was not an intellectual, but she was very savvy about people, which I liked. Very candid, surprisingly candid – particularly about other members of the Royal Family to somebody that might quote this stuff in books or journalism. And there was an unspoken thing – she never said once, 'For God's sake don't print that!' She called Buckingham Palace the 'leper colony', and if you want to know what she thought about the Queen Mother, she called her the 'chief leper'.

If I was being manipulated, well, it was a very nice way to be manipulated, and so long as I was aware of it, I didn't see the harm.

Diana assiduously courted other influential writers and journalists. And so did friends of Prince Charles, including Camilla Parker Bowles, who maintained her own discreet line of communication with Stuart Higgins's *Sun*.

We had a very civilised relationship over the phone. We met a couple of times. And that was it, but she was a very good sounding-board for what was going on.

Camilla Parker Bowles never badmouthed the Princess. She was never openly critical of the Princess until very, very late on, and then not to me but to other people, and then it got fed back through a route that was obviously part of the damage limitation process for the Prince.

She really became almost like an unofficial adviser if you like, or an unofficial shield to all the gossip. But I would ask her about her own marriage, and I would talk to Andrew Parker Bowles about it. I'd say, 'Can you put the record straight about this?' – you know – 'We've heard rumours that you're going to break up.' 'Absolutely untrue, we will never divorce.'

But now I look back on it, everything that I said to Camilla must have gone back to the Palace or gone back to the Prince. I think she got more out of me than I ever got out of her.

Anthony Holden never got close enough to Diana to experience the drawbacks of friendship with her. Vivienne Parry, a friend for twelve years, recalls a pattern of difficulties that did not change with the separation:

There wasn't one friend that she hadn't fallen out with at one time or another and I think part of it was that she felt rather difficult in the company of people who were very close to her, particularly if they started to criticise. And what she didn't understand was that sometimes people criticise you because they love you, not because they don't.

For a time there would be a friend that was there all the time that she would ring at all hours of the day and night, and then suddenly that person would be dropped. And it would usually be because they had been truthful, or because Diana had tested their loyalty in some way and she felt that they had not lived up to her test. I don't know why she felt the need to do that, but she did do it and it harmed her. I saw her doing it and it broke my heart. There were countless people I knew

> who were friends of both Diana and myself, who would come weeping to me because Diana had dumped them.

Some of Diana's busier friends, like financial adviser Joseph Sanders, grew wary of getting too close:

> She thought I was looking after her, making her money, and she respected my opinions. So from time to time she asked me about things that were troubling her. But I didn't take it upon myself to ask her if there was anything troubling her, she would've been on the phone twenty-four hours a day. And she did have a lot of other people that she asked about things.

James Colthurst's wife complained at the number of late-night phone calls and Colthurst became irritated with Diana's angry reactions to constructive criticism, as he told Felix Lyle:

> It became too much for him. In the end there was a parting of the ways and a painful one. She turned on him. She had a little bit of a problem with loyalty. If you weren't a hundred per cent with her, you must be against her. She had that black-and-white way of looking at friendship and so James became ostracised, he became a sort of pariah. He said that she used to refer to him as 'that shit', which I think is a great shame and the end to a rather sad story.

Colthurst still counts himself one of Diana's strongest admirers, is proud of his role in her life and remains an angry critic of the Royal Family's behaviour towards her.

Meanwhile, Diana expanded her small army of alternative counsellors: psychic Rita Rogers, therapist Susie Orbach, colonic irrigator Chryssie Fitzgerald, acupuncturists Oonagh Toffolo and Lily Hua Yu, energy healer Simone Simmons, and fitness trainer Jenny Rivett to accompany Carolan Brown. On Brown's advice, she also engaged the actor Peter Setterlen to give her voice coaching and help write her speeches. Joseph Sanders, with some exaggeration, recalls that:

> I once went to a large drinks party she gave at Kensington Palace and there were seven hundred of us there and she was very good, she knew everybody on their first-name terms. She spoke to every single person there, and there were six hundred therapists out of the seven hundred.
>
> I don't think the therapists did her any good at all, except they took her mind off things. She used to keep one for two or three years and then fall out with them and get another one. And she had so many of them she couldn't have possibly seen them all, even once a year.

Diana's therapists and healers have similar stories to tell: Diana presented herself as a damaged and unhappy woman, there was an intense period during which she was highly dependent, then she said she was making progress (and there must be a dozen people in London who claim to have cured Diana's bulimia), then she lost interest. The next therapist down the line was greeted with the opening line of misery again.

Diana's bulimia came and went, triggered by arguments and stress. It's likely that she succumbed to it intermittently right up to her death, although she sought advice about it from many experts on eating disorders. Patrick Jephson was alarmed by the confusing variety of physical and emotional stimuli coming into Kensington Palace, and the contents of Diana's medicine cabinet, where Prozac and sleeping pills figured large.

There is even a question about how severe Diana's bulimia really was. Her personal beautician, Janet Filderman, accepts that Diana made herself sick at moments of stress, or after occasional 'comfort food' binges, but says that

> I don't think she had bulimia as I know it. I have two or three clients who really have been like that, and are like that, and believe me there is no comparison because Diana had a super

figure, wonderful teeth, good-quality hair, skin was good, eyes were bright. I don't think you can have any of those outward signs if you have bulimia badly.

If Diana's private life remained troubled, her public performances in 1993 were triumphant. One powerful new ally was the Minister for Overseas Development, Lynda Chalker. In March 1993, they went together to Nepal, where Diana was no longer greeted with the National Anthem but met the King and visited British aid projects.

She was trying to expand her schedule and further build up her international interests. Jephson recommended an increased involvement with the International Red Cross. Lynda Chalker was well placed to encourage this and to maintain a line of communication with the Prime Minister. In a series of private meetings, John Major was able to make his own judgment as to Diana's capabilities, and to decide whether, in Jephson's words, 'the anxious young woman he met . . . was the demonised inadequate portrayed by certain establishment sources'. She clearly was not.

The Prime Minister and his representatives in numerous foreign outposts had many reasons to thank the Princess for the goodwill she generated during these trips, on which she behaved with grace and intelligence throughout. Jephson, who cheerfully admitted his own fondness for first-class air travel, was frequently taken to one side by Britain's ambassadors and consuls and told that Diana's visit had swung a crucial contract or soothed a niggling dispute. All wanted her to come back in a hurry and several compared her favourably to other royals who had passed their way, news that Diana was always happy to receive. This was a princess in her prime, a gala princess fully meriting the 'R' word again, radiating empathy and goodwill and looking a thousand times healthier and happier than during her last tours with Charles.

Although 1993 was turning into a good year, back in London the court's response to the royal separation was predictably petty, driven by protocol and precedent. According to Vivienne Parry:

> The most ridiculous, demeaning and diminishing things were done to her. And silly things, like she was taken out of the Court Circular and her public engagements were not mentioned in an attempt to make people believe that she was less royal.

Diana planned a visit to British peace-keeping troops in Bosnia. The Palace blocked it because Charles was due to make a similar trip. She was told that an Irish visit was also out of the question. At times the two competed to play the part of national figurehead. Charles represented the Queen at the memorial service for the two children who died in the IRA's Warrington bomb attack. Diana was instructed not to go. But she made a typically personal contribution by calling and then visiting the grieving parents at their homes.

There may have been no more national anthems in Kathmandu, but Diana was far and away the most popular member of the Royal Family. There was a trip to the ballet in a minibus, an economy flight to the Caribbean, a visit to London's Trocadero Centre to play video games with her sons. Invariably the press attended – sometimes summoned by an image-conscious Princess, sometimes as the inevitable consequence of her own celebrity.

Royal Ascot brought Diana no invitation and so she drove the boys to Planet Hollywood and blew the Windsors off the front page. As her estranged relatives waved stiffly from a carriage, Diana looked royal in blue jeans. In August the Queen Mother's birthday party took place without the next Queen. With no invite to Clarence House, Diana went go-karting instead. 'First we cauterise, then we heal' had been the Windsors' approach to Wallis Simpson and King Edward VIII, who were ruthlessly frozen out in the years after he left the Royal Family.

It had worked in the 1940s and 1950s, but it wasn't working now.

Richard Aylard wanted to relaunch his Prince. He offered Jonathan Dimbleby eighteen months of what television producers like to call 'unprecedented access' to the royal household, to the royal archives and to Charles and his closest friends. The plan was to make a feature-length documentary accompanied by a heavyweight book, a truly authorised biography. The project was *not*, it was repeatedly stressed, a rejoinder to Andrew Morton. Instead it was presented as a serious and respectable celebration of Charles's twenty-fifth anniversary as Prince of Wales, due in 1994. Throughout 1993, as Diana stole headlines and bathed in the light of foreign flashbulbs, Dimbleby and his production team went about their work.

From the start, Dimbleby says, he had a royal injunction ringing in his ears.

> The one thing that the Prince implored me to do, the only thing, was that I should do nothing to hurt the Princess, whatever I might hear from those of his friends who might be indiscreet enough, despite his injunctions to them that they would cease to be friends if they spoke poorly of the Princess.

This can be taken at face value or with a pinch of scepticism. If Charles, or perhaps Charles's office, felt a need to counter-attack but did not wish to be seen to be doing so, this would have been a convenient disclaimer. Like Diana with Morton, Charles would need 'deniability', some distance between the intention and the act, so that later he could tell the world that he was not responsible for what was being said and written about the Princess.

What *was* written, in the opinion of its author, was fairly harmless.

> My book and my film contain not a single word of criticism by the Prince of the Princess. No single word of criticism from any of the friends. Everything about the Princess that I have published was recorded – as we now know – with her approval, by others, beforehand.

We know that Dimbleby cut out a lot of very damaging material, and dropped his Borderline Personality Disorder chapter altogether. And yet his book did contain hurtful stories – like her alleged resentment of the public interest in the Falklands War at her expense – that had not appeared in Morton.

Penny Junor was familiar with the background to Dimbleby's book because, for a while, *she* was going to write it. She was set aside because St James's Palace thought she was tainted by her previous public support for the Prince. Despite her irritation at this, Junor believes that when the project started Charles genuinely did not want to hurt his wife.

> It was the friends and I think they went rather farther than the Prince might have liked. When he [Dimbleby] was first told about the way Diana behaved I think he did think, I'm being told this by friends of the Prince. This marriage has broken down and is just one lot slagging off the other side. . . . But he did, I think, eventually come to believe what he was hearing.

It's possible that naïvety was the problem. That's what Max Hastings believes.

> I remember when I was first told about the Dimbleby project, right back in the beginning, and I was asked what I thought about it privately by one or two of the Palace people, and I said, 'This is absolute madness. There's only one thing anybody's going to want to hear about and that's the marriage. And the consequences will be disastrous.'
>
> And I remember one of the Prince of Wales's closest aides saying, 'But we've got to do something.' And I said, 'But this is the fundamental huge mistake at the heart of your thinking

> – that this is a sort of public war which can be waged by public relations means.'

Just before Dimbleby finished his book, Patrick Jephson arranged for the author to meet Diana.

> My intention . . . was to confront him with the reality of what she was like so that he could compare it dispassionately with what he had been told by sources close to the Prince. This, I mischievously hoped, might at least pull a brick from the foundations of the edifice created for his benefit.

Diana was on top form: informal, considerate and friendly – although the author did look uncomfortable for a second when she said, 'Oh well, I suppose it's *your* turn to be his guardian angel now.' As they left Kensington Palace, Jephson artlessly asked Dimbleby whether his views had changed. To Jephson, the distinguished broadcaster, veteran of a hundred bruising political interviews, appeared dazed. Jephson alleges that Dimbleby said to him, 'If I can't believe what I have been told about her . . . then I can't believe any of it.'

Jonathan Dimbleby will not respond to Jephson's story about the lunch 'as – unlike him, apparently – I propose to honour the terms which he set for my conversation with the Princess – that it should be conducted on a confidential basis'.

While Dimbleby continued to write, Jephson successfully managed Diana through more of the best moments of her career. In July 1993 she visited Zimbabwe and was extremely professional during a demanding and stressful trip. She charmed the notoriously anti-British President Robert Mugabe and she met five-year-old AIDS sufferers with only months to live. She attended other African projects run by Help the Aged and the Leprosy Mission. On this tour Jephson was delighted to find that Diana was now getting favourable coverage from Max Hastings's traditionally royalist *Daily Telegraph*. Hastings's high-minded boycott of royal marriage stories had softened when he heard that Dimbleby's book, like Morton's, was being offered to his great rival the *Sunday Times*.

> When one found that both the Prince and Princess of Wales were willing to flog enormously valuable commercial properties to the Murdoch press then you feel 'What's the point?' [of helping them out] . . . if it's a commercial game now, then everyone's out for themselves.

Diana took the boys to Disney World, Florida for a summer holiday. She was almost invited to present the BBC's prestigious Dimbleby Lecture, named after Jonathan's father Richard. She attended the Hollingsworth Dinner at Spencer House, where for the first time she met Henry Kissinger. She visited Luxembourg and met Jacques Santer, soon to be President of the European Union. She had tea with Queen Fabiola of Belgium. She opened the new library at Emmanuel College, Cambridge. On 14 November she attended the Remembrance Day service at Enniskillen in Northern Ireland, where, in 1987, an IRA bomb had killed eleven people. Jephson and his solo Princess roadshow were successfully infiltrating the diplomatic and establishment worlds in which he felt she could make the most positive contributions, despite her separation from the Prince and in spite of St James's Palace.

Then, just when everything was going so well, Diana's equilibrium was disturbed by a nasty privacy scandal. In November 1993 the *Daily Mirror* published candid photographs of the Princess exercising wearing a leotard. She was still seeing Carolan Brown, and now used the LA Fitness Centre in Isleworth, where the fitness trainer worked.

> We never dreamed that he [gym owner Bryce Taylor] would plant a camera in the ceiling. And I felt a little bit responsible

On holiday at Lech, Austria, March 1994

A few days later Diana shows her anger towards photographers, March 1994

'Why don't you put your head up and start acting like a fucking Princess?': avoiding photographers, July 1994

Diana passes Glenn Harvey;
Mark Saunders makes way
as Glenn Harvey 'whacks' her;
Diana breaks down as
Mark Saunders waits for
her to turn

"You filthy pervert! I'll call the police – Oh! sorry Charles I didn't realise it was you."

Two hundred years of royal satire: the *People* newspaper, 1993, and *His Highness in Fitz* showing George, Prince of Wales with Maria Fitzherbert, 1786

HIS HIGHNESS IN FITZ

Lord Palumbo meets Diana outside the Serpentine Gallery on 29 June 1994, the night Charles admitted his affair with Camilla during a televised interview with Jonathan Dimbleby

PRIVATE EYE

No. 886
Friday
1 Dec. 1995

£1

DIANA: QUEEN RESPONDS

I don't think a divorce will be necessary

PRIVATE DI
IT'S A CROWDED MAGAZINE

Following Diana's *Panorama* interview, broadcast on 20 November 1995, *Private Eye* commented on the troubled royal marriage

Diana leaves the English National Ballet on the day of her divorce, 28 August 1996

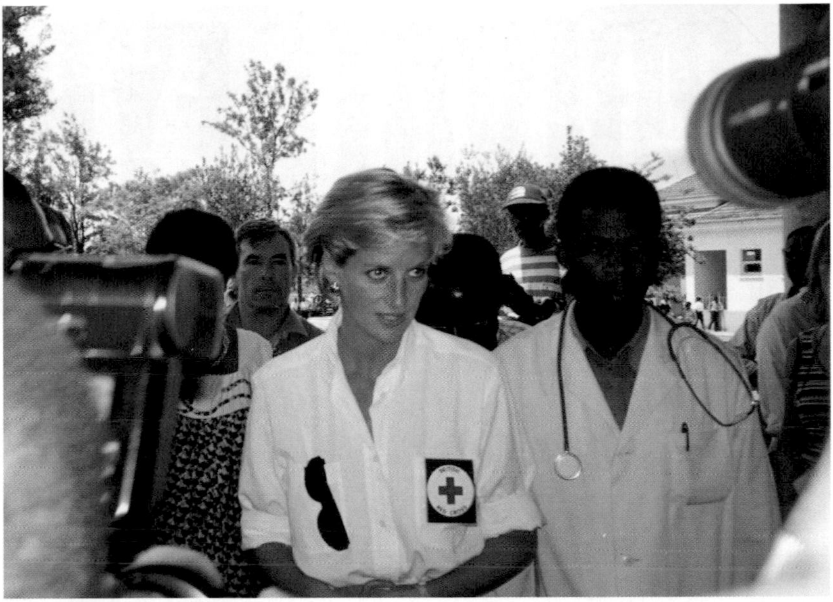

War reporter Christina Lamb's snap of Diana at a hospital for landmine victims at Huambo, Angola, January 1997

The sea of floral tributes outside Kensington Palace, September 1997

No. 932
Friday
5 Sept. '97

PRIVATE EYE

£1

MEDIA TO BLAME

The cover of *Private Eye* that led to the magazine receiving a record number of complaints

> because I was the one that had suggested that we trained there. The picture really upset her, she was disgusted. She said to me, 'I feel as if he's raped me through a camera.'

The photographs were sold for over £100,000 to a *Mirror* no longer edited by Richard Stott. The paper published them, claiming as a thin excuse that they exposed a terrible lapse in royal security. Diana's long-serving, loyal and supportive detective, Ken Wharfe, James Hewitt's old poker-playing chum, had already left her service. No one detected a cunningly concealed camera that was put in place after the initial security sweep.

Every other tabloid paper poured scorn on the *Mirror*, and the Press Complaints Commission thundered its condemnation. Diana decided to take the paper to court. More immediately she decided she had had enough of this sort of thing and was going to withdraw from public life. Let the tabloids see how they managed without her. 'For some months,' Jephson writes, 'the Princess had been musing aloud about her wish to find a quieter life.' He had evidently been struggling to keep this wish suppressed. Now he had to explain to the allies he had gathered around him that the Princess needed a break. For Mike Whitlam from the Red Cross:

> It came as a bit of a shock when I had a phone call from her private secretary to say could we just talk about some concerns he had. And then the issue of her pulling out of public life came up. I hadn't any inkling that this was even on the agenda. So we talked briefly about it and then I talked with the Princess about what might be involved. My concern was here was someone who had a very active involvement in a number of charities who was thinking of doing something quite extreme that would perhaps harm her and the charities about which she was so concerned.

The phone call took place three weeks before Diana was due to give a speech to a conference for Headway, the spinal injuries organisation. Jephson was worried that Diana would not let him see the text. He did not get his hands on it until a few days before she was due to deliver it. Believing that whatever she said she would not retire from public life for long, Jephson secretly briefed the Queen and 10 Downing Street to this effect. As soon as he could, he showed the Queen's office the speech. They were alarmed, believing that the Royal Family would be blamed again. At the last minute Jephson and the Queen's deputy press secretary, Geoffrey Crawford, persuaded Diana to change the text 'to excise the more histrionic references to a self-imposed and irreversible exile'. Nevertheless, all involved knew that the speech was going to cause another huge row.

On 3 December 1993, at the end of a year of consistent success, Diana bade her public farewell.

> I hope you can find it in your hearts to understand and to give me the time and space that has been lacking in recent years . . . When I started my public life twelve years ago I understood that the media might be interested in what I did. I realised then that their attention would inevitably focus on . . . our private lives . . . But I was not aware of how overwhelming that attention would become; nor the extent to which it would affect both my public duties and my personal life in a manner that's been hard to bear.

Most of the charities had received no warning and were shocked at the loss of their patron. Some of the *Mirror*'s rivals blamed the gym photos, but most accused the Prince and the Palace of driving her out. Diana's decision to declare her retirement on a public stage was directed primarily against the tabloid media. But the conclusion the Palace had jumped to was partly correct as well. Diana herself briefed the *Daily Mail*, which declared 'Charles Drove Her To It'. Even the sober *Times* demanded to know 'Did Diana Go or Was She Pushed?'

Diana was handed her diary sheets for the following year. They were blank.

The faction fighting was getting ever nastier. Lord Palumbo had once been able to describe himself as a good friend of both the Prince and the Princess, but not any more.

> You were either in one camp or you were in the other. You couldn't really be in both. I can think of very few examples of those who were in both. And the tendency clearly was to drive the two people at the very centre of the drama apart . . . And the warfare is total, in such circumstances. The warfare is very nasty and very deep and very bitter.
>
> 'The Princess was unbalanced', 'the Princess was this', 'the Princess was that', 'she was unstable', she was so on and so forth. And similarly damaging things [were being said] about the Prince of Wales and his relationship with Camilla Parker Bowles.
>
> And all these things should have remained private if humanly possible, but it was not possible because things get out of hand. Once those lorries start to roll downhill without any brakes there's no stopping them.
>
> The Princess talked to me on occasion about what might have been. And that prompted me to feel, perhaps wrongly, that there was some hope . . . maybe it was not too late to find some sort of formula. But the two camps had become so entrenched and so deeply divided and the feelings so bitter . . . the constant sniping and the press briefing . . . that it was not possible to find any common ground.

On 29 June 1994, fourteen million British television viewers watched Jonathan Dimbleby's documentary about Prince Charles. On it he admitted to adultery, after 'it [the marriage] became irretrievably broken down'. Next day Richard Aylard confirmed in a press conference that Camilla Parker Bowles had been the woman involved. The immediate tabloid reaction was very hostile. 'Not Fit to Reign,' the *Mirror* proclaimed, supporting its headline with the results of a poll taken in the immediate aftermath of the broadcast. 'So Cruel and So Selfish: That's your verdict on the Prince,' it announced. In its enthusiasm the *Mirror* was somewhat cavalier with its own poll results. In fact a relatively modest 32 per cent of those polled had said Charles was unfit to reign and 46 per cent that Diana should divorce him for his adultery; 55 per cent said that his confession made no difference to the monarchy, 54 per cent that he was right to admit to the affair, and 61 per cent that he was fit to be King. Nevertheless, the loyal monarchism of the British people was wavering.

And the tabloids had made their minds up. Both the *Mirror* and its arch-rival the *Sun* were on the side of the elegant woman in the black dress pictured down the side of their front pages. 'Revenge is Chic,' commented the *Sun*.

On the night of the Dimbleby broadcast Diana had made one of her now rare public appearances, wearing a bejewelled black dress designed by Christina Stambolian to a *Vanity Fair* party at London's Serpentine Gallery, escorted by Lord Palumbo.

Vanity Fair had a strange attitude towards Diana. It couldn't print enough photographs of her, especially when she bestowed what the magazine called her 'gala charm' on American high society. Yet the magazine's star cultural columnist was Christopher Hitchens, still Diana's number-one public critic. Editor Graydon Carter was Diana's host for the evening ahead.

> She showed up and she looked fabulous and I don't think anybody knew what Charles was going to say on TV that night – at least I didn't. And it was a very nice night and if she felt any signs of distress or betrayal, she didn't show it.

Soon it was Hitchens's turn to be introduced.

She looked terrific – she was drop-dead gorgeous, in a beautifully cut dress and very daring. But it occurred to me that what she was thinking was, If I do this right, my ghastly hubby's interview with Jonathan Dimbleby will not be on page one tomorrow and instead it will be 'Di Knocks 'em Dead at Serpentine Bash' . . .

And I thought I'll have to wing it, so I said, 'It's delightful to meet you, we republicans must stick together,' and she laughed prettily. The men around her sort of reared back and whinnied and snorted a bit, and there was a bit of 'I say, what d'you mean by that?' And I said, 'Well, she's done rather more to subvert the monarchy by accident than I have been able to accomplish on purpose' . . . she seemed to get the joke.

14
Not Easy Being Me

'What is a Princess for? A Princess is for looking at.' Jayne Fincher remembers the good days.

> Whenever we went on a trip we'd always have a cocktail party with her. She loved getting together with us. She wanted to know who was getting married to who, who was having an affair with who, who'd got a new car, who had a new suit or a new haircut. She knew everybody's nicknames. She loved it. The first thing she'd say when she came in was, 'What's the latest gossip?'

By the winter of 1993/4 the relationship was very different. As a newly single woman, Diana was determined to lead as normal a life as possible. But press attention grew ever more intense, and the woman who had courted the media grew increasingly to hate and fear it, or at least the part of it that pursued her through the streets of London. She had freed herself from her protection team. The police were uncertain what to do, and maintained a group of four officers for her to use if she wanted. She rarely did.

London's freelance photographers could not believe their luck when Diana started to walk the streets without police protection. In November 1993 Glenn Harvey was staking out her colonic irrigation clinic in Beauchamp Place when Diana came out alone. He ambushed her from a shop doorway, got his photos, and rang the *Sun*. Ken Lennox, new boss of the picture desk, was intrigued to find that the rumours that Diana had dropped her police protection were true. Harvey's partner, Mark Saunders, recalls the ensuing frenzy:

> It then became common knowledge, and there was just a tremendous excitement among the paparazzi based in London, who kind of thought, Well, this is not gonna last. And so it was approached in the same way that now, if Jack Nicholson's in town for a week or if Brad Pitt is in town for a week, the paparazzi get excited and they'll do that person for a whole week. And that was the initial approach – that was how it was done. How long are we gonna get this for? Probably a week, maybe two, and then obviously common sense is going to prevail and she'll have to have protection.
>
> If there had been police protection for the Princess, whenever she came out of one of these restaurants they would come out first and they would say, 'There's the line, don't cross it.' And you wouldn't have crossed it. It's in your interests not to.

A bad tempered game began. Diana would be out shopping or on her way back from the gym. Men with cameras and mobile phones would appear. She might stop and pose or she might cover her face and run. The photographers would chase after her 'like puppies after something that moves', says Ken Lennox. 'The older heads would have said, "Oh my God," and drawn in; the younger ones just ran, still trying to take pictures.' There were no reassuringly bulky detectives around to say, 'Stand back, boys, that's enough,' or 'You don't want me to step on that fancy camera by accident now, do you, mate?'

Fincher had been photographing Diana for thirteen years. She was horrified by the behaviour of the new breed of self-styled 'paps' that now dogged her.

> They would be right up close in front, so that she couldn't walk one step, so she's got to keep dodging. It's physically oppressive. It would be like being hunted in a pack. And they would be verbally aggressive to her, they would say, 'Take your clothes off because we need to earn some money.' They'd use foul language at her and be completely abusive and horrible.

Judy Wade witnessed similar scenes.

And they used language that was aggressive – they'd say, 'I've whacked her,' meaning I've done a picture of her; or 'I've hosed her up and down,' that meant doing a full-length picture; and 'I've blitzed her' – that was, you know, firing off the flashgun at her non-stop.

Mark Saunders explains the terminology of his trade:

To take pictures rapidly – whether you are taking pictures of a starving baby in Somalia or the Princess of Wales in Beauchamp Place – in our business to take pictures rapidly is to 'blitz', to 'hose', to 'whack', to 'hit' . . . I mean it does sound aggressive when you read it – I was banging, blitzing, hosing – yeah, it can read quite bad, but it wasn't done like that.

Speed was ever more important as photographers raced to be first to get a shot to the picture desks. Market forces were at work. Diana's empty official diary had reduced the supply, and so raised the price, of her photograph. Moreover, the shots that they now got of Diana using a parking meter or getting a parking ticket were more interesting to the tabloids than shots of her opening a school or launching a ship. For Mark Saunders it was a bonanza that he was constantly expecting to come to an abrupt end.

But it didn't. It just went on and on. You'd have Princess Diana in a newsagent's, Princess Diana in a restaurant, Princess Diana parking her car, Princess Diana at the Chelsea Harbour Club, it was just snowballing all the time. The prices of the pictures were going through the roof. So suddenly sitting on Princess Diana's tail for twenty-four hours a day, seven days a week, became very much worth it. And they weren't doing it with any bad attitudes, they were doing it purely because the chance had arrived for them to make a lot of money from a person who was becoming more famous than ever.

A routine set of Princess Diana shopping, looking at some gowns, possibly buying a gown, coming out with the gown

> packaged? Maybe fifteen hundred pounds, maybe two thousand. Swimming-costume stuff was picking up ten thousand, ten thousand pounds for a set of pictures, and then remember you would be selling that abroad as well, so you'd be picking up money on the foreign rights. As a rule of thumb a good internationally selling picture should make three times as much money abroad as it does in London.

By the early 1990s the same products were selling in every market, and the same stories were playing on every one of the new cable and satellite television channels. It was called 'globalisation'. But universal sales were only possible where everyone was interested in the same subject, and so the range of news contracted to a small number of widely appreciated topics. International celebrities were ever more a staple, and Diana was the princess of international celebrities, one of a very select few whose photograph was valuable almost everywhere. As Mark Saunders' accountant was to discover.

> I look at my sales reports sometimes from those days and there are some countries there I didn't even know existed – I think they probably grew out of Russia or something like that. It wasn't an amazing amount of money in that everybody was making millions and millions of dollars, but the people that were making money were making enough money to earn a good living. And it was also a good lifestyle.
>
> Most of Fleet Street was making it quite clear to the paparazzi that they did not want the paparazzi pursuing the Princess of Wales, but if the paparazzi were insisting on pursuing the Princess of Wales, they certainly would be prepared to buy the pictures that they did not want taken.

The lure was difficult to resist. The *Sun*'s sale might jump by 60,000 copies on even a minor Diana story. The editors of *Hello!* found that Diana on the cover would increase sales by 10 per cent. A compromising photograph was an enormous temptation.

In May 1994 Eduardo Junco, proprietor of *Hello!*'s Spanish parent *Hola!*, phoned Jephson to tell him that a paparazzo had a photo of the Princess adjusting her bikini while on holiday in Malaga. At Jephson's request the chivalrous proprietor bought the offending picture and suppressed it.

Diana's reaction to the attention of the paparazzi could be unpredictable. Sometimes she would be friendly and smile for their cameras. More often she was frowning. This puzzled them:

> What have we done wrong? What are we doing today that we weren't doing yesterday? You could never understand it until you read the press reports and then you would see either that picture was taken to negate some bad publicity that was coming in from another angle, or else there would have been a lovely picture of Camilla Parker Bowles in the paper the day before which Diana would hate.

Such observations made them cynical and reduced their sympathy for her when she was distressed or angry. Mark Saunders, who followed her for months, confirms that 'the stuff about Diana making secret trips to see sick children and stuff like that – it's not a myth, it's actually true. She really did things like that.' The photographers were impressed by such occasional 'private' mercy missions but noted that they invariably appeared, with accompanying photographs, under Richard Kay's name in the *Daily Mail*. Jephson recognised whole sentences in Kay's articles as phrases of Diana's. Finally, in June 1994, photographs were printed of Diana's clandestine conversations with the reporter in her car.

When confronted, Diana developed an unnerving habit of challenging her pursuers to justify themselves. As Mark Saunders recalls:

> When Brad Pitt, Christian Slater, Princess Di, Madonna says, 'Can you not take my photograph,' you just ignore it because

you expect that. They make their complaint and then they go. But she wouldn't go. So then there would be . . . a kind of embarrassing silence and then she would say something, 'Why does this have to go on all the time?' . . . How do you answer a question like that? When the most famous woman in the world, a woman who is never, ever out of papers, says to you, 'Why do you have to keep photographing me?'

And then she would say, 'It's not easy being me,' and you would say, 'Yes, of course, I understand.' Well, you wouldn't understand! Why would I understand what it's like to be the Princess of Wales?

I always got the feeling that she wanted to talk, but not necessarily about being photographed or being upset by being photographed. And it's not just me that had this feeling, the other paparazzi she would talk to always said the same thing. God knows why someone didn't just say, 'Why don't we go and have a cup of tea and try and sort this out?' Because maybe, just maybe it might've worked.

This unpredictable atmosphere around Diana gave rise to an 'in-joke'.

When you asked, 'Where is the Princess?' somebody would say, 'She's in Kensington' and as an in-joke you would say, 'Is it a loony lunch?' which would mean 'What's the situation? Is it all clear today or is she in a bad mood?' And if the answer was 'Yeah, it's loony tunes,' that meant keep a low profile.

And obviously 'loony tunes', 'loony time', 'loony trip' evolved [into] 'the loon' in reference to her, and from that became the verb to 'loon' – I loon, you loon. To 'loon' means to shout and scream at someone and tell them to go away, basically. So it became a verb. But it's not – we always say it was a term of endearment, and everybody laughs at that and says, 'How, how on earth could it be?' It was genuinely a term of endearment, a laugh, an in-joke.

There was a demand for pictures of Diana angry or in tears, and so she would be provoked. She said they tried to trip her, and shouted obscenities looking for a reaction – 'You're the fucking Princess of Wales, stop carrying on like a fucking tart'; 'You're a real fucking loon, aren't you?' Mark Saunders does not remember the provocation being quite that bad:

> I don't think I could really say that we acted respectfully or diplomatically and gave her a status greater than any other celebrity we were photographing, because it's kind of hard to think of using the right knife and fork when you are operating a camera. And it would be a lie for me to say we were always polite. I mean, certainly we weren't rude, but you could say we were being rude by virtue of the fact that we were there.
>
> I remember once where she got into a taxi and put her head down between her legs. And there were . . . members of the paparazzi all around the taxi. She put her head right down between her legs and put her hands over her head, and one of the Spanish photographers said, 'Why don't you put your head up and start acting like a fucking Princess?' And she shot up. And she just looked as stunned as any woman would be who had been so insulted. And I thought, don't look on this as if you're not involved because you are involved. I myself as a photographer was there, was part of that. And that's certainly not something I would look back on with any sort of pride.

One day a passer-by with a home video camera filmed Diana trapped by a crowd of photographers in a London street. Her arms were wrapped around her face and she was whimpering like a wounded animal.

After a few months Jephson persuaded Princess Diana to slip back into what he considered real work. Through Mike Whitlam she was induced to become a British board member of the advisory committee of the Red Cross Federation and the International Committee of the Red Cross. She attended some meetings in Geneva during the summer of 1994, but as the serious meetings got under way Jephson 'watched my boss's eyes glaze over' and she quit in September. Even the Palace occasionally extended an olive branch. She was invited to join the celebrations of the fiftieth anniversary of D-day and accepted enthusiastically. Less pleasant was the leaking – widely blamed on sources in Prince Charles's office – of Diana's yearly grooming bill, £160,000 worth of dresses, make-up, haircuts, facials and massages.

Diana could still be great company – warm, gossipy and mischievous. Kensington Palace would echo with laughter and chatter, as if its mistress was back in Colherne Court, a carefree single girl again.

Vivienne Parry frequently saw Diana in this mood.

> Diana was like a light. I knew Diana for a very long time and I remained loyal to her. She could be difficult, she could be awkward, but you always, always forgave her. She earned your loyalty a hundred times over. And, on good form, she was the most sparkling and energetic person you're ever likely to meet.

But the friends who shared the chatty lunches and the animated evenings could find Diana on the phone to them, later that same night, in sudden distress at some real or imagined slight. For much of her marriage Diana had been fragile like this. In the 1980s she had often dreamed of independence, of having her life back again. But freedom wasn't making her better. The buffeting she received from the press, the reports she received of high-society gossip, the leaks against her from 'the enemy camp': they all made her needy and dependent.

Joseph Sanders, on good terms with several newspaper

proprietors, received his share of late-night calls, and early-morning ones too:

> I think she was a permanent little girl lost. She'd keep phoning up from seven o'clock in the morning and she used to read all the papers. So if there was anything in them that she didn't like, that she was dating a man, or there was a photograph she didn't like, she used to phone up and say, 'Joseph, why have they written this about me?'

Another recipient of calls was AIDS clinician Mike Adler:

> There were a number of us who recognised that we could become close friends, that she could pull us in. And I know three or four of my friends took a very conscious decision, as I did, that we were not going to be pulled into a sort of inner circle where we would be called up at four o'clock in the morning.

One source of anxiety was James Hewitt. The affair had again been extinguished, but Diana was fearful that he might talk. The press carried much speculation but as yet had never been able to print the truth. Since returning from the Gulf, Hewitt had been under incessant pressure. Cheques for hundreds of thousands of pounds had been waved in front of him. He had been told that there were compromising tapes in newspaper safes and that the whole story was about to break at any moment.

Despite being mentioned in dispatches for his conduct in battle, Hewitt had seen his military career collapse. He was trailed and taped and photographed wherever he went. And he was cut off from Diana.

> I still hadn't said anything at all. I wouldn't return any calls from the papers. The hacks and the paparazzi were using extraordinary tactics in order to try and glean more information . . .

And I had to try and handle the situation as best I could. I had no professional advice or agent.

I didn't know what tape recordings or pictures were in existence and I was bribed and blackmailed into meeting these people. Which is a ghastly thing.

From time to time he would speak to Diana on the telephone, asking her how to react to the latest approach from journalists. She encouraged him to give a misleading version of his story in the hope of throwing the other royal reporters off the scent. He decided to meet a journalist from the *Daily Express* called Anna Pasternak.

We had to find out how much they knew. It was suggested, I mean by Diana, that I put my side of the story, which was to be a sort of an anodyne account of the situation, to a newspaper, which was the *Express*, I think. And I tried to do that and it didn't work.

Some of Diana's friends recall that she asked Hewitt to speak to Richard Kay rather than Pasternak, but that he did not favour the *Daily Mail* reporter. Hewitt's denials to the *Express* were ridiculed by the other tabloids.

Pasternak learned more than perhaps was healthy. I was persuaded that it would be a good idea if I gave Pasternak a certain amount of information because she would then put the situation a little more favourably than it had up until that moment been put in the press. I was coming under a lot of attack and criticism, unnecessarily so.

People have all sorts of ideas on what you should be paid for and what you shouldn't be paid for . . . but I really do regret getting involved in the media, full stop. But, you know, they know their business and they're good at it. And I didn't know the business and I was hopeless. And that is my biggest crime. And I've had to live with that.

In early August Diana went on holiday to America with her friend Lucia Flecha da Lima. There she learned that Hewitt had told their whole story to Pasternak, who was writing it up in a hurry for a book that would come out in October, the same month that Dimbleby's was expected and just in time for the Christmas market.

Diana's turmoil that summer owed much to a more recent relationship that was rapidly going wrong. Throughout much of 1993 and 1994, Diana had been seeing a married art dealer called Oliver Hoare. One of the reasons she had dispensed with her protection officers was she that wanted to conduct her private life without detectives following her everywhere.

Diana made several hundred telephone calls to his home. Sometimes the line went dead when Hoare's wife, Diane, answered. Mrs Hoare called the police. They quickly traced the calls to private numbers inside Kensington Palace and to phone boxes nearby. Oliver Hoare asked Scotland Yard to drop their investigation. But in August 1994 someone leaked the story to the *News of the World*. Under the headline 'Di's Cranky Phone Calls To Married Tycoon', the paper printed the story in detail, including the results of the initial police investigation. To Richard Kay, Diana admitted making some of the calls, but said she was not responsible for the majority of them. Several of her friends knew better. Joseph Sanders got an admission direct from a very fearful Diana:

> Diana told me that she made probably three or four hundred telephone calls to Oliver Hoare. She made them from phone boxes from different addresses. She wore disguises to go to the phone boxes, she wore gloves and she really covered her tracks. But she did make the phone calls. If he didn't answer the phone she normally put the phone down. And she was really very worried about it . . . She was actually worried that she might be arrested and charged with making nuisance calls.

> I shouted at her and I said, 'You know, you're a very silly girl to behave like this, you really shouldn't do it, and you shouldn't think that you can get away with it.' And that evening I thought about it and I thought maybe I'd been a bit cruel to her. So the next day I saw her and I apologised. I said, 'I'm sorry, Diana, maybe I was a little harsh on you.' She said, 'Oh, don't worry, the Palace are shouting at me the whole time.'

Diana assumed that St James's Palace had leaked the story to bring her down. She may have been right. However, policemen have long handed stories like this to newspapers without any encouragement.

The *Daily Mail* printed Diana's plaintive response: 'What have I done to deserve this? . . . I feel I am being destroyed,' but it made little difference. She was faced with a barrage of bad publicity, all of which she read and reread, brooding over the unfairness of it all.

Elsa Bowker was close to Diana at this time, and a conduit between her and Oliver Hoare. Before Bowker died in 2000 she gave us a dramatic portrait of Diana's friendship with him, suggesting that when anxious or upset Diana wanted the comfort of hearing Hoare's voice, and, in need of his approval, became fixated with the idea of speaking to him.

Free speech and liberty! The British have long laid proud claim to their right to discuss whatever or whoever they like, in whatever terms they like. When Britain acquired a German royal family in the eighteenth century, Germans became very interested in British culture, and especially this notion of free speech. In 1804 a journalist from Hanover was shocked to discover that the Englishman:

> talks about his King, his Princes and Princesses just as he might talk about the lowest of his fellow countrymen . . . The private affairs of the royal household are discussed with no regard for

majesty, just as one might discuss how well or badly a valet runs a household. If a man's actions expose him to the mercy of the public, it doesn't matter whether he is an Esquire or a Lord; he must put up with being discussed in detail and criticised by everyone who has heard the whisper of Rumour's hundred tongues. One is most aware of this shameless freedom in the English literary lampoons and caricatures which are published in such numbers . . .

Saturday night in the West End of London. Groups of young people hurry down Oxford Street or Piccadilly to the Tube, across the Strand to Charing Cross and the last train back to suburbia. The Sunday papers are on sale from roadside trestle tables. 'Oh, go on, get the *News of the Screws* as well. We want all the goss.'

The cheerful cruelty of the British tabloid press grew from deep roots. Before 1800 unsteady late-night promenaders would have walked these same streets, hurrying home on foot, by chair or coach or river-boat, past Holland's caricature print shop, or Fores' or Darly's. By day, to the horror of respectable visitors from Hanover, crowds of ordinary folk would gather round these windows, all laughing like drones at pictures of princes or prime ministers. At Fores' print shop in Piccadilly they might have marvelled at a picture of the Prince of Wales having sex with his mistress, Maria Fitzherbert, a Catholic widow six years his senior – *His Highness in Fitz*, ha! ha! ha!; at Darly's there was no mistaking the crude innuendo of *The Scotch Broomstick and the Female Besom*, in which the young Queen Mother holds the bushy head of her besom, protruding from between her thighs, ready to receive the end of the Earl of Bute's broomstick. 'Come lassie, let's make the most of the game for I am strong in hand & we are above the vulgar,' exclaims the Scottish favourite.

Camillagate and Squidgygate: they were tame compared to the print and pamphlet mockery of the sex scandals of the Georgian courts. George, Prince of Wales, the later Prince Regent, actually married Mrs Fitzherbert and then denied that it had happened. With him and his brothers (and uncles and forebears) one shocking affair whetted the appetite for another until the Prince's own career culminated in an orgy of scandal when he barred his estranged Queen, Caroline, from his coronation. If Charles and Diana had done every scandalous thing that rumour imagined they might have done, they could not remotely have matched the children of George III. The Georgian public loved their glimpses of the caricatured hedonism and debauchery that was supposed to go on behind aristocratic screens. And in the 1990s the public reaction was very similar. A voracious appetite for sex stories about the royals had developed. People expected to see ever more lurid and partisan accounts of their lives delivered up for their entertainment. Just the thing to make the train ride home pass a little quicker.

After a lousy summer, 1994 got even worse. The phone pest story was hard evidence of the kind of abnormal behaviour that her husband's friends had been telling Jonathan Dimbleby about. Right on cue, Dimbleby's book came out, accompanied by a much-advertised serialisation in the *Sunday Times*. The next blow was *Princess in Love*, the book written by journalist Anna Pasternak, based on her interviews with James Hewitt.

A year before Diana had seemed serene and unassailable. Now every bookstore and newspaper was full of stories of her adultery, her mental instability and her bizarre relationship with Oliver Hoare.

Hewitt's tempters became his tormentors. The same men who had spent three years trying to get him to speak now turned on him for doing so, giving him his first taste of headlines like 'Britain's Biggest Bounder' and 'Love Rat and Cad', while at the same time publishing lengthy extracts from Pasternak's book. The *Sun*'s 'Eight-Page Special on the Book that Betrayed Diana' revealed 'They Did It at Althorp', 'They Did It in the Bathroom' and 'She Begged to Do It on Dartmoor'.

Hewitt soon became one of the tabloids' favourite caricatures, a heartless ladies' man in uniform who seduced a vulnerable young princess; a scoundrel who kissed and told. It was a parody of the true history of their relationship – and especially its early years – but it was widely believed.

> People do *not* know the history of events. What has been suggested in the press is not the truth [and] in many instances it's a lie. I did not kiss and tell. That is a fallacy. Yes, I was paid for an interview. I regret that very much. The fact that I did it at all I regret and it was a mistake. And I'm sorry, very, very, very sorry, for that.
>
> I don't think it's damaged anybody particularly other than myself. So people can rest assured that that's the case . . . I damaged myself and I've been paying the price.

Despite all their years of closeness, Diana and Hewitt were now estranged. Joseph Sanders heard her complain about him many times.

> Diana told me that her relationship with James Hewitt had ended because she didn't want to see him any more. Diana changed her number and he had to phone up on the switchboard. I was there on one occasion when he phoned and she just refused to take the call.
>
> She had great difficulty when she finished a relationship. Instead of meeting somebody and saying, 'I don't think we ought to see each other any more, this is goodbye,' having a meal with them, or doing it in a pleasant way, she literally would not speak to them from one day to the next. So they didn't know where they were. One minute they'd been on very friendly terms and the next minute they couldn't speak to her.

How to find trust in an echo chamber? Diana found it difficult to maintain confidence in other people – a problem amplified by friends or advisers eager to question another's loyalty. Trust rarely existed in her marriage. With Hewitt it was present in the early years, underpinned by secrecy and regular personal contact. But once the parties were geographically separated, and once the press was after the story, it was easy for both to suspect the actions of the other.

> How much she loved me I don't know . . . She said she did, but who knows exactly what one individual is really thinking?

Fierce perjury laws mean that courtroom cross-examination by London's bewigged QCs can easily lead the unwary into further legal trouble. This thought preoccupied Diana's friends as she prepared to go to court in her privacy case against the *Daily Mirror* over the illicit gym photos. The *Mirror* had selected Geoffrey Robertson, QC, one of the most aggressive courtroom performers in town, to represent it. Robertson's team had been doing their research and had dug up many recent occasions when supposedly private events had been photographed with the Princess's help. They had also investigated rumours of other relationships between Diana and men she had met at the same gym.

Diana thought this was meaningless. She was a single woman now. If she chose to have lovers, it was no one's business but her own. But those advising her believed that, after the Oliver Hoare disaster, further disclosures about her sex life would not look good in court, especially if they involved other married men.

Joseph Sanders played a central role in this affair.

> I don't think she realised what she had coming. I told her very strongly that she really should not go into the witness box, and be cross-examined by Geoffrey Robertson, who is a brilliant QC. He would have asked her very relevant questions about

> her past affairs, the men that she'd been out with, and it would have been very, very embarrassing.
>
> He would've asked her how many times she went to the gym, who she'd met at the gym, whether she'd had a cup of coffee with them, whether she'd had more than a cup of coffee with them. And these were very difficult questions to answer truthfully. And any answers that she gave would have had her in great difficulties.
>
> So I spoke to the chief executive of the *Mirror*, and arranged a meeting.

In February 1995 the case was settled out of court. The *Mirror* apologised, Diana declared victory. In reality she had backed down. Lord Palumbo, who had also advised Diana to settle, was delighted. 'There was a great sigh of relief all round when she didn't have to go through that experience.'

After the battering she had received in 1994, Diana tried during the following year to charm a few of the papers back to her cause. An early opportunity came when she received an invitation from Rupert Murdoch. Could she do him a favour with a New York charity that he supported?

It was the United Cerebral Palsy Fund, and they were looking for someone to honour at their gala dinner later that year. Finding someone to accept honours like this was a major problem in New York. Ed Mathews was the charity's chief executive.

> Getting a high-profile 'honouree' is very important. About ten per cent of our annual budget comes from donations, which is a little over seven million dollars a year, a lot of money in this town. To raise that kind of money you've got to be in the public eye. Being high profile gets us people at the dinner, it gets us corporate sponsorship and gets us in the media.
>
> It's very difficult to get somebody to accept an honour. When I first started in this business about eleven years ago I thought

it must be quite easy, everyone would want to be one of their 'awardees'. Far from the case. The most high-profile people get thousands of requests from charities like this. It takes individual relationships to even get them to entertain the notion.

Princess Diana was a unique figure from the American point of view. So we set out to get her, using the relationship that we have with our own board member, Rupert Murdoch. He simply wrote her a note. It said: 'I would be most personally appreciative if you would consider this. Love, Rupert.'

The news about the Princess and her extramarital affair, the break-up of her marriage, was prevalent at the time. We thought, She just won't do it. We were working on the back-up honouree when I got a call saying that Mr Murdoch was on the line. And he said, 'She's all set.'

We knew that we had lightning in a bottle when she accepted.

As Ed Mathews began to market bottled lightning, Diana continued her love affair with America on a holiday with her sons in the Wild West. They rode horses in Colorado and white-water-rafted through the canyons of Utah. Lucia Flecha da Lima arranged for them to spend some time on actress Goldie Hawn's ranch in Aspen. It was summer, and things were turning good again.

Then came a short but disastrous relationship with Will Carling, the England rugby captain. 'Another married one,' Diana's friends groaned. Carling met her at the Chelsea Harbour Club gym and visited her at Kensington Palace. The press reported that Carling was 'advising her on her workout'.

Julia Carling had known nothing about her husband's friendship with Diana until she read about it in the *News of the World* on 6 August. When Carling said that he barely knew the Princess, his wife defended him vigorously, declaring in the next weekend's *News of the World* that Diana 'had picked the wrong couple to do it with this time'. 'An affair could not have been further from her mind,' said a friend of Diana's. Unfortunately Carling was spotted entering Kensington Palace, and on 24 September the paper returned to its theme, 'Will and Di at it again'. The *Mail* ran two parallel articles with Paul Johnson arguing the case for sympathy and Rhoda Koenig accusing Diana of childishness. Julia Carling asked for a divorce; Diana blamed the press.

Diana's friends agreed about one thing. She needed a decent man in her life: stable, discreet and unmarried. Diana thought so too, but as she asked Joseph Sanders, 'Who will have me now?'

> Diana was desperate to meet the right man, to have the right relationship, and she never completely found it. She used to see men and she was continuously disappointed. Or if she got on particularly well with somebody the press would ruin it because they'd publish the relationship and the man would say, 'Look, I'm sorry, Diana, I can't see you any more. I can't be in the papers every day. I can't face all this publicity.' If she went away somewhere she could have a hundred and ten photographers following her, all with zoom lenses. And it was a lot for anybody to take on. She said to me one morning when she was feeling particularly down about all this that she thought she'd never find a man. And I showed her her horoscope and said she actually would find somebody.

Then finally, in September 1995, Diana found her 'Mr Wonderful'.

Diana first met Dr Hasnat Khan when visiting Joseph Toffolo, husband of her acupuncturist Oonagh Toffolo, in London's Royal Brompton Hospital. Khan was one of a team of specialists who performed a triple heart bypass operation on him. Diana fell deeply in love, visited Toffolo practically every day and later would slip in to see Khan on the pretext of visiting other patients in the wards.

A lot of convalescing heart patients never realised why the Princess of Wales was spending so much time at their bedside. One night at the beginning of December, when leaving the hospital, Diana was cornered by a photographer from the *News of the World*. Instead of running for it, she paused for photographs and then phoned the newspaper's royal reporter to explain that she regularly visited the hospital at midnight. 'I try to be there for them,' she told him. 'I seem to draw strength from them.' What she said was intended to deceive the *News of the World*, but it was only partly untrue. Nevertheless, she would never have been able to get away with it if she had not just scored a massive propaganda coup of her own to claim the sympathy of the *News of the World*'s readers.

Diana had been approached, originally through her brother, by a television reporter named Martin Bashir, who worked for *Panorama*, the BBC's top current affairs series. Bashir impressed Diana, and eventually proposed to her that she might put her own point of view across effectively by giving him a long television interview.

She asked various friends for their opinion, but not Patrick Jephson, from whom she was slowly becoming estranged. Jephson wanted her to leave the bitterness of the past behind and move under the protection of the Queen and her household. He had a vision, which turned out to be unrealistic in the extreme, of keeping his Princess 'in the fold' and out of the divorce court.

Film producer David Puttnam and broadcaster Clive James counselled against the interview. She appeared to take their advice, but she didn't. Joseph Sanders believes that Diana knew that divorce was inevitable and decided to go on *Panorama* with that in mind.

> She was trying to put herself in a better position vis-à-vis the divorce and getting a good settlement . . . She felt a bit like a rat in a trap. She wanted to get away from the Royal Family – she wasn't getting anywhere negotiating with them. She just felt that she had to do something really serious and really outrageous and that's why she did the Panorama interview.

Max Hastings had just been invited for lunch:

> I said, as I always do on these occasions – 'Ma'am, I should just let the other side make the mistakes. Just stick with the principles: "say nothing, say nothing". You still have tremendous public support but you are not going to serve your interests by saying a lot publicly.'
>
> Now nothing is more unflattering than finding your advice not taken. And I've never had my advice so *resoundingly* not taken.

Vivienne Parry thinks the moment was going to come sooner or later.

> When the Prince of Wales admitted to adultery with Mrs Parker Bowles in the Jonathan Dimbleby interview, it was like setting a fuse which would lead to an enormous great explosion. That explosion was *Panorama*. It was inevitable.
>
> Of the people that she did talk to, those that had media experience said very firmly, 'Don't do it.' But she ignored them.

Diana demanded total secrecy, stipulating that the BBC Chairman, Sir Marmaduke Hussey, must not be told in advance of transmission. He was married to Lady Susan Hussey, still a lady-in-waiting to the Queen. On the evening of 5 November, Diana gave her Kensington Palace staff some unexpected time off and ushered Bashir and his crew through a rear entrance. As soon as they saw the result, BBC executives realised that they too had lightning in a bottle. The programme was broadcast on 20 November to twenty-three million viewers in Britain alone.

'All I want to be,' Diana said, 'is queen of people's hearts.' It was a bravura performance. Diana talked through her eating disorders, her attempts to hurt herself, and her miserable marriage. She turned on Camilla, explaining that her marriage had always been crowded since there had been three people in it, and she turned on James Hewitt, who, she said, she had loved and adored but who had let her down. She raised the possibility that Charles did not want to be King – indeed, might not be suitable for the 'top job' at all – and that William might be a more suitable heir. Of her own future she said, with some menace, she would not 'go quietly, I will fight to the end'.

Newsnight, the BBC's late-night news magazine, had rapidly planned a discussion programme to follow. Anthony Holden and Nicholas Soames had agreed to appear. As *Panorama* began, these representatives of the rival royal factions watched in growing amazement.

> It was a weird and quite funny experience, because the show followed straight on, and we were all thinking, Well, she's not going to say anything very interesting. I think I'd even written that she might trash Charles a bit but I don't think she'll be admitting adultery.
>
> We were just chatting among ourselves. I'm quite friendly with Nicholas Soames, we can rise above our disagreements. But then: 'Wait a minute, did she just admit adultery with Hewitt? My God!' And suddenly this moved into a different stratosphere. Then when she came out with 'I want to be queen of people's hearts', Soames, who was by this time getting very indignant, turned to me and said, 'I bet you wrote that, Holden!'

By the time *Newsnight* started, Soames was shaking with rage. He tore into Diana, accusing her of being 'in the advanced stages of paranoia'. The British public finally got a sense of the angry partisanship that had lain behind the royal marriage.

> He let rip, which I thought was a rather dangerous thing for a government minister to say, about a woman who was still at the time the Princess of Wales, wife of the next King and mother of the future King. And I thought that this was really the endgame now.

Lord Palumbo watched Soames's outburst and thought the same.

> I'm sure that those people who were advising the Prince of Wales said, 'I told you so, that's what she's all about.' It gave ammunition to those people who opposed her, unnecessarily. It had a pretty devastating effect. It made the situation irretrievable . . .

Patrick Jephson arranged to watch *Panorama* with Anne Beckwith-Smith. Diana had told him of the interview less than a week before transmission. He had tried to smooth things over with the Queen's office, while privately blaming Diana's 'inner child' for stamping its feet and demanding yet more attention be paid to its tale of injustice. Continuing with his spoilt-child analogy, Jephson describes waiting for the programme to start:

> it was the kind of foreboding that parents experience when returning home after a dinner party in the knowledge that the nursery will have been left in a bit of a shambles.

The current private secretary and the former lady-in-waiting both felt it was ghastly. Both knew that it meant the end of Jephson's strategy of reconciliation with the Queen. Both sensed he would have to resign.

James Hewitt watched apprehensively and with mixed feelings:

> It was a complete shock. I didn't think that she would speak about me. Golly. A whole load of thoughts flashed through my mind. I think that the overwhelming thought was that she's admitted [it] . . . that's good, and I think that's wonderful and thank you very much. People might be less sceptical about this 'Lothario playboy', 'woman hater', 'woman user', or whatever

had been written up until that point. She went on to say 'He let me down' but she didn't explain why, it wasn't asked of her: 'Why?'

But I think she came across completely differently to the person I knew. I'm thinking that she was natural and carefree and generous in spirit. And the person on the *Panorama* interview was calculated and not any of those things.

But at Wapping Ken Lennox couldn't believe his luck.

By that stage I was picture editor on the *Sun*, and it was probably the most exciting night I've ever had on the picture desk of a national newspaper. We could not change our editions quickly enough. We were changing them on the phrases that were coming out. When it got to the marriage – 'there were three in the marrriage, it was a bit crowded' – we were ripping our front pages and improving on them. We were giving more and more pages over to it.

The next day the tabloids took up the 'I Loved James Hewitt' theme while the broadsheets were concerned with the 'I will not go quietly' threat. In *The Times*, William Rees-Mogg admired what he took to be 'a dazzling display of sheer political skill'. Ken Lennox's *Sun* eventually gave the first nine pages to the interview and page twenty to Hewitt. On page nine the *Sun* established its people's paper status with an account of readers' reactions. The vast majority were positive: 'You were magnificent Di: Thousands call the Sun to praise brave Princess.' The paper quoted twenty-five readers, of whom twenty-two were women. Only three readers were critical, and two of them were men.

Some viewers watched a piece of ham acting by a vindictive woman bent on revenge. But it was immediately apparent that they were a small minority. *Panorama*, more than anything else, formulated the image of Diana the defiant victim, the brave survivor. From now on she had an army.

15
Decree Absolute

In December 1995 Diana flew to New York to fulfil her promise to Rupert Murdoch. There, in the Hilton grand ballroom, before 1,500 thousand-dollars-a-plate guests, she received the United Cerebral Palsy (UCP) Humanitarian of the Year Award from Henry Kissinger.

A press baron calls in a favour, a princess has a PR problem and Henry Kissinger presents a *humanitarian* award.

It's easy to cry 'fake', but simplistic too. This is how good deeds get done in Gotham City. UCP had worked hard to solve its 'honouree shortage' and the evening would make a huge contribution to its funds, especially as *Panorama* had just brought Diana right back into the spotlight.

> We [UCP] had requests from all over the world. It was simply overwhelming. We hadn't had anything like that before. Any number of celebrities in this town offered to up their donations. There was one gentleman who used to buy a ten-thousand-dollar table; he offered fifty thousand if he could sit next to the Princess.
>
> To minimise possible criticism for raising money for an American cause, we thought we'd cut the British in on the deal. We offered a small sum of the proceeds to a cerebral palsy organisation in the UK and that was gratefully accepted.
>
> Henry Kissinger got to sit next to her, and there are lots of famous pictures of that because Diana was very tall and our former Secretary isn't. So he came up to about bosom level.

Kissinger spoke about Diana's 'luminous personality' and praised her for identifying herself with 'the sick, the disadvantaged and the suffering'. Ed Mathews had heard many such speeches, but he had never met anyone like Diana:

> The rest of the Royal Family are cold fish, frankly. Diana was a more interesting person because she seemed to have a feeling for people's plights. And she wanted to use her fame and title to do something about it. And she seemed to be trying to fit in to some place that she no longer could.
>
> She was very warm with the children but she appeared sad to me. I'm a psychologist by training and by trade, so maybe I'm just reading too much in, but that was how she came across, and she stayed that way for the entire dinner. Regal, but sort of uncomfortable and sad.
>
> She spoke not about the organisation, but about what it meant to be a volunteer. She spoke very seriously about commitment, what it meant to her and what it should mean to people to do things outside of themselves.

Diana spoke about her children. One of the dinner guests stood up, walked to the back of the room and yelled out, 'Where are your children, Diana?' A hush fell over the crowd. Diana looked to the back of the room, coolly replied, 'At school,' and proceeded with her speech. Security came over and escorted the heckler out. Diana got a standing ovation when she finished.

> The dinner made all the local news shows. I was grateful for the effort that Diana was putting in sincerely to benefit others. I never thought, Is she doing this for some other motive that I don't understand? It didn't really matter to me. Two point two million dollars that night is what mattered, and all the free publicity, and we've never come close to it since, nor do I ever expect to.

Soon after she returned from New York, Diana received a letter from the Queen urging a rapid divorce. *Panorama* had been one provocation too many. Diana's mother-in-law had consulted John Major and George Carey, the Archbishop of Canterbury, before writing to her and Charles. Diana made a tearful phone call to Patrick Jephson. She told him she had never wanted this to happen. He shook his head. She had just *made* it happen.

She had been fine in New York, but in London she was soon in a bad way, convinced that her rooms were bugged, believing that someone had taken a pot shot at her in the park and telling Jephson that the brake wires had been cut on her car.

Tiggy Legge-Bourke had been hired as a nanny by Prince Charles in 1993 to help look after the children when they were in his custody. She had long been an object of suspicion in Kensington Palace. Jephson had drafted several letters asking for clarification of Tiggy's duties and demanding, on Diana's behalf, to be involved in all decisions relating to the boys' care. At the 1995 staff Christmas party on 14 December, Diana snapped. She crept up behind Legge-Bourke and whispered, 'So sorry about the baby.' The nanny had to be helped out of the room in tears.

Diana believed that Tiggy had recently had an abortion. The identity of the supposed father did not take much guesswork. There was not a scrap of truth in it. But Diana, who was proud of having confronted her enemy in this way, told a shocked Jephson that she simply *knew* Tiggy had been carrying her husband's child. Through her lawyers, Legge-Bourke demanded an apology. Diana refused.

Diana saw conspiracies everywhere. She left disturbing messages on her staff's answering machines, and then one arrived on Patrick Jephson's pager: 'The Boss knows about your disloyalty and your affair.' After *Panorama* and Tiggy, this was the last straw. Jephson decided he had better leave before he was pushed.

But just before he went, Jephson headhunted a replacement for Diana's press secretary, Geoff Crawford, who had resigned because she had not consulted him about *Panorama*. Jane

Atkinson, a public relations executive with heavyweight media experience, was only told who her prospective client was when she was placed on the short list. Atkinson would not work directly for Diana but would keep her own independent company going and deal with the Princess from a relatively safe distance:

> She asked me what I thought of the *Panorama* interview, she asked me a few personal questions. It was more whether the chemistry was right. Clearly it was. I felt that we would be able to work together. I liked her. I actually hadn't thought that the *Panorama* interview was a very good idea. But I did tell her that she had got some of her points across very well.

Jephson told Atkinson that she would be expected to read the newspapers very early each morning and then ring Diana to discuss what was in them. Diana then made her new press officer a promise that had Jephson looking at his shoes.

> If she was doing some private visits, then she would tell me what she was doing so that I wouldn't be surprised if the media rang me to say they had seen her in various places. She was going through a divorce and she obviously wanted to have as clean and good a reputation as possible.

Jephson left in late January 1996. Atkinson's job was not too difficult at first. One early task was looking after a trip to Centrepoint, a charity devoted to helping homeless young people. Diana had visited a Centrepoint project in 1991 and, impressed by what she saw, had become Patron in 1992. Her patronage had raised Centrepoint's profile enormously, and she introduced new donors to them. Victor Adebowale, young and not at all posh, had been appointed Chief Executive of Centrepoint in the autumn of 1995 and had visited Diana at Kensington Palace in an attempt to get her to resume an active involvement with his charity. In the immediate aftermath of *Panorama*, on 7 December, she had made an emotional and effective speech for him about the plight of homeless young people. Now another project visit was arranged. Berwick Street, Soho, is the site of the only emergency accommodation project for sixteen- to twenty-one-year-olds in central London. Diana told Adebowale that she wanted to make a private visit because she wanted Harry and William to see what she had seen. He said 'fine'. And then private turned public again, as Adebowale remembers:

> I remember being absolutely petrified. The street was awash with reporters and flashlights. There were metal barriers all the way down it. Reporters were hanging from windows, up lampposts, up ladders, there were flashbulbs going off and she wasn't even due to arrive for another hour. It was a siege.

The press were excited because this was the first time Diana had brought her sons to such a gritty, and politically loaded, location.

> The police were looking worried. The car door opened, she got out of the car with her sons and we got them into the building as quickly as we could. We had to push people back, and the door was barricaded to stop reporters coming in. Lights were flashing through the windows; it was unbelievable.

Diana was ever conscientious with her post, but she had refused to respond to the Queen's divorce instruction for several weeks. Then, in late February 1996, she suggested to Charles that they meet in private at St James's Palace. She told him she would agree to a divorce by mutual consent, but she wished to keep living at Kensington Palace, to retain an office at St James's, to share custody of the children, and to keep her title Princess of Wales. Once back at Kensington Palace she immediately issued a press statement, saying she had agreed to Prince Charles's request for a divorce. She added the sentence 'The Princess of

Wales will retain the title and will be known as Diana, Princess of Wales', even though at this stage the Palace had agreed to no such thing. The Queen responded with a rare and immediate public rebuttal.

During Morton, *Panorama* and the public unravelling of her marriage, Diana had frequently told her friends and supporters that it was all being done to break free, to get a good settlement and a bright new life. She and Sarah Ferguson had joked together about their 'Great Escape'. In her positive 'sisters are doing it for themselves' moods, that is doubtless how she felt. But she still mourned her lost love, the summit of all her teenage hopes, and still speculated about a reconciliation. 'Divorce was the very last thing that Diana wanted,' says Vivienne Parry, 'and she was devastated by it. I remember she was sobbing her heart out. She was utterly desperate about it, because she felt that she had failed. She continued to have the silliest hopes of getting back together with her husband.' Soon she was complaining to friends like Vivienne Parry and Elsa Bowker that her life was ruined.

The stories about Diana that really hit home – the Tiggy slander, the nuisance phone calls, the messages on the pagers – cannot be dismissed as smears from her estranged husband's camp. These are real stories about how Diana was capable of behaving in these last years of her life. The way she treated Victoria Mendham was another example.

Mendham, a junior secretary at Kensington Palace for seven years, became a favoured confidante. Diana invited her to go on holiday with her to America and the Caribbean and paid for them both. Then, at Easter 1996, Diana again invited Victoria to go with her to the Caribbean. They had a great time. Halfway through the holiday, Diana told Victoria that she would be getting a bill for her share of the cost. It would be for about £5,000. Quietly, Prince Charles paid the bill. They went on holiday again at the beginning of 1997 and Diana presented

Mendham with an even larger bill. When she found out that Charles had paid for the previous holiday she was furious. Diana, who frequently complained that others freeloaded at her expense, pursued the secretary remorselessly over the money. Eventually Prince Charles had to step in again, but Mendham left in distress.

Diana told Joseph Sanders all about the incident.

> Diana shouted at her so she started crying, and in the end she got the sack, and Diana thought it was terrible. That's just an illustration of somebody who was very close to her, went on holiday with her and the next minute, she's discarded.

Other friends attempted to intervene on Mendham's behalf. But it was no good. Diana, so gracious, so thoughtful, so full of compassion for so much of the time, was playing the role of household tyrant.

Diana and Hasnat Khan visited clubs and restaurants together, she disguised in dark wigs, scarves and sunglasses. Khan insisted that their relationship remain private. They spent weekends at the Stratford-upon-Avon home of his British relatives. Other nights were spent in the doctor's on-call flat at the Brompton Hospital.

She was drawn to his calmness and dedication to the sick; also to his large, warm family. She happily told friends that she had learned to cook pasta, and had stood unrecognised in a supermarket queue buying the ingredients for a microwave feast. She said that she teased Khan about his spreading waistline, lack of exercise and fondness for the high-cholesterol pleasures of Fulham Road takeaways.

Diana wanted to live openly with Khan, but he remained wary. She wrote to the famous heart surgeon Christian Barnard in South Africa, enquiring about a job for Khan. Her brother already had a house in Cape Town, so perhaps she could move there too. But none of the plans came to anything. Khan was committed to his work and his research – and, for the moment, that meant London.

For all the love she shared with Khan, Diana was never consistently happy. Or rather, as Vivienne Parry realised, she was never consistently self-confident.

> One day she rang me up at home. I was in my dressing gown, at half past eight in the morning, and Diana said, 'Don't ever stop sending me your notes, Vivienne, they mean so much.' And I just thought, My God, this poor girl, just a little note from somebody of no consequence telling her that she's valued is so important.

The Khan relationship led to Jane Atkinson's first big PR problem. In April 1996, Khan was performing a heart operation with surgeon Sir Magdi Yacoub, and Diana came to watch with a Sky News crew in tow. The film showed her wearing make-up and jewellery in the operating theatre. Jane Atkinson recalls the setting up of the session:

> The Princess had asked me whether I thought that she should go and observe the operation. I talked to a few people and generally we all thought that it wasn't a very good idea. And she said that she would decide at the last minute. I was on my way to Chicago to do a recce trip for her subsequent visit when she rang me in the departure lounge to say, 'I've decided to do it, and I'm at the hospital.' I held my breath and got on the plane. And then at four o'clock the next morning, I was woken up by the media because it was all over the press.
>
> The Princess wasn't happy about the coverage. She thought she had been misunderstood. I don't think she had done herself any favours in the way she handled it.

The press – still unaware of Hasnat Khan's role in her life – accused her of tasteless self-promotion. Anthony Holden asked her why she had done it:

> I said, 'My God! How can you watch that stuff, don't you feel faint or keel over, why do you do that?' And she said, 'No, no, if I'm going to comfort the suffering, I have to understand what they've been through.' Now that's a classic example of something where cynics will sneer, but if you knew her at all you believed it.

Atkinson believes that Diana understood how to manipulate the media, but not how to manage them. There's a big difference, she says – the difference between short-term thinking and long-term.

> I was told by the journalists themselves that most of them didn't believe what she was saying because she had tried to manipulate them too often in the past.

If being Diana's press officer could be taxing, so could being her friend. Diana was spending so much of her time in America now that Lucia Flecha da Lima decided she needed some more social and emotional support there. And so she decided to search for a woman of Diana's age who could be a reliable and trustworthy companion.

Lana Marks is an expatriate South African running a successful accessory design and retail business from Palm Beach, Florida. She was delighted to be approached.

> Over a period of nine months Lucia and some of Diana's people spoke to me very extensively about my views on various things, and after that Lucia called me up and said would I consent to being the friend of the Princess of Wales? And I was deeply, deeply honoured and said that I would never let her down and that I would be a loyal and terrific friend. And she said, 'Lana, we know, and Diana will be so delighted.'

It was an unusual way to begin a relationship, but Flecha da Lima had chosen well. Marks had two children the same ages as William and Harry. She had studied to be a ballet teacher at the South African Royal Academy of Ballet. She was a regular on the American fashion and charity scenes. And she'd enjoyed twenty years of stable marriage to a distinguished psychiatrist. After a brief introduction in Washington, Diana invited Marks to lunch at Kensington Palace.

> I called Lucia and said, 'Lucia, I'm going to be a nervous wreck.' And Lucia said to me, 'Lana, just be yourself, Diana has a way of making people feel comfortable.'
>
> I arrived at Kensington Palace. Her butler opened the door and said, 'Mrs Marks, welcome to Kensington Palace. The Princess of Wales is waiting for you.' I felt, Oh my goodness, this is really quite something. It was fantastic. Diana came bouncing down. So I curtsied and she said, 'Oh, that's not necessary at all, but how lovely of you.' And she threw her arms around me and kissed me on both cheeks and said, 'Welcome to my home.'
>
> Lucia was right. Diana put me at ease completely, and we chatted so intensely for three hours, it was quite lovely.

Marks would stay at the Lanesborough Hotel, on the southern fringe of Hyde Park. Discreet lunch parties were a speciality.

> The first time she came in a little Ford Escort. When the car arrived I said, 'Oh my goodness, she's cancelled.' And of course she was crouched down in the back, and she sat up and there were no reporters, she looked round and she was so surprised and I said, 'See, it can be done.'

The two subsequently saw a lot of each other on the American dinner circuit.

> She would call me after the various galas in the United States, and we would dissect everything that had gone on. We would laugh so hard about who was wearing what. She was just like somebody who had gone to a party and afterwards wanted to discuss it with one of their friends.

Soon Diana was sharing everything with Lana Marks – including her continued ill feeling towards Camilla Parker Bowles, who was now being subtly rehabilitated in the British press with the help of Charles's press officers.

> Diana's way of dealing with it was putting an unflattering cartoon of Camilla in her bathroom. She did the same later on with Elton John when she had the disagreement with him. She said, 'Oh, he's in the bathroom with Camilla.'

Jane Atkinson was less interested in becoming Diana's friend.

> I could see that there was a temptation to get sucked into the whole personal vortex that surrounded the Princess. She was very informal and very amiable and very charming. But I rationalised to myself that I really wanted this to be a professional relationship only. I really didn't want to become a confidante.

But Anthony Holden did not see the darker side of life at Kensington Palace.

> Diana's apartments in Kensington Palace were immensely relaxed and the atmosphere was almost festive. She had a great succession of people there, very informal.
>
> I arrived in my battered blue Mondeo and she skipped out, it was the school holidays, the children skipped past the car too. I made a feeble attempt to lock it and she said, 'I don't think that'll be necessary around here. There are policemen in every bush.' The relaxed naturalness of it was something I'd never encountered in any other royal residence.
>
> I asked her at my last lunch if she ever thought she would remarry and she said, 'Yes, if I can find somebody who understands what I'm about,' so that gave me the chance to say, 'Well, what are you about?' And she said, 'I'm about caring. I thought I'd married a man first time around who cared about caring but

I was wrong.' Put like that it sounds like the quintessential Di – stage Di, as it were – but two-thirds of her meant it.

Diana and her sons went to stay at Lord Palumbo's house in Paris. They flew by private jet and for two days were completely unrecognised. They wandered around and did ordinary tourist things – went up the Eiffel Tower, ate ice cream in the Bois de Boulogne. On the third and final day of her long weekend she was spotted, inside the Louvre, looking at a Matisse exhibition. From then on she was shadowed everywhere.

> We ate in a café, and the best table was in the window and she wanted to sit there. The problem with sitting in the window was that you overlooked the street and somebody could see you. So she got over that by pulling the curtain across her.
>
> The press by that time were outside on their motor scooters, but the curtain was drawn and they couldn't be quite sure that she was there. But at the end she just pulled the curtain back and they knew very well that she was there. Then when we left the café, the whole horde of photographers were waiting. It was a sort of little cat-and-mouse game she was playing – a tease really, I think.
>
> We went to Notre Dame and she arrived in a really grumpy mood. Of course, as soon as she went into it, somebody spotted her and immediately there were fifty or sixty people around her, some of them trying to kiss her hand and so on. And the grumpiness left, it was as though the spotlight had gone on and she became animated and full of laughter.

One day Jane Atkinson was telephoned by a contrite photographer.

> He rang me to apologise. He had followed her to and from a private lunch, and had driven his scooter very close to the car

> and shouted at her through the car window in the hope of getting a picture of her crying or a picture of her snarling at him, and he was very upset by her reaction and he rang me, and asked me to apologise for him.

Jayne Fincher had become so sickened by the behaviour of the paparazzi that she decided to do something about it. She recruited a group of photographers into an unofficial corps, like the press corps at the White House in Washington, with the aim of producing its own code of conduct and penalties for those who stepped out of line.

> We asked the Palace if they could assist us, so if people did paparazzi pictures they would be excluded from official jobs, trips and photo calls on royal property. It seems logical to me: if somebody abuses you, you don't invite them in for a cup of coffee the next day.

Fincher is convinced that if a handful of photographers had been refused accreditation for a big royal trip – their 'bread-and-butter work' – then it would have made them and their colleagues think twice before chasing Diana down the street again. But Buckingham Palace staff said that they couldn't help.

> I don't really know why they couldn't, I never really got to the bottom of that. So nothing was done. They said we had to police it ourselves. Of course, we couldn't police other photographers, it wasn't for us to do that. So the whole thing fell apart.

As her secret romance with Hasnat Khan continued, Diana fantasised about sharing her future with him. She visited Pakistan twice in 1996, ostensibly to see her old friends Jemima and Imran Khan (no relation). She visited Lahore to help raise money for the Shaukat Khanum Memorial Cancer Hospital, founded by Imran in memory of his mother, who had died of cancer. She visited again in July. Another reason for both trips was to persuade Hasnat's mother, Naheed Khan, that she would make a suitable wife for her son. But Mrs Khan wanted him to marry one of his own Pathan clan. Diana professed an interest in everything Pakistani, burned incense sticks at Kensington Palace, wore kaftans and watched Pakistani videos, much to the bemusement of her staff. In November 1996, the *Sunday Mirror* published a detailed account of their affair. To appease the media-shy doctor, Diana denied the romance to Richard Kay.

Diana had, by now, confided in Lord Palumbo. 'Hasnat Khan is a very honourable man. He seemed a very decent person and she seemed very happy with him.' She had also told her new friend Lana Marks all about him:

> Emotionally she needed somebody who could give her security, who could help her through this very difficult time when she was breaking up with Prince Charles. This was a gentleman who was very highly educated, very bright, very compassionate with the work that he was doing. He shared many of the same views as Diana, and was an enormous source of strength for her at a difficult time.

But Marks is not convinced about Diana's marriage plans.

> Diana told me that Hasnat Khan was wonderful. She had met his family, she had met various of his relatives and she had the greatest respect for him. But in terms of marriage, I really don't think this was something that Diana would have gone through at all.

Diana owed much of her international reputation as a humanitarian to her early work with AIDS. But she was about to fall out with the man who had organised those first bedside visits, and watched them with such admiration.

Mike Adler was planning to open a new department of

sexually transmitted diseases and wanted the patron of the National AIDS Trust to be at hand. Diana agreed to come:

> The day before her visit I received a message to say that Diana had decided that she was going to bring Aileen Getty with her. Now Aileen Getty was a high-profile American woman with HIV and AIDS and she was travelling around every television and radio studio in the capital talking about it, and she had latched on to Diana.
>
> The Princess was going to bring Aileen Getty to this visit, and Aileen Getty wanted to bring two or three of her hangers-on. I rang up Jane Atkinson and went bananas down the phone, saying, 'She can't just bring all these people in, these are patients that we are dealing with! This is not a zoo! This is not an aquarium!'

Jane Atkinson had been expecting the call.

> The objective was for Mike to raise the profile of the work that he was doing with AIDS. Then she announced that she was going to take Aileen Getty with her because this was a opportunity to draw attention to the fact that AIDS could also affect women.
>
> Mike was absolutely furious. He felt that this wasn't the main part of the issue he was involved with, and that it was hijacking the visit, and he was very angry. He did shout at me down the telephone as to how I could have allowed this. I rang the Princess and she was quite adamant that she was going with Aileen, so I rang Mike back and I said, 'I think the only thing to do under these circumstances, Mike, is for you to ring her directly.'

Adler said he would do just that.

> Jane subsequently told me that the phone melted in her hand as I bawled her out. Of course, it wasn't Jane's fault. She didn't know what was going on. About half an hour to go before the

event, Diana came on and I said, 'Ma'am, listen, as far as I am concerned it doesn't matter to me whether you come or not, OK? It really doesn't matter. But I am not having you treating us in this way. I am quite happy to call it all off now.'

She went, 'Oh, Michael, Michael, you must trust me, it will all be all right,' so I said, 'OK, but you do realise the conditions under which you are coming?'

Anyway, she arrived and we had got the whole thing worked out: Aileen Getty would be taken by one of us, sat at the back of this room while I did a short presentation with Diana sitting in the front. Having sat next to Diana, I got up to do a presentation and Diana beckoned to Aileen Getty, who came from the back of the room to the front and they held hands together the whole time. The only photograph that appeared of Diana was her holding hands with Aileen Getty.

Not the worst thing a charity patron could do. After all, Aileen Getty's cause was valuable too. But it wasn't the reason this particular event had been organised.

It was just an example of how she lost focus, how she would try sometimes to use an event that was very serious for a completely different agenda, and it was highly inappropriate. We were very bitter about it.

Here was Diana forgetting the promises that had been made. We were fairly curt with each other. You have to hang on to what is important to you, and what is important to me was the integrity of what I did clinically, and being chairman of a trust.

And frankly, if people try and misuse the opportunities then it is not worth the candle. Frankly, it is just not worth it.

On 15 July 1996 the decree nisi was announced, followed six weeks later on 28 August by the decree absolute. Diana received a lump-sum payment, estimated at £17 million. But she lost the title 'Her Royal Highness'.

Diana blamed the loss of her title for her immediate decision to drop her involvement with a hundred charities, including favourites like the Red Cross and Help the Aged. Jane Atkinson was against it, saying it would look petulant and sulky, but she refused to listen. None of the charities, bar six she kept working with, was informed of her decision until the last minute. Many found out only when the announcement was made public.

Diana told friends that she wanted to spring-clean her life, cut down her workload, and concentrate on the few charities that most appealed to her. She kept the National AIDS Trust, Victor Adebowale's Centrepoint, the Royal Marsden NHS Trust, the Great Ormond Street Children's Hospital, the Leprosy Mission and the English National Ballet. Atkinson waited for the bad press to arrive.

> I don't think that I ever thought there was a good time to do it. We always knew that it was going to be a negative media story. She tried to do it as a story which would give her some sympathy for losing the HRH title, and it backfired! We all of us knew it wouldn't work. It seemed like a cold-hearted thing to do, but I think it was done as part of her trying to structure her life after divorce. I can honestly say that I don't know what the rationalisation in her own mind was. She talked about it as genuinely wanting the charities to feel free, and not be tied to her: she was no longer royal and they should have another royal patron.

Mike Whitlam was one of those who was dropped.

> I heard [about it] one morning at about eight-thirty in a phone call. She was trying to explain to me that we were not one of the six. She felt she owed it to me to tell me, rather than just get the letter which arrived about ten minutes later. The conversation was very amicable. But I guess I was personally

hurt. I was surprised, disappointed, maybe even shocked. Particularly as I felt we had a very good working relationship. And also because the Red Cross was an organisation which she was very close to. She'd been made a vice-president. She had even accepted a role within the International Red Cross making policy. I suppose I had wonderful visions of her being with us for ever.

In Soho, Adebowale was counting his blessings:

I think she realised that abandoning Centrepoint wasn't just abandoning an organisation that was going to do all right anyway because it was a 'sexy charity'. She realised that if she was to walk away it might affect our future and she didn't want to see that.

Centrepoint has always had to struggle to stay financially afloat. We need every penny and her walking away at that point might well have sunk us. So her being with us meant a lot in every sense, and she knew that. I think that made the decision about Centrepoint just that little more urgent: I should keep this one because they really need me. I think that's why she stuck with us.

Despite their recent argument, Mike Adler's National Aids Trust was also one of the lucky ones, but he didn't find her taking an increased interest:

When she kept us as one of the six charities we were delighted. I don't know why we were one of the chosen few. I imagine it had to do with the fact that she had been involved with us right from the beginning.

But the moment she dropped it down to six charities was the time, even though we were all very flattered, that she began to disengage. It was very difficult for a charity like mine to rely on her. I think she was confused about what she was meant to be doing – there were so many other things going on in her life. I think she became distracted by that, and it became very difficult to be able to know that she would deliver on things that you would ask her to do.

For example, if you were trying to arrange a charity concert she would never say yes or no. It was very difficult because when you are trying to do charitable events, there is a long lead into things, and unless you can get her to sign on early on you can't run things. Towards the end, because you knew getting an answer was going to be difficult, you stopped asking.

She just found it difficult to focus. That was one thing; the second thing was that I increasingly realised one was getting caught up in her own personal agenda and her own personal confusion.

To be quite honest, by the end of her life we hardly asked her to do anything. It just wasn't worth it. It was better to plan to do things knowing that she wouldn't be there. We began to operate as a charity with a patron but without her.

After a stressful spring, Jane Atkinson was looking forward to another American visit.

The trip to Chicago to raise money for breast cancer treatment was a great success. We'd overcome the negatives of Harefield, and she and I and her staff worked very hard to make Chicago work for her. She behaved impeccably. She was absolutely wonderful, the Americans loved her, she liked the Americans. It was hard work, but the publicity was great.

After that, one or two articles appeared about me and her staff, and I'm told that she didn't like them very much. She felt that it had been a team effort. I was very, very careful, if you read any of the publicity, to say that it *was* a team effort, and it's certainly not anything that I engineered. But she just became distrustful.

She'd always helped me considerably with background things that I didn't understand, maybe things that had happened before. And then just suddenly I would ring her and say, 'Can you explain about this?' and she would just be unhelpful and say, 'Well, tch, you should know that!'

When she resigned the charities, she had already written the press release and discussed how it should be handled. Then later in the day she rang me and was very angry because of the way that the media had treated the story. She felt it had been very negative to her. I explained that I'd only answered the questions in the way that we'd agreed, but she accused me of not doing so. And then one of her friends was on the ten o'clock news saying almost exactly the same things that I'd said. And when I rang the Princess and asked her if she knew that her friend was on the news she said no, she didn't know. I think her words were, 'You can't always stop your friends talking.'

It was impossible for me to do my job in an environment like that. I thought, Well, that's it. I can't continue to function properly as a media adviser, so I ought to resign.

Diana came to rely on her friends for PR advice. And she had one more triumph to come.

16
Miracle in Huambo

> Mike, it's Diana, could you come over for a cup of tea some time soon? I'd like to talk about those landmines again.

Diana's ambition to become a roving envoy had so far been thwarted by the government and the Royal Family. Some thought her insufficiently well informed and astute, and some dismissed her as an attention-seeker. Lord Palumbo told her to make the best of it. If 'she wouldn't be permitted to roam the world as an ambassador at large', he said, 'she should target certain specific issues which would be left up to her.' So she did.

Veteran *Daily Telegraph* man Bill Deedes had been involved with the anti-landmine cause since 1991. Promoted by the arms industry as an effective weapon of defence, millions of landmines had been laid since the Second World War. Very often, when the armies went away, the minefields were left behind, to kill or maim unlucky civilians and make farmland unusable. Now a major effort was under way to clear existing minefields and prevent further mines being laid. It was a difficult issue because powerful interests were opposed to the ban. Deedes appreciated how useful Diana could be to the cause, and how her participation might go some way to fulfilling her ambition.

The Red Cross was one of the hundred charities that Diana had recently abandoned, but now she called Mike Whitlam and offered to help. He told her that she had to see the plight of landmine victims for herself, and suggested she should visit a country that was clearing up after a war. Inevitably she would bring the world's attention with her. With luck this might generate some progress on a planned global landmine treaty which had become mired in bureaucracy in several nations that had said in public they supported it, notably Britain, Canada and America.

At first they planned to go to Cambodia, but with a hostage crisis in progress they were warned off by the Foreign Office. Bosnia was also considered too dangerous. And so Angola was chosen, where it was estimated that fifteen million mines were scattered among a population of twelve million people. A BBC documentary crew asked if they could accompany her. Whitlam said 'yes please'.

> I was very clear, as was she, that this was going to be a working visit, not an official visit. She was travelling as part of the Red Cross. It was not a Palace or government visit. There was quite a lot of pressure for her to take part in major fund-raising events, such as big dinners in Angola, and we refused. Occasionally, when I wavered, thinking that this might not be a bad idea, she would say, 'No, Mike, we've agreed.' Then when she wavered and said, 'Well, maybe I ought to,' I'd come in. So we worked as quite good support for each other. We wanted to show the destruction and devastation caused by landmines: we didn't want it to be sidetracked.
>
> And suddenly, just before Christmas, I had a panic phone call from one of the more senior staff in the Red Cross in Geneva, saying he was extremely worried about this visit. I said, 'It's too late, you've said yes and it's all set up.' I had to fly to Geneva for a whole day of meetings, to reassure people about how we would get round some of the difficulties.

Diana sought Mike Whitlam's advice on what clothes to wear, as she did not want to detract from the focus of her tour. 'I found that highly amusing, as even my wife wouldn't ask that question of me.' Chino trousers and an open-necked shirt were his recommendation.

Christina Lamb had been thinking about clothes too, uncomfortably imagining a Princess rubbing tailored shoulders with African amputees. A war reporter for the *Sunday Times*, Lamb had been asked by a hesitant editor to accompany Diana on this tour. She was a couple of years younger than Diana and remembered having her hair done in the short style with highlights just after the royal wedding. But she had little interest in Diana now, or in the breathless royal revelations that filled most British papers.

> I was very cynical about Diana, but I thought the trip was important because I'd worked a lot as a correspondent covering the issue of landmines in Mozambique and Angola which her trip was meant to highlight. But I just saw it as a big publicity stunt, another chance for her to be photographed in front of victims, looking beautiful.

Lamb promised her equally sceptical friends that her pen would be sharp and that she wouldn't be falling for any charm offensive.

There was chaos at Heathrow in January 1997 as a small army of cameramen and sound recordists, journalists and photographers all tried to check in stacks of metal boxes and piles of bulging bags alongside Whitlam and Diana. Eventually airline staff took the VIPs around the back. But that was as far as the special treatment went. They were completely surrounded by journalists on the plane. But Diana was buzzing. Always good when focused and fired up, she was her old confident and chatty self.

They changed planes at Brussels and flew to Luanda. All the way Diana was amending a speech she was due to give on arrival, taking it out, reading it, scribbling on it, pacing up and down the aisle, reading it again and putting it back in her bag.

Coming down into Luanda, Diana and Whitlam could see the

reception party from a thousand feet up: yet more journalists clustered under arc lights and, to Diana's astonishment, dozens of dignitaries too, all lined up in a receiving line, resplendent in suits, uniforms or national costume.

> And suddenly she said, 'I'm going to have to change – we've got it all wrong.' And I said, 'Look, no, we're running this, this is our visit. We have to set the scene when we arrive.' 'OK, you're in charge,' she said.

Christina Lamb was waiting below:

> Luanda airport is completely wrecked. It's just a sort of shell of a building. There's not much of a runway and it was extremely hot and dusty. So we were waiting, lots of military around because it was a war zone, and waiting for her to arrive and come down the red carpet. And I was surprised, pleasantly surprised, when she arrived at least wearing very casual clothes. I'd expected her to arrive looking very glamorous. I mean she looked beautiful, but she was wearing just jeans and a T-shirt.

So the Princess shook hands in chinos, gave her speech and moved on to her hotel. Outside, a bemused Angolan selling chewing gum pulled at Christina Lamb's sleeve and asked her who the tall blonde lady was.

> The other journalists that were there were all royal hacks who were used to going to Klosters and those kinds of places. They were all, almost without exception, horrified to be in Luanda. They refused to eat the food – they lived on omelettes, because they thought they were safe. They wouldn't go out at night, and they were kind of not very keen on this new Diana going to difficult places.

Sun photographer Arthur Edwards thought Angola was the worst place he'd ever been.

The next day, the hundred-strong party of officials, journalists and charity workers set out for one of the Red Cross health centres. As they left the centre of Luanda, they drove past shanty-towns and markets, crumbling apartment blocks and police barracks.

> It was very hot, it was very dusty. Angola is a completely destroyed country, there're no roads to speak of, there are flies everywhere, lots of people, amputees walking around, and there're more amputees per capita than there are anywhere else. And so it's very traumatic travelling around there.

Diana asked questions about what she saw. 'Why are those children playing on that rubbish heap?' They stopped next to a Red Cross health centre. Sewage ran down the centre of the street. Diana thanked Whitlam for letting her see Angola as it really was, as a worker getting closer to the issue and to the people.

And, slightly to his surprise, Diana *was* on top of her subject:

> We were talking about the numbers of landmines there were in various parts of the world; in Angola it was disputed whether there were ten or fifteen million. I said, 'Don't forget there are ten million landmines left by the British in the deserts of North Africa.' To which she promptly replied, 'Mike, I think you'll find it's twenty-three million.' And she was right.

Diana wanted to visit Cuito, reputed to be the most heavily mined town in Africa. Completely ringed with minefields and largely in ruins, Cuito was an extremely dangerous place. They had planned to go there as part of a trip to nearby Huambo, but when they got to Angola the local Red Cross workers were told it was too hazardous and the government wouldn't allow it.

Diana refused to accept the decision. She pestered officials and then raised it with the President's wife. Whitlam didn't want to take any serious risks, but she was determined. One of her staff went and checked the town out, while the rest stayed in Luanda. The message came back that it was possible, but difficult, and it meant completely reorganising the schedule.

The journalists knew nothing about any of this, and when Diana was strongly advised not to take the full entourage into Cuito, she and Whitlam worked on the problem until midnight. They had to find an extra small plane and come up with a strategy to separate the tour into two parties. Eventually the UN offered a flight.

That same night a political argument broke out in London, where Diana was accused of being a 'loose cannon' and a 'self-publicist' by Conservative MPs. Whitlam was now trying to deal with two crises at once.

> At about two o'clock in the morning, after being up until midnight sorting the logistics of the Cuito trip, I got a phone call to say there were reports coming out of London about some politicians being highly critical of her taking this particular trip, that she was in conflict with government policy. As it happened, and unusually for me, in this rather grotty hotel I was staying in I had the British government's policy on landmines next to my bed. I was able to quote from it directly and immediately. I spent the next two or three hours sending messages back to ministers saying, 'Look, there is no conflict here. Please do something back in London about it.' The result was that there was a joint statement in London from the Foreign Secretary and from the Ministry of Defence, saying that there was no conflict at all, that what she was saying was in line with both British government and Red Cross policy.

At 5 a.m. Whitlam went to brief the British ambassador about what had happened overnight. He explained everything to Diana too when she came down at five-thirty to set off. They agreed that she must not be drawn personally into any argument about the MPs' critical statements. Then there was the Cuito trip to deal with.

We had two planes, put most of the journalists on one, and a few, the pool crew, on ours. After takeoff they were told that one group were going to Huambo as planned, and the smaller group was coming with us to Cuito, *en route*.

I had some explaining to do to some of the journalists. And the pool crew shared their material, so it worked out in the end. But she was a very determined woman, and thank goodness she was because it was one of the highlights of the visit.

And then suddenly Diana was confronted by the BBC's Jenny Bond, one of the journalists travelling with the pool crew. She demanded a reaction to the stories coming out of London. Diana fended her off, but was very angry in the Landcruiser afterwards. The BBC crew filmed her questioning Whitlam.

'Why is this being said? Why do people want to do this? What do I have to do?' She was quite upset about it. And I said, 'Look, we'll stick to the line we've taken. I'll deal with it. You just carry on with the visit and do what you have to do.'

On the trip to Huambo the thinned-down staff did not include a Red Cross interpreter, so Christina Lamb volunteered her services as a Portuguese speaker.

We arrived in Huambo, which is one of the most devastated towns in Angola. We flew in, and it was quite scary, we flew in a transport plane, landed on this airstrip, bumpy landing. It's an area where there's been intense fighting and it's still a disputed area, so it is right in the centre of the war zone. And we came out of the plane and walked through the town, and you had to walk very carefully, because it was heavily mined, so we were following in the footsteps of an anti-mine engineer.

So we were walking in a single file and being very careful where we trod. And the town itself is just like a ghost town. It's strange, the fronts of buildings are there, but there's nothing behind. So we walked through the main street, and we walked to this small hospital which has nothing – I mean, there's no equipment. The staff were all very nice and they took us in and they'd clearly done their best to clean up the hospital for their important visitor. But it was very, very basic.

There were not enough beds, so people were lying on the floor, people in terrible condition. One of the doctors showed us the pharmacy, and there was almost nothing, so few drugs. Then we went into various wards to see people. It was just huts really, with people in makeshift beds.

These people had no idea who she was, the patients. Because of the war, people had been completely cut off from the outside world. There's no electricity, no television, no newspapers outside of Luanda. So it's probably one of the few places she could go to and people really had no idea who she was. They'd never heard of Princess Diana. They just saw her as a sort of beautiful, white lady who appeared, they didn't really know why. So she went to some of the bedsides, and I actually interpreted for her because I speak Portuguese. I was trying to do my job as a journalist and get into places where I could hear what she was saying.

We went into one particular ward with children. And there was a little girl who was clearly in a terrible condition. She'd gone to fetch water and had stepped on a mine and basically had her entire insides blown out, and everything was sort of hanging out. It was horrific. And the hospital said that she wouldn't survive – they were just making her as comfortable as possible. You could see that she probably wouldn't last, maybe even that day.

After Diana moved on, I stayed and just asked the girl a few more questions, because I thought I would write about her. And she said to me, 'Who was that?' And it was quite hard trying to explain Princess Diana to somebody who didn't know. And I said, 'She's a princess from England, from far away.' And she said to me, 'Is she an angel?' And I found that really moving. This little girl probably died a few hours after that – I know she died – and it somehow seemed nice that that was the last thing that she saw, this beautiful lady that she thought was an angel.

While she was touring Angola, having just returned from another Caribbean holiday with Victoria Mendham, Diana found a few spare minutes to pursue her secretary over what she deemed to be her share of the cost. Since they had been staying in beachside villas at a cost of £1,200 a night, this came to rather a lot.

Diana leaving the hospital to make a phone call to Victoria Mendham is perhaps the defining paradox in a story that's so rich in them.

How to weigh up and value a life? Not, perhaps, by algebra. A bad act does not cancel out a good one. And some of the greatest philanthropists have been bullies. As Diana was – no, as Diana *could* be, by the end. But because of Angola, because of Henry Street, she was forgiven. When Diana died, Victoria Mendham volunteered to come in to her old office and help arrange the funeral.

After the hospital Diana was scheduled to walk through a half-cleared minefield. The idea had been conceived when Whitlam had talked to the Halo Trust, the mine clearance team, about what they could show the Princess. They wanted her to see the range of landmines that had to be taken out of the ground and some of the risks that their mine clearance workers took every day.

All around, young men and women were prodding very carefully into the dusty African soil. Exposed and half-extracted mines were there for her to inspect. In Cuito she had just heard a story about children who were playing on the local football field, which was supposed to have been cleared. Seven were killed when one of them trod on a large mine that had somehow been missed. Mike Whitlam was feeling nervous.

> The Halo Trust guys took over. It's not a job I would like. They gave her a very full briefing, saying not to move away from them and how to react if she saw anything a bit odd. I think by the end of the briefing she was beginning to wonder whether this was a good idea. But she did it.
>
> We all walked through this cleared area, to a point where they had almost completed clearing a mine that they'd found. You could see this landmine buried in the ground. I think it had been deactivated. I don't know – they never told me – but I hope it had been. Then she walked back on her own from the minefield, wearing the visor and the body armour, and this was the shot that the journalists were really looking for, so we all stayed way out of the way.
>
> One or two journalists, for whatever reason, hadn't quite got the shot they wanted and jokingly asked her if she'd mind doing it again. And she was quite happy to do this. She realised that this was one of the shots that was really going to make a big impact around the world. So she did the walk a second time.
>
> When we got back she pressed the button which blew up the mine she'd just seen. It had been wired to explode. And that was one less landmine.

Immediately after the walk, the journalists switched back to the story coming out of London. Whitlam held an impromptu press conference next to the minefield.

> I remember trying to answer their questions and I was just aware out of the corner of my eye that Diana was creeping closer and closer to the group. Until at one point she just couldn't hold it any more and she said, 'I'm here on a humanitarian visit.'
>
> They were pushing me into saying this was an ill-advised statement, or something along those lines. I said that this seems to me to be somebody making mischief.

Throughout the Angola trip Christina Lamb watched Diana closely, waiting for the caring mask to slip. She noticed that Diana had an eye for a photograph. To that extent her scepticism was confirmed.

> She knew the photo opportunity. I mean, she had an instinct for it. That was fascinating to watch. She would go into a hospital or school and she would immediately spot, you know, the girl with two stumps but amazing, appealing eyes who would look great sat next to her. There is that famous photograph from the Angola trip. It was not a photographer who put Diana with that girl, Diana walked straight over to her. There were many other people there, equally sad victims of the war in Angola and the landmines, but there were few that would have looked so captivating in a photograph as that girl. And she knew.
>
> And I saw the same thing in another hospital where there was a little boy, a real character, who had lost both his legs, had got artificial legs and was trying to walk and play football. And she spotted him immediately and went over, and you could see that out of the corner of her eye she was looking for the cameras. I didn't like that at all.

But Lamb began to see even this as an aspect of an assured professionalism rather than an insatiable hunger for attention. And she hadn't forgotten the angel story.

> Diana had an incredible empathy with these people. I found it really astonishing because she somehow managed to transmit to them this feeling of really caring about what had happened. It didn't seem cynical at all once you were actually there with her. And she had this kind of aura about her, which I've only seen really I would say with Nelson Mandela – he has the same thing – where he somehow is able to transmit this force of personality and of caring to people.

I was very impressed. It changed my view of her.

I spend a lot of time in developing countries, writing about issues that people back here are not very interested in. And it's very difficult to get people's interest. Having Princess Diana in the middle of Angola, talking to landmine victims, immediately means that people like my mum and dad, and people back here, would read the story, because they'd see the picture of her.

Christopher Hitchens has a view of Diana's African trip that doesn't square with those of the converted sceptics in the Land-cruisers.

I do quite a lot of public lecturing in the United States, and at question time I ask people, 'Who was the last American to win the Nobel Prize for Peace?' Americans are very proud of their Nobel Prize winners – it's like the Olympics for them. And the prize for peace is one of the most respected and it hasn't been won by very many Americans. And I say, for a clue, that this is in the last two or three years. Nobody knows. Absolutely nobody knows. I've never had anyone put their hand up and get the answer right. And I don't blame you if you don't know. Do you?

No. Well, it was Jodie Williams for the landmines campaign, for bringing up the question of landmines and the appalling damage they do to civilians. I then say to the audience, 'Well, is there anyone here who doesn't know that Princess Diana once spent a day in Angola, being filmed near a landmine?' And they have to admit I've got them – they all did know that. I say, 'Well, is this not possibly substituting the phoney for the real thing? Is it not wolfing down the wrapper and throwing the truffle away?'

It may be unfair that Diana attracted more attention than Jodie Williams, but it was important too. Arthur Edwards, who had taken the first photograph of her ever printed, was there in Africa and now took perhaps the most important. And neither Arthur nor his paper would have gone anywhere near Angola for Jodie Williams.

For eight gruelling days, Diana and Mike Whitlam had hit every news bulletin. The criticism from London only added to coverage that instantly created a wave of interest in the subject, taking the question of the stalled landmines treaty directly into the public arena.

> I can't think of anybody now who could give such a very simple, global message, and get people to listen, and take notice. Not a single individual. And she did it on that visit, without any question whatsoever. If a politician stands up and does it, then the opposition will start to argue against it. If it's a religious leader, there's some other argument against it.
>
> It raised the profile so that governments really couldn't escape that, and it certainly helped the Red Cross and a number of other agencies to be able to argue the case for governments to ratify. Without her intervention, it would have been a struggle, I think, to make it happen in Canada.
>
> I think, had she lived, this would have been the new way that we'd see Diana working. Whether overseas, or in the UK. She just enjoyed it. She was a natural. I think Diana's motivation for the landmines campaign was no different from her motivation for many of the other things that she became involved with. She was particularly good at raising issues that were unpopular. She wanted to make a difference. The campaign was a global campaign and needed lifting. She felt she could do something.

A meeting was due in Canada – a meeting of all the governments that had said they were going to ratify the treaty. In was set for December 1997. Diana was planning to be there.

It's possible that Hitchens is right, that Diana's most celebrated good works *were* the result of a leap on to a rolling bandwagon, an over-rehearsed photograph, a wrapper without the truffle.

Against that there's Mike Whitlam, who thinks she changed the world for the better that week in Angola, and Christina Lamb's glimpse of the same unaffected charisma that had worked its magic down Henry Street. And perhaps real change takes more than the day-to-day slog of activists like Jodie Williams. Perhaps, as Ed Mathews discovered in New York, you have to cut a few deals to get good things done in a bad, sad world.

Was she an angel? No, of course she wasn't. She was a woman who was capable of behaving in strikingly unangelic ways, even in Huambo. But at that moment by the bedside, to that dying girl, and for that great cause, Diana was the only angel in town.

17
Last Summer

On 1 May 1997 the Labour Party swept the Conservatives out of government after eighteen years. Diana was at a dinner along with businessman Gulu Lalvani, one of several friends who had recently switched political allegiance. He had an invitation to Labour's late-night victory party at the Festival Hall. Although she was very tempted, Diana felt she should not go with him. Instead he rang her several times from the party to discover her sitting up late, excitedly watching the election results come in.

For Mike Whitlam the change of government made an immediate difference:

> [It] enabled me to discuss with at least three government ministers why the British government were not first to ratify the landmines convention, even though they'd signed it. And so people like Robin Cook [the new Foreign Secretary] and others quickly came together and we managed to make it happen.

Labour brought other new possibilities for Diana. She told Lalvani that she got on well with Tony and Cherie Blair and had given Cherie some advice on how to dress in public. She was invited to Chequers, where Blair said he was going to offer her the long-dreamed-of 'ambassadorial role'. He had, he said, already discussed it with Bill Clinton, a man Diana also admired. By July nothing had been arranged, but Diana was optimistic. She wanted some kind of peacemaker's role and was confident that she could achieve something by mediating in Ireland.

'You'll never guess who just dropped by. My ex!'

Diana's relationship with Charles had improved, as her trainer Jenny Rivett recalls:

> I remember one time that he had popped into Kensington Palace and I was there for some training, and she came bounding in and said, 'Oh, Charles says I've got great legs,' and was just kind of really happy and pleased. And I just thought, That's great, they obviously have got some form of a relationship that's working.

Charles visited Diana several times at Kensington Palace in the spring, dropping in for tea when he used the nearby helipad. They appeared comfortable together at William's confirmation and Harry's school sports day. Charles offered to take her and William with him to Hong Kong, where he was due to hand over control to the Chinese. She said she'd think about it.

In March, *Vanity Fair* commissioned New York photographer Mario Testino to shoot a special set of portrait pictures for their July cover. They were among the best ever taken. Under the headline 'Diana Reborn', she looked confident, fresh and relaxed.

But thoughout this period personal relations remained stormy. Diana argued with her acupuncturist Oonagh Toffolo and her energy healer Simone Simmons, both of whom had become friends and had done much to comfort her throughout her relationship with Hasnat Khan. She pursued her vendetta against Tiggy Legge-Bourke, her office issuing hostile statements about the nanny after she was seen pouring champagne at an Eton picnic. When she was criticised for this, Diana blamed Michael Gibbons, her new secretary. She also blamed Stuart Higgins editor of the *Sun*.

> We ran the story about what the Princess had said about Tiggy Legge-Bourke, which came from the Princess's office . . . [Later] her aides ring up and say, 'How could you do that? It's totally

untrue.' They had clearly been told by the Princess, 'Get on the phone and give that Higgins bloke a bollocking, now!' And I said, 'But you know it's true. You told me!'

Diana's relationship with Hasnat Khan remained difficult, as she confided to Joseph Sanders:

> She hoped they would be married and have a family. One of the problems was that Hasnat Khan's family were Moslems and they didn't really want Hasnat to marry anyone who wasn't a Moslem. She went from great joy to great despair. Sometimes she said, 'Oh God, it's never going to work. He doesn't want to see me any more.' Sometimes she said, 'Oh, it's fantastic, you know, I am so happy.'

In May, Diana revisited Pakistan for a two-day visit, including lunch with sixty Pakistani MPs, each paying a thousand dollars towards Imran Khan's hospital. She also visited Hasnat Khan's family once again. She did not tell Khan that she was going, and the visit forced their relationship into crisis. After a series of newspaper articles the previous autumn, Khan suspected that a press campaign was being orchestrated to push him into marriage. To find that Diana had visited his family behind his back, and that this visit had also been leaked to the press, was too much. On her return, Diana said that the doctor was withdrawing from her and she was very distressed according to Simone Simmons and Elsa Bowker. In June, Diana was photographed leaving Annabel's nightclub with Gulu Lalvani at 2 a.m. Khan was further angered and would not take her calls for several days.

Le Monde is a heavyweight Parisian newspaper covering political and economic stories in great detail. Annick Cojean worked mostly on foreign reports. The paper followed British politics very closely, but found Royal Family stories of little interest. When they heard that Cojean wanted to interview 'Princess Di', her colleagues laughed and said, 'She'll say "no", that's obvious, and anyway it's ridiculous, *Le Monde* doesn't deal with princesses.' But Cojean was persistent. She had been commissioned to write a series of articles for the summer, each based on an influential photograph: the little girl in Vietnam, burned by napalm; Gorbachev saved by Yeltsin; Arafat signing the peace deal with Rabin. And among the images that most struck her were several of Diana. She called Kensington Palace and described the idea.

> I said that I wanted to interview the Princess in the same way as I was going to interview Gorbachev, Arafat and Lech Walesa. I spoke to someone very friendly, who said, 'But you must write to her.' I said, 'She must get five hundred letters a day!' And then the secretary laughed and said, 'The Princess reads all the letters!' I think that the very day she received it, we got a phone call saying, 'The Princess is delighted. When do you want to come?'

When Cojean arrived at Kensington Palace, she showed Diana the other photographs. She was interested in the little girl from Vietnam and said, 'But she's alive! That's incredible! Where is she? What country does she live in?' Then they turned to the fifteen pictures of Diana that the Frenchwoman had brought.

> Each time she looked at a photo she'd say, 'Oh yes, I remember, that was at the hospital in London. Ah, that was with Nelson Mandela, that was wonderful.' And then suddenly she saw a photo of the little boy and said: 'That was in Lahore in 1996. I'll always remember, I held him in my arms and I found out later that he had died very soon afterwards. He had cancer.'

Diana reminisced about the tenderness she had felt while holding the boy.

> I asked her, 'Why did you pick this little child up?' And she said, 'I knew that he was going to die, I spoke to his parents. I asked if I could take him in my arms and I held him like that for a long time.' The little boy, who was blind, lifted his eyes towards her at one point. He heard them laughing and he said, 'Please don't make fun of me!'

Then Diana came up with some harsh remarks about British newspapers. 'The press is ferocious. Whatever I do, wherever I go, it waits for me, it tracks me down. Whatever I do, whatever I say, it will always look for controversy and contradiction. It will always criticise me.'

They talked about the Angola trip, and Diana explained how important the landmine campaign was to her, and that she hoped the convention would be signed by the United States. Cojean said, 'But there is a new British government that has just made a very important announcement to ban landmines.' Diana replied, 'Yes, it's terrific. It's what he promised and he's doing a terrific job. The last government was hopeless!'

> That day I met a Princess who seemed to be happy, who was very relaxed and had a cheerful sparkle in her eye. She spoke with such warmth and conviction about what she did and about her life. She said that she had a very strong and special contact with people and that she had to be close and tender. This was the impulse which would propel her towards other things. She said, 'Wherever it is in the world that someone calls me in distress, I will run to them.'

Mike Whitlam had organised a trip to Washington to launch the American Red Cross's anti-landmine campaign. Diana flew there on 16 June in time to attend Katherine Graham's eightieth birthday party. The *Washington Post* publisher had recently become one of Diana's expanding number of American friends. The next day she gave a press conference with Elizabeth Dole, president of the American Red Cross. That night there was a gala dinner for five hundred at the Museum of Women in the Arts. Mike Whitlam remembers what a difference her presence made:

> We raised six hundred and fifty thousand dollars in the one evening, which for Washington was a very good result.
>
> We stayed with Lucia Flecha da Lima and were very well looked after. I'd been out at a series of meetings and then I came in and one of the staff said would I like to join the Princess for tea in her suite? So I said, 'Yes, I would be very happy to' and went into the lounge to find her not quite how I'd imagined, but with Lucia Flecha da Lima, relaxing before the evening event with a face pack on! I blushed, and she commented that I'd blushed, which made me blush even more. I turned to leave, saying, 'I thought we were having tea?' And she said, 'No, no, come and join us and have some girl talk.'
>
> And so we had a cup of tea and talked about the day, and then I left her. That evening we were due to be at the event at seven or eight o'clock and I was waiting in the lobby. She came down the stairs in this stunning red dress. She really did look good. She walked down the stairs and spotted me, and I must have looked absolutely ridiculous because she just came up to me and pushed my chin up to close my dropping jaw.

Diana wanted to speak to the President about her future. Instead she got a breakfast meeting with Hillary Clinton. She flew to New York to visit Mother Teresa, saturating the Bronx with TV crews and security, and then returned to Washington to complete her Red Cross commitments. She returned to New York on 24 June for the preview party of a charity sale of her dresses, an idea suggested by Prince William. The party, hosted by Lord Hindlip of Christie's, was also for charity, and eight hundred guests each paid over £100 to attend. Kate Moss, Zandra Rhodes and Barbara Walters were there, amid rumours that

Walters was about to record another confessional interview with Diana.

Americans loved Diana, not least, as Graydon Carter explains, because they saw her as a rebel:

> I think it may have reflected a love-hate relationship with England. Americans don't really like royal families. They only like the 'theme park' aspect of a royal family, the amusement park icons of this little fantasy kingdom across the ocean. She represented both a connection to that and somebody who was rebellious against it. And I think America was founded out of rebellion and they like rebels by and large. And here's one who looked fabulous in an evening gown too.

The sale raised $3.26 million. It was split between several charities, with the bulk going to the Aids Crisis Trust.

Back in London, Hasnat Khan was still agonising about his relationship with Diana.

New York was a second home now. In July, Diana had lunch with two of the city's most influential women – Tina Brown, editor of the *New Yorker*, and Anna Wintour, editor of *Vogue*. They met at the Four Seasons restaurant, the epitome of understated Manhattan chic. Behind the shimmering gold-chain curtains, and alongside the cherry trees, mahogany and Picassos, Diana told a slightly incredulous Brown that Tony Blair was about to send her on 'missions', and that she was looking forward to spreading peace and love and 'sorting people's heads out'. Perhaps, as Brown had once predicted, Diana had now reached 'Graceland'. But if so, she still ventured out. She spoke of secret visits to hospices, to comfort the dying, and of how such moments brought her release. Brown thought her strangely intense, but mature too, 'a woman in earnest'.

POV stands for Point of View. It's a film-making term for the moment when you cut to the world as seen through a particular character's eyes. We thought hard about the best way to render Diana's POV in our television series, or whether we should even try. With a video camera set to record three or six frames a second, the perspectives lurch and then settle, a face in a crowd emerges from a blurry background, the lights of passing cars smear across the screen. Is this how she saw her world – her worlds? For by now she was moving quickly through so many of them. Thinking of Angola at the Four Seasons, thinking of Manhattan in Luanda. Absorbing the taste and refinement of one, the amputations and shantytowns of the other, her internal camera lurching first one way then another. And all the time, the montage speeding up.

Mohamed Al Fayed had cultivated royalty for years. Harrods, the famous London department store that he owned, prominently displayed its many 'by royal appointment' crests, and he sponsored the annual Windsor Horse Show. He was even closer to Raine Spencer, a non-executive director of Harrods. Diana was a regular visitor to the store, and Fayed gave generously to her favourite charities. Hearing that she had no firm summer plans, he invited Diana and her sons to join his family on a holiday in St Tropez.

Diana wanted her sons to have a great summer holiday, their first since the divorce was finalised, and she thought it would be good for them to have Fayed's four youngest children around. After letters were sent from Harrods to Kensington Palace promising total privacy, Diana decided to ignore the negative advice she received, saying that Fayed was an old family friend and she trusted him to take great care of her and her sons. The day after Diana said yes, Fayed completed the purchase of a new £20 million luxury yacht, the *Jonikal*.

Within twenty-four hours of the arrival of Diana and her

sons, the St Tropez photographers were tipped off. Jean-Louis Macault usually worked the summer season, taking pictures of visiting celebrities:

> It was about seven o'clock in the evening when I received a phone call from the chief editor of my agency in Paris saying, 'Diana's in St Tropez!' My reaction was this is going to be very difficult because this girl keeps herself hidden the whole time. She'll be in some villa that will be impossible to find, or on a boat. Then they told me she's staying with someone called Al Fayed, who had a villa in the park area, plus a boat and a private landing jetty, just after Brigitte Bardot's place.
>
> Then, for the first time in my life, I saw Diana. She was being taken towards a huge yacht. This, the woman who ran away, who stole the keys of photographers' motorbikes. One had always had the impression that it would be impossible to get a photo like this of her. And now I could see her wearing a swimming costume! I waited there for the best part of the day. There weren't many of us, only the five or six who were usually in St Tropez. I saw her come back again that evening wearing the same costume, walking along quite calmly. She climbed out of the motor-boat, stopped for a moment to say something to the boatman, and then she went back into Al Fayed's house, glancing right at us towards her right, she looked at us. Zap! I thought that she would run or that bodyguards would put a towel in front of her, but no. This seemed incredible!
>
> The next day I returned. At about eleven o'clock in the morning we saw William and Harry arrive, at which point we said to ourselves that all we needed now was Prince Charles, the Queen of England and the Pope.
>
> Diana was playing, joking with her children, grabbing them by the neck, kissing Harry. We took vertical shots, wide shots, shots of William, who was on jet-skis. It was like Christmas!

> William went past and sprayed her all over. He went round and round her, spraying her, she was laughing.

While most of the world enjoyed Macault's images of family fun, the coverage in Britain made much of Diana's choice of holiday companion. The *News of the World* led with 'Di and Sleaze Row Tycoon'; the *Sunday Mirror* chastised royal free-loading with 'Di's Freebie'.

On Monday, 14 July Diana set off in a boat to meet the press. Arthur Edwards, who had arrived with a posse of British journalists, photographed the approach of an agitated Princess:

> The first thing she said was, 'How long are you going to be here?' And I told her and she said, 'I don't know why I don't live abroad like my boys want me to.' You'd say, 'All right, I'll speak to the editor and we'll pull off.' And she said, 'I don't want that. I just want to know how long you're going to stay.'
>
> She was saying things like, 'I'm not here as a guest of Mr Fayed. I'm here as a guest of his wife.' And then she said, 'You'll be surprised what I'm going to do in the next two weeks.' And to this day I do not know what she was talking about. The only thing I can say is that as she left our boat she was close to tears. And then she did an amazing thing, she went back to the villa and jumped on the back of one of the jet-skis and roared round our boat several times, making fabulous pictures. She jumped off, went to the edge of the jetty and did a most beautiful dive into the sea and swam around laughing and as though she was having a wonderful time. It was the most amazing thing. One minute she was saying, 'When are you leaving? You're upsetting the boys!' And the next minute she was giving us the most fantastic photo call.

Edwards and his colleagues left the Fayed party alone during the evenings, as Macault explains:

> You shouldn't imagine that she was shut up in a huge villa with Al Fayed's bodyguards. She went out every evening, to restaurants, to nightclubs, and no photographer ever went into St Tropez during the evening to photograph her – there was a tacit understanding.
>
> The photographers were saying to themselves that if they wanted to have the same thing the next morning, it was better to stay quiet and let her lead her life as a woman at night-time. Then the following morning was for us again: she arrived, she put on her show, because, you know, it was a bit of a show. It was a real fashion parade, really rather enjoyable.
>
> The bodyguards would tell us that Diana was leaving by boat and that she would be back at around four in the afternoon; they didn't hide anything from us. Sometimes one of Al Fayed's men would come down and say to us: 'That's enough for today, there won't be anything more today.' They would only have had to make a telephone call and the police would have made us leave.

More holiday pictures were splashed across the world's front pages, outshining the coverage of Camilla Parker Bowles, whose fiftieth birthday party was hosted by the Prince at Highgrove on 18 July.

The day after Diana's conversation with the British photographers, Fayed telephoned his eldest son Dodi and asked him to join the party. Dodi Al Fayed was forty-one years old and had spent the better part of his life spending his father's money: on celebrity girlfriends, on fast cars, on cocaine and, occasionally, on producing movies. However, Dodi's American friends described him as generous and affectionate, given to sudden declarations of friendship or of love. Several bad debts had arisen from this enthusiasm for handing out expensive gifts. He was also said to be charming and a good listener.

Dodi had been staying at his apartment in Paris along with his girlfriend, an American model called Kelly Fisher. The relationship had lasted eight months, almost as long as Dodi's marriage in 1986 to another model, Suzanne Gregard. Dodi had given Fisher a ring and they were planning to live together in a new apartment in Malibu, California. Fisher and her family considered the couple engaged, although this would later be contested, and she was planning a wedding ceremony in Los Angeles.

Dodi received the phone call from his father, as a result of which he told Fisher he had to go to London. Instead, he flew immediately to St Tropez. In a later phone conversation with Dodi, Fisher discovered that he wasn't where he had said he was. They argued and then, two days later, Dodi sent a private plane to bring her to the South of France to join him. While Fayed, father and son, entertained Diana and the children at their villa and on board the *Jonikal*, Kelly Fisher was kept out of sight on another family boat, moored close to the house. One evening Dodi rented a disco just for Diana and her sons. He spent the days and evenings with his father's guests and spent the nights with Fisher. At the end of the holiday, she flew home to America unaware that a romance between Dodi and Diana had started yards from where she was staying.

Some of Diana's friends later suggested that she romanced Dodi Fayed to make Hasnat Khan jealous and so force his hand in marriage. But things were not that simple. Diana did have qualities in common with Dodi, the ability quickly to form an emotional attachment being one of them. They shared an interest in movies and movie stars too, and both enjoyed lying in the sun reading magazines and exchanging endearments. And Dodi had one crucial advantage over Diana's previous boyfriends: he had 'all the toys', as she put it. He was able to keep up with Diana's own lifestyle, lavishing time, attention and money on her and offering her protection and privacy when she wanted it. Lucia Flecha da Lima believed that she was captivated by a man who had no full-time occupation and could dedicate all of his time to her, something she had never had in her life before then.

Diana and her sons returned to London on 20 July. Hasnat Khan, unaware that Dodi and Diana had grown close, informed her that he had decided to end their relationship. During these same few days, piles of gifts and flowers arrived from Dodi, accompanied by requests for further meetings.

Diana made a brief visit to Paris to see him on 26 July. She stayed in the luxurious Imperial Suite of the Fayed-owned Ritz hotel in the Place Vendôme. A Fayed family chauffeur, Philippe Dourneau, saw the couple walk hand in hand along the River Seine. Diana and Dodi were then together in London for a few days before flying back to the South of France on 31 July for a second holiday, alone this time, cruising to Corsica and Sardinia aboard the *Jonikal*. René Delorm, Dodi's butler, observed them happily lying around in the sun, reading, talking and being very affectionate. Meanwhile Kelly Fisher was back in Los Angeles planning her wedding, scheduled for 8 August.

The author Kate Snell believes that Diana was in shock at the news from Khan and wanted to make him jealous. This, she says, was Diana's motive for helping Mario Brenna take a photograph of the couple kissing during this cruise. Brenna acted on a tip-off from his London colleague, photographer Jason Fraser. The day before Diana left, Fraser received a call from someone close to her, telling him that the Princess was on her way to the Mediterranean. He was told the name of the boat, who she was with and approximately where the couple could be found. The caller made it clear that there would be no complaints if photographs were taken. All Brenna had to do was to shadow the boat to Corsica and wait for the right moment. Some of his pictures were taken from just ten yards away. Brenna then telephoned Fraser in London, who contacted the press. A furious bidding war broke out, which the *Sunday Mirror* won.

The *Jonikal* visited Monaco, where Dodi took Diana to the Repossi jeweller to choose a ring from the 'Tell Me Yes' range. The manager promised that it would be ready for collection from his Paris shop on 30 August.

Brenna's kiss photo was the hottest property in years, as Ken Lennox was quick to realise:

> Diana kissing Dodi, a million pounds. I think it earned in total three million pounds around the world. We were the first daily to get it. It went to a Sunday before us. We paid a sensational amount of money for it. Most I've ever been involved in. In fact it's ten times anything I've ever been involved in and I was there at the *Sun* for nearly seven years.

On 7 August, the *Mirror* published the first news of the couple's romance with the headline 'Di's New Man is Al Fayed's Son'. 'Hasnat broke her heart' three months ago, it told readers. Three days later, the *Sunday Mirror* published the Brenna photographs of the couple locked in an embrace. The paper speculated that an engagement was forthcoming, quoting some of Diana's unnamed London friends. 'Dodi's to Di for,' said the *Sun* the next day, reproducing, on page three, Brenna's picture. They protected their spectacular investment in the pictures with the warning '(Any reproduction prohibited) OUR LAWYERS ARE WATCHING'. Kelly Fisher received a fax of a British newspaper front page. Her wedding was obviously off. She called Dodi in London but never spoke to him. Mohamed Al Fayed took the call and, she says, told her never to call him or his son again. On 14 August, Kelly sued Dodi in Los Angeles, claiming he had dumped her after insisting she give up her career for him. She then told her story of duplicity and abandonment to the *News of the World*.

Quite what Diana was trying to do remains mysterious. Some level-headed friends like Lord Palumbo thought she was merely having fun:

> I thought that it wasn't serious, but that she was probably just having a good time. After all, she was divorced and why shouldn't she? The Al Fayeds are controversial people and to some extent she was controversial too. So I think they found a certain amount of common ground on that basis. I don't think myself that it would have led anywhere. I think she was going through one of her periods of confusion and at the end of it, had the tragedy not happened, she would have sorted it out. I thought that she was very much on the rebound from Hasnat Khan.

When the *Sunday Mirror* published the photographs, Diana was in Bosnia, further promoting the Red Cross landmine campaign. The trip, lasting from 7 to 10 August, was run jointly by Norwegian People's Aid and the Landmine Survivors' Network of Washington. Diana visited landmine projects in Travnic, Sarajevo and Zenezica. Bill Deedes accompanied her. Like Lamb in Angola, the veteran reporter Deedes was struck by Diana's silent stillness, how good she was at hearing and dealing with grief, simply stretching out a hand to touch, applying her own brand of soothing tranquillity, even in the face of stories that made Deedes, a journalist with fifty years of war experience, blanch. One afternoon he saw her embrace a woman by a graveside and stand motionless with her for what seemed like half an hour. He thought – as Mike Whitlam had thought in Angola – that there was no one else in the world who could have fulfilled this role. Deedes described Diana as a human being with ordinary faults, but an unusually big heart.

She returned to London on 11 August and made Rosa Monckton listen to Dodi's voice on her answering machine. On 12 August she flew with Dodi in the Harrods helicopter to see Rita Rogers, her psychic. Rogers had previously told Diana that she would meet a dark man at sea, and Diana wanted to show her this first-hand evidence of her prognostic skill.

Lana Marks was surprised by the incessant press coverage.

> I asked her what she had thought about the press reports. And she said, 'Lana, I really can't sit at home and watch the four walls of Kensington Palace. To get out and have a good time is just so nice for me.' There's one thing that people don't understand about Diana's personality – if she did permit you to enter her life she was very warm and loving and trusting. And this was so badly misinterpreted by people who really didn't understand Diana. She was just showing somebody, who she was having a good time with, some warmth.

Diana then flew with Rosa Monckton to Athens on the Harrods Gulfstream jet. There the two women boarded another yacht for a holiday cruising around the Greek islands. She told Monckton all about Dodi and appeared to be very much in love. She spoke about his many presents of jewellery and anticipated the arrival of a ring – which was destined, she said, for the fourth finger of her right hand, not her left. She said how nice it was for her to be made welcome by the whole Fayed family, and how nice to be with a man who obviously cared for her and wanted to share that with the world, rather than being embarrassed or ashamed to be seen with her.

They came back on 20 August. Dodi had gone to America the day before to see his lawyers about Kelly Fisher's lawsuit. Diana had planned to see Lana Marks next

> Diana had spoken to me twice about going on vacation with her. We finally got both of our schedules together and decided we would go to Milan. I'd told her so much about the Four Seasons Hotel in Milan, and La Scala, how lovely it was, and Lake Como too. We had decided to spend four days together at that time. The reservations were made and we had booked flights. Then my father passed away very, very suddenly and I had to dash down to South Africa for his funeral. Diana was so supportive and kind and sympathetic and she completely understood.

But this left her with a free week at the end of her summer. And when Dodi asked whether she would come back to the South of France, she agreed.

On 21 August, Diana saw Dr Lily Hua Yu, her Chinese medicine specialist, in London and gave her a positive health report: 'she told me she had never felt so physically well in all her life.' Later that day Diana returned to the Mediterranean on the Harrods jet for her second private holiday with Dodi on board the *Jonikal*. Bodyguards Kez Wingfield and Trevor Rees-Jones accompanied them. Dodi also brought his Los Angeles masseur and therapist, Myriah Daniels, who described herself as a 'Missionary of Natural Spiritualism'.

Once more Jason Fraser was tipped off. But this time the calls didn't come from an intermediary but from Diana herself. Fraser came to France to take his own photographs. The *Jonikal* was moored at Portofino, where Fraser photographed Diana on a bed of yellow cushions with Dodi. The following morning Diana called Fraser in his hotel room to ask why the pictures had been so grainy. Fraser wasn't the only one to enjoy Diana's collaboration. French photographer Jean-Louis Macault was also still in close attendance:

> She came down, I started taking photos. We were really very close to each other. I had my feet in the water, she came right above me, click-click, zap-zap. I started taking photos for all I am worth and she looked at me and slowed down. She slowed down for Dodi to catch up with her . . . so I kept taking photos at which point there was a slight gust of wind and she made a movement like that, put her hair back in place, at one side. Then she looked at me and made a little smile.

She had often encouraged happy holiday snaps, but never before with a lover. Once again she seemed keen for the world to see her happiness.

Diana spent a lot of this week on the telephone. Annabel Goldsmith later wrote an article saying that she, Elsa Bowker and Robert Devorik were all called and told that Dodi was Diana's 'summer fling'. Goldsmith also said that Diana rang members of Hasnat Khan's family in Britain during the week to say that there was 'nothing in it' and that she was hoping to see them all again soon.

But those who downplay the Dodi relationship choose to ignore his attraction. Here was a man who demonstrably worshipped Diana. No more sneaking about, no more 2 a.m. denials to Richard Kay of what she knew to be the truth. It must have been liberating to be loved so straightforwardly at last, and by someone who made few demands in return. Perhaps that was all the reason Diana needed for wanting the world to share her pleasure. 'Here I am,' the pictures said, 'happy at last, with a good-looking boyfriend and on a millionaire's yacht to boot.' That was what Ken Lennox, one of the men paying for the pictures, believed.

> She wanted to show Prince Charles she was having a great time . . . It was, 'You've got Camilla, you've got the Rottweiler, but look at me!' It was there in so many pictures. And she was a beautiful woman. She looked sensational in those swimming costumes.

In the care of the Fayed family, Diana thought that she could control the press's access to her at last. When she wanted them, they would come. When she didn't, she could disappear into the private jets, luxury suites, the family's hideaways in Paris, Malibu and the Swiss Alps. Diana had worked hard in Angola and then skulked around London in the back of Hasnat Khan's old car. But here with Dodi was the fun side of being rich and famous, and she was letting her hair down, luxuriating in the Imperial Suite, champagne on ice.

On 28 August the *New York Times* printed a long and favourable profile of Mohamed Al Fayed. In the passages about Dodi's relationship with Diana its interview stressed parallels with Edward VIII and Mrs Simpson. Perhaps this romantic royal reject was also finding love in a world of millionaires' yachts and Paris villas. That evening Diana and Dodi toasted the first anniversary of her divorce on a deserted Sardinian beach under the stars. For the Fayeds the summer was going perfectly. For Diana too. 'Yes, it's bliss,' she told Rosa Monckton on her mobile.

Annick Cojean was in Washington when her feature about Diana and the photograph appeared in *Le Monde*.

> There was a knock at the door. It was the director of the hotel, who said, 'What is going on? I'd like you to tell me who you are! The telephone exchange can't handle it! People have been asking for you throughout the night and there are several television crews downstairs who want to meet you.' I replied, 'I'm not at all famous but I interviewed Princess Diana and it has set something off in Europe and I'm not quite sure what it is.'
>
> It was a small hotel, and as soon as I arrived in the foyer there were people following me with a camera. The questions came thick and fast: 'Why did the Princess give you an interview?' 'Do you know that it's the first time that she has done this?' 'Why does she want to talk about politics?' 'Why did she criticise the Major government?'
>
> And I kept saying, 'But it isn't a scoop. She has been campaigning against landmines and so she's delighted and cheers when the government decides to ban them, and she says that the previous government, which didn't want to ban them, was wrong. Where's the surprise? Where are the revelations?'
>
> I sensed that they wanted to whip up a storm. I remember sitting on my bed and saying to myself, 'But it's incredible, it's incredible!' Kensington Palace was distancing itself from it all, saying, 'The Princess never criticised the Conservative government.'
>
> All of a sudden I was in the public eye. One paper published

two photos, of me and Diana, facing each other, with the caption: 'Two women, one word, "hopeless"'. I could have cried, I was totally overwhelmed. I wanted to telephone Diana at that point. But how could I? Who was I to ring her? But I really wanted to say to her, 'Wait, I didn't want this. You know what took place during our conversation, you know that I was very respectful of your words.'

And then all of a sudden it was being turned into something controversial, incendiary, explosive. It was horrifying. I had just realised the nature of the British press.

Mohamed Al Fayed says that he spoke to Dodi on the *Jonikal* and his son told him that he and Diana were going to get married, and would soon go to Repossi's in Paris to pick up the ring. Rings can mean different things to different people, as Kelly Fisher had recently discovered, and it is far from clear that Diana was aware of this particular ring's importance to Dodi.

Dodi, says his father, added that he also wanted to take Diana around the Windsor villa in Paris (Edward VIII and Mrs Simpson's old home, now a Fayed property) because he planned to live there with her once they were married. But however warm the feelings between the couple, an engagement after a month doesn't sound like Diana's style. She would surely have wanted to talk it over with her sons. Diana's friends tell various stories. Vivienne Parry:

> She wrote to me to say that she had never been happier and I was thrilled for her. But I was also concerned about her, because this was very short term. I do not believe for an instant that she planned to marry him. And in fact even Diana, in the first flush of romance, could see that marrying Dodi would cause immense problems.

No one will ever know how long Diana and Dodi would have lasted, but it seems wrong to dismiss their relationship. Diana told as many people she adored the Egyptian as she told it was a simple fling. She talked to Joseph Sanders at length from the *Jonikal* and he's convinced that the relationship could have continued.

> I think Diana wanted to find a husband and she wanted to find a new family. And I think she felt at one with Dodi. I think she could have got married, and it could have been the fairytale ending that she wanted.

Lana Marks disagrees:

> I spoke to Diana about a week before her accident and she told me that she was really enjoying her summer and having a lovely time. And in the second breath she told me that she was so looking forward to getting back to London because she was meeting William and Harry on the Sunday. They had spent time with Charles as part of their vacation and then it was Diana's turn to be with them. And in fact she had even tried to cut her last vacation with Dodi short by two days. She had asked Paul Burrell [her butler] to try and change the reservations for two days earlier and Dodi had persuaded her to stay. She told me that she was looking forward to catching up with some of her friends that she hadn't spoken to in the summer. And she just wanted to be back in her own surroundings.
>
> Diana was very subtle. She didn't spell things out and say, 'Oh, I'm chucking the fella, I'm over with that now and I'm moving on.' That wasn't her style.

18
Paris

On the morning of 30 August, Kez Wingfield and Trevor Rees-Jones learned that their boss wanted to take the Princess to Paris later that day. The bodyguards had little time to make security arrangements. When they reached Le Bourget airport, they found a dozen photographers lying in wait for them, and they were followed from then on.

They drove to the Windsor villa, where Fayed's security chief, Ben Murrell, met them. For forty minutes Dodi showed Diana around the house and then they left.

From this point everything is disputed by Mohamed Al Fayed. His initial challenge to the exhaustive two-year official French investigation has been rejected, but his bid to prove that agents of British intelligence killed Diana and his son did uncover the possibility that some staff at the Ritz may have been dealing with intelligence agencies. However intelligence services in every major city keep a close eye on the comings and goings at top hotels, habitually paying staff for information. Security experts point out that the couple's ever-changing plans gave very little time to set up a complex operation like staging a car accident.

From the Windsor villa the couple went on to the Ritz. Dodi and Rees-Jones drove the hundred yards around the Place Vendôme to the Repossi showroom and picked up the ring Dodi had ordered for Diana. She, meanwhile, was phoning Richard Kay to tell him that she was blissfully happy, would be retiring from public life in November, but would continue with some charity work. This sounded like another of the semi-retirements

Kay had seen twice before. She spoke of setting up a chain of hospices around the world, some funded by Fayed. Kay later said that Diana that evening was the same woman he had met in Nepal in 1993, unsure of herself, in search of approval and understanding. Nevertheless, she was in love and in Paris and looking forward to a swanky evening out.

The couple drove to Dodi's apartment on the Champs Elysées near the Place Charles de Gaulle. A small army of paparazzi stood outside, and the two bodyguards had to push their way through the crush. As he dressed for dinner, Dodi told his butler René Delorm that he was going to propose to Diana when they returned later that night. Then, changing plan once again, Dodi, Diana and the bodyguards were driven towards a restaurant called Chez Benoît. The bodyguards had no idea what awaited them there. Philippe Dourneau remembers how disconcerted Dodi was as the paparazzi pursued the car. There were motor scooters all around it. Once again he changed his mind and redirected the driver to the Ritz.

Security cameras at the Ritz showed a solemn-looking Diana walking into the hotel followed by Wingfield, then Dodi and Rees-Jones. Once inside, Diana began to cry.

Tension was mounting, fed by the last-minute changes of plans. All of Dodi's team were now on a hair trigger, tired and frustrated by the changing plans, excited by the press pursuit, pumped up with adrenaline, fearful of a temper outburst from Dodi or his father, who was monitoring the evening closely from London.

Inside the Ritz, Dodi's perfect romantic evening was coming unstuck. There was an argument, and he blamed the bodyguards for the 'fuck-up'. Wingfield and Rees-Jones forcefully told him it was his fault for doing everything in such a rush. Everyone calmed down and the couple ordered food to eat upstairs in a suite. As they dined, Henri Paul, deputy head of security at the hotel, was summoned. He joined Wingfield and Rees-Jones in the bar. They later stated that he did not appear to be drunk to them and was drinking what looked like pineapple juice. But their bar bill included two Ricards, a brand of pastis that could perhaps be confused with pineapple juice when diluted with water. Not that there was any reason for the bodyguards to study his intake, because at that point he was not due to drive anyone anywhere. The real chauffeur, Philippe Dourneau, was sitting outside, waiting.

Kez Wingfield went upstairs and stood outside the suite. He heard laughter coming from inside. The evening was back on track. Dodi rang his father, who says he tried to persuade him to sleep in the hotel, but Dodi was keen to get back to his apartment, his luggage and his proposal. He had a plan: a decoy vehicle would leave from the front entrance, taking the bodyguards, while he and Diana left by the back. Henri Paul popped out of the suite to tell Wingfield and Rees-Jones. Paul would drive them and there would be no back-up car. The bodyguards were alarmed; the plan ran contrary to all their security training, which stipulates that guards must accompany VIPs at all times, followed by a back-up vehicle. But Dodi told them his plan had already been approved by his father and their boss. Mohamed Al Fayed denies this, and much else in the bodyguards' accounts, blaming them for allowing Dodi's plan to proceed. Whoever had or had not been told of the decoy idea, Dodi agreed to Wingfield's firm insistence that Rees-Jones would travel with him and Diana.

Was Paul fit to drive?

None of the so-called conspiracy theories begins to work unless the French autopsy's conclusion that Henri Paul was drunk is challenged. But at his autopsy five samples were taken, all showing him to be three times over the French legal limit for alcohol in blood at the moment of his death. A second set of samples was then taken on the Thursday after the crash under the personal supervision of investigating Judge Hervé Stéphan. Every step of the process witnessed by Stéphan was photographed. The new results confirmed the old. They also showed the presence of antidepressants, known to slow reactions, drugs that carry written warnings not to combine them with alcohol and not to drive under their influence.

Both bodyguards reported that Paul did not appear drunk immediately before leaving the hotel, but Paul was an experienced drinker, they had not been expecting him to drive, and they were hardly going to admit that they had allowed him to do so while obviously roaring drunk. It might be argued that it was mildly suspicious that Mohamed Al Fayed was refused permission to carry out a second autopsy on Paul or to have any of his blood samples tested privately, but this was a most unusual request.

Some have raised the possibility that the blood could have been switched. But such a thing is far easier to allege than to carry out. To switch Paul's blood would have required the co-operation of hospital staff, some of whom came in unexpectedly and so could not have been previously 'squared'. Meanwhile, someone else would have had to prepare the fake sample of exactly the right age and blood group, to match a man who was not even supposed to be driving the car until half an hour before the crash.

It's overwhelmingly likely that the driver was drunk.

Henri Paul had already wandered outside the front door of the Ritz to taunt a group of photographers that included Romuald Rat and Pierre Honsfield. Perhaps he was trying to persuade them that a departure from the front was imminent. But several began to think that the couple might use another exit and so some went around the back. At 12.20 a.m. Dodi and Diana emerged. Henri Paul shouted 'You will never catch us' at the knot of photographers by the back door.

Paul went the long way round to avoid traffic lights that might have brought photographers alongside the clear glass windows of the Mercedes. He followed a dual carriageway along the river which tunnelled under major junctions. The second tunnel on his route, cutting under the Place d'Alma, was an accident black spot. There had been thirty-four crashes there in the previous fifteen years, and eight deaths. The problem is a sudden dip and a slight bend to the left. There are no crash barriers between the road and the central concrete pillars.

As he had promised, Paul easily outdistanced the paparazzi by driving at 65 mph in a 30 mph limit. No photos of the car were taken during its journey to the tunnel. Some photographers gave up and went straight to Dodi's apartment by the direct route. As he entered the tunnel, Paul veered suddenly to the left, travelling at between 74 and 97 mph. The police found no tyre marks caused by braking – the car simply careered into the thirteenth pillar. No one was wearing a seat belt.

When they checked the Mercedes, the police found traces of paint that they considered to have come from a white Fiat Uno. In response to their appeal, a couple remembered seeing a Uno leave the tunnel, being driven erratically with a dog in the back. But the car was never found. The police did find a Uno owned by a Vietnamese immigrant who had had a dog grille fitted, but he was working that night.

First on the scene was photographer Romuald Rat, who took photographs of the wreckage. Others did the same. Dodi and Henri Paul had been killed instantly. Rat entered the car and spoke to Diana. 'Be cool, a doctor is coming,' he said. Another photographer, Christian Martinez, got into the car to take photos. Rat says that he tried to stop Martinez. Within minutes a doctor called Frédéric Mailliez arrived. He was returning after a night out with friends. There was a terrible noise in the tunnel as the Mercedes's horn was stuck full on and it was making an echo. Mailliez had worked as an emergency doctor and offered what help he could.

Diana was moaning and semiconscious. Mailliez had no idea who she was. Rees-Jones was alive but looked unlikely to survive fearful head injuries. Mailliez attended to Diana because, in his opinion, she had a better chance. He is adamant that the paparazzi did not get in the way as he tried to help the woman in the car. In fact, if anything, he recalls one of them suggesting that he speak to the woman in English. But some kept on taking pictures of the injured and the dead. Mailliez's friend Marc Butt had been keeping an eye on the car that they had left parked on the other carriageway. He recalled seeing lots of camera flashlights going off. He also remembers a crowd gathering and arguments breaking out. He didn't know what this was at the time, but assumes that it must have been between the photographers and members of the public who had stopped to offer help.

Two policemen, Sébastien Dorzee and Lino Gaggliardone, arrived at 12.30 a.m. and had to fight their way through a crowd around the wreckage. Unpublished photographs of the crash show Dodi slumped across the back seat, his leg broken and twisted. Diana is kneeling with her back against the front passenger seat. Gaggliardone remonstrated with the dozen-strong group of photographers who were still taking pictures. One, Martinez, is reported to have said that he was just doing his job. Passers-by shouted at photographers too.

Seven photographers or their drivers were arrested that night, including Rat and Martinez. Gaggliardone was damning in his comments on their behaviour, Mailliez less so. Police developed their film. It appeared that pictures had been taken only after the crash. And so camera flashes were unlikely to have triggered the accident, as many first assumed.

The emergency services arrived soon afterwards. Mailliez estimated that his total involvement lasted no more than fifteen minutes. Once the fully equipped ambulances had arrived he thought it best to leave matters to the doctors who had arrived with them. It was only when he was watching the TV the next morning that he realised who it was that he had treated the night before.

Diana had to be cut free. She was stabilised at the scene by a resuscitation specialist, Dr Jean-Marc Martino. According to Martino, she was agitated and crying out. It took nearly an hour to get her loose, during which time she suffered a heart attack, the result of heavy internal bleeding. The ambulance set off for the La Pitié Salpêtrière hospital at 1.25 a.m. It is normally a ten-minute journey, but this time it took over thirty. The vehicle drove slowly so as not to cause further damage to the patient whose condition was critical.

It has occasionally been alleged that the ambulance did not get Diana to the hospital fast enough. Thierry Meresse, the spokesman for the hospital, explains that such allegations are based on a misunderstanding of French medical practice:

> The moment the Princess of Wales was placed in the SAMU ambulance it was as if she already had one foot in the hospital. It isn't just an ambulance with a stretcher – it's an actual hospital that goes to the site of the accident. In France, the system is such that the best doctors for resuscitation, the very top specialists in serious road traumas, are actually present in the ambulance.

News of the crash reached London immediately after it happened. Picture editors were woken by calls from Parisian photo agencies, Ken Lennox among them:

> The phone rang and it was a Paris agency, saying there'd been a car crash in Paris. I looked at the time, it was just after twelve o'clock in London. They said that Dodi had been very badly injured but Diana was all right. They thought she had maybe a broken leg. This agency had the photographs and wanted three hundred thousand pounds from the *Sun* to run them exclusively on the Monday. I said automatically, 'Yes, we'll

> have them. I want to see them. I'm heading towards the office now.' I arrived at the office with no socks and a T-shirt and a pair of jeans.

Lennox faced a night of excitement, dread and tumbling, troubling memories. This was the girl behind the tree, the clever one with the compact, the girl who'd borrowed his *Private Eye* and made him cocoa, the one who'd asked him 'How am I doing, Ken?' in the Welsh rain. She'd been in a big black car then too. And now here he was, haggling with a French photo agency for a picture of her propped up next to her dead lover. Other calls came into the office, and Lennox soon realised that photographers were going to be blamed, probably the ones he was dealing with on the telephone.

> There's a dreadful finality about a still photograph. It doesn't go away, it sits there, balefully looking at you.
>
> I felt for the whole thing. I felt ill with the thought of this. I felt guilt and sadness and how brief a life it'd been. And how that she, at the end, couldn't find that peace that would have let her live a normal life of some kind. But it would never have been normal because no matter what anyone, any editor, said, 'We will not cover her again', somebody would have. But I must admit at the time I felt dreadful.

But Lennox still had a job to do.

> They sent the first tranche of photographs over – photographs of Diana and Dodi and the driver, etc. I then phoned my editor and I phoned my chairman and I phoned everyone I could think of. I got a friendly photographer in Paris to go straight to the scene. I got Arthur Edwards on a private jet. I got a photographer in Kent to go across on a ferry . . .

At the Salpêtrière, Thierry Meresse was waiting for the ambulance to arrive. In late August, Paris is empty but for tourists.

During the night there was not much more than a skeleton staff at work.

> I saw in the darkness the ocean of flashing lights which filled the road leading to the hospital. The Prefect of Police said to me, 'I am requisitioning your hospital.' It was as if a head of state were about to come. There were moments of great, great silence throughout the corridors. It was the middle of the night, and it was the evening of a holiday, when half the hospital wasn't working.

Sami Naïr was assistant to the French Interior Minister, Jean-Pierre Chevènement. He had been on duty that night but in late August there was little going on, and so he had left the office at about half past ten and gone home to have dinner with some Spanish friends. He was phoned with news of an accident that the police thought may have involved Princess Diana. After making absolutely sure that the victim of the crash really was Diana, he phoned Chevènement.

> I said to the Minister, 'I have to go very quickly to the hospital, and you'd better come too.' I left my friends, there, at my house, and I took my official car. You can switch on a signal to show it's a police car, so I turned on the signal and I got there very quickly.
>
> I arrived at the Salpêtrière hospital at about ten past one in the morning, and I busied myself preparing for the arrival of both Lady Di and the Minister. The atmosphere was extremely tense – meeting like that in a hospital at one o'clock in the morning, ten past one, with those colours, that yellow light, it was a little surreal.
>
> When the ambulance arrived, I was with the Minister outside. There were only two stretcher-bearers so, the Minister on one side and me on the other, we helped to lift out the body, we pulled the stretcher out. The Princess had a breathing apparatus on her face, she had swellings on her eyes, but she still looked

beautiful. Her face was extremely lovely, very fresh, very serene, very young. It was very moving. She had this blond hair which made her look Raphaelesque, and the Minister said to me, 'She's beautiful, isn't she? She's beautiful.'

She was obviously still breathing. The stretcher-bearers immediately took charge of her and took her very quickly to the resuscitation room, where she was immediately operated on to try to save her.

As Naïr and Chevènement were helping carry the stretcher into the hospital, Meresse was trying to master the switchboard:

> The press, the media, the politicians and Mr and Mrs Everybody in Paris, who were listening to the radio, heard that the Princess of Wales has had an accident, that she is in hospital, the Pitié Salpêtrière. Beyond that we communicate nothing. But we have to divert the flux of important people who have only one resource, which is to telephone the hospital. People telephone but to such an extent that the switchboard is blocked.

Soon after 1 a.m. at the British embassy the duty officer was woken up by a call telling him that Princess Diana had been involved in an accident. Dodi was reported dead, and Diana badly injured. It was 2 a.m. before the ambassador, Sir Michael Jay, was informed. He passed the news to Robin Janvrin, the Queen's deputy private secretary, at Balmoral. Janvrin woke up the Queen and Prince Charles. The Prince telephoned his deputy private secretary, Mark Bolland, in London and asked him 'What's going on?' Bolland couldn't shed much light. He'd been woken up by the *News of the World* and Stuart Higgins of the *Sun*, each giving conflicting reports of the accident. If anything, Ken Lennox was marginally better informed:

> Just before two o'clock, the photographer who had gone to the hospital in Paris said, 'I think Diana's dead. There's a rumour here that she is dead – or so badly injured that she is dying – and I've just seen someone who I think is a British embassy

guy fainting in the corridor of the hospital, and being picked up by two hospital staff and stuffed into a side room.' I think what he'd seen was the duty man at the British embassy who had suddenly realised that it was his job to phone the Foreign Secretary and tell him that the Princess of Wales was dead. I thought, Oh my God, and by this time my chairman was standing behind me and the *News of the World* had been told and were just replating. I saw the editor of the *News of the World* in the corridor – he'd been out for dinner that night – with his bow tie hanging round his neck, with his executives in a corridor talking to them. And I said to the chairman, 'I think Diana's dead.' And just then I got a call from ITN and they said, 'Have you got anything on Diana?' I said, 'Yeah, I think it's fairly serious.' And I knew the guy from the newsroom at ITN and he said, 'They have got word that she's dead coming from Paris.' And I said, 'Well, so have I.' He said, 'Well, I'll keep you informed, we'll keep each other informed.'

Then we watched the news coming up – it seemed to strike everybody connected with it. I had photographers too stunned to speak on the phone. I got a girl to come in and help me on the desk – she was useless, poor girl just cried for five hours. Couldn't answer the phone. And that's the effect.

In Paris, press attaché Tim Livesey and ambassador Sir Michael Jay drove to the hospital. The White House called at three o'clock in the morning to find out the latest news. Between 2.30 and 4 a.m., Jay made a series of phone calls to Balmoral, the Foreign Office and the Foreign Secretary, Robin Cook, who was in Manila. At Balmoral, all the Royal Family except the boys were up, waiting for news.

The first television news reports were confused. Some reported that Diana had escaped with relatively minor injuries, others said she had got up and walked away from the scene. There was even discussion on live TV as to how Diana would cope with Dodi's death. Photographs taken at the scene showed the

Mercedes in the tunnel and its occupants in the first minutes after the crash. The photo agency in Paris e-mailed the photographs to the US and British papers. Offers flooded in – \$250,000 from the *National Enquirer*, £1 million from British newspapers.

Meresse now had a team working on the switchboard:

> It is very time consuming because you have people in tears on the phone, telling you their life story, who say: 'No, it's not possible, she can't have had an accident, a princess doesn't have accidents!' You have to reassure people, you must try not to hang up on them, you have to reply to everyone, but everyone includes the head of state, foreign ambassadors who have close relations with Great Britain, you receive calls from all over the world, as soon as they all know your telephone number. So there are calls waiting, a blocked switchboard, an exploding telephone! There must have been three hundred calls a minute coming in.
>
> We knew that the chauffeur had died, that Dodi had also died, that the bodyguard was in a critical condition. So there was little hope. When the doctors who have spent two hours trying to resuscitate her, when they come up, one can sense that it's all over. One can read it in their faces, their body language, their attitude; when one works in a hospital one can sense when a doctor has just suffered a failure. For a doctor, life is important and death is always experienced as a terrible failure.

Adrenaline injections were given to keep Diana's heart beating, and her heart was massaged by hand, but it would not beat unaided. At 4 a.m., the medical team told Chevènement that Diana was dead. They told him she'd suffered a second massive cardiac arrest when she arrived at the hospital. They'd tried to resuscitate her for two hours, but to no avail. With Sami Naïr watching, Chevènement took Jay aside and broke the news to him.

It was at about four o'clock in the morning. The Chief of Police, Massoni, came back into the room, he came to have a coffee with us, and then went out again; and at that moment I saw him give a little sign to the Minister. The Minister went out, I went out behind him; he said to the Minister, 'She is dead.'

So the Minister staggered at the shock, then he recovered himself, came back in and said to the ambassador, she is dead, and he presented all his condolences. And the ambassador began to weep.

The ambassador asked when he could see the body. We told him that he couldn't see the body until it had been removed from the resuscitation room, because no one is allowed in the resuscitation room. So the Chief of Police, Massoni, asked if the body could be brought up to the room on the second floor where she would await transfer to the morgue.

At about half past four a table was put in the room and she was put on it. The Minister asked me and the Chief of Police to prepare a press release for him. We were very sad, but we were also very angry with the photographers, because we understood that the car had been pursued by the photographers. We were saying, 'These paparazzi! It's a terrible thing to destroy the lives of people like that.'

At 4.15 a.m. the Queen's private secretary, Diana's brother-in-law Robert Fellowes, rang the hospital and spoke to an embassy official, who broke the news. Thierry Meresse realised that there were no decent clothes for the Princess.

She was about the same size as the ambassador's wife. So she suggested she donate one of her black dresses and a pair of shoes to go with it.

It was necessary to allow certain journalists to come into a section of the hospital which was cordoned off behind barriers so that they could carry on their job of filming the departures and arrivals of famous people and the imminent arrival of

Prince Charles. But at that actual moment the paparazzi are being accused of having killed her. So everyone who has a camera is accused of being guilty. Among the press, there are a few baying onlookers, a bit excited, who want to fight it out. There are insults flying.

I notice there are a few overexcited people who need calming down. I try to argue with them, to make them understand that there are no paparazzi here, to calm them down. I have to go and explain to every person who appears to be a bit worked up, who wants to let rip, that we are waiting for the Prince of Wales and that I am counting on them to give a dignified welcome to a man who has just lost his wife, who is coming to collect her body.

People took note of what I said, and when the Jaguar arrived, all that could be heard was the screech of the tyres on the tarmac, there was total silence for the arrival of Prince Charles.

I was moved by his humanity and by how responsive he was, by the way in which he spoke very correct French, and one really felt that he was shattered by what was happening. His entire attitude from start to finish was one of concern for the Princess of Wales, over details; nobody could find her second earring and he kept saying: 'No, she can't go without her second earring!' Details like that. One could feel he was truly, truly distraught.

When he went into the room alone he was calm and collected. It was another man who emerged from the room, a man utterly shattered by what was happening. Very human, totally unlike all the images one might have of him of a very formal person, all uptight, austere and reserved. You could sense the same reserve, but at the same time immense pain and great humanity.

The Accident and Emergency wing has a roof on which helicopters can land. So we suggested to the Prince of Wales that they leave by helicopter, to avoid the crowds. And he said: 'No, she arrived by car so she will leave by car. There are people who love her waiting outside.'

19
Funeral

Suddenly there were people who loved Diana everywhere.

Earl Spencer stood outside his house and accused the media of 'having blood on their hands'. Jean-Louis Macault was reluctant to leave his home: 'I thought, This is the end. It's a disaster. I don't think that I can go on doing this kind of work. As soon as we went past, people would say: "Ah-ha, paparazzi, murderers!" We hid ourselves away, we were almost ashamed of being photographers. People were extremely nasty, very, very nasty.'

What had felt like fair comment on Saturday night had turned into a hideous embarrassment by Sunday. In the days before the crash many newspaper writers had been critical of Diana. Despite frantic efforts to recall and reprint, a series of negative articles reached the grieving public. 'Any publicity is good publicity' and 'She seems to relish her role as a martyr, God help her if she ever finds happiness – it would make her miserable,' said the *Sunday Express*. And the *News of the World*'s 'exclusive' read: 'Troubled Prince William will today demand that his mother Princess Diana dump her playboy lover.'

In America that week's *National Enquirer* was already on the news-stands blaring out 'DI GOES SEX MAD'. Whether or not hounds with cameras had literally pursued her to her death, evidence of the hunt was writ large in headlines like this. And so by Monday the press was on the defensive. The *Mirror* played the xenophobia card, pointing out that Diana's pursuers had been French. The *Sun* simply begged, 'Don't blame the press.' On Tuesday the Paris police announced the results of Henri Paul's first blood tests: *France Soir* proclaimed '*Le Chauffeur de*

Lady Di était Ivre' – 'Lady Di's Driver was Drunk'. The sound of exhaled breath was audible in newsrooms all over the world. Now the media pounced on Al Fayed, alleging he had allowed Diana to be driven by a drunk, and Prince Charles, for forcing her into the arms of such untrustworthy guardians. Meanwhile Diana was bleached virgin white.

Private Eye summed up:

> The Late Princess Diana: An Apology. In recent weeks (not to mention the last ten years) we at the *Daily Gnome*, in common with all other newspapers, may have inadvertently conveyed the impression that the late Princess of Wales was in some way a neurotic, irresponsible and manipulative troublemaker who had repeatedly meddled in political matters that did not concern her and personally embarrassed Her Majesty The Queen by her Mediterranean love-romps . . . We now realise as of Sunday morning that the Princess of Hearts was in fact the most saintly woman who has ever lived, who, with her charitable activities, brought hope and succour to hundreds and millions of people all over the world. We would like to express our sincere and deepest hypocrisy to all our readers on this tragic day and hope and pray that they will carry on buying our paper notwithstanding.

But if the public was ready to blame the press, the press had a question in return: just who exactly had been buying all these terrible newspapers in the first place? *Private Eye*'s cover, which brought the magazine a record number of complaints, read 'Media to Blame'. The picture under the headline showed a crowd assembled outside Buckingham Palace, and in speech bubbles mourners said to each other, 'The papers are a disgrace.' 'Yes. I couldn't get one anywhere.' 'Borrow mine, it's got a picture of the car.'

BBC newsreader Martyn Lewis wept on air as he read the death announcement. On 31 August and for days afterwards there was simply no other news. Other events passed entirely without comment as TV stations in Britain, Europe and North and South America devoted hour after hour to Diana tributes and Diana analysis. It began immediately, while Annick Cojean was still in shock in front of her hotel room TV in Washington.

> I was glued to my TV, I zap from channel to channel for two hours, till two, three o'clock in the morning, and then at that moment the world's press landed on my telephone! I don't know how they got my phone number. I got fifty calls, I have the list, 3.01, 3.02, 3.04, and after that they came to fetch me, CNN, NBC cable, and then regular NBC, and then CBS and CNN's car came, and then TF1 called me and I'd talked so much that I said, 'No, I don't want to talk any more, I want to sleep for two hours,' and the correspondent said, 'But it's for French TV, you're going to be live, it's very important, it will have a lot of impact!' And I said, 'Impact, I don't give a damn about impact, I've had enough, that's all I have to say.'

The Prince of Wales was acutely aware of the depth of public sympathy for Diana and concerned for the feelings of their children. Quite apart from that, independent witnesses who saw Charles in Paris and on his return say he was genuinely distraught and personally determined to treat his wife's death with as much respect as he could. But he found that even his determination to go immediately to Paris was opposed, as television newsreader Jon Snow was informed by a man from Charles's entourage:

> The row was over the most microscopic and ludicrous things like whether Queen's Flight planes should be laid on for Charles to go to Paris. Should he go to Paris at all since this was not a royal personage?
>
> I was told by two sources, one inside the royal circle, one ministerial, that an almost immediate breakdown occurred

within hours of the discovery of Diana's death. The Queen did not want the body anywhere near a royal palace, anywhere near a royal chapel. She wanted her left at an undertaker's in the Fulham Road. Charles, driven by the boys, wanted a proper royal send-off and all the protocol to kick in. The whole thing deteriorated into the most appalling slanging match, which at one point found Charles shouting at Sir Robert Fellowes, Diana's own brother-in-law, the Queen's secretary, 'Why don't you just go and impale yourself on your own flagstaff?' Extraordinary phrase. And another royal official saying, 'Would you rather, ma'am, that she be taken away in a Harrods van?'

The tension continued the whole week, but was expressed very clearly on the flight-deck of the plane that Charles did eventually take to Paris. It was a place which effectively became his office because, denied royal protocol, he now had to find some way of getting all the things which protocol would normally have provided. And therefore an open line was established on the flight-deck with Number Ten, and such minute details as the flowers that were to be put on the coffin had to be called up.

A Cabinet minister confirmed to Snow that:

Charles had been unable to call on the royal protocol in any form. Normally, if a royal person dies, all sorts of things kick in immediately: how the body is to be carried, where it is to land, what kind of a coffin, the provision of flowers, a guard of honour, flags, all the rest of it comes out of the woodwork. There is a formula for doing it.

He had no alternative but to call on the government and see what they could do. And I think Number Ten, conscious of the public reaction, already realised that they would have to do whatever could be done.

On the Queen's instruction, Robert Fellowes had arranged for Diana's body to rest in Fulham mortuary, commonly used by the royal coroner. At Charles's insistence, plans were quickly changed and Diana's body was taken instead to the Chapel Royal at St James's Palace. From Northolt to central London, knots of people, heads bowed, watched the hearse go by. That Sunday the Royal Family went to church as usual at Balmoral, where no mention was made of the death either by them or their preacher, and so it was left to Tony Blair to give voice to the swelling public mourning. He grabbed the opportunity with both hands, speaking emotionally to television cameras outside his own local church in County Durham. His voice cracked, his eyes were wide with sincerity and repressed tears, his fingers reached out as if trying to grasp the desolation that he sought to share with the nation. Alastair Campbell, Blair's press spokesman, had beefed up the Prime Minister's original draft, inserting one of Anthony Holden's old phrases: 'the People's Princess'. That set the tone for the week. No doubt Blair felt sad, but he and Campbell also appreciated that it was politic for him to be seen to be sad. The Queen and Prince Philip did not appear to have worked this out for themselves.

Margaret Jay was in a television studio when the Prime Minister made his statement. As the one member of the Cabinet who knew Diana well, she had spent all morning recording TV and radio interviews. She'd also been among the first to be consulted about what Blair should say:

> People have looked back and slightly sneered at what the Prime Minister said on that occasion, but in fact it was very much capturing the mood – the mood of people feeling that this was somebody very valuable who had been lost; who had a particular connection with people. That she was, at one level, an amazing star, an amazing celebrity, and yet she was somebody with whom lots of people, who were watching what the Prime Minister said on the occasion, felt they had a personal connection, because they'd once shaken her hand, or they'd once been in a crowd and given her a flower.

> I think as events emerged, it was very important that he said something on that day, because the whole atmosphere became so intense and so confused and there were so many thousands of people involved that the fact that the Prime Minister had said this very appropriate thing did give it a framework.

It was Annick Cojean's umpteenth interview of the day: 'On the panel, Annick Cojean, who was a friend of the Princess's.'

> And I said: 'No, no, I wasn't a friend, I interviewed her once in the context of a series of articles.' And nobody wanted to hear the rest! The controversy about landmines, the controversy about the Major government or the Blair government, nobody gave a damn, it was no longer an issue. Everything was about how she had been. Did she smile? Was she in love? Did she get on well with you? How was she dressed, was she warm? I realised how everything that touched her was controversial, important, exciting, it put the most sensible of people into unheard-of states, there was a sort of hysteria, and one has no idea of it until one has experienced it first hand in the way that I did for those few hours.

Tony Blair's public sorrow began a week of confessional distress. The handful of people who came to Buckingham, Kensington and St James's Palaces early on Sunday morning with wreaths and bunches of flowers soon swelled into an army bearing cellophane. Acres of park and gravel driveway were quickly swamped with flowers, cards and teddy bears. One image dominated: the Queen of Hearts, lifted from packs of playing cards, drawn in crayon on hand-made posters. People wept on the steps of the Victoria Monument, their friends consoling them.

At St James's Palace a book of condolences was opened and soon queues four hundred yards long stretched down the Mall.

The number of books was multiplied to ease the congestion, but the queues grew longer still. People waited for twelve hours to sign their names. As they did, they talked to strangers, a phenomenon considered so un-English that it generated great comment. They talked of their own lives and sadnesses and made, they said, new friends.

Many of the people carrying the flowers and the gifts would have agreed with the previous week's newspaper criticism of Diana. But not now. Now she was a saint – no, a martyr. A martyr to love, to compassion, to everything that was good. And so, of necessity, killed by everything that was not good: by the press, by the royals, by 'them'. Journalists were drawn to these scenes, but their presence was not always welcome. Scuffles broke out as mourners jostled, spat at and abused photographers.

The television crews decided that this was the place to interview their pundits, and so Anthony Holden found himself with an American TV crew on a platform outside Buckingham Palace. Soon he was:

> live on a breakfast show at noon London time trying to explain to an American audience why there was no flag at half-mast on the Buckingham Palace flagpole. The camera panned around and every other public building in Whitehall and Westminster had a flag at half-mast, and I was trying to explain that the flag never flies at half-mast, that the monarch never dies, and anyway they don't have a regular flag, they have the Royal Standard. It shows whether the monarch's in residence or not, and she's not because she's at Balmoral.

Before long television pictures of the Royal Standard flying high at Balmoral illustrated his point, and irritated the crowd some more. Why was it not at half-mast? As Holden dispensed royal lore to North America, voices from the crowd urged him to speak out on their behalf. He turned to thank them:

and I got this voice in my ear from New York saying, 'This is great, do it, do it.'

The Queen should have been leaping into action because a national icon was dead in tragic circumstances, regardless of whether it was her daughter-in-law and regardless of what she thought of her and all the trouble she'd caused the monarchy.

It made it clear to me that although Diana had begun life as a very establishment figure, the daughter of an earl who married a future king, by the end of her life she *was* anti-establishment. She had come to represent all sorts of minority groups, the people who turned up, people who would never otherwise have dreamed of turning up to any kind of royal event.

Who were these people? Early television coverage had focused on those who claimed Diana as their anti-establishment Princess. But by mid-week the mourning had swept through Britain's suburbs and shires and brought their representatives to SW1 in tens of thousands. The trains of south-east England were filled with women carrying flowers, as florists scoured Europe for fresh supplies. The *Observer* undertook its own analysis for the following Sunday's issue: outside the gates 80 per cent were women, and most were aged between twenty-five and forty, claimed to be middle class and read the *Daily Mail* or the *Sun*. The mothers of Middle England were camped in front of the Palace, behaving most strangely with little shrines and pictures of Diana. The knick-knack makers ran off T-shirts with slogans such as 'In Loving Memory of Princess Diana: Born a Princess, Died a Saint'. Another bore the legend 'Fuck off Paparazzi'. The pilgrims who bought such souvenirs were not natural republicans: 72 per cent thought William should succeed to the throne. But they were distinctly unimpressed with Prince Charles and, with every passing day she spent in Balmoral, with the Queen as well.

ANTHONY HOLDEN: I certainly thought that if they didn't respond to this public mood it was going to be some sort of bloodless revolution. What was interesting was that the royal machine for once clearly *was* at a complete loss as to how to handle this. I called Christopher Hitchens and said this was the most extraordinary manifestation of some sort of public feeling that had happened in our lifetimes and that he should get his ass over to take a look.

CHRISTOPHER HITCHENS: Anthony rang me insistently and said, 'If you don't come over here now and see this, you'll be really sorry, you won't believe it if you don't see it, what's happening to public opinion, I almost think the Royal Family could be swept away this week.'

ANTHONY HOLDEN: The crowd who I moved among every day were saying to me that they thought unless something happened the Queen would get booed at the funeral on the Saturday and that Charles, if he wandered more than six feet from his sons, would get pelted with rotten tomatoes. And the atmosphere was such that I believed it.

CHRISTOPHER HITCHENS: I doubted he was right, and I differ with him. I wish he hadn't ventriloquised that crowd, in fact, because it became a sort of sentimental surrogate royalism, the 'show us you care, ma'am' royalism.

Mass hysteria is never attractive. I couldn't see what Tony claimed to see, which was the embryonic development of a grown-up republican and democratic political style. I can tell you I've been a soapbox artist myself, and if you can get a crowd worked up there's no feeling exactly like it, but if you don't distrust yourself when you're doing it a little bit, even if you're sure you're in the right, then you ought to.

Derek Draper had been political adviser to Cabinet minister Peter Mandelson, Tony Blair's chief strategist. Draper was well aware of the currents of opinion flowing through the government machine that week:

> Alastair Campbell [Blair's spokesman] and Angie Hunter [Campbell's deputy] had to go from Downing Street to Buckingham Palace to have all these meetings about the funeral. They were going through the crowds and Alastair reported back to Blair that it was like when you come out of a football match and a team has lost and there is something in the air, there's a crackle in the air.

ITN's royal reporter, Nicholas Owen, felt the crackle too.

> About the Tuesday, I think it was. I went to the Mall and a woman came up to me and said, 'Oh, you're that chap from the telly, can I just ask you this: why isn't the Queen here? That's what I want to know, why isn't the Queen here?' The woman was really angry, and she wasn't one of those nutty people who turn up at royal events. She was a straightforward sort of lady, but she was jolly cross. And I went back to the studio and told my bosses about all this, and their reaction was exactly the same as I know newspaper editors reaction was. 'This is dangerous stuff.'

Police reports confirmed both views, and made their way, via the Home Office, to Downing Street and Balmoral. Nicholas Owen heard the result.

> A very good source told me that there was a meeting to discuss the funeral, at which senior police officers and royal officials and Special Branch were involved. A senior police officer at that meeting, I am told, expressed the view that the Prince of Wales would be booed or worse if he was to turn up in London at such a sensitive time.

The Queen and Prince Philip appeared paralysed in the face of this advice. Tony Blair considered his own position. Those close to him say that he wasn't immediately attracted to the idea of helping the Windsors. He had once expressed republican views and many in his party still did, including, it was said, at least half the Cabinet. But as the crowds grew larger, and the headlines nastier, the mood in No. 10 hardened. Blair, Mandelson and Campbell all came to believe that a constitutional crisis was not what their new administration needed.

A friend who phoned Lord Palumbo from Argentina told him that labourers were crying in the fields. In New York Ed Mathews thought that it brought 'the greatest outpouring of common grief for someone other than John Kennedy'.

> In a jaded world you're always looking for somebody that's just trying to go out and make a difference. We decided to put a book of condolences in our lobby on Twenty-Third Street here in our main building in Manhattan. And we received an endless stream of visitors. The police had to cordon off the block to deal with the line of people.
>
> I think that there are cases where the media make the story larger than it is. In this particular case they simply reported the story. Throughout the city and throughout the United States people were trying to find some public way to say that they were sorry that this happened. To say to her children, I guess, or maybe to themselves, that they were sorry that this happened, that this was one person that had touched them.

There were some who thought that the blanket coverage was overblown and that sentimentality was stifling good judgment. Predictably, Hitchens was one, so he was repeatedly invited to be the token bolshy pundit on American television.

> We were not told by objective reporters, 'There are masses of people mourning her death in very intense ways'; we were told, '*We are all* mourning her death' – which I object to because I wasn't, and nor was anybody I knew.

Few indeed dared remind the public that Diana had had faults. After her funeral A.N. Wilson pointed out that she had recently abandoned most of the charities represented there, and that, rich throughout her life, 'in latter years she was extravagant on a scale that would have made Marie Antoinette blush'. His explanation for this public forgetfulness was that people were in love with Diana – men for obvious reasons, women 'because she went public with many of their concerns'.

Martin Amis wrote of 'a bereavement uniquely contaminated by the market forces of fame'. Diana was beautiful, had a gift for love and believed she could heal. But she was 'a phenomenon of pure stardom' and 'if power corrupts the self, then absolute fame must surely distort it'. In the end, Amis concluded, 'Diana was a mirror, not a lamp.'

It was an apt description. Throughout this story of magic and manipulation, Diana had reflected back different facets of the millions who had gazed fascinated upon her. Kindness and compassion had sometimes shone, at their brilliant best, and courage too. But, at other times, she had mirrored her onlookers' weakness for gossip and for feuding. She was the people's princess after all: the people who run the shelters and the hostels, the people who buy those sleazy newspapers when the pubs are shut.

By Wednesday evening, Anthony Holden had been joined by other television and press reporters in wondering aloud what the Queen and her family were doing at Balmoral. Apart from a terse statement on Sunday morning, nothing had yet been said by Britain's head of state about the death of her daughter-in-law, the mother of a future King. Protocol about flags at Buckingham Palace sounded more ridiculous each time it was repeated. Clearly something needed to be done differently, even if it was only to find a second flagpole. Jon Snow's sources kept him informed about discussions within the Palace and within the Cabinet:

> There were real worries, according to my ministerial source, about what kind of reception the Queen was going to get if she

should set her face out publicly in the Mall. The worry was things would be thrown, that people would jeer or shout, or abuse her.

On Thursday the royals returned. Diana's brothers-in-law were the first to emerge among the crowds. It was not an accident, as Derek Draper well knew. It was a testing of the water.

When they agreed to the walkabouts what they agreed was that Andrew and Edward would go out first and see what happened. Blair and Campbell and the Queen were watching that to see what happened. Would they be jostled, spat at? I mean, people had been calling Buckingham Palace and swearing at whoever answered the phone. Now, as it happened, the deference of the great British people took over and everyone sort of immediately doffed their cap and said, 'Oh, now they're here we're going to treat them like the royalty they are,' and so it was diffused.

And of course they always had the ace up their sleeve of the two boys, because they weren't *seen* as part of the House of Windsor. They were seen as her kids. Ironic, because of course they literally *are* the future of the House of Windsor.

The coast was clear. Next it was the Queen's turn to brave the crowds. Jon Snow's contact in the Palace told him about the continued royal anxiety.

The decision was taken that they should do it as near the gates of Buckingham Palace as possible, so that an escape route existed if anything went wrong. But my royal source says that even the Queen was worried about what kind of a reception she was going to get: eggs, rotten tomatoes, abuse. There was a real fear, fear perhaps that she'd never previously experienced in her reign. As it happened, despite the fact that they did it right at the very tip of the Mall and as near Buckingham Palace as they could do it, it went like a charm.

And so Charles, William and Harry walked out among the mourners too and marvelled at the carpet of flowers. Many messages expressed sympathy for the boys, but few for Charles. The one that said 'Diana may you rest in peace. Charles may you *never* rest in peace' was not exceptional. In a most unroyal moment, Charles held Harry's hand.

On Friday evening the Queen spoke to her people, her image projected on screens specially erected so that the crowds could watch television images of the funeral the next day. She did not indulge the nation's grief as Tony Blair had done, but her upper lip quivered more than it had ever been seen to quiver before. She spoke, she said, to her people from her heart, and 'as a grandmother'. Derek Draper knew the story behind the words on the royal autocue.

> When the Palace officials finally agreed to facilitate that, they said, 'She's going to do it at four o'clock,' and Alastair Campbell said, 'Well, that's no good, she needs to do it live into the teatime news,' and one of them turned round and said, 'The Queen does not do live.'

But she did, speaking words finessed in Downing Street.

> The draft of her speech came into Downing Street and there was no emotion in it at all, but Alastair, being very smart, managed to get phrases like 'as a grandmother', blah, blah, blah, and all those kinds of things into the speech.

There had been immediate disagreements about the funeral. The Queen's office argued for a private family ceremony, feasible to arrange and in keeping with Diana's recent status as a private individual. Prince Charles's office and the Prime Minister were both in favour of the large-scale national event that seemed to be what the people wanted. They felt that this would help to unify the country and provide catharsis for the turbulent emotions aroused by Diana's sudden death. Lord Airlie chaired a funeral committee that was not always harmonious, but which produced a stunningly effective event. Time was only one of the problems they had to cope with, as Vivienne Parry explains:

> In many ways the funeral was a nightmare to organise. The people who were running her [Diana's] office at the time had only been there for a matter of months. So there was no sense of past history, of who she'd been involved with previously. Also Diana lived her life in compartments and there were people that actually nobody knew about at all who were friends.
>
> In the end a number of her former staff were approached and they went through some of the events and organisations and people that she had been involved with in their time, and so a list was compiled in that way.

On the evening before the ceremony, Victor Adebowale, invitation in pocket, wandered through London's candlelit parks.

> The evening before the funeral, thousands of people had come down to London just to be able to be together. It was a very odd event. I remember picking my way through these crowds to get to the studio to do an interview, and just bumped into this friend of mine who I'd not seen for a good few months. I'd always thought he was a bit of an anti-royalist really, and there he was with his mother, wirh a tent on the pavement, kipping out.
>
> I'm like, 'What are *you* doing here?' And he just said he had to come. I was just like, 'Wow!' This was not somebody I was expecting to be there at all, he was taking meaning out of this event that I didn't expect him to take, and there he was with his mother of all people, who was incredibly emotional about it. . . . I remember sitting on the top of Westminster Hall looking down on a crowd of a couple of hundred thousand people camped out; and talking to people and seeing people absolutely gobsmacked.

By the next morning more than a million extra people had moved into the city. People in sleeping bags, sitting around, surrounded by flickering candles, and around and above them the technology of the world's media with arc and floodlights and cameras on giant cranes. No other event in the history of television received such intense coverage. It bettered even the wedding. The BBC broadcast pictures to 187 countries, ITN to 45, CNN to 210. The American networks flew over their most famous names with hundreds of support staff. A hundred camera positions commanded the procession route. Helicopters were ready to escort the coffin to Northamptonshire. In Tokyo, coverage was displayed on giant video screens in main shopping centres. In America, millions rose before dawn to watch.

Jayne Fincher had thought hard before going to the Abbey:

> I felt very uncomfortable going with a camera. I really in my heart of hearts did not want to do it. I felt like a leech. But my father said to me, 'Look, you were there at the beginning, it's very historic. You've photographed her all those years. You must go and photograph the end.' So in the end I went, but I didn't want to be seen walking around with a camera, I remember having them in my bag and being very discreet.

She took up position alongside her colleagues, with real paparazzi among them, on a wooden platform raised above the crowd opposite the Abbey. The people below were hostile. Police stood nearby in case of trouble. The photographers began to snap the guests arriving at the Abbey. Victor Adebowale was one of them:

> My abiding memory was queuing outside the church with Sting, Tom Cruise and all these people, queuing to enter the church: and we were levelled, we all had to queue to go in. I thought to myself, She would have liked that. That would have made her smile.

It was a strange gathering. Stars of politics, show business and fashion mingled with charity workers and people that Diana had once personally helped.

As the funeral cortège left Kensington Palace, the crowd, lining the road by Hyde Park, was twenty deep. The muffled Tenor Bell of Westminster Abbey tolled once every minute as the procession travelled past Buckingham Palace, up the Mall and Horse Guards, along Whitehall to Parliament Square and then to the Abbey – the same route, more or less, that Diana and her friends had taken in their little car on that exciting engagement night sixteen years before.

There was silence but for the hooves of the horses, the wheels of the gun carriage and the weeping of the crowd. The service began conventionally enough with the National Anthem and 'I vow to thee my country', the hymn Diana had chosen for her wedding. Her sisters and the Prime Minister read lessons. Then Elton John sang a version of his song, 'Candle in the Wind', with the lyrics altered to suit Diana rather than Marilyn Monroe. Then her brother, Charles Spencer, made his tribute, an electric moment, partly because he was so close to tears. He spoke of the tens of millions who were mourning Diana and of the qualities in her that had caused them to mourn, of her childhood and her bizarre life afterwards. Then he turned on the press, describing how she had wanted to leave England because of the way she was treated by the newspapers and how she had never understood why her genuinely good intentions were sneered at by the media.

The speech was broadcast through speakers to the crowd outside. Jayne Fincher listened in horror.

> They all turned round and hissed at us. It was horrible. I just wanted the earth to open up and be swallowed by it because I didn't want to be seen there. I didn't want to be seen looking through a camera at the children in their time of grief, and I just found it really unpleasant and horrible, the whole thing.

Spencer reached the climax of his tribute, promising that Diana's blood family would look to the interests of her children and implicitly criticising the Windsors for depriving her of her title. Then emotion finally got the better of him. The crowd outside began to clap, making a noise that was audible within the Abbey. People began to clap there too. The Queen looked straight ahead.

More hymns and prayers, 'Cwm Rhondda' and the Commendation. Echoes of the music bounced off the buildings on the fringes of Hyde Park, and slowly dissipated down empty streets. London had never felt so quiet nor so dignified. The Welsh Guards took up the coffin once again and the cortège left the Abbey as the choir sang John Taverner's haunting anthem 'Flights of Angels'. The hearse set off northwards to Althorp, and all along the route people stood at the side of the road and on bridges. By the time the car reached the north of London the driver had to stop and clear the flowers off the windscreen.

Afterword

In the years that followed Diana's funeral, the royal scene appeared serene. Under the guidance of Mark Bolland, Prince Charles made peace with the newspapers that once tormented him. He made frequent appearances with Camilla Parker Bowles at his side, smiling for the camera alongside Diana's old showbiz friends. He visited AIDS wards and Centrepoint, looking happier than he had for years.

The Press Complaints Commission celebrated its tenth anniversary with a huge party. Persecutors and persecuted mingled with the conviviality that characterised the early Charles and Diana tours. Meanwhile news reporters complained to us that their editors wouldn't print stories about Camilla's royal privileges for fear of antagonising the Palace and losing what they called 'William points', for it was William they all wanted.

From time to time the young Prince appeared on television, the image of the teenage Diana, and accompanied in Britain by TV commentaries reminiscent of the unctuous 1970s. The new royal performer was impressive. Charming, uninhibited, he knelt to play with children and pulled on the yellow Marigolds to do the washing up. We recalled his mother doing the same in her kindergarten days. This could be the face of the reconstructed, modernised monarchy that she dreamed of. William began university at St Andrews in October 2001. There was a well-ordered photo call and the Press Complaints Commission issued an instruction to 'leave the young man alone to study'.

But then, suddenly, there was a row, the nastiest in years. A team from Prince Edward's television company was discovered filming in the town after everyone else had left. Was William being 'stalked' by his own uncle? The newspapers had no doubt that he was, and castigated Edward for cashing in on his royal relatives. Earlier in the year Edward's wife Sophie had come in for similar treatment after reporters from the *News of the World* had secretly recorded her boasting of her connections and making disparaging comments about other members of the family.

The news management of the Diana years had not gone away. We had become aware while writing this book that there was a major rift between Charles and Edward; also that members of Charles's staff were briefing journalists against his younger brother.

Then the opposition struck back. Articles in the *Daily Telegraph* and the *Spectator* described anger in Buckingham Palace, where Charles was being accused of trying to boost his own popularity at the expense of other family members. Courtiers and ex-courtiers from Buckingham Palace were behind the stories, generating speculation about a disagreement between the Queen and Prince Philip and their eldest son on the whole question of 'royal spin.'

To add more spice, the October 2001 issue of *Vanity Fair* contained a remarkable feature entitled 'A Court of His Own'. In this Charles and Camilla were photographed together for the first time while entertaining inside royal property. A starry collection of American socialites had been invited for a four-day series of lunches, dinners and picnics at Highgrove, Buckingham Palace and various polo grounds. Assorted Trumps, Rockefellers and Bloomingdales trooped up and down royal staircases and in and out of royal banquet halls as the cameras flashed. The magazine described it as the moment when Charles finally 'emerged from under the shadow of his late wife'.

But the one really emerging was Camilla, and the guest list was no accident. These king and queen-makers of American high society had all been Diana's people. Mark Bolland had established a bridgehead with them earlier in the year when he'd accompanied Camilla on a 'meet and greet' trip to New York, but this was her moment of real acceptance.

Meanwhile, what of Diana's legacy? Britain's first official monument to her, a children's playground in Kensington Gardens, was opened while we were writing this book, and so we went along to watch the ceremony. Not one member of the royal family turned up. Diana's old friend Vivienne Parry was not surprised:

> What the Establishment wanted more than anything else while Diana was alive, was for her to be back in her box. The great horror for them when she died was that she was out of the box again. Her memory, her face, were everywhere. Since her death there has been an absolutely concerted attempt to try and get her back in that box, to try and stop her memory lingering on.
>
> One particular example has to do with the Diana, Princess of Wales Memorial Fund, of which I was a trustee. There was a huge cry, which I think was promoted for all it was worth by St James' Palace, that all the money should be spent straight away. Our feeling as trustees was that some money should be spent immediately, but that the rest should be put in trust and the income spent every year; so that in twenty years time there will still be people saying: 'Lord love that Princess of Wales'.
>
> In that way her memory as somebody who cared for those who were on the margins continues.

Bibliography

Barry, Stephen, *Royal Service: My Twelve Years as Valet to Prince Charles*, London: Macmillan, 1983

——, *Royal Secrets: the view from downstairs*, New York: Villard Books, 1985

Bedell Smith, Sally, 'Diana and the Press', *Vanity Fair* (Sept. 1998), pp. 108–16 and 151–52

——, *Diana: In Search of Herself*, New York: Random House, 1999

Berry, Wendy, *The Housekeeper's Diary: Charles and Diana before the breakup*, New York: Barricade Books, 1995

Bloch, Marc, *The Royal Touch*, written 1923, English edn pub. 1973: Routledge & Kegan Paul Ltd and McGill-Queen's University Press

Brown, Tina, 'The Mouse that Roared', *Vanity Fair* (Oct. 1985), pp. 58–65 and 118–19.

Burnet, Alastair, *In Private – In Public: The Prince and Princess of Wales*, London: Michael O'Mara, 1986

Campbell, Lady Colin, *Diana in Private: the Princess Nobody Knows*, New York: St Martin's Press, 1992

——, *The Real Diana*, New York: St Martin's Press, 1998

Cannadine, David, *The Decline and Fall of the British Aristocracy*, New Haven: Yale University Press, 1990

Carling, Will, *Will Carling: My Autobiography*, London: Hodder & Stoughton, 1998

Carpenter, Humphrey, *Robert Runcie: The Reluctant Archbishop*, London: Sceptre, 1997

Dimbleby, Jonathan, *The Prince of Wales*, London: Little, Brown, 1994

Edwards, Anne, *Diana and the Rise of the House of Spencer*, London: Hodder & Stoughton, 1999

Edwards, Arthur, with Judy Wade, *I'll tell the Jokes Arthur*, London: Blake Publishing, 1993

Fincher, Jayne, *Diana, Portrait of a Princess*, London: Callaway, 1998

Gregory, Martyn, *Diana, the Last Days*, London: Virgin Publishing, 1999

Hall, Trevor, *Charles and Diana: The Prince and Princess of Wales*, New Malden: Colour Library Books, 1982

Hewitt, James, *Love and War*, London: Blake Publishing Ltd, 1999

Holden, Anthony, *Charles Prince of Wales*, London: Weidenfeld & Nicolson, 1979

——, *Charles: a Biography*, London: Weidenfeld & Nicolson, 1988

——, *Charles Prince of Wales*, London: Weidenfeld & Nicolson, 1998

Howell, Georgina, 'Making the Best of It', *Vanity Fair* (Sept. 1988), pp. 168–74 and 259–60

——, *Diana: Her Life in Fashion*, London: Pavilion Books, 1998

Jephson, P. D., *Shadows of a Princess*, London: HarperCollins, 2000

Junor, Penny, *Charles*, New York: St Martin's Press, 1987

——, *Charles and Diana: Portrait of a Marriage*, London: Headline, 1991

——, *Charles: Victim or Villain?*, London: HarperCollins, 1998

Kear, Adrian, and Deborah Lynn Steinberg, *Mourning Diana: Nation, Culture and the Performance of Grief*, London: Routledge, 1999

MacArthur, Brian (ed.), *Requiem: Diana, Princess of Wales 1961–1997*, London: Pavilion Books, 1997

Morton, Andrew, *Inside Kensington Palace*, London: Michael O'Mara, 1987

——, *Diana's Diary*, London: Michael O'Mara, 1990

——, *Diana: Her True Story*, London: Michael O'Mara, 1992

——, *Diana: Her New Life*, London: Michael O'Mara, 1994
——, *Diana: Her True Story – in Her Own Words*, London: Michael O'Mara, 1997
Pasternak, Anna, *Princess in Love*, London: Bloomsbury, 1994
Pearson, John, *Blood Royal: the Story of the Spencers and the Royals*, London: HarperCollins, 1999
Pimlott, Ben, *The Queen*, London: HarperCollins, 1996
Rees-Jones, Trevor, with Moira Johnston, *The Bodyguard's Story: Diana, the Crash, and the Sole Survivor*, London: Little, Brown, 2000
Robertson, Mary, *The Diana I Knew*, New York: HarperCollins, 1998
Sancton, Thomas, and Scott MacLeod, *Death of a Princess: The Investigation*, New York: St Martin's Press, 1998
Saunders, Mark, and Glenn Harvey, *Dicing with Di*, London: Blake Publishing, 1996
Simmons, Simone, with Susan Hill, *Diana: the Secret Years*, London: Michael O'Mara, 1998
Wardroper, John, *Kings, Lords and Wicked Libellers: Satire and Protest 1760–1837*, London: John Murray, 1973
Whitaker, James, *Diana vs Charles: Royal Blood Feud*, London: Penguin, 1993
Wilson, Christopher, *A Greater Love: Charles and Camilla*, London: Headline, 1994
York, Sarah, Duchess of, with Jeff Coplon, *My Story*, London: Simon & Schuster, 1996

Royals and Reptiles: Channel 4 series, transmitted autumn 1997 (R & R)
The Accident: Channel 4, August 1997
Independent on Sunday, 7 September 1997
The Secrets of the Crash:, ITV, June 1998

Notes on sources

Passages transcribed from interviews for the series are mentioned in the Notes only where the interviewee is not clearly identified in the text. Interviews were also conducted with people who were unable or unwilling to appear on camera or to be named as contributors to the book. Where their views have been consulted, the source is given as 'confidential interview'. Other sources are noted below. The 1997 edition of Andrew Morton's *Diana: Her True Story* is cited for quotations from the transcripts of Diana's taped recollections and for events that occurred after the publication of the original 1992 edition.

Chapter 1

p. 1 'So we had lunch', Morton 1997, p. 38.
p. 2 'We all heaved a sigh of relief', confidential interview.
p. 2 'The Lord Chamberlain ventures', Pearson, p. 202.
p. 5 'She later told her biographer', Morton 1997, p. 24; reflected in Morton 1992, p. 10.
p. 5 'Frances says that this was an idea', Shand-Kydd interview, *Daily Express*, 2 September 2000, p. 3, and Saturday magazine, p. 16.
p. 14 'When these things were doing', Pearson, p. 14.

Chapter 2

pp. 25–6 'She knew nobody', 'fresh and unsuperficial', 'She was quite clear about her destiny', confidential interview.

Chapter 3

p. 34 Mountbatten's advice, Dimbleby, p. 248.
p. 36 'Mr and Mrs Parker Bowles were there', Morton 1997, p. 33.
p. 38 'From his childhood this boy', Holden 1978, p. 271.
p. 38 'All the world and all the glory of it', W. Bagehot, *The English Constitution*, cited in Holden 1988, p. xiii.
p. 38 'He had a lot of charisma', confidential interview.
p. 42 'I knew your legs were good', Morton 1992, p. 51.
p. 42 'More and more press', Kay Seth-Smith interview.
p. 43 'I do hope he gets a move on', confidential interview.
p. 44 'I couldn't understand why she kept saying', Morton 1997, p. 33.
p. 44 'feeling of emptiness', Dimbleby, p. 232.
p. 45 'No sooner had Lord Soames', *Private Eye*, 4 January 1980, p. 6.
p. 45 'HRH is very fond of my wife', Wilson, pp. 73–4.
p. 46 'What a sport', *Private Eye*, 18 August 1978, p. 6.
p. 48 'She was young, insecure, shy', confidential interview.
p. 51 'I'm afraid we've upset the Palace', R&R interview with Roy Greenslade.
p. 51 'She rang up one day', confidential interview.
p. 53 'The people in my dormitory', Charles correspondence in Dimbleby, p. 78.
p. 54 'I do very much want to do the right thing', Dimbleby, p. 342.
p. 54 'The truth is she got swamped', confidential interview.
p. 56 'Why don't you go away?', Holden 1998, p. 187.
p. 56 'Darling you must understand', Morton 1997, p. 36; Dimbleby, p. 340.
p. 57 'Charles was an insecure person', confidential interview.
p. 58 'He was a bachelor, loved the single life', confidential interview.
p. 58 'He got bounced into this', confidential interview.
p. 59 Call to Camilla, Junor 1998, p. 73.

Chapter 4

p. 62 'positively delighted and frankly amazed', BBC interview; Dimbleby, p. 331.
p. 62 'I said, "I love you so much . . ."' Morton 1997, p. 34.
p. 63 'partly because of the press', confidential interview.
p. 64 'Never underestimate the Palace', confidential interview.
p. 65 'Over the four months', York, p. 82.
p. 66 James Boughey in *Private Eye*, 13 March 1981, p. 6.
p. 68 'If I hear the word "caring"', Dimbleby, p. 359.
p. 74 *Private Eye*, 26 December 1980, 3 July 1981.
p. 75 'Such exciting news'; 'To Gladys from Fred', Morton 1997, pp. 38–9; Junor 1998, pp. 86–8.
p. 79 'I was longing to walk over to Her Majesty', Robertson, p. 99.
p. 79 'Well, bad luck, Duch', Morton 1997, p. 39.

Chapter 5

p. 81 'My dear you look simply enchanting', Shanley in *Sunday Mirror*, 10 February 1985.
p. 82 'I'm so proud of you', Morton 1997, p. 41.
p. 85 'I knew about *that* already', Carpenter, pp. 222–4.
p. 86 'a princely marriage is the brilliant edition', Bagehot, cited in Holden 1998, p. 206.
p. 87 'Church as usual', confidential interview.
p. 88 'He did a lot of reading and painting', confidential interview.
p. 88 'It was terribly difficult for Prince Charles', confidential interview.
p. 89 'Diana screamed and shouted', Junor 1998, p. 94.
p. 89 'the Prince was perplexed', Dimbleby, p. 355.
p. 89 'The bulimia was appalling', Morton 1997, p. 42.
p. 90 'His idea of enjoyment', Morton 1997, p. 43.
p. 91 'I remember crying my eyes out', Morton 1997, pp. 43–4.
p. 91 'At dinner one night the Queen cornered me', confidential interview.

p. 92 'brown envelopes of ten-pound notes', confidential interview.

p. 92 'stuffed shirt' stories in *News of the World*, 13 September 1981, and *Sun*, 18 September 1981.

p. 93 'go to bed at night and sleep', Morton 1997, p. 44.

p. 96 'I caught Charles kicking a pebble', confidential interview.

p. 97 'Diana: the Queen of Hearts', *Brecon and Radnor Express*, 5 November 1981.

p. 97 'entirely to the effect my dear wife', Hall, p. 132.

p. 97 'Moving into Buck House', confidential interview.

p. 98 'She was terribly conscious of her image', confidential interview.

p. 98 'When are you going to stop', Wilson, p. 97.

p. 101 'Andrew Morton's 1992 biography told how', Morton 1992, p. 73.

pp. 101–2 'She said that is why', Bedell Smith 1999, p. 130.

p. 102 'Lady Colin Campbell announced'. See Campbell 1998, p. 104.

p. 102 'I threw myself down the stairs', Morton 1997, p. 45.

p. 103 'haplessly trying to soothe her' and 'unfathomable', Dimbleby, p. 361; 'inexplicable', p. 400; 'aberrant', p. 365.

p. 103 'those of their friends', Dimbleby, p. 361.

p. 104 'As her pregnancy advanced', Dimbleby, p. 367.

p. 104 'They were all oiling up', Morton 1997, p. 40.

Chapter 6

p. 110 'The Princess also seemed', Dimbleby, p. 367.

p. 112 'Thank goodness he hasn't got ears', Morton 1992, p. 79.

p. 113 'We looked at her big eyes', confidential interview.

p. 114 'She rang up and asked, "How did I do?"', confidential interview.

p. 116 'I stumbled across the term BPD', letter from Dimbleby to Phil Craig.

p. 116 'The Prince of Wales was concerned throughout', ibid.

p. 117 '. . . there appeared to be a terrible conflict', Dimbleby, pp. 477–8.

p. 118 '"Rubbish", a spokesman said', *Daily Mirror*, 31 January 1983.

p. 119 'So badly is the Princess of Wales treating husband Brian', *Private Eye*, 3 December 1982, p. 10.

p. 120 'If the *Daily Mail*'s Reptile', *Private Eye*, 31 December 1982, p. 17. For tabloid coverage, see Bedell Smith, pp. 136–8.

p. 122 'help to preserve my sanity', Charles correspondence in Dimbleby, p. 402.

p. 124 'What is a Princess for?', *Time*, 28 February 1983, quoting Suzanne Lowry, *Sunday Times*.

p. 124 'Princess thrills 35,000 children', *Auckland Star*, 18 April 1983.

p. 124 'Diana's spontaneous manner', *Northern Advocate*, 30 April 1983.

p. 124 'The terrifying part, as always', Dimbleby, p. 403.

Chapter 7

p. 125 'In the autumn of 1983', Holden 1998, pp. 225–6.

p. 127 'learned that, among other feelings', Jephson, p. 63.

p. 128 'as Harry was born it just went bang', Morton 1997, p. 51.

p. 129 'offensive, reactionary and ill-considered', quoted in Holden 1988, p. 164.

p. 129 'self-conscious, deeply vulnerable', Holden 1979, p. xx.

p. 129 'He will need to prove himself', Holden 1979, p. 270.

p. 130 'a tortured, self-doubting, almost monkish introvert', Holden 1988, p. 139.

p. 134 'the man who really knows', *Daily Star*, 4 February 1985.

p. 134 'pussy whipped from here to eternity', *Vanity Fair*, October 1985.

p. 135 'As always on these occasions', correspondence in

Dimbleby, p. 407.
p. 135 'I've thought of a good idea', *Vanity Fair*, October 1985, p. 63.
p. 138 'Here They Come', *Time*, 11 November 1985; Dimbleby, p. 463.
p. 138 'Why? What's wrong?' Carter Brown interview.
p. 139 'Well, we had a press conference', Carter Brown interview.
p. 139 'A gentleman of the press', *London Evening Standard*, 11 November 1985.
p. 139 'cream coloured evening dress', *London Evening Standard*, 11 November 1985.

Chapter 8

p. 143 'Just keep smiling', York, p. 72; 'Why can't you be more like Fergie?', York, p. 75.
p. 143 'absolutely amazed', Morton 1992, p. 91.
p. 144 'What is it now, Diana?' Berry, p. 53.
p. 144 'Everything is such a mess', ibid., pp. 50–1.
p. 147 'Barry, how do I look?' Berry, pp. 24–5.
p. 148 'Look at this fucking shirt, Evelyn', ibid., p. 52.
p. 148 'fifth columnist', Pimlott, p. 482.
p. 153 'the one light in her life', Hewitt, p. 31.
p. 154 'There is no need for me to do all this', Holden 1988, p. 190.
p. 154 'I have been brought up', ibid., p. 191.
p. 159 'She was clearly nervous', Adler interview.
p. 160 'Sunday evenings at Highgrove', Berry, pp. 56–7.
p. 161 'Difficult Di causes Malice', ibid., p. 60.
p. 161 'Who is getting the benefit', ibid., p. 78.
p. 161 'The emotional temperature', *Time*, 9 November 1987.
p. 161 'It has been impossible to disguise', *Time*, 9 November 1987.
p. 162 'air of relaxed domesticity', Berry, p. 87.
p. 166 'When I arrived at Buckingham Palace', confidential interview.

p. 170 'That anxiety was heightened', Jephson, p. 189.
p. 171 'I said: "Camilla, I would just like"', Morton 1997, p. 63.

Chapter 9

p. 175 'Princess Diana has asked', *Today*, 30 January 1989.
p. 177 'Shopping, isn't it, Darling?' Jephson, p. 67.
p. 177 'Patrick, what do you get', based on Jephson, pp. 36–7.
p. 178 'As I watched her at a dying child's bedside', ibid., p. 40.
p. 185 'If an institution marked out for particular ends', Bloch, p. 48.
p. 186 'Countless witnesses have testified', ibid., p. 6.
p. 186 'Public opinion was unanimous', ibid., p. 234.

Chapter 10

p. 192 'Some people are even beginning', *Vanity Fair*, December 1989, p. 219.
p. 192 'DID CARING PRINCESS DI', *Sun*, quoted in *Vanity Fair*, December 1989, p. 221.
p. 194 'Long and sometimes incoherent', Jephson, p. 163.
p. 206 'She was very concerned', confidential interview.
p. 206 'How flirty Di captures', *Sun*, 19 March 1991.
p. 207 'Charles the Absent Royal Father', *Daily Mail*, 4 April 1991.
p. 208 'The sadness was that immediate staff', confidential interview.
p. 208 'The Princess was lunching', based on Morton 1992, pp. 117–19, and Holden 1998, pp. 301–2.
p. 208 'With the Princess at lunch', based on Dimbleby, pp. 575–6; see also Bedell Smith, p. 208.
p. 210 'Wills in Brain Scan Scare', *Sun* 4 June 1991.
p. 210 'He thought he had checked out', confidential interview.
p. 211 'Fincher's photograph', e.g. *Sun*, 25 October 1991.
p. 212 'Diana and Charles: cause for concern', Dempster in

Daily Mail, 2 July 1991.
p. 212 'stuffy old friends', Morton in *Sun*, 3 July 1991.
p. 213 'I like her a lot', Jephson, p. 100.

Chapter 11

p. 216 'It was over a plate of bacon', Morton interview for Royals and Reptiles, Blakeway Productions.
p. 221 'The straightforward deal', ibid.
p. 224 'To further satisfy Morton's desire', Bedell Smith, p. 216.
p. 227 'And we had an awful week', Morton interview for Royals and Reptiles.
p. 228 'They also needed to send a warning', York, p. 200.

Chapter 12

p. 234 'Patrick . . . What do people think', Jephson, p. 244.
p. 234 'this family had this book', ibid., p. 243.
p. 234 'those whose motives', ibid., p. 241.
p. 235 'peel yourself to death?' Campbell 1992, p. 256.
p. 236 'the situation has to end', *Sunday Express*, 5 July 1992; incident is Berry p. 167 but not the quote; SBS 362 confirms *Sunday Express*, 5 July 1992.
p. 237 'passive, philistine, bewildered, anachronistic', *Financial Times*, 8 February 1992, cited in Pimlott, p. 542.
p. 238 'not the adulterous kind', *Today*, 6 July 1992.
p. 238 'Why don't you save yourself', Morton 1997, p. 218.
p. 239 'second honeymoon'.
p. 242 'Diana told me, "It's dishonest"', confidential interview.
p. 243 'their friends', Dimbleby, p. 594; 'they're all *his* friends', Jephson, p. 267.
p. 243 'Just think Patrick,' Jephson, p. 268.
p. 244 '1992 is not a year on which', Pimlott, p. 558.

Chapter 13

p. 248 'Well ladies! We all know what men are like', Jephson, p. 288.
p. 248 'Sisters are doing it for themselves!' ibid., p. 289.
p. 253 'the anxious young woman he met', ibid., p. 283.
p. 255 'The one thing that the Prince', Royals and Reptiles.
p. 256 'My book and my film', ibid.
p. 256 'I remember when I was first', ibid.
p. 257 'My intention ... was to confront him', Jephson, pp. 292–3.
p. 257 'as – unlike him, apparently', letter to Phil Craig.
p. 259 'For some months', Jephson, p. 313.
p. 260 'to excise the more histrionic references', ibid., pp. 315–16.
p. 260 'I hope you can find it in your hearts', ibid., pp. 317–18.
p. 262 'Not Fit to Reign', *Daily Mirror*, 30 June 1994; 'Revenge is Chic', *Sun*, 30 June 1994.

Chapter 14

p. 271 'watched my boss's eyes glaze over', Jephson, p. 332.
p. 275 'What have I done to deserve this?' *Daily Mail*, 22 August 1994.
p. 275 'talks about his King', *London und Paris*, 14 (1804), 3–4 in C. Banerji and D. Donald (eds), *Gillray Observed: The Earliest Account of his Caricatures in* London und Paris, Cambridge: CUP, 1999, p. 203.
p. 277 'Britain's Biggest Bounder', *Daily Mail*, 2 October 1994; 'Love Rat', *Sun*, 4 October 1994.
p. 283 'I try to be there for them', *News of the World*, 3 December 1995.
p. 286 'it was the kind of foreboding', Jephson, p. 365.
p. 287 'a dazzling display of sheer', *Times*, 21 November 1995.
p. 287 'You were magnificent Di', *Sun*, 21 November 1995.

Chapter 15

p. 289 'luminous personality', *Daily Mail*, 13 December 1995.
p. 289 'Where are your children, Diana?' 'At school.' *Daily Telegraph*, *Daily Mail* and *Sun*, 13 December 1995.
p. 290 'So sorry about the baby', Jephson, p. 373.
p. 290 'The Boss knows about', ibid., p. 374.
p. 293 'The Princess of Wales will retain', Morton 1997, p. 251.

Chapter 17

p. 323 'You'll never guess who just dropped by?' Kay in 'Diana: the Untold Story', Bedell Smith, p. 326.
p. 328 'sorting people's heads out' Tina Brown, *Vanity Fair*
p. 331 'Di and Sleaze Row', *News of the World*, 13 July 1997.
p. 331 'Di's Freebie', *Sunday Mirror*, 13 July 1997.
p. 335 'Dodi's to Di for', *Sun*, 11 August 1997.
p. 338 'she told me she had never felt', Gregory, p. 44.
p. 338 'Missionary of Natural Spiritualism', ibid., p. 45.

Chapter 18

p. 344 'fuck-up', Gregory, p. 65.
p. 346 'You will never catch us', ibid., p. 73.

Chapter 19

p. 367 'in latter years', Wilson and Amis, *Time*, 15 September 1997.
p. 371 'Diana may you rest in peace', *Observer*, 7 September 1997.

Index

Index

Index

Index

Index

Index